# The Motley Fool®

# MONEY GUIDE

*Answers to Your Questions About Saving, Spending, and Investing*

## Selena Maranjian

FOREWORD BY DAVID GARDNER

Published by The Motley Fool, Inc., 123 North Pitt Street,
Alexandria, Virginia, 22314, USA

Third Printing, August 2001
10 9 8 7 6 5 4 3

This publication contains the opinions and ideas of its authors and is designed to provide useful information in regard to the subject matter covered. It is sold with the understanding that the author and publisher are not engaged in rendering legal, financial, tax preparation, or other professional services. Laws vary from state to state, and if the reader requires expert assistance or legal advice, a competent professional should be consulted. Readers should not rely on this (or any other) publication for financial guidance, but should do their own homework and make their decisions. The author and publisher reserve the right to be stupid, wrong, or even foolish (with a small "f"). Remember, past results are not necessarily an indication of future performance.

The author and publisher specifically disclaim any responsibility for any liability, loss, or risk, personal or otherwise, which is incurred as a consequence, directly or indirectly, of the use and application of any of the contents of this book.

ISBN 1-892547-11-2

Printed in the United States of America
Body set in Apollo MT 11.5/13.5. Questions set in Syntax Med 13/13.5. Titling set in ITC Veljovic.

Distributed by Publishers Group West

Cover design by Johnson Design

Interior Design & Production by Pneuma Books: Complete Publisher's Services;
(for info visit www.pneumadesign.com/books/info.htm)

Printed by United Book Press, Inc.

# The Motley Fool

The Motley Fool's mission is to educate, amuse, and enrich. Begun as a newsletter serving 60 readers in August 1994, the Fool now reaches millions of people every month as it plays host to a celebrated community of individuals dedicated to helping each other achieve financial security and independence. The Motley Fool's products and services are available across a variety of media: on its website at Fool.com; via its four Simon & Schuster books, all *New York Times* bestsellers; through its premium products, including online seminars, self-published books, and Motley Fool Research; through its syndicated weekly newspaper column, currently carried by more than 200 newspapers around the U.S.; via its daily "Market Minutes" and weekly "Motley Fool Radio Show," both joint ventures with Cox Radio that can be heard on more than 150 stations nationwide; and on America Online (keyword: Fool). The Fool's international website can be found at www.Fool.co.uk and on America Online (keyword: FoolUK).

---

## Become a Fool!

Join the millions of people who call themselves Fools and are taking control of their financial destinies. When you become a Fool you'll get:

- Access to The Motley Fool's informative and acclaimed website, Fool.com
- A wide variety of personal finance solutions and exciting investment ideas
- Foolish product discount alerts
- Answers to all of your questions about money

Get started on your journey to financial independence today by registering at **www.Fool.com!**

# About the Author

Selena Maranjian is a senior writer at The Motley Fool. She lives in New Hampshire with her two dogs. (Whoops! Scratch that — that's every *other* writer.) Armed with a Wharton MBA and a Masters in Teaching from Brown University, one of Selena's missions in life is to render the incomprehensible comprehensible. She writes the Fool's nationally syndicated weekly newspaper feature and has also written *Investment Clubs: How to Start and Run One the Motley Fool Way* and co-written *The Motley Fool Investment Tax Guide*.

 # Acknowledgments

Few Foolish products are created alone. Foolishness is all about community — about people conversing and learning together, asking and answering questions, sharing opinions, and making each other laugh. Even though I have an MBA, most of what I know about investing and personal finance was learned in Fooldom. Most of what you'll read in this book also comes from Fooldom, directly or indirectly.

I'm grateful to the many community members of the Fool who spend time on our discussion boards, sharing their wisdom. I'm also indebted to my many Fool colleagues, from whom I've learned much. I hesitate to name any names, but when it comes to personal finance and tax issues, Roy Lewis and Dave Braze are the ones who've most often made me look smart. Much of this book's car buying and home buying information, as well as the glossary, is drawn from the work of Bill Barker, Paul Maghielse, and David Wolpe. The colleagues who've taught me about investing are too numerous to name.

Many Fools worked hard helping make this book a reality, heroically reading and reviewing every page and making it a much better work than it otherwise would have been. I thank them most sincerely: Brian Bauer, Reggie Santiago-Bobala, Alissa Territo, Robyn Gearey, and Debora Tidwell. Thanks to Alicia Abell as well, for her guidance as the book was shaped.

*For my family,*
*who made me who I am,*

*and my Fool colleagues,*
*who always make me look good.*

# Table of Contents

# Foreword by David Gardner

Every year, The Motley Fool executes its own April Fool's Day prank. We design each of the pranks in accordance with our public mission: to educate, to amuse, and to enrich. That means the jokes themselves must not only be funny, but must also teach people to make better financial decisions.

Our 1998 joke provided a perfect example. On our home page at Fool.com, as evening blended into early morning on April 1, 1998, we put up a public apology, front and center. "We've been telling you for five years now that most mutual funds underperform the market averages," it began. "We were wrong."

We were of course completely right. In case you didn't already know, the vast majority (on the order of more than 80%) of managed stock mutual funds have in fact lost to the market's *average* over the past five years! It's one of the most damning statistics out there — that mutual funds managed rather expensively by humans do *worse*, after fees, than the stock market's average performance each year. Given that you're paying fees to a manager, do you not find it pretty shocking and disappointing to be paying someone to lose to the market for you? And not enough people know this, which is the educational purpose of our joke, once we came clean.

Anyway, we claimed in this April Fool's apology that we'd been wrong, wrong, wrong. You see, we had been *misreading a graph*, we said. For five years, we had been looking at a graph of these numbers that had, unbeknownst to us, been printed *upside-down*. So rather than 80% of all mutual funds *losing* to the market, our April Fool's letter stated that 80% of mutual funds had actually *beaten* the market. And we had been telling all our customers to steer clear of managed mutual funds as a bad idea! Egg all over our faces.

Now if you're not clear on what "stock mutual funds" are, or what "market averages" even means, these are irrelevant for the purpose of this Foreword. I'll just say now that you've come to the right book; Selena is here to teach you.

No, the singular aim of this Foreword is to get across to you that if you don't "know it all," you're not alone! In fact, you might be surprised to learn of the company you keep...

Later that day, April 1, 1998, a vice president of a regional brokerage firm in Charlotte, NC who also hosts a popular regular radio broadcast in that city dispensing financial advice — castigated The Motley Fool for being so wrong about mutual funds. We'll call him "Fanny." In 10 minutes of radio we will never forget, we listened to Fanny explain to his listeners how he knew we had *always* been wrong about mutual funds, that 80% of them had *beaten* the market, that we were completely wrong and that our apology wasn't even enough. "If I had my way," Fanny said in an emotionally charged address, "I'd put those guys up against a wall and shoot 'em."

That's right, a man who had risen to become VP at a regional brokerage firm and a daily radio personality dispensing financial advice to a large Southern city had actually fallen for our joke.

He had actually believed that 80% of all mutual funds were beating the market! (He'd *"known"* we were wrong.) This Wise "expert" who held sway over the money management of many did not himself even realize how poorly managed mutual funds had performed. Given his career focus, you'd think he'd have had his eye on the ball, especially given his senior level. You'd think so, wouldn't you? Without ever intending to actually bait professionals with our April Fool's joke, we had snared a big shot who actually lacked a simple knowledge of one of the financial world's most basic truths.

In her introduction, Selena calls it a secret that most of us don't know much about personal finance and investing. Guess what? She writes: "Most of your friends, relatives, neighbors, and colleagues probably feel the same way. Just as you're pretending that your financial house is in order, so are they."

In this handy, plainly worded, and humorous guide are many of the answers to questions most of us think everyone else *but* us already knows. Keep it nearby, go back to it as needed, and put these answers to work for you in your daily life.

And don't believe a word you read on our site on April first. But you'll be surprised who does!

— David Gardner

*To read the 1998 April Fool's Joke visit: www.Fool.com/AprilFools98/*

# Introduction

Chances are, you're moving through your life with a big secret. It makes you feel bad, but you're too embarrassed to address it or confess to it. The thought of your colleagues at work or your children finding out is mortifying. No, I'm not talking about the fact that you love Doris Day movies. Or that you were the one who somehow managed to explode that frozen pizza in the microwave. Or that the reason your new diet isn't working is that you keep stopping at Taco Bell on your way home from work.

No, it's a different secret... and a *big* one. Here are some of its facets:

- I don't know much about personal finance and I know even less about investing.
- I have no idea what kind of insurance I need or what "market capitalization" means.
- I haven't planned for my retirement because I don't know how.
- I'm just a big financial ignoramus.

If any or all of these ring true for you, you're not alone. Far from it. Most of your friends, relatives, neighbors, and colleagues probably feel the same way. Just as you're pretending that your financial house is in order, so are they.

You shouldn't feel bad about this secret. It's not your fault. Very few people are ever taught these things in school. Don't think that it's a hopeless situation, either. You *can* learn this stuff. It's not difficult or mysterious, and the Fool is here to help you. The Motley Fool exists to help people learn about and manage anything financial. This book is here to serve you — to answer all those questions you're too embarrassed to ask, to make you think about some issues that need your attention, to help you save money when you spend, and to help you make money when you invest.

Much of the information in this book is drawn from the Fool's nationally syndicated weekly newspaper feature. At the time of this writing, roughly 200 large and small newspapers across the U.S. and Canada carry it. (If your local paper isn't among them, just give the editor a friendly jingle and ask for it.) I write most of the feature, and I've often heard from readers that they crave a compilation of the information in it. This is the answer to those requests. It's not exactly a compilation, though, as half of the content is new and the other half is revised and updated.

I hope you find answers to most or all of your financial questions in this book. If any questions are left unanswered, come visit us at Fool.com, where you can ask more questions and get speedy responses.

Here's to a rosy future of smarter spending and successful investing!

---

## What is Foolishness?

Keep in mind as you read this book that, to us, "Foolish" is a positive adjective. The Motley Fool takes its name from Shakespeare. In Elizabethan drama, the Fool is usually the only one who can tell the king the truth without losing his head — literally. We Fools aim to tell you truth, too — that you can learn enough about money and investing to build a secure financial future for yourself. To learn more about The Motley Fool, drop by our website at www.Fool.com or on America Online at keyword: FOOL.

---

# PART ONE
# Personal Finance

**CHAPTER ONE**
**ANSWERS TO YOUR QUESTIONS ABOUT**

# Saving and Budgeting

*At The Motley Fool, one of our main goals is to get everyone on Earth investing and building a financially secure future. It's a tall order, we know. Lots of people are not even close to the point where they are ready to begin investing, though. Instead, they need to focus on generating more money to invest. Enter the world of saving and budgeting.*

## 1 Why should I bother with budgeting?

Most of us would rather poke ourselves in the eye than sit down and plan a budget. Many would rather slam a door on their hand than actually live according to a budget. That's just wrong thinking, though. We should budget with delight. We should even have trouble getting to sleep at night, as we eagerly anticipate tending to our budget in the morning.

Budgeting can be very valuable because it permits you to optimize your spending. You might think that all is fine with your spending habits, but a little time spent on budgeting might reveal that you're spending a surprising amount on something that you don't care that much about. If so, you could tweak your habits a little and end up with more to spend on things you care about more, such as entertainment or investing.

Budgeting is even more vital if you're having trouble making ends meet. A little analysis of your spending patterns should show you where your money is going and might help you see where you could cut back. Knowledge is power, and going through the budgeting process gives you a lot of self-knowledge.

## I know that budgeting is important, but for the life of me I just can't muster up the energy to tackle it. Is there any way you can inspire me to just do it?

Instead of thinking of it as an enormous lifestyle change that will have you miserably pinching pennies for the rest of your life, focus on the positives. Try thinking of it as a game — or something close to that. Or, think of it as one of those self-quizzes you take in a magazine or online, to learn more about yourself. People who budget know a lot about themselves. In many cases, figuring out where your money comes from and where it goes may even liberate you to some degree. You may learn that you have more than you think!

## How should I go about setting up a budget for myself?

A budget is all about tracking and reporting all your *sources* and *amounts* of income, and all your *uses* of income. It should answer the questions "Where's all my money coming from and how much is there?" and "Where's it all going?"

Before you get started, and to make the process more suspenseful and fun, jot down how much you *think* you're spending on food, entertainment, travel, clothing, charity, investing, etc. Then record how much you *want* to spend on them.

Next, gather information. For one to three months, record all your financial inflows and outflows. (One month will do, but a few more will maximize accuracy.) Try to account for big expenses that occur once or twice a year, such as car insurance, too. Jot down how much they amount to per month. During this two- or three-month period, save every single receipt you get for any expense. If you don't normally ask for or keep receipts, do so during this period. Also, carry a small notebook to write down any cash transactions. If you spend a few dollars for coffee at a local coffee shop each morning, jot down each time you do so. If you do some odd jobs for a few extra dollars now and then, record that too.

After the information-collecting months are finished, sit down with all your records — the big bunch of receipts, your checkbook, your pay stubs, credit card and bill statements, and that little notebook of cash transactions. You'll also want a pad of paper, a pen or pencil, and a calculator. Start making lists of all the inflows and outflows. Group them into categories and total the amounts for each item. For example, you might list all your eating-out expenses and all your supermarket expenses, and lump them together in a "Food" category. Then calculate what percentage of your income is spent on food.

Make sure you're accounting for *all* your expenses. Even a $12 check written for a magazine subscription should be counted. As you're classifying expenses, notice that some of them are fixed, while others are more flexible.

Now, step back and see what you've got. You should be looking at a fascinating detailed record of where your money comes from and where it goes. Compare your actual expenses with your initial estimates and see how close you were. Assess whether you're saving and investing as much as you want to. See what changes you need to make in your habits to meet your goals.

Perhaps you can hit your savings goal simply by cutting out HBO and your subscription to *People* magazine. Buy a water filter instead of endless jugs of bottled water. Use a fan sometimes instead of air conditioning. You might be able to save a tidy sum by giving slightly less-extravagant gifts. Also, don't assume that fixed expenses are completely fixed. You might be able to refinance a loan at a lower rate. Or, a little comparison-shopping might turn up a less-expensive insurance policy.

A later chapter in this book addresses living below your means. Once you decide that you need to cut back on spending in some areas, you'll find lots of useful tips there.

## 4  Is there a handy budgeting worksheet I can use?

I'll include a worksheet here that you might use — or just use as an example. Know that you might get more value by making a worksheet of your own, where you can be more specific. For example, if you lump

# BudgetingWorksheet

Enter all figures as monthly amounts. You'll need to adjust some. (For example, if you pay $300 twice a year for car insurance, you'd enter $50 per month.) Fill out amounts for two or three months.

| Item | Month 1 | Month 2 | Month 3 |
|---|---|---|---|
| Rent / Mortgage | | | |
| Utilities | | | |
| Telephone | | | |
| Food | | | |
| Household Repairs | | | |
| Household Maintenance | | | |
| Automobile Payments | | | |
| Automobile Repairs | | | |
| Transportation Cost | | | |
| Clothing | | | |
| Medical, Dental, & Glasses | | | |
| Child Care | | | |
| Vacations | | | |
| Non-vacation Travel | | | |
| Gifts and Christmas | | | |
| Charitable Contributions | | | |
| Home Insurance | | | |
| Car Insurance | | | |
| Health Insurance / Major Medical | | | |
| Child Support | | | |
| Alimony | | | |
| School Tuition | | | |
| School Expenses | | | |
| Home Improvement | | | |
| Purchase of Furniture/Appliances | | | |
| Taxes (auto, etc) | | | |
| Real Estate Taxes | | | |
| Loan Payments | | | |
| Credit Card Payments | | | |
| Savings and Investments | | | |
| Other | | | |

all entertainment expenses into an "Entertainment" line item, you won't get as much insight into your spending habits as you would if you broke entertainment into movies, eating out, cable TV, theater tickets, etc. Add any relevant items that you spend money on regularly, such as golf, dry cleaning, music lessons or books. It's important to see where all significant chunks of your income go.

Enter all figures as monthly amounts. You'll need to adjust some. (For example, if you pay $300 twice a year for car insurance, you'd enter $50 per month.) Fill out amounts for two or three months.

## 5 Are there any software packages that will help me with budgeting and financial planning?

There sure are. Intuit's *Quicken* is probably the best-known software package. Microsoft offers an alternative, with its *Money* software.

Both Intuit and Microsoft also offer money management tools online at their websites, www.quicken.com and www.moneycentral.msn.com, respectively. Fool.com offers many similar features, as well.

## 6 What are reasonable amounts to spend on common household expenses?

It varies widely, of course. Where you live is a major factor in how little you can manage to pay for some products and services. Car insurance, for example, can cost very little in some regions, and an arm and a leg in others. Likewise, housing costs can be sky-high in some parts of the country and quite reasonable elsewhere.

Here are some very rough guidelines on how much of your after-tax income you might aim to spend on various categories:

- Housing and utilities: 25-30%
- Food: 10-15%
- Vehicles: 10-15%
- Insurance: 5%
- Saving and investing: 10-15%

- Entertainment: 5%
- Clothing: 5%
- Medical: 5%
- Childcare and education: 1-8%
- Gifts and charity: up to you

---

**7** **If I know what I spend on something like food in terms of dollars, how can I figure out what percentage of my income I'm spending on it? How do you do the math?**

Grab a calculator. Let's say that you earn $45,000 per year after taxes and spend $3,000 per year on food. Take $3,000 and divide it by $45,000. You'll get 0.07. Take that, multiply it by 100 and tack a "%" sign on the end. *Voila* — the answer is 7%. Here's the formula:

$$\underline{\hspace{3cm}} / \underline{\hspace{4cm}} = \underline{\hspace{2.5cm}}$$

annual expense          annual post-tax income          portion spent

$$\underline{\hspace{4cm}} \text{ x 100 + "%" = } \underline{\hspace{3cm}}$$

portion spent                                              percentage spent

As another example, imagine that you're spending $1,100 per month on rent and you and your spouse earn a total of $60,000 per year, after taxes. Take $1,100 and multiply it by 12 to get an annual number — $13,200. Divide $13,200 by $60,000 and you'll get 0.22, or 22%. With the formula above, you can substitute monthly or weekly numbers for the annual ones — just be consistent and don't mix annual numbers with weekly or monthly ones.

## 8 Do I need to keep 3 to 6 months of living expenses available as an emergency fund?

It's certainly smart to have *some* emergency funds available for unpleasant surprises that occasionally rear their ugly heads. (Your employer relocates to Siberia and your spouse isn't keen on moving, so you're out of work. Your child is discovered to be a tuba prodigy and you suddenly need to cough up a lot of money for costly Tuba Camp — and a costly tuba.)

You shouldn't park any emergency money in stocks. That's too volatile a place for short-term money. Keeping it in a savings account that earns little interest isn't so hot either, though. You have other options. You could keep the money in a money market fund, which will pay you more than a savings account. You might also park the money in short-term certificates of deposit (CDs) or bonds, perhaps staggered so that a portion of it is always close to maturity.

Here's another option, if you don't have any or much credit card debt. You might decide to charge expenses on your credit card, up to a certain amount, if you run into temporary trouble. Be careful with this approach, though. If you keep a significant balance on your credit card and are charged a steep interest rate, a bad situation can get worse quickly.

Loans are another possibility. If you have family members or close friends who could easily lend you enough to cover your temporary needs, that could work out well. If you own your own home, you might be able to take out a home equity loan to generate some temporary cash.

If you have a brokerage account chock full of stocks, you might be able to borrow what you need from your brokerage, on margin. People usually borrow on margin from brokerages to buy addition stock, but you can borrow for pretty much any purpose. Your portfolio serves as collateral. Just be careful — if you borrow a lot and your stocks suddenly plunge in value, you'll be hit with a "margin call" and may end up losing some of your stocks. We recommend only using margin sparingly, if you use it at all.

If you have a 401(k) at work, you might be able to borrow against that in an emergency.

The main idea behind these unconventional alternatives is that, by counting on one or more of them, you'll not have to keep a sizable chunk of money tied up where it's not earning much for you. You can concentrate on building wealth, while having a solid plan for emergencies.

Again, be careful, though, because planning to tap 401(k) money or establishing significant credit card debt can end up making matters worse in the long run, if you're not able to recover fairly quickly. If these options make you nervous, then stick with the more conservative alternatives. The safest approach is to have some emergency funds socked away.

## 9 How might I teach my children about budgeting?

Instead of just sitting them down for an abstract lesson (or worse, a sermon that has them rolling their eyes), get them involved in your own budgeting. Show them how much the family is spending on various items and what your goals are. Explain what things such as cable TV and lawn-care services cost. You and your kids can work together to decrease some spending — or at least to keep expenses within your budget. They may even be more understanding when you have to say no to a plea for a new toy.

## 10 Once I've created a budget, any tips on how to successfully live with it?

One big problem many people face is that, while they may *mean* to save and invest 10% of their salary, by the end of the month they don't have that much left. They have good intentions, but not enough discipline. There's a well-worn maxim that addresses this problem: Pay yourself first. In other words, take out money for saving and investing as soon as you get your paycheck. Then you can use what's left for your other needs.

If you want to be super-organized, you might even take it a step further. You could create envelopes for your major spending categories (such as food, clothing, entertainment, wigs, etc.), and put the money that you plan to spend on each category in the respective envelope. Then, once your entertainment envelope is cleaned out, you're out of luck until the next payday. You won't end up spending money on one thing that was meant for something else.

## 11 Where can I learn more about budgeting and organizing my life financially?

Here are a few helpful websites:
- www.buildabudget.com
- www.rightonthemoney.org/shows/104_budget
- www.houseclicks.com/owning/budget.html
- www.njscpa.org/students/mm9909.asp (for college students)
- www.wife.org
- www.juliemorgenstern.com
- www.Fool.com/calcs/calculators.htm
- http://financialplan.about.com/library/blbudgets.htm
- www.studyweb.com/links/5072.html

And some books:
- *The Budget Kit* by Judy Lawrence
- *10 Minute Guide to Household Budgeting* by Tracey Longo
- *Bonnie's Household Budget Book* by Bonnie Runyan McCullough

Another handy resource is a later chapter in this book on "Living Below Your Means."

CHAPTER TWO
ANSWERS TO YOUR QUESTIONS ABOUT

# Credit Cards and Debt

*There are few things as insidious as credit card debt. You can probably take out a car loan for around 9%, but credit cards are eager to charge you twice as much or more for the privilege of borrowing from them. Many people get caught up in the spiral of credit card debt. Once they rack up a lot of debt, the best they can usually manage is paying the interest. If they're not very disciplined, their debt just keeps rising. Worse still, credit card companies are targeting college kids now. Too many young people graduate from college with a degree, a lumpy futon, and several thousand dollars in credit card debt. Talk about an inauspicious beginning!*

## 12 How can I get a copy of my credit report?

There are three credit-reporting bureaus that keep credit records on us:

| | | |
|---|---|---|
| Equifax | 800-685-1111 | www.equifax.com |
| Experian | 888-397-3742 | www.experian.com |
| Transunion | 800-888-4213 | www.transunion.com |

You should be able to contact any or all of them to get a copy of your credit report. Some experts recommend getting all three reports, as some information may have been reported to just one bureau. Last time we checked, you could order a copy of your combined credit report from all three bureaus at www.truelink.com.

In some circumstances, getting a report from one of these bureaus is free — such as if you live in certain states (Colorado, Georgia, Massachusetts, Maryland, New Jersey, and Vermont, last time we checked), or within 60 days of being denied credit, employment, insurance, or rental housing. Otherwise, it may cost you about $8 per report, or more for a three-in-one combined report.

## 13 If there are errors on my credit report, what can I do?

You can have them corrected. Somewhere in the report, often at the end, there should be instructions on how to dispute anything that you believe is an error.

## 14 Is there anything I can do about accurate but negative information?

That information will remain on your report for seven to 10 years (usually seven, but 10 for bankruptcies). You can still lessen the sting of that information, though, by paying your bills on time. Credit issuers tend to give more weight to your recent bill-paying history, so a clean record for the last year or two can make a real difference.

## 15 Is it worth it to use the services of a "credit repair clinic"?

According to the Federal Trade Commission, these are often scams. The credit bureau Experian concurs, noting that "consumers pay so-called credit clinics hundreds and even thousands of dollars to 'fix' their credit report, but only time can heal bad credit."

## 16 Is some debt okay? For example, is it wrong to have a mortgage or student loan debt?

Not all debt is alike — and not all debt is bad. It's very reasonable to carry a mortgage, a car loan, etc. You simply need to pay attention to the cost of the debt. If you're carrying revolving debt on a credit card that's charging you 18% per year, you're in a bad situation. If your student loan is charging you 7%, that's much less worrisome.

Another consideration is what else you might do with the money you'd use to pay off a low-interest loan. Imagine that you've borrowed $5,000 at 6% and you now have the money to pay it off in full. You could do so, but consider the alternative. If you're bullish about a stock or two and are fairly sure that, over the next five years or so, you'll earn at least 15% on them per year, on average, then you might choose to keep the loan and pay it off gradually, as you originally planned. You might take the $5,000 and invest it. If the stocks perform as expected, you'll be earning more than you're paying out in interest.

That's why mortgages, for example, are not necessarily a bad thing. If your mortgage rate is low, it makes perfect sense to keep paying it off gradually. (If your rate is high, consider refinancing it, if you can.) Mortgage interest brings with it some tax benefits, too.

## 17 Why is credit card debt so bad? Is it really such a big problem?

Unfortunately, it is. Americans owe nearly half a trillion dollars in credit card debt. The average American household with credit cards owed about $7,000 in 1997. Aggregate credit card debt more than doubled between 1990 and 1997, according to the Consumer Federation of America.

Once you've fallen prey to the easy-money attraction of credit cards, it's very hard to dig yourself out. It can be tempting to simply ignore your balance and pay the minimum requirement on your card. This is a dangerous approach, though. Let's consider an example.

Morris owes $5,000 on his Zirconium MegaCharge card, which extracts 16% in interest each year. If he manages to scrape together enough money to pay it all off in a year, he'll be forking over about $450 per month and will pay more than $400 in interest. In contrast, if he takes his time paying it off and does so over 10 years, he'll be paying roughly $84 per month and will end up paying a whopping $5,080 in interest. This means he will have paid more in interest than he originally borrowed!

Building up credit card debt is kind of like investing — in reverse. With investing, your money grows. Mired in plastic, it shrinks. Think back to Morris and that $84 per month he paid on his debt for 10 years. If he'd been parking it regularly in the stock market and earning its historical annual average of about 11%, he'd end up with more than $23,000 after 10 years. (And, if he'd invested it in the stock of a company like Wal-Mart a decade ago, he'd have more than $40,000.)

Aim to pay off all your credit card charges in full each month. If you're in too deep to do that, visit our debt area online at www.Fool.com/Credit to learn more about your options. One is to try renegotiating your interest rate. If you have a sound credit history and explain that you'll be moving your debt elsewhere if your rate isn't lowered, the credit card company may knock it down a few percentage points. That can make a big difference.

Credit cards may be convenient, but they can devour your financial future. Use them carefully.

---

## 18 What are some ways to reduce my debt?

Here are a few ideas:
- Stop borrowing. It might seem obvious, but if you're just charging a little more than you can pay here and there, those expenses add up. If you're having trouble managing your credit card spending, consider cutting up your cards and only paying for things with cash or by check. Some Fools suggest putting your cards in a bag of water and popping them in the freezer. When you're tempted to use them, you'll have to wait until they thaw, giving you time to rethink your urge.

- Consolidate your debt under a more-favorable interest rate. Depending on your circumstances, you might be able to get a bank loan to pay off your credit cards and other debt. Or, you might roll your credit card debt from various cards onto a single, more-favorable card.

- Allocate as much money as you can to paying down your debt.

You could raise some extra funds by holding a garage sale. Or, in these online times, you might sell your old lunch boxes, woks, books, and CDs at sites such as www.eBay.com, www.auctions.yahoo.com, and www.Half.com.

- If you have debts at several different interest rates, concentrate on paying down the higher-rate debt first.

- Continually remind yourself that credit cards are not mere conveniences. Accumulating charges on many credit cards is like taking out a 16% to 21% loan.

## 19 Where do I turn if my debt is so out of control that I need professional help?

You can use the services of a nonprofit credit counseling organization, ideally one that's a member of the National Foundation for Consumer Credit (NFCC). To get the name and number of an office near you, call the NFCC at 800-388-2227 or visit www.nfcc.org. The NFCC website contains additional information that might help you, and they offer some online counseling, as well.

## 20 Is there any way to get a credit card company to waive its annual fee?

There's no harm in asking. Call your card company and explain that you'd like them to waive the fee and that, if they won't, there are plenty of cards with no fee you can switch to. With some companies, it'll work; with others, it won't.

Some card issuers have actually imposed annual fees on cardholders that pay off their bill in full each month, essentially penalizing them for not generating enough income from interest charges. Sheesh. If your card company is that obnoxious, tell them you'll take your business elsewhere unless they waive the fee.

## 21 Is there any reliable place online where I can compare

## various credit cards to see which one is best for me?

There sure is. Many spots on the Web offer just such information. One good place to start (and probably to finish) is www.bankrate.com. It offers a wealth of information to help you get the best deals on all kinds of loans, credit cards, and accounts. Click on "Credit Cards" there, and you'll be able to find lists of the best credit card deals, with interest rates and grace periods detailed for you. You'll find more information at sites such as www.cardtrak.com.

## 22 What's the ideal kind of credit card? What should I look for when choosing one?

Look for a credit card with no annual fee. If you're Foolishly planning to pay off the balance each month, the interest rate on the card won't be of paramount importance. Do pay attention to the grace period, though, and aim to get a card with at least a 25-day grace period. That's the period of time when you don't accrue interest charges on your new balance. The longer the grace period, the more time you have to send in your check.

If you're not going to be able to pay off your balance each month, look for a card that excludes new purchases from the interest calculation period. That means they don't base the interest charges on two months of billing cycles. Some cards are set up to calculate interest that way, and it ends up costing you more.

## 23 How can I effectively warn my son, who's heading to college soon, about the dangers of credit card debt?

Here's what we might say to him:

College can be great. No parents nagging you with curfews. You can eat ice cream for breakfast and popcorn for dinner, if you like. And, best of all, America's banks keep offering you credit cards!

Fast-forward to your graduation. You've racked up $5,000 in debt on your card. (That's just $104 per month for four years.) Are you worried? Naaaah. Your minimum monthly payment is only 2% — just $100 per month. Consider a few other things, though. When you signed up for the card, it offered that low 6.9% interest rate. But, you did notice, didn't you, that the rate swelled to 18% after six months? Sneaky devils, those card companies.

Now, even if you don't accumulate any more debt, it will take you more than *43 years* to pay off the balance if you just make minimum payments. Holy guacamole! All told, you will have paid nearly $18,000 just for the privilege of charging $5,000. No wonder the banks keep sending you unsolicited credit card applications.

Here's another danger. Let's say that you're fired up to invest in stocks, but you still owe that $5,000, paying 18% annual interest on it. If your $5,000 stock investment nets you an 11% return, you're *still* losing money — 11% in, 18% out. Investing doesn't work well if you're deep in debt at high interest rates.

Don't worry, though. We're not going to tell you to use credit cards only as shoehorns, eye patches, and after-dinner snacks. It's okay to have a credit card. Just make sure that you're only charging what you can afford to pay, and that you pay the bills off in full each month. Choose your cards carefully, using an electron microscope to read the fine print. Look for a low interest rate; no annual fee; no unreasonable penalties; and a protected, interest-free grace period. Then, when the bill arrives, take five minutes and scrutinize your statement for mysterious charges.

Finally, if you find it difficult to manage a revolving-debt card, consider getting the type of charge card that *requires* full payment each month — like an old-fashioned American Express card.

The typical American household owes thousands of dollars on credit cards. Be above average, Fool. Graduate without credit card debt.

---

## 24 How long would it take someone to pay off a credit card if they only pay the minimum amount due each month? Is it structured to last forever?

It will take longer than an entire lifetime — if you're a gorilla. For us *Homo Sapiens*, it'll take about half a lifetime. It all depends on the size of the balance you're carrying on the card and the card's minimum percentage due. Most cards have a minimum due of between 1.5% and 2.5% of your outstanding balance. Let's say that you owe $4,500 on your card. If so, it'll take you about 44 years to pay it off — and you'll end up paying a total of $17,000. Yowza. That's a pretty powerful demonstration of how vital it is to pay down your balance.

## 25 Is it true that if someone steals my credit card and charges hundreds of dollars on it, I'm only responsible for $50?

Yup. By law, consumers can't be held responsible for more than $50 if they are the victims of fraud and report the theft promptly. So, you should contact the card company as soon as you notice that a card has been lost or stolen.

In addition, be careful with "pre-approved" offers you receive in the mail. If you toss them out and a dastardly sort picks one up, he can change the address on it to his own and get a card in your name. This is one way that identities are stolen. It's not a bad idea to buy a paper shredder to destroy credit card offers and documents with confidential information. At office supply stores, you should be able to pick up a modest shredder for around $20 or $30.

## 26 I'm tired of getting so many credit card offers in the mail. I already have a card and don't want any more mail offering me new ones. How can I stop it?

There are three main credit bureaus in the United States, and they've agreed that if someone contacts one of them and asks to be removed from junk mail (er, "direct mail") lists and telemarketing phone lists, they'll all honor the request. Call them at: 888-5-OPT-OUT. Here are the three and their websites: Equifax (www.equifax.com), Experian (www.experian.com), and Trans Union (www.tuc.com).

While we're on the subject, you can opt-out of even more junk mail and telemarketing calls by contacting the Direct Marketing Association (DMA). Here are the addresses:

Mail Preference Service
Direct Marketing Association
PO Box 9008
Farmingdale, NY 11735

Telephone Preference Service
Direct Marketing Association
PO Box 9014
Farmingdale, NY 11735

Opting-out through the DMA won't stop mail from local merchants, religious and charitable associations, professional and alumni associations, politicians, and companies with which you conduct business. To stop those, you'll have to contact each organization directly.

## 27 Do you have any other tips on managing credit cards?

People on our online discussion boards share thoughts on this every day. In our "College Fools" discussion board, for example, people have been posting messages discussing how tempting and dangerous credit cards can be to college students. (Much of America's whopping credit card debt begins in the college years.) The consensus is that credit card bills should be paid off in full each month. Fool Steve Koch had this interesting contrary take, though:

> "I just wanted to point out that credit cards aren't as bad as you make them out to be. You say you only use credit cards if you have to. I believe in the opposite — I use my Yahoo!, Visa or Discover card at every possible opportunity, even when buying my $2.39 lunch. My wife does the same.
>
> Then, we get a bill from First USA and Discover every month for $1,200 or so, due in a few weeks. You know what my wife does? She writes a check from our Waterhouse Securities money market checking account, puts it in an envelope, and notes on the outside of the envelope the last possible day to send in the check (usually 7 days before due, I believe).

This means that we pay for most of the stuff we buy more than a month after we receive it. We average about $1,500 in debt at any given time. But, the funny thing is, we pay 0% interest on this debt and, because of the debt, our money market account has roughly $1,500 extra in it at all times. That works out to about $70/year extra cash, beyond the 1% cash back and 1% gift certificates we receive.

So, while your system is good, I believe you are missing out. Interest-free debt is not a bad thing, as long as you are not living from paycheck to paycheck. If you don't trust yourself to pay off the bill, then by all means, take your credit card out of your wallet. But, once you can trust yourself, I believe a smart move is to start taking money back from First USA. Believe me, I feel no burden whatsoever from my credit card debt."

## 28 What are some resources that will help me learn more about digging out of debt?

Here are some that should prove useful:

**Websites**
- www.nfcc.org
- www.debtproofliving.com
- www.Fool.com/credit

**Books**
- *How to Get Out of Debt, Stay Out of Debt and Live Prosperously* by Jerrold Mundis
- *10 Minute Guide to Beating Debt* by Susan Abentrod
- *Downsize Your Debt* by Andrew Feinberg
- *Credit Card & Debt Management* by Scott Bilker
- *Credit Card Debt* by Alexander Daskaloff

**CHAPTER THREE**
**ANSWERS TO YOUR QUESTIONS ABOUT**

# Insurance

*The thought of insurance may not get your heart racing, but if you ever find yourself looking at a grease spot on the asphalt where you last saw your car or at the smoldering remains of your home, and you're not insured, you'll find your heart racing plenty. Insurance is not a luxury, but a necessity. It's not something to put off thinking about, it's something to deal with now. It's not just for your car and health. There are other forms of insurance you should consider, as well. So read through this section and you'll be prepared to get your insurance house in order — and to save some money on it in the process.*

## 29 What are the main types of insurance?

Here are the biggies:
- Life insurance
- Disability insurance
- Long-term care insurance
- Health insurance
- Dental insurance
- Eye/vision insurance
- Renter's insurance
- Homeowner's insurance
- Mortgage insurance
- Auto insurance
- Monster-under-the-bed insurance

Okay, I was just kidding about that last one. There are a host of other kinds of insurance, though, such as pet insurance, "pre-need" (funeral) insurance, etc. And, within the categories listed above, you'll typically find many sub-categories, such as whole life insurance and term life insurance.

## 30 What kind of insurance makes the best investment?

Don't think of it as an investment. It's true that some "investments" in insurance will appreciate in value, but the main point of insurance is protecting you against the financial consequences of losses, not serving to increase your wealth. If you're looking for long-term investments, there are many options more attractive than insurance — chief among them stocks. If you're looking for protection against floods, car accidents, appendicitis, or death, you need insurance. (And, if you're looking for company on cold winter nights, you may need a cat.)

## 31 What are a "premium" and a "deductible"?

An insurance policy's premium is the amount you have to pay for the policy. For car insurance, as an example, your premium might be $800 per year (or more or less, depending on many things). The premium is the amount you pay to keep the policy in force.

The deductible is the amount or portion that *you* will have to pay on any claim. For example, let's say that you have a car insurance policy with a $250 deductible. If you have a small accident and the repair will cost $600, you'll have to pay the first $250 of that, and your insurance policy should cover the rest. If you have another mishap a few months later, you'll again have to pay the first $250 of the cost.

The lower the deductible you choose, the higher your premium will be. So, unless you are particularly accident prone, it's often smart to carry a fairly steep deductible to lessen the cost of the policy. A good rule of thumb is to determine how much you could afford to pay out-of-pocket, without causing severe financial hardship, if you have a claim. Then make that amount (or the closest option offered by the policy) your deductible.

Before you agree to any insurance policy, ask about and make sure you understand what limitations there are to claims being paid, so you don't pay for insurance that won't serve your needs.

## 32 What are some common mistakes people make with insurance?

A major one is buying unnecessary insurance. Keep in mind that insurance is meant to address financial losses. Without health insurance, a serious illness could wipe you out financially. Similarly, life insurance is just insuring against loss of income due to someone dying; it can't do much else about death. That's why it doesn't necessarily make sense to insure the lives of your children... or even yourself, if you're single and dependent-free. The death of a child is catastrophic in countless ways, but not usually financially. And, if a dependent-free, single person bites the dust, it's not likely to put financial pressure on anyone.

Depending on your point of view, flight insurance is another unnecessary expense. Airplanes are just about the safest means of transportation — especially compared to cars — yet people who don't carry sufficient auto insurance routinely buy flight insurance.

Another mistake is looking at insurance as a way for your loved ones to get wildly rich when you expire. You need to view insurance as financial protection, not a lottery ticket. Many people take out more insurance than they really need, and it costs them more than it needs to.

Finally, many people, after paying into a policy for years and years, will stop paying for it due to some short-term budget crisis. This is rarely a smart move, as insurance is vital and they're leaving themselves unprotected. If years go by and you don't have any claims, you might feel like you've been pouring money down a drain, but you haven't. All that time, you've been protected against financial loss — which could have happened during the time period.

## 33 What's the difference between whole life and term life insurance?

These are the two main forms of life insurance you should understand. (It's also good to learn about universal and variable, which are variations of whole life insurance.)

With term insurance, you're covered only during the life of the policy, while you're paying the premiums. If you carry a term life insurance policy for 50 years, regularly pay the premiums, and then quit paying and die a year later, you're out of luck. (Well, you'd be out of luck regardless — but, in this case, your beneficiaries are out of luck, too.)

There are several forms of term insurance:
- **Level term** is where you pay a fixed premium for up to 20 years. This can be a good deal, as it protects you against the effects of inflation and unexpected changes in your health that would warrant higher premiums.

- **Annual renewable term** gives you the option of renewing your policy regularly, but at increasing premium rates.

- **Decreasing term** policies feature a steadily decreasing death benefit. This might seem undesirable, but it can be sensible for many people. You may need a bigger benefit when you're a young breadwinner for your family than when you're a retiree with grown children and a nice nest egg.

Whole life insurance, meanwhile, is designed to cover you for your whole life. These policies charge you a fixed premium each year, one that's typically higher than term insurance. The advantage touted by insurance companies for whole life insurance is that, while part of the premium covers what term insurance would cost, the surplus resides in an account that pays interest and accumulates a cash value. As this "accumulation account" grows, your premiums can decrease over time. Eventually, in some cases, the interest earned can pay the premiums for you. So, you won't be paying any more premiums, but you'll still be covered for the rest of your life.

The problem with whole life insurance is that insurance companies tend to offer low interest rates to policyholders, while they typically earn much greater returns because they invest the money in stocks and bonds. Policyholders are indeed earning a bit of money through the policy, but as an "investment," it leaves a lot to be desired.

Enter "universal" life insurance, a form of whole life insurance. With universal life, in years when the insurance company earns more on policyholders' accumulation accounts than they promised, they pass along the extra gain. This sounds good but, in some situations, due to overly optimistic assumptions insurers make about returns customers will earn, customers can end up paying more than they expected to. "Variable" life insurance policies, which invest in sub-accounts that look like (but legally are not and cannot be) mutual funds, carry the same danger.

With universal and variable insurance, the higher the initial assumed rate of return, the lower the annual payments will be. This is how some unscrupulous agents can sign you up—through very attractive policies based on unreasonable assumptions. Since most insurers invest to a great degree in bonds, be skeptical of any promised universal rates much higher than the 30-year Treasury rate. With variable insurance, since most mutual funds have trouble beating the S&P 500's average historical return of 10-12% per year, we'd be skeptical of any projected rates in that neighborhood.

## 34 Do you recommend term life insurance or whole life insurance?

For most people, it probably makes the most sense to stick to term insurance. Buy just as much insurance as you need, and only for as long as you need it. With term insurance, you won't be paying anything extra as an "investment." Instead, put the money you save on premiums into better long-term investments — such as stock market index funds, stocks you've selected on your own, or whatever you're most comfortable with. Your own investments are likely to outperform any investment an insurance company makes for you. By combining term insurance with investments on your own, you'll be minimizing your insurance costs and maximizing your investment potential.

Another plus for term insurance is that it's a very competitive segment of the insurance business, with companies lowering costs to win customers.

---

## 35 | How much life insurance do I need?

You're actually the one best able to answer that question. Ignore blanket formulas that suggest you need something like five to 10 times your annual income. Each person's situation is different. Look at insurance not as a lottery-like payoff, but as filling a specific need. If you're insuring your own life, you need to think about the financial impact of your demise on your family. Take out a pen and paper. List yourself and the members of your family. List how much money comes in from various sources. List how much is needed by various people each year. Think about how these numbers will change over time.

For example, let's say you contribute $45,000 per year to your family, and your spouse contributes $40,000. That's the extent of your family's income. Perhaps you have two teenage children. Take a deep breath and begin imagining the unimaginable. What if you and your income stream disappear from the picture? Will your spouse and children get by on just the $40,000? Think about how much additional income they'd need. If your kids are in their late teens, they're probably not too far away from being able to support themselves. You'd need greater insurance coverage if the kids were still toddlers.

Think about the contributions you would have been making over the years to any college funds or to your retirement nest egg. You'll want your insurance policy to fill those gaps. Are you also supporting your mother-in-law? If so, you'll want to make sure that she isn't left in the lurch should you get run over by a bus.

You also have to consider additional expenses your spouse will face as a single parent. With two toddlers or an aging parent to support, for example, will she be able to pay for the extra childcare help she'll need, maybe a lawn-care service for the house, daytime help for her mother, and still be able to work if you die? If not, you need insurance to cover her lost income and the added expenses she'll face.

If your kids' future educational costs are already covered and your mother-in-law has sufficient insurance of her own, you may not need very much in the way of insurance. Spend some time thinking about how much coverage you need to protect your loved ones from financial hardships posed by your death. You may need a lot of coverage now, and much less a few years down the road.

You might take advantage of some online calculators that help you estimate your insurance needs. State Farm's website offers one at www.statefarm.com/jscript/cashneed.htm. Poke around New York Life's website at www.newyorklife.com and you'll find another. Don't use these as more than general tools, though. They shouldn't be making any decisions for you. That's what the gray matter between your ears is for!

## 36 Is it smart to buy disability insurance?

It sure is. Disability insurance provides an income if you become... you guessed it, disabled. According to some reports, nearly half of all mortgage foreclosures are due to disability. Are most people taking steps to prevent this? Nope — less than 15% of life insurance purchasers opt for disability insurance.

Think of it this way: If you're 35 years old, earning $50,000 per year, and become disabled for the rest of your life, you'll be losing roughly $1.5 million in income from age 35 to 65. Disability insurance serves to help make up for that loss. (Being disabled from age 35 to 65 will also mean that you'll miss out on something like 7,500 or more hours of office meetings, too. Unfortunately, insurance can't make up for this. Sorry.)

We often worry about and plan for death, but we tend to give little thought to the possibility of an extended period of disability. If you make your living as a chimney sweep and you suffer a bad wrist break, you'll likely be unable to work for quite a while. Here's where disability insurance would kick in, protecting you from that loss of income.

Depending on the kind of coverage you have, disability insurance might pay you a fraction of your salary while you're disabled, or your entire salary. It might continue until you reach retirement age, or stop after a number of months or years. Many people are covered by their employers. Check and see what coverage your company offers you, and evaluate whether it's good enough. You may want to purchase additional coverage, either through your employer or separately.

Disability insurance can seem expensive, but that's largely because there's a high probability you will use it. Many people become temporarily incapacitated at some point in the course of their lives.

## 37 How likely is it that I'll need disability insurance in my lifetime?

Take a gander at this table. It shows how likely you are to become disabled for various periods of time before you reach 65 years of age, depending on your current age:

| If you are now | for 6 months | for 1 year | for 2 years | for 5 years |
|---|---|---|---|---|
| 25 | 35% | 22% | 17% | 13% |
| 30 | 33 | 21 | 16 | 13 |
| 35 | 31 | 20 | 16 | 13 |
| 40 | 28 | 18 | 15 | 12 |
| 45 | 25 | 17 | 14 | 11 |
| 50 | 14 | 12 | 17 | 10 |

As you can see, even if you're 40, the odds are nearly one in five that you'll be disabled for an entire year. The higher odds for younger people might surprise you, too. But, remember that childbirth and recovery are considered medical disabilities for women and can last six months or more. Disability insurance is a dangerous thing to ignore.

## 38 What does disability insurance consider "disabled"?

It varies by policy, so make sure you understand the terms of any coverage you have or are considering. With some policies, they're in effect only until you can be employed in some way. So, if you were a dentist and, after being on disability awhile, you regain enough mobility to become employed as a receptionist, your disability payments will end. With other policies, you're considered disabled until you can resume your original line of work.

## 39 What should I look for in a disability policy?

If you can find them, look for policies that are guaranteed and non-cancelable. Guaranteed means the payment is fixed. Non-cancelable means that the policy will remain in effect as long as you keep paying the premiums.

Examine the policy's definition of "disabled" and make sure it's what you want. Ideally, you'll want it to cover any disability related to working in your current occupation.

Finally, carefully evaluate how the policy will pay you, in the event that it needs to. Make sure that the payment will increase as your income increases. (If you buy the policy when you're earning $30,000 and become disabled when you're earning $45,000, you don't want your benefit based on the initial salary.) Some policies offer riders that will permit the payment to increase with inflation, as well.

Check out how long the policy will pay you. A good one will cover you until you reach retirement age. Others may stop after five or 10 years. See what percentage of your salary the policy will pay. Some pay 60% or less, others pay 75% or more.

One good way to save money on the policy is by increasing the waiting period. Some policies kick in very soon after you become disabled. Others require a waiting period of up to several months. You'll typically have to pay more for more immediate coverage. But, if you're prepared with a bit of an emergency nest egg, you can opt for a lengthy waiting period to reduce your cost. Invest the savings and you might well surpass the value of that little nest egg.

One last consideration is a "return of premium" rider that you might get offered. With this, you pay a higher premium and get some of your money back if you don't ever use the policy. We're not big fans of this, as we'd rather invest that extra premium amount ourselves.

## 40 | What is long-term care insurance for, really?

Many people assume it's for nursing home care, and it often is, but that's not all. It can also cover at-home care. Basically, it's there to help you if you're having at least a certain amount of trouble performing "daily living" activities such as bathing, dressing, eating, transferring in or out of a bed or chair, and using the toilet. To a lesser degree, it can also aid in activities such as managing money, doing heavy or light housework, taking medications, shopping, preparing meals, and using the telephone. It will typically pay a certain amount per day, which may cover all or part of your needs.

Another misperception about long-term care insurance is that it's for old people. Remember that even young people can become temporarily or permanently incapacitated due to illnesses or accidents. In many cases, disability insurance can cover these risks. But, if you're young, you might still want to look into long-term care insurance and what it can offer you. A bonus is that premiums are low for young people. And, some policies permit you to pay for a number of years in your youth and will then cover you for the rest of your life. A little exploration can turn up some valuable coverage.

## 41 | Is buying long-term care insurance a good idea?

Possibly. Here are some scary statistics to help you take this issue seriously:
- At 65, the average person's chances of being admitted to a nursing home at some point in the future are more than 4 in 10. (Source: Long-Term Care Campaign)
- One person in three who turned 65 in 1990 will stay a year in a nursing home. One person in 10 will stay five years or more. (Source: National Association of Insurance Commissioners)
- In 1994, 7.3 million Americans needed long-term care services at an average cost of nearly $43,800 per year. By 2000, this number will rise to 9 million Americans at nearly $55,750 per year and, due to inflation, by 2060 it will skyrocket to 24 million Americans paying more than $250,000 per year to receive long-term care. (Source: Long Term Care Insurance National Advisory Council)

- Recent studies report that two of every five people age 65 and over will enter a nursing home and stay an average of 2.5 years. (Source: *Life Insurance Selling*, December 1995)
- Within a year after admission as private-pay residents, more than 90% of nursing home residents are impoverished. (Source: *Life Savings* by Harley Gordon, 1994)
- Nursing home care costs, on average, about $40,000 per year. (Source: State Farm website)

As with all scary statistics, though, take them with a large grain of salt, as they can be and often are misleading. For more on this topic, see the article "Those Dratted Statistics Made Easier" written by The Motley Fool's retirement expert Dave Braze. The article may be found at the following web address, if you have the stamina to type it in: www.Fool.com/retirement/retireeport/2000/retireeport000222.htm.

---

## 42 How can I figure out if I need long-term care insurance?

There's no one answer that applies to everyone. The United Seniors Health Cooperative, a nonprofit consumer organization devoted to the issues of the elderly, suggests that long-term care insurance is appropriate provided it costs no more than 7% of your retired income and:

a. You have $75,000 or more per person in assets, excluding a home and a car.
b. You have a retirement income of at least $35,000 per person per year.
c. You can pay the premium without adversely affecting your lifestyle.
d. You could absorb up to a 30% increase in future premiums, if necessary.

If you're fairly wealthy, you may not need this insurance. Figure out what the kind of nursing home care you'd want would cost, and see how many years you could easily pay for it. If it won't present that much of a problem, you may be better off not paying out hefty premiums to cover expenses you might not incur, since you have alternative means of paying for them should they materialize.

## 43 Do you have any tips for buying long-term care insurance?

First, these policies vary widely in terms of cost, what they cover, and when they will actually pay. This makes it very tough to compare them.

One good strategy is to start early. If you wait until you're 75, the cost will be fairly steep. Many policies allow you to buy in your 50s and enjoy a fixed premium for the rest of your life. This can be a good deal. It's also smart, because you can suffer ill health at any time and, once you do, you may have trouble getting long-term care insurance. Better to sign up while you're still healthy, if possible.

Another strategy is for a couple to shop for coverage together. Some companies will offer a substantial discount if you're buying two policies together.

If at all possible, get a policy that hikes the amount of your benefit to keep pace with inflation. This is especially important if you're buying the insurance relatively early in life. You may not need it for 20 or 25 years. But, when you need it, you don't want it to have become a pittance.

As with disability insurance, you can decrease your cost if you're willing to accept a lengthened waiting period between when the need occurs and when the benefits kick in. You might also limit the policy's payments to include only part of a nursing home's costs, planning to make up the difference with Social Security or some other income or savings.

Other things to look for in a policy:
- No prior hospitalization is required. (Some policies require this before paying for nursing home expenses.)
- Home health care is covered (in case you don't want to and don't need to go to a nursing home).
- You're covered no matter what kind of nursing home you choose.
- The policy doesn't limit its coverage to just "skilled care." This is required by a tiny fraction of long-term care patients and is one way insurers can try to dodge payments — by severely limiting what they'll pay for.

## 44 Where can I learn more about long-term care and nursing homes?

We offer more detailed information in our retirement area at Fooldom online (www.Fool.com/retirement.htm). At www.ushc-online.org, the United Seniors Health Cooperative offers additional useful information.

Here are several books recommended by the Fool's retirement expert, Dave Braze:

- *Beat the Nursing Home Trap: A Consumers Guide to Assisted Living & Long-Term Care*, by Joseph Matthews
- *Long-Term Care Planning: A Dollar & Sense Guide*, available from the United Seniors Health Cooperative. To buy it, contact the U.S.H.C. at 202-479-6615.
- *Insider Secrets to Long Term Care Insurance*, available from Health-Watch Group, Ltd. It can be purchased as an electronic document at www.booklocker.com/bookpages/lsauls.html.
- *Shoppers Guide to Long-Term Care Insurance*, available free on request from the National Association of Insurance Commissioners. Click over to www.naic.org/webinfo.htm, call 816-783-8300, or write them at NAIC Publications, 2301 McGee St., Kansas City, MO 64108.

## 45 What factors influence car insurance rates?

Your age and your driving record are two biggies. The more experience you have driving, the fewer accidents and traffic violations you're likely to have. The more tickets and convictions for violations you have, the steeper your premiums will be.

The car's model, age, and how you use it are additional factors. A 1999 Maserati 3200 GT is likely to command higher rates than a 1977 Dodge Dart. Insurers may also factor in annual mileage driven and how much the car is driven for business vs. pleasure.

Where you drive and park your car also matters. People living in cities tend to pay higher rates than people in the suburbs or small towns do. That's because of higher crime rates and higher costs of repairs or medical expenses.

## 46 How can I save money on a car insurance policy?

One simple thing you can do is increase the amount of your deductible. The lower your deductible, the higher your premiums. Ask yourself how likely you are to incur expenses, and how often that might occur. Compare that with the extra amount you're paying on your policy. For many people, it makes sense to carry a deductible of about $500 and pay lower premiums. Hiking a deductible from $200 to $500 can sometimes save you 15-30%.

Another option is to make sure you're not over-insuring your car. If you're driving an old clunker, you may not want to bother with collision and comprehensive coverage on it. Cars worth less than $1,000 are often not worth repairing. If you have an accident where the cost to repair the car exceeds its fair value, the insurance company will usually opt to "total" the car. That means your car is labeled a "total loss" and the insurance company is only obligated to pay you the "Blue Book" value minus your deductible, rather than paying the higher amount necessary to fix the car. They also will no longer insure the car, so you'll be left looking for a new set of wheels.

Many insurers will give you a significant discount (up to 10%) if you hold more than one policy with them. So, look into buying both auto and home insurance from the same insurer. Whichever company you choose, make sure you investigate all possible discounts. Some insurers will knock off a few dollars for safety devices such as airbags or anti-theft devices such as passive engine disablers.

Oddly enough, paying a little *more* for your policy can save you money, too. Most policies, for a few dollars per month, will pay for a rental car should your car be damaged and unusable. This can be a big savings, so it's something to think about. Something else to include is coverage that protects you if an uninsured or underinsured motorist hits you. (According to some experts, as many as half or more of all motorists fall into these categories.) Most policies offer a degree of coverage in this area, but it might not be as much as you need or want.

And finally, do some comparison-shopping! Don't assume that the price differences among various insurers are small, because they're often not.

P.S. If you're a shareholder in Warren Buffett's company, Berkshire Hathaway, you may be in luck. Berkshire Hathaway owns car insurer GEICO and offers discounts in the neighborhood of 8% to shareholders. GEICO also offers discounts to members of various organizations too. Call GEICO at 800-861-8380 for more information.

---

## 47 I rent an apartment. Should I bother with renter's insurance?

You betcha. Here's what it can do for you:
- Protect you against theft of or damage to your personal property.
- Cover some or all of your personal liability.
- Sometimes pays for temporary housing, if your rented home is damaged.

With renter's insurance, you decide how much total dollar value of property you want to insure. Some policies will pay you enough to cover the depreciated value of various items at the time of loss, while others will cover replacement costs. This can be a big deal. Let's say you bought a computer for $2,500 a few years ago and it's now worth $250 (don't laugh — this isn't an extreme situation!). It's suddenly ruined by water dripping onto it from an apartment above you. One policy might pay you just the $250 that it's worth, while another policy may pay you enough to buy a new computer with similar features.

Renter's insurance can cost as little as $100 or less per year. Compared with the losses you might incur, it can be well worth it.

---

## 48 Are there any important, little-known facts about renter's insurance?

Yup, here are a few:
- If you have an unrelated roommate and you get renter's insurance, your roommate isn't likely to be covered. Standard policies cover relatives living with you, but that's it.
- Don't assume that your policy covers everything. Read the details. For example, most standard policies don't cover earthquake damage. So, if earthquakes are a real threat to you, ask about additional earthquake coverage.

- You might be able to save money by getting renter's insurance from the company that insures your car. Insurers often offer discounts for multiple-policy holders.
- You might also pay a lower rate if your rental property has a burglar alarm, sprinkler system, fire alarm, or smoke detectors.

## 49 What do I need to know about homeowner's insurance?

There's too much to cover in detail here, but basically homeowner's insurance covers two things: your personal property and your personal liability. Just about any homeowner should carry this insurance. If you have a mortgage on your home, the lender will be listed on your homeowner's policy and will require you to carry the policy because it protects the lender against non-payment of the mortgage balance. If your house burns to the ground, you have little incentive to keep paying that mortgage. After all, there's no "house" any more. That's why your mortgage company will be the first to be paid on the loss because, technically, they "own" the house (the structure and land) until the mortgage is paid off.

As with any insurance, when buying a homeowner's policy, first determine exactly how much coverage you need and want in order to cover your property and your personal liability. Once you know exactly what you're looking for, take some time to do a little comparison-shopping.

## 50 How are my personal possessions protected with homeowner's insurance?

Just as with renter's insurance, you want to pay attention to whether your losses will be paid on an "actual cash value" basis or a "replacement cost" basis. The former will cover just the depreciated value of the property at the time of loss. The latter is preferable, covering what it will cost you to replace the property at a current price. You typically will have to cough up extra to get replacement cost coverage.

Ask the insurer what they show as the total value of your personal property. Usually it's an estimate the insurance company makes based on the size of your home and where you live. But, it may be out of whack with the actual value of your possessions — you might live in a modest abode, but have very expensive taste in clothing, furniture, and accessories, for example. Or, conversely, you may have just purchased a sprawling estate, but it's basically empty because you need to save up for furniture. Walk through your home and mentally add up the cost of things. Then make sure your insurer's estimate is in the right ballpark. If not, ask to have the amount adjusted to reflect your own estimate. This will change your premium up or down, but you won't be faced with a horrible surprise if you have a loss and you won't be paying for insurance you don't need. Review this every year or so, to make sure your insurance keeps up with you.

Also, as with renter's insurance, make sure you understand exactly what's covered and what isn't, and to what extent. There are often limits on how much you can claim in various categories (such as jewelry, art, or cash). If this is the case, and you own a lot of expensive jewelry, you should purchase additional coverage.

## 51 If my property is stolen or burned in a fire, how will I prove what I lost for an insurance claim?

As noted earlier, based on where you live and the number of rooms in your house, the insurance company assumes you have a certain amount of clothing and other possessions. So, if the claims are within reason, there usually isn't too much trouble as long as you can provide reasonable descriptions and cost estimates for your possessions. If you lose everything, the insurance company will generally cut you a check for the total estimate they used for your policy coverage, not an item-by-item payment.

That being said, most people who experience significant losses due to fires and other disasters find that they have a difficult time remembering everything in each room, let alone model numbers and descriptions. A great way to prevent having to remember every detail is to make use of a camcorder (yours or one borrowed from a friend). You might be surprised at just how many individual items you actually own! Walk through your house and videotape the contents, describing things as you film. Open drawers, closets, and cabinets to film the contents. Turn appliances around and videotape model numbers and other characteristics. Show measurements and describe the materials things are made of that might not be apparent on videotape (e.g., a leather chair versus vinyl, an oil painting versus a print, a granite countertop versus ceramic tile, etc.), to help place an accurate value on your possessions.

Then, put this videotape somewhere it won't be damaged by whatever happens to your house — a fireproof safe, a bank safe deposit box, a strongbox in your detached garage or shed, or even at a trusted friend or family member's house. Update or redo the video every few years, depending on your needs.

## 52 What about earthquake damage to my home?

As California residents will tell you, most homeowner's policies don't cover earthquakes — if you live in an area with a high risk of earthquakes and you want earthquake coverage, ask about it and have it added on.

## 53 Will my homeowner's policy cover damage from flooding?

A very common tragedy that often catches people by surprise is that most homeowner's policies do not cover losses due to flooding. If you live in an area prone to flooding or where there is any potential for flooding from rivers, lakes, mountain snow packs, or storms, it's a good idea to purchase flood insurance. The Federal Emergency Management Agency (FEMA) offers flood insurance at reasonable rates. See the FEMA website at www.fema.gov or call FEMA and ask for information on the National Flood Insurance Program at 1-888-CALL-FLOOD. The insurance does not kick in immediately, so call and get coverage well before you expect to need it.

## 54 What's an "all risks" policy?

It's a term you'll commonly see on homeowner's insurance policies. "All risks" means that you're covered for any kind of loss to your property except causes that are specifically listed as excluded. If your policy isn't an "all risks" one, you probably have a "named perils" one. Named perils policies only cover your property losses when they're caused by perils listed on the policy, such as fire, flood, hail, etc. If a peril isn't listed, it's not included.

## 55 Are there any special insurance considerations if I have an older home?

You might want to consider homeowner's coverage that includes any building-code upgrades needed if you suffer a loss and have to rebuild your home. Most policies will just cover what it costs to put things back exactly the way they are now. If building codes in your area have changed significantly since your house was built, they may require something that your house doesn't have (better wiring, more substantial foundation, different easement restrictions, etc.). You will have to pay for improvements to bring your house up to code if your policy doesn't cover these expenses, and the total cost can be substantial for older homes. Check on the building requirements for your community to see if this is something you should be concerned about.

## 56 How can I save money on my homeowner's policy?

Here are some ways:
- Buy just as much insurance as you need, and no more. Ask yourself how much it would cost to replace your personal property, rebuild your house, or buy another like it in the same neighborhood.
- Look into discounts. Some policies offer them for burglar alarms, deadbolt locks, and perhaps some construction features. You can often also get a discount if the same insurer is covering your home and your car.
- Increase your deductible. If you don't expect to file claims very often, then the higher the deductible, the more you'll save each year on your premiums. (Just make sure you can afford to pay the deductible if and when the need arises.)
- Comparison shop. Contact agents from a variety of companies and also do a little shopping online, at sites such as www.insure.com.

## 57 How should I calculate how much personal liability insurance I need in various insurance policies?

A good rule of thumb is to ask yourself how much you have to *lose* if you're sued. Add up the value of your home, your belongings, and your financial assets. Tack on more for the cost of legal defense. (In some cases, the insurance company will take care of providing a lawyer.) You want to be sure that a lawsuit won't wipe you out or cause severe financial strain.

If your total assets are substantial, ask your insurance company about an "umbrella" personal liability policy. Umbrella policies generally offer much more liability coverage ($1 million or more) at lower premiums than individual policies such as homeowner's, renter's, and automobile.

## 58 Is it better to buy insurance through an agent, through a website such as www.insure.com, or directly from the company (via phone or the company's website)?

Sometimes you'll find the best prices by skipping the middleman (the agent). But, some agents still offer competitive prices, and the best among them will give you sound advice and guide you through the learning process.

Insurance agents have sometimes been portrayed in a negative light. That's because the shiftier among them prey on the less informed among us, selling unnecessary insurance, insisting that policies are "investments," and not making it clear that they're compensated via commissions.

If you find a good agent who's providing a valuable service to you, you might buy through him. If you haven't met such an agent, though, don't be afraid to explore the world of insurance online.

## 59 Do you recommend "pre-need" funeral insurance?

Many experts think this is an unnecessary expense. This question is answered in more detail in a later chapter covering death and funerals. Flip over there for the scoop.

## 60 Do you recommend pet health insurance?

Pet insurance can be extremely worthwhile, but consider your own situation first. Without it, you face the possibility of one day having to fork over hundreds of dollars to repair Buster's leg or, worse yet, having to decide whether to spend thousands of dollars to save Frisky's life.

The value really depends on the type of pet you have, its age and health (some breeds, older pets, and pets with chronic or terminal illnesses are usually not approved for coverage), and what your personal feelings about pet healthcare are. You may have personal limits to what extraordinary measures you are willing to consider for a pet, or you may be willing to do absolutely anything possible to treat an unexpected health problem. In the latter case, pet insurance premiums are fairly reasonable, ranging from $100 to $300 per year. The premiums can increase as much as 50% as your pet ages (usually after 9 years of age for dogs and 11 years for cats).

More and more companies are now offering pet insurance to employees. If yours doesn't and you are interested in the option, ask your human resources department to look into it. In the meantime, check out insurers such as Veterinary Pet Insurance (www.petinsurance.com and 800-872-7387) and Premiere Pet Insurance (www.ppins.com and 877-774-2273).

## 61 Where can I learn more about various kinds of insurance?

As you might have suspected, we offer detailed information in Fooldom online, at www.Fool.com/insurance. You can get additional details at www.quicken.com/insurance. Another very useful site is the previously mentioned www.insure.com, where you can read up on just about any kind of insurance.

You'll find another good resource in the websites of many major insurance companies. There's a host of consumer information at AIG's www.aigdirect.com site, for example, if you poke around. You'll also find info at sites such as www.allstate.com, www.chubb.com, www.newyorklife.com, www.statefarm.com, and www.metlife.com. To find the website of any other major company, try looking it up at company information site www.hoovers.com or via a search engine such as www.google.com.

If you're interested in health insurance, try www.hiaa.org and www.ehealthinsurance.com. The latter has a good collection of answers to frequently asked questions.

Just remember where you are when you're at an insurance company's website. Realize that they're in the business of selling you as much insurance as they can. So, learn what you can from them, but don't immediately sign up for lots of policies.

Here are some books that might also be of interest:
- *The Complete Idiot's Guide to Buying Insurance and Annuities* by Brian H. Breuel
- *A Comprehensive Guide to Understanding Your Homeowner's Insurance Policy* by Gerald J. Curren, Jr.
- *How to Save 25% Plus on Your Auto Insurance* by Alan Abler
- *Getting the Most from Your Insurance Claim* by Patrick M. Catania
- *How to Win the Insurance Claim Game* by Ron Alford
- *Long Term Care Planning Guide* (9th Ed., 1999) by Phyllis R. Shelton
- *Long-Term Care Insurance Made Simple* by Les Abromovitz

**CHAPTER FOUR**
**ANSWERS TO YOUR QUESTIONS ABOUT**

# Buying a Car

*Vroom vroom! You can go through all of your life having bought a house just once, but you'll likely buy a car five to 10 times — if not more. Add all those expenses together, and they'll probably amount to the cost of a house. Buying a car involves a significant amount of money. Don't enter into an agreement to buy anything with wheels and cup holders until you've read through at least this chapter. You can probably save hundreds, if not a thousand or more, dollars on your next purchase with some of the tips and strategies that follow.*

## 62 What kind of car makes the best investment?

Don't think of cars as investments. For most of us, they're simply necessary means of transportation. Remember — good investments appreciate over time. Cars, on the other hand, tend to decrease in value over time. That's why it's generally true that the less you spend on cars, the better. That doesn't mean that you should always buy the cheapest available car. Spending a little more on a car that will be reliable and last a long time can be a very smart strategy.

## 63 How quickly do cars depreciate in value?

It depends on the make, model, and year. Some vehicles remain highly desirable in the used car market, so they depreciate more slowly.

In general, expect your new set of wheels to lose 20% or more of its value in its first year. (Some vehicles drop by twice as much.) In fact, a car loses a big chunk of its value as soon as you drive it off the lot! In year two, expect a loss of around 15%. Year three: roughly 13%. Year four: about 12%. If you buy a $20,000 Mazdolet Vroomster, it may be worth just $8,500 in only 5 years — with depreciation amounting to $11,500.

If you buy new cars and drive them for only a few years before trading them in for other new cars, you'll be taking big depreciation hits. The longer you can safely and reliably drive your car, the longer you're putting off spending a big chunk of change for something that will quickly depreciate.

Depreciation is a key reason why it's worthwhile to consider buying a used car. Let's return to our imaginary $20,000 car. After two years, it's likely to have depreciated by around $7,000 or more. So, it'll be worth roughly $13,000. Let's say that it has, conservatively, another seven years of life left in it. If you buy a $13,000 two-year old car and drive it for seven years, you'll have paid roughly $1,860 per year for it.

But, think of how much it cost for the first two years: It went from $20,000 to $13,000 in value, costing about $3,500 per year. If you bought it new and only drove it for two years, that's what it would have cost you (excluding maintenance and repairs, of course).

If you buy a car new and drive it for many years, the average cost per year drops considerably. And, if you buy a good used car and drive it for many years, the cost falls further still. This is clearly a simplified example, but it offers some useful food for thought.

## 64 What are the steps involved in buying a car?

Here are the main steps you can follow:
- Decide how much you can spend on the vehicle.
- Decide whether you're going to buy a new or used car.
- Decide which cars fit your needs and interest you.
- Research the candidates.
- Select one.

- Determine exactly how much it costs and how much you want to pay for it.
- Negotiate for the best price.
- Buy — and enjoy!

## 65 How can I figure out what kind of car I need?

Here's one way. Take a sheet of paper and draw a vertical line one third of the way from the left. You'll have two columns now, the first half as big as the second. In the first column, list all the kinds of vehicles there are:
- Sub/compact
- Family sedan or station wagon
- Sports car/coupe/convertible
- Minivan
- Sport utility vehicle
- Pickup truck
- Full-size van or conversion van
- Luxury sedan

In the right hand column, jot down answers to the following questions:
- How many miles per year do you think you'll drive the vehicle?
- How much time, on average, do you think you'll spend in it each day?
- What type of driving will you be doing? (What percentage of the time will it be on city roads, highways, off-road?)
- How much can you afford to spend?
- List all the reasons you want and need the vehicle (such as for commuting, shuttling kids to activities, camping, antiquing on weekends, etc.).

Now, begin reconciling the two lists and eliminating the vehicle types that don't meet your needs. If you spend a lot of time buying antique furniture, for example, or transporting large animals between zoos, you probably won't want a small sports car with leather seats. If you drive 90% of the time in the city or in heavy, slow traffic, you might not want a gas-guzzler or something that's difficult to park.

Your goal is to get down to one vehicle category. Once you do that, you can begin narrowing the field even further.

## 66 If I'm trying to figure out how much a car will cost me over its life, what should I take into account?

This is a great exercise to go through, as it can help in your budgeting. Below are the main factors to consider. For each one, estimate how much you'll spend on it each year, and then add up all the values for all the years that you expect to own the car.

- Purchase price
- Maintenance
- Repairs
- Gas (or other fuel)
- Insurance
- Taxes
- Registration and plate fees
- Accessories such as fuzzy dice

These considerations are also important if you're thinking of buying a pricey car that you can just afford. You may be able to swing the purchase, but will you be able to afford other steeper costs that might come along with the car, such as higher insurance premiums and premium gasoline?

Some trim models of the same car get placed into higher-premium "sports car" categories by insurance companies, and the cost difference to insure them can really pack a punch to your wallet. Call your insurance company and get an estimate on insurance premiums before you finalize a car purchase, so you won't face any surprises. If a car does seem to cost a lot more to insure than you expected, ask the insurance company why. They may help you choose another model with more reasonable premiums.

## 67 Is it better to buy a new or used car?

Since a car loses much of its value in its first few years, it can make a lot of sense to stick to buying just used cars. In an ideal world, buying used cars will save you a lot of money. But, the world is not ideal. If you're not too savvy about cars and their inner workings, you might get taken advantage of. Used cars are riskier than new ones. You never know the car's full past history. It might be a lemon disguised as a peach.

Still, for some people, buying used cars is the way to go. Here are some questions to ask yourself, to see if you're among this group:
- Am I a skilled negotiator?
- Am I good at determining the real value of things?
- Do I enjoy shopping for vehicles and scouring car lots?
- Am I mechanically inclined, or do I have access to someone handy with cars?
- Am I patient?

The more "yes" answers you have, the more suited you are to used vehicles.

Even if your answers were mostly "no," you might still tap the used vehicle market, via the many dealers now offering "re-warranted" off-lease vehicles.

If you plan to explore the used vehicle market, a very helpful website to check out is www.carfax.com — especially before you finalize a purchase. Private sellers and often, sadly, even car dealerships have been found guilty of repairing "salvage" (seriously damaged) vehicles, taking them across state lines, registering them and getting a "clean" title in the new state, and then putting them up for sale without revealing their true history to prospective buyers. The car you think is one heck of a great deal might have been pulled from a swamp a couple of months ago in another state. Jot down the vehicle identification number (VIN) of any car you're seriously interested in buying and run it through Carfax's free "Instant Lemon Check" service. It could keep you from being taken by unscrupulous car sellers trying to unload some sour automotive citrus fruit (if you catch our drift).

## 68 Once I know what kind of vehicle I want, how should I decide which specific car to buy?

Research. Read up on the many possibilities out there — online and/or in magazines. Stroll around parking lots and get ideas there. Start assembling a list of candidates.

Notice that I haven't mentioned visiting dealerships. That's intentional. If you end up deciding to use our "Fool Fax-a-thon" method (which is described later), it'll be to your advantage not to have visited local dealerships. Also, stepping foot onto dealership lots means that you'll soon be sweet-talked by salespeople who'll be telling you what you want before you've made up your own mind. Don't let them play their tricks on you — they do this for a living.

Fortunately, there are many resources online where you can learn more about cars than you can imagine. (A big bunch of them are listed a few questions later.) Your goal is to winnow down your list of candidates to just *three* models. Some websites offer nifty search functions, where you can specify features you want and will get a list of models fitting those specs.

As you narrow the list, keep in mind the factors most important to you. These might include: price, safety, reliability record, resale value, responsiveness, size, mileage rates, and the ability to turn heads. See which models are closest to your perfect vehicle.

## 69  What should I be on the lookout for when I test-drive a car?

Ideally, you should test-drive it in the various driving conditions you expect to use it in, such as busy city streets and highways. Below are the categories of things you should evaluate as you drive. If you're test-driving without a salesperson in the car, having a friend with you who can jot down your impressions will be helpful. If you're driving with the salesperson, then hold off on jotting down your impressions until just after you leave the dealership. (But, do it immediately after leaving, within a few minutes, before you forget important details.)

In our Buying a Car area online, we've got a very detailed checklist that you can print out and take with you. You can view the checklist at www.Fool.com/car/step7car.htm. In the meantime, here's an abbreviated overview of what to examine:

- **Drive Train Performance and Acceleration**. Pay attention to how well the car accelerates and shifts gears, and how it takes hills. Listen for any noises.

- **Safety Systems & Braking.** Try the brakes on level ground as well as downhill. Listen for any worrisome noises. Make sure the braking feels solid and even.

- **Steering and Handling.** Check out how the vehicle responds to your steering and how well it takes curves. Find a legal U-turn spot and see how tight the turning radius is.

- **Ride Comfort & Suspension Systems.** See if the ride is too hard, too soft, too bumpy, too smooth, or just right. See how it handles itself when you shift gears, change speeds, or brake.

- **Cabin Noise Levels.** Pay attention to all the noises you can. Start with the fan off, vents shut, and the radio off. Listen for engine noise, road and tire noises, wind noise, buzzes, squeaks, rattles, vibrations, etc. Open and close various windows and the sunroof, if there is one. Make sure there aren't any worrisome or annoying noises.

- **Overall Impressions.** Now it's time for the big picture. Is the car a pleasure to drive, or a pain? Are you comfortable and can you see well in all directions? Jot down a list of all the details that stand out as big plusses and big minuses. You'll want to refer to these later.

- **Dealership Impressions.** Finally, take a few notes on how friendly and comfortable the dealership was.

## 70 Are there any other aspects of a car to examine before or after a test-drive?

Yes, indeedily doodily. Much of the examination that you should undertake is best done while the vehicle is parked. Below is a quick overview of the kinds of things to check out. It's best if you do this on your own or with a friend — ask any salesperson breathing down your neck to leave you alone for a little while.

Examine these items:
- **Interior Fit, Finish, and Color.** Examine whether all the seats are comfortable and offer adequate support, whether the fabric is sat-

isfactory, whether the space is roomy enough, and whether the color scheme is pleasing. Also, spend some time in the driver's seat, making sure all the controls are logically laid out, easily reachable, and whether the line of sight is good. Test the sound system and various buttons and levers (e.g., the windows, turn signals, wipers, etc.). If things like cup holders and glove compartment layout are important to you, check them out. Don't forget to try all the seats in the vehicle for comfort, support, and elbow room.

- **Exterior Fit, Finish, and Color.** Here you want to consider whether the color appeals to you; how practical the design is inside and out; how well pieces fit together; how easy it is to operate the doors, trunk, and hood; are there any paint or surface imperfections… and so on.

- **Engine Compartment.** Here you should assess the engine compartment layout and how practical it is. Find out where everything is located, evaluate how easy it is to jump-start the battery, and how easy routine maintenance will be to perform (such as checking oil or adding washer fluid).

- **Trunk and Storage Space.** Evaluate whether there's enough room and if it's configured appropriately for your needs.

---

## 71 What tips can you offer for dealing with car salespeople?

Well, for starts, have the proper perspective. Remember that you only buy a car once every few years, but these people negotiate sales all day long, every day, for years. Who's more skilled at this game? You're clearly at a disadvantage.

Some tips:
- Remember that *you* have the upper hand.
- Think about this old adage from the world of negotiations: "Whoever speaks next, loses."
- Don't offer any more information about yourself than you have to. The more a saleswoman knows, the more she can tailor a strategy to you.
- Rein in any enthusiasm. No drooling in the showroom. Don't let the

sales guy see your hand trembling in excitement as you caress a fender. If you must buy a car this day or this week, don't reveal that. Any urgency on your part transfers some bargaining power to the salesman.

• Understand that, if you're talking to a salesman on the phone, he desperately wants to get you into the showroom. If you're in the showroom, he desperately wants to sell you a car right then and there. If you're ready to buy a particular car, he desperately wants to switch you to a more expensive car, or at least get you to pay as much as possible for whatever car you buy.

• Be prepared. Do a lot of reading and researching so you're not thrown for a loop if you're suddenly offered an extended warranty or some feature you don't know much about. Better still, by doing a lot of reading, you'll also be prepared for the many ways that salespeople will try to manipulate you into buying something you don't want or paying more than you need to.

• Don't negotiate alone. Take some friends or relatives with you.

Our online collection of articles on how to buy a car (at www.Fool.com/car) will offer you many glimpses into the mind of a salesperson.

If you can type the following long web address into your browser, you'll find a special collection of articles we ran online — confessions of a former car salesman. It's full of some shocking revelations about what goes on at dealerships:
www.Fool.com/Specials/1999/sp990309CarConfessions.htm

The best advice I can offer you, if you don't look forward to negotiating with a salesperson, is: *don't do it*! That's right — you actually don't have to. At the Fool, we've developed a nifty way to keep the car-buying advantage in your court the whole time. It's our Fool Fax-a-thon.

## 72 So what's this Fool Fax-a-thon method of buying a car?

Glad you asked! It's a crafty strategy you can use to shift the bargaining power back to you. Once you know exactly what car (and options) you want to buy, gather the fax numbers of the appropriate dealers closest to you — and get yourself to a fax machine. Ideally, you'll want a list of at least one or two dozen dealerships. The more you include, the better chance you have of getting a great price. If there aren't too many dealerships in your immediate area, spread your net wider. You won't mind driving 90 minutes once to pick up a great bargain.

To locate fax numbers, check manufacturer websites or just call the dealerships and ask for the fax number of their sales department — without letting them rope you into any discussions.

Ideally, you won't have shopped at the dealerships you fax to. If you have shopped at one, and took up the time of a salesperson there, then it's not really right to go behind the salesperson's back with the Fax-a-thon. If you've not shopped the dealership, address your fax to the fleet manager, and ask that any sale be considered a "house sale," which is non-commissioned. If you have shopped at one, perhaps address your fax to the salesperson you spoke to at that dealership.

Once you're all ready with fax numbers and names, fax a letter to all the dealers (ideally a dozen or two — the more you include, the better price you're likely to get). In it, specify exactly what car you want to buy, including all the options, the color, etc. Include your fax number (but not your phone number) and invite them to fax you an itemized price offer, including options, fees, and taxes. This way, you can compare apples to apples when the bids arrive.

Give them a firm deadline by which to respond — ideally a few days, but no more than a week. Some dealers won't reply, but others will, and you'll probably get a wide range of prices. If you get an utterly amazing bid among the responses, rush to that dealership, checkbook (and faxed bid) in hand. If you think there's still room for improvement on the price, take the lowest bid and do one more round of faxing. In the second round, include the itemized best price you have, and invite all the dealers to beat it. Then walk into the winning dealership with the firm offer.

Online at the Fool, we've heard from many people who've saved thousands of dollars using this tactic. Give it a shot!

## 73 Can you give me a sample of the kind of letter I'd fax to dealers?

Sure can. Here's one:

(date)

Dear (Fleet Manager's Name — or "Sir or Madam," if you don't have a name),

I am looking to buy a new car this week. On the second page of this fax, please find a listing of the specific vehicle features I'd like included with the vehicle when I make my purchase.

I'm faxing this letter to many dealerships in a wide radius. Over the next three days, I'll be taking bids from any dealers interested in my business. After selecting the most attractive bid, I will formally secure financing for purchase within one week.

If you bid, please include all costs, and *itemize* these costs specifically to the options that I have listed on the next page. The bid should also include an *itemized* listing of all other fees and tax liabilities, including dealership preparation fees, title costs, and licensing fees. Any bid that is incomplete or not per the option listing will not be considered in my purchase decision. If you have an option package alternative or other changes, please list these as a separate bid and note the exact specifics of the changes in the bid.

I have not "shopped" your dealership in more than one year, and have had no sales contact with any employees operating in the dealership's interest during that time. Because of this, please consider this bid to be a "house sale." In addition to that, I will accept no bids after (time) on (date).

I thank you for your time and interest. If you choose to bid, please fax your fully itemized bids to (your first name) at (XXX) XXX-XXXX. I look forward to doing business with you.

(your signature)
(your name printed here)

Note: Make sure that you do not include your phone number. You don't want to negotiate over the phone. You just want to receive faxed bids.

---

## 74 What do I need to know about how cars are priced to get the best price?

The main thing to remember is that "MSRP" stands for manufacturer's suggested retail price, and you should focus on the word "suggested." It's far from the actual cost of the vehicle and, in most cases, it's well above the price you should actually pay.

Here's how the system typically works. The manufacturer ships a bunch of Rocket 900XZs to the dealership. The dealership is billed at and pays the invoice price. Once a Rocket is sold, the manufacturer deposits a certain percentage of the vehicle price into a kitty for the dealer. This is the "holdback" percentage, which varies but is usually between 2% and 5%. You'll find the holdback percentage for any particular vehicle listed at many of the auto supersites online.

Regularly, perhaps once per quarter, the manufacturer clears out the kitty and sends the dealer a check. This holdback system permits the dealer to swear to you that he's paying a certain invoice price for the vehicle, while not mentioning that he gets a certain percentage of that price back. On a $20,000 car, a 3% holdback comes to $600 — and it's an amount you don't have to surrender in full to the dealer.

There are additional incentives for dealers, as well, which you can learn about by doing a little digging online or in trade magazines such as *Automotive News*. As a very rough example, imagine that you're looking at a vehicle with an invoice price of $20,000 and an MSRP of $22,000. A dealer might be telling you that he'll give it to you for just $20,500, fully $1,500 off the MSRP. But, he might not be mentioning that he's getting a $600 holdback, plus a special dealer incentive of $1,000. (Here and there, some special dealer incentives amount to several thousand dollars.) In other words, the $20,000 car is really costing him $18,400 and he's asking $20,500 of you — looking for a whopping $2,100 profit. Naturally, car salespeople have to earn a living, but that profit sure looks larger than it needs to be.

With a bit of research under your belt before you approach a salesperson, you can create a win-win result, with the dealer netting a modest profit and yourself not getting taken to the cleaners.

## 75 Where do trade-ins fit in the new-car buying process?

Don't mention your trade-in until you've finished negotiating the price of your new car. Bringing it in early will only allow the salesperson to confuse you by making the negotiation more complicated. Once you have a firm price for the new car, you can make arrangements for the trade-in, and then attend to financing matters.

## 76 Is it better to buy or lease a car?

For some people, leasing makes sense. But, for many it doesn't. If you plan to keep your car for a long time, buying is often the best choice. But if you're short on cash, or don't plan to own a car for many years, sometimes leasing is smarter. If there's much chance that you'll damage the vehicle (not so unlikely, with a truck), you might get socked with extra charges if you lease — after all, vehicles coming off leases are later sold. If your credit rating isn't too hot, buying might be best, as good credit is often required for leases.

Here are a few things to keep in mind as you deliberate:
- Is the leasing deal you're being offered a good one?
- What will you be using the car for? (If it's being used for business, you may have some tax deductions coming.)
- How many miles will you be driving the car? (Excessive mileage or wear and tear can end up costing you more.)

As you compare leasing vs. buying, consider these costs and factors as they relate to each option:
- What's your initial outlay?
- How much will you be paying while you possess the vehicle?
- What final costs are there, at the end of your possession period?
- What options rights do you have, if you're leasing, and what will they cost you?
- Will you be able to deduct any of these expenses?

The ins and outs of leasing can get fairly complicated. Take some time to do some research before opting to lease. You can learn a lot more about leasing at these sites:

- www.edmunds.com/edweb/leasingby.html
- www.ricedelman.com/planning/basics/buylease.asp
- www.consumerlaw.org/consumer/lease.html
- www.carbuyingtips.com/lease.htm
- www.Fool.com/car/step11car.htm

And check out this book, too:
*How to Buy or Lease a Car Without Getting Ripped Off* by Pique Lyle

---

## 77 What's the best way to finance a car — getting a loan through the dealer?

Once again, a little preparation will serve you well. If all you do is ask the dealer to arrange financing for you, you're not likely to get a great interest rate on your loan. If you shop around, though, you'll be surprised at the range of rates available to you. Your bank, credit union, or other local banks can offer loans, as can some car insurance providers such as State Farm. Your local AAA office can help you out, too. And, of course, online is perhaps the easiest place to comparison-shop.

Once you have a good rate, you might take it to your dealer and see if he can beat it. He'll often be willing to do so.

---

## 78 What are some good online resources for studying up on the car-buying process, as well as researching and buying cars?

There are many. (Really — *many*.)

Extremely detailed and easy-to-read information on how to save a lot of money:

- www.Fool.com/car
- www.edmunds.com/edweb/advice

Super-sites, where you can research details on specific cars, as well

as get general advice and information:
- www.edmunds.com
- www.autobytel.com
- http://carpoint.msn.com
- www.autoweb.com
- www.autosite.com
- www.thecarconnection.com
- www.consumerreports.org (a for-pay site, costing about $24 per year. It can be worth it, though, as it features a wealth of information on all kinds of other products.)

Sites that report crash test results:
- www.nhtsa.dot.gov
- www.crashtest.com
- www.hwysafety.org

*Kelly Blue Book*: The standard source for new and used car prices:
- www.kbb.com

Some of many sites to help you with loans and leasing:
- www.leasesource.com
- www.bankrate.com
- www.peoplefirst.com
- www.wheels.eloan.com
- www.aaa.com
- www.ge.com/capital/auto

Some of many sites with information on car insurance:
- www.insure.com
- www.insweb.com
- www.progressive.com
- www.geico.com
- www.aaa.com

Auto magazines online:
- www.cartalk.com (public radio's Click and Clack brothers' site)
- www.automobilemag.com
- www.motortrend.com
- www.caranddriver.com
- www.autoweek.com

# CHAPTER FIVE

ANSWERS TO YOUR QUESTIONS ABOUT

# Buying a Home

*Buying a home can be traumatic. For starters, it's a complicated process. You're relying on all kinds of professionals you never dealt with before — like real estate agents, home inspectors, and mortgage bankers. You're talking about enormous sums of money, as the houses you'll look at cost much more than you make in an entire year. It's scary. But, it doesn't have to be that scary. Take some time to read through the information in this chapter and some of the follow-up resources listed. The more you know, the calmer you'll be, and the better decisions you'll make.*

## 79 How much house I can afford to buy?

This is a good question, and one that mortgage lenders seek to answer before qualifying you for a mortgage. To get an answer, you might apply some formulas lenders use — like the front-end and back-end ratios. The front-end ratio addresses your ability to afford mortgage payments, and the back-end ratio addresses your debt load. Let's look at an example:

Imagine that your gross income is $4,000 per month and you owe $1,000 per month in debt — perhaps for your car, student loans, and some credit card debt.

Lenders will typically want you to spend no more than 29% or 30% of your income on your mortgage. This is the front-end ratio. In this example, 29% of $4,000 is roughly $1,200, so a lender might assume that you can reasonably pay as much as $1,200 per month in mortgage payments.

Meanwhile, your debt payment-to-income ratio is $1,000 divided by $4,000, or 25%. Lenders will balk if much more than 40% of your income is going toward debt.

Once you know how much you can afford for a down payment and how much you can pay each month, you just need to plug them into a formula. You can do this at our online home-buying area (at www.Fool.com/house), where we've got calculators and worksheets to help you with much of the mathematical gymnastics involved.

Fill in amounts in the workshhet provided here to reflect your average costs over a full year. (If you know what you spend on something each week, just multiply it by 52; multiply monthly amounts by 12, of course.) Note that this worksheet is just for you, not a lender. It has more information than they need to know. Note also that current rent or mortgage payments are left out of the expenses because they'll be replaced by your new home purchase arrangements.

Divide your discretionary income by 12 to get a monthly figure. This is how much you have left over each month after you pay all your expenses and sock away your savings. See how much you have and determine how much of that you're willing to apply toward housing expenses each month.

## 80 What percentage of what I'm paying for a house should be my down payment?

There's no single best amount, and it will likely vary according to your situation. Mortgage lenders typically like to have you pay 20% or more down (which means you're only financing 80% of your purchase price), but some special loan plans can get that down payment into the low single digits. By using private mortgage insurance (see the next question for more information on PMI), you can also swing a down payment that's less than 20% of your home's purchase price.

# How Much House Can You Buy?

Fill in amounts below to reflect your average costs over a full year. (If you know what you spend on something each week, just multiply it by 52; multiply monthly amounts by 12, of course.) Divide your discretionary income by 12 to get a monthly figure.

| | |
|---|---|
| **INCOME** | |
| Salary, tips, wages | |
| Dividends and interest from investments | |
| Bonuses | |
| Any other income | |
| **Total Income** | |
| **EXPENSES** | |
| Income taxes | |
| Social Security taxes | |
| Other taxes | |
| Savings | |
| Food | |
| Insurance | |
| Health bills not covered by insurance | |
| Car loan | |
| Car expenses (gas, maintenance, repairs) | |
| Credit card bills | |
| School loans | |
| Other loans | |
| Child care | |
| Clothing | |
| Education expenses | |
| Entertainment | |
| Vacations/travel | |
| Charity | |
| Miscellaneous | |
| **Total Expenses** | |
| **RECONCILIATION** | |
| Total income | |
| Less total expenses | − |
| **Discretionary income** | = |

Note that this worksheet is just for you, not a lender. It has more information than they need to know. Note also that current rent or mortgage payments are left out of the expenses because they'll be replaced by your new home purchase arrangements.

If you're fairly flush with funds at the moment, and you work in a profession where you never know exactly how much you'll make in any given year, you might consider paying more than 20% as a down payment. The higher the down payment you make, the lower your mortgage loan and, therefore, the lower your monthly payments will be.

Of course, it's also reasonable to pay only as much as you need to, and invest the rest. It's up to you. Just remember that you need to be comfortable with the amount you're putting down and with your monthly payments.

## 81 What is private mortgage insurance (PMI) all about?

Private mortgage insurance is extra insurance a lender may require you to buy if you're paying less than 20% of the property's value as a down payment. This is because people who put down small amounts are more likely to default on a loan. And that's frowned upon in the lending business.

If you opt for mortgage insurance, once you have 20% equity in your home, you should be able to cancel the insurance. (An appraisal may be required beforehand, though.) In our online home-buying area, we've got a calculator that will help you explore how to reduce mortgage insurance costs.

(An important thing to understand about PMI is that the 20% equity threshold relates to your home's *value*, not necessarily 20% of the mortgage amount. If you get a great deal and buy your home below market value, buy a fixer-upper and fix it up to increase its value, or pick an area that suddenly becomes popular and appreciates in value rapidly, your mortgage amount might be very different from the value of your home. If you are required to pay for PMI, keep tabs on the changing value of your home.)

## 82 Should I check out my credit report before applying for a mortgage?

That's a smart thing to do. Flip back to the chapter on credit cards and debt, where you'll find details on how to go about doing that — as well as information on how to correct any errors. After all, it would be a bummer to get turned down for a mortgage because your credit report inexplicably says that you missed six payments on a hovercraft. Make sure your report is error-free before you apply.

## 83 If I'm only going to live somewhere for a few years, should I rent rather than buy a house?

That may be a good strategy. Let's say you buy a house and then have to sell it within two to three years. The various buying and selling costs alone will probably be a significant amount of money. Will the house have appreciated enough to cover those costs? It's possible, but not likely. Besides, in the first years when you're paying off a traditional mortgage, your payments are mostly going towards interest, not towards building equity (paying off the principal balance). So, after living in the house for only a few years, you'll probably technically own just a tiny part of it.

Renting is always an option to consider. It's true that mortgage interest is tax-deductible, and it can be cost-effective to own rather than rent. But, if you're renting a place for considerably less than you'd have to cough up in mortgage payments, you might invest the difference and watch a nest egg grow. (Pop over to our online calculators at www.Fool.com/house/worksheets/worksheets.htm to use our "Am I Better off Renting?" calculator.)

## 84 What are these "points" I hear about people having to pay when they buy a home?

A "point" is 1% of the value of the mortgage loan. So, if your mortgage is $150,000, one point is $1,500. When someone takes out a mortgage, "points" are often involved. Typically, these are "origination" and "discount" points.

Origination points are charged for originating, or launching, your mortgage. You pay these points upfront when you begin the mortgage. Discount points serve to lower your interest rate (and thus your payments). The idea here is that if you cough up a little extra at the beginning, you can pay less over time.

Although it may appear that your interest rate is the one officially listed on your mortgage, it's not necessarily a reflection of the actual rate you'll have paid over the life of the loan. You should incorporate the effect of points into the rate. For example, if your mortgage is for $150,000 and you pay a total of two points, then you're really paying $153,000.

## 85 | What are the pros and cons of a 15-year mortgage vs. a 30-year one?

Let's compare them:

| 15-year mortgage vs. 30-year mortgage | | |
| --- | --- | --- |
| Length | PROS | CONS |
| 15-year Mortgage | Ends more quickly | Larger monthly payments |
| | You'll build equity sooner | |
| | You'll pay less in interest over the life of the loan | |
| 30-year Mortgage | Flexibility: you can pay more when you have more and pay it off in fewer than 30 years | You'll pay more in interest over the life of the loan (often twice as much as with a 15-year mortgage) |
| | Smaller monthly payments | Takes longer to pay off |

## 86 | What's the difference between a fixed-rate mortgage and an adjustable-rate one?

These are the two main types of mortgages — the Coke and Pepsi, the cats and dogs, of the home-lending world.

A fixed-rate mortgage is very straightforward. The borrower knows from the beginning what the interest rate will be for the entire duration of the mortgage, and the monthly payments due are likewise fixed. Simple.

Slightly less simple is the adjustable-rate mortgage (ARM). It changes from year to year, to reflect the interest rate environment. If rates are plummeting, your rate will also drop — and vice versa. ARMs typically have an extra-low "teaser rate" for the first year, as well as an upper limit, or cap. In addition, the amount that an ARM rate can rise each year is also limited, so that it won't rise too quickly.

Fixed-rate mortgages are good because they come with no surprises. But, for this benefit, you'll likely pay a slightly higher rate than you would with an ARM. Fixed-rate mortgages are good for people who enjoy stability. They're also especially attractive during periods when interest rates are low. At these times, fixed-rate mortgages permit you to lock in low rates for many years.

Conversely, if the prevailing interest rates are very high, an ARM might make more sense, if you think rates are more likely to fall than rise. In addition, since ARM rates are typically slightly lower than fixed rates, they permit borrowers to borrow a little bit more. This difference can help you buy a slightly spiffier house. ARMs are often recommended for those who will only be in a house for a few years — as the rate is not likely to change too much in that time. Beware, though — don't enter into an ARM unless you're sure you'll be able to handle the worst-case scenario — if your rate quickly rises to the cap.

Again, I point you to our online calculators, which can answer such questions as "Which is better: fixed or adjustable?" (They can be found online at: www.Fool.com/house/worksheets/worksheets.htm)

## 87 What is a mortgage broker?

A mortgage broker sets you up with a mortgage. There are other ways to get mortgages, though: via banks, credit unions, savings and loans, and mortgage bankers. In exchange for setting up the mortgage, most lenders charge origination fees. Mortgage brokers charge a broker's fee (and are sometimes compensated by the lenders they work with, as well). More than half of all mortgages in America originate with mortgage brokers.

Depending on the fee they charge and the kind of deal they can get for you, mortgage brokers are sometimes your best bet. They have access to a wide variety of lenders and programs and can be especially helpful if your credit history is checkered or if you have any other special circumstances.

So, should you go with a mortgage broker or not? It depends. See what your alternatives are and go with the best deal you can find. It may well be with a mortgage broker. It's smart to do a bit of research before talking to mortgage brokers, though. You'll delay their hard sell and you'll be more informed as you listen to them.

Mortgage brokers tend to charge higher closing fees. A fee of $700 isn't uncommon, but you might also see some charge as much as $1,200. Make sure you learn of all fees before making any decisions.

### 88 Okay, so where can I find various mortgage lenders to compare, as I seek the best deal?

First, start with your bank, savings and loan, or credit union. (If you are eligible to join a credit union, but haven't, look into it — they can offer very competitive rates. And, with many, you simply have to open an account with as little as a single dollar to join.)

Next, if you're without a computer, get your local newspaper and scour the real estate section, looking at other banks' ads. If you do have a computer, things are much easier. (And, actually, even if you're unwired at home, you might avail yourself of a computer at a friend's home or your public library.)

Pop over to our Home Center at www.Fool.com/house/mortgage and you'll find links to several mortgage lenders or, better still, consolidators of mortgage lenders — where you can easily compare among many different lenders. Another good spot is www.bankrate.com, which highlights exceptional values in loan rates across the nation.

### 89 When in the home-buying process should I shop for a mortgage?

It's best to do this before you even begin house hunting. You'll have a leg up, knowing exactly what you can afford, and you'll clearly strike sellers as a serious buyer. Don't let yourself feel intimidated by the process. Remember that lenders serve *you*, not the other way around. You'll be paying a lot in interest for many years, so you want to find a lender who'll serve you well and fairly.

You should not only shop for a mortgage before you shop for a house — you should also get "pre-approved." With a pre-approval or pre-qualification letter in hand, you'll be in a stronger negotiating position when it comes time to negotiate a purchase.

A pre-qualification letter is somewhat informal. It typically costs nothing and isn't binding. It merely says that, based on what you've told the lender, they're ready to lend you the money — and states a ballpark amount you will be able to qualify for. Of course, they may change their mind, especially if you've misrepresented any information. There isn't any (or just minimal) background checking done with a pre-qualification letter.

Pre-approval is a bigger deal. It means the lender has checked out your employment and salary information, your credit record, your assets, and your debts. Many lenders don't charge for pre-approvals, but some do.

## 90 What's this "6% solution" I've heard about?

It's a "seller concession" that can save you some money. (But, not necessarily 6% of the home's value.) Here's how it works, in an example swiped from our online Buying a Home area:

Imagine that you and the seller agree on the price of the house at, say, $200,000. You then ask the seller for a 6% seller concession. What this means is that you add (up to) 6% to the price of the house. That's right, you're now going to pay $212,000 for that house — but the seller is going to give you that $12,000 back when the sale takes place. You're going to use that money to cover all of your closing costs.

If we pretend for a moment that those costs add up to precisely $12,000, then what you've done is folded those closing costs into the mortgage. Title search, recordation fees, and all other closing costs — most of which are not tax-deductible — have effectively been included in your mortgage. Since your mortgage interest is tax-deductible, these costs have effectively become tax write-offs.

In addition, you don't have to come up with all that extra cash at settlement. Your down payment will be somewhat higher, (if you're putting down 20%, then in the current example your down payment would be $42,400, versus $40,000) and, of course, your mortgage payments will be higher, but it ends up saving you money.

The seller has no reason to refuse this — after all, the agreed-to price is still the same.

## 91 What's the catch with this 6% solution?

The catch is that the house has to appraise for the higher value. If the appraiser comes back and tells you that this house won't appraise for more than $200,000, you can't do it.

Let's look into this a little further. Say you buy the house for $200,000. Your $40,000 down payment leaves you needing a $160,000 mortgage. You get a 30-year loan at 8%. Your monthly payments for principal and interest are $1,174.

Now, say you decide to use the 6% seller concession strategy. You buy this house for the price of $212,000. You put down 20%, and this leaves you needing a $169,600 mortgage. Your monthly payments will be $1,244, or $70 more per month. Is it worth it?

To begin with, many people aren't going to feel an enormous pinch paying the extra $70 per month — not nearly as much as they would feel having to fork out an extra $12,000 all at once to cover closing costs. But, what about the fact that now you have to pay this extra money over the course of 30 years? Well, over the course of 30 years, you're paying $25,200 more for that extra $12,000 ($70 more per month x 12 months in a year x 30 years = $25,200).

However, remember that's $12,000 less out of your pocket at the time of closing. If you take $12,000 and invest it at 10% (less than the market average has returned over the past 35 years), then your money will grow to more than $200,000 (before taxes) at the end of 30 years. So, in this scenario, it's well worth it.

Naturally, you'll want to run the numbers for your particular loan to see whether it would be worth it for you.

Note: there are certain rules under certain mortgages as to what the seller can actually pay for at closing. If you get $12,000 from the seller and all of your costs are $12,000, this does not necessarily mean that you won't have to pay anything. Be sure to ask your lender what costs the seller may cover.

## 92   What are some other ways to save money on a mortgage?

Here are a few:

You might "assume" the existing mortgage on the house you're buying, if there is one. This is a good deal if the existing mortgage is at a lower rate than prevailing interest rates. To do this, you'll need to make sure the existing mortgage is "assumable" or transferable. And, you'll have to cough up whatever difference there is between the purchase price and the outstanding debt. You might do this by tapping your nest egg, if it's large enough, or by taking out a second mortgage.

Another strategy is "seller financing." Here, you make your monthly payments to the seller, not to an institutional lender. The advantage is that you can often arrange a lower interest rate — especially if the seller has had trouble selling — and you avoid the many costly administrative fees involved with institutions. (If the seller has had trouble selling, though, find out why!) In addition, you avoid private mortgage insurance.

Why would a seller take on this kind of risk? It's actually not that risky. The house is the collateral. Default on the loan, and the seller keeps the house — just like a bank would. Sellers might also appreciate getting regular checks from you over time, rather than a lump-sum payment — it'll be an additional income stream. And, depending on the seller's circumstances, this arrangement might also save him some capital gains tax. One caveat is that sellers typically will want a shorter term than the traditional 30-year mortgage.

You might also save some money by playing with points and other elements of the mortgage. Maybe pay more discount points and get a valuable lower rate. Perhaps consider a 15-year mortgage instead of a 30-year one. (Of course, if you'd rather pay less each month with a 30-year mortgage and invest the rest in something like stocks, it could be better than a shorter-term mortgage — especially if your interest rate is low.)

It's also effective to pay off your mortgage sooner than you're scheduled to. The more you pay, the less you owe. And, the less you owe, the less interest you'll pay.

Finally, remember that mortgage lenders want your business and will usually compete to get it. Don't be afraid to negotiate. Let one know what another is offering you. Don't assume that published rates are final. If your credit record is good, you'll be in a particularly strong position to negotiate. Knocking a quarter percent off a published interest rate is a reasonable goal.

## 93 Do you recommend bypassing the real estate broker or agent when buying a house? Is it smart to seek out "for sale by owner" offerings?

In theory, yes. Real estate agents are middlemen (or middlewomen). They typically take a percentage of the sale price — usually around 6% — as a commission for their services. It's true that this commission is paid by the seller, not you the buyer; but, if the seller isn't paying the 6%, perhaps the price of the house could be a mite lower.

The plus side of working with an agent is that he has access to a wide variety of available properties. He's also well versed in the home-buying process and can guide you through the various legal and administrative steps.

If you're attracted to the idea of buying a home that's "for sale by owner" (FSBO), you'll run into a few problems. For starters, there aren't many of them. You might drive around the neighborhood of interest, looking for signs on lawns. Or, check out your local newspaper for ads. An online search is also good, but so far the sites that list these homes for sale don't always list too many in some regions. For example, at the time of this writing, I checked one major site and there were just 38 FSBO homes listed for the Atlanta metropolitan area. In Fresno, California, which isn't a hamlet anymore, there were only three homes listed. In Providence, Rhode Island, just two.

Still, it doesn't hurt to look. As time goes by, these sites will probably be showcasing more and more homes. Here are some websites where you can check out available FSBO homes — or list your own!
- www.sellyourhomeyourself.com
- www.fsbonetwork.com
- www.owners.com
- www.forsalebyowner.com
- www.fsboonline.com

Here are some sites offering guidance to FSBOers:
- www.homebuying.about.com/realestate/homebuying/msub9.htm
- www.fsbohelp.com

The fsboonline.com site offers the encouraging (and admittedly surprising) statistic that, "Over 29% of home sales are FSBOs and are completed without real estate agents! (Bureau of Labor Statistics — 1992)."

If you take the FSBO path, you'll still probably have to fork over some fees to various professionals, such as lawyers, to guide you through administrative formalities. But, these fees will likely pale in comparison to what you'd spend taking the road more traveled.

---

## 94 What's the difference between a real estate broker and a realtor? Are they the same thing?

Not exactly. Someone with a real estate license is a licensed real estate professional, or an agent. This person may also be a REALTOR®, but isn't necessarily one.

We often think of any real estate agent as a REALTOR®, but to be a REALTOR®, he or she must be a member of THE NATIONAL ASSO-

CIATION OF REALTORS®, which has trademarked the word "RE-ALTOR®." I'll use the word "agent" from now on, as I don't want to run out of my allotted supply of capital letters or cause any eyestrain.

A real estate *broker*, meanwhile, has had additional training and holds a different license. Don't think that you need a broker and not an agent. Either can serve you very well. Although many people casually refer to those who show and sell homes as brokers, they're often actually agents. Most people use the terms interchangeably.

---

## 95 What's a buyer broker, and do you recommend using one?

A buyer broker represents the buyer and not the seller. Many people don't realize that traditional real estate agents are working for the *seller* of a property. Yes, they're working *with* you, perhaps spending many days showing you dozens of homes. But, they're devoted more to the interests of the *seller* than to your interests. The simple reason for this is economics — their pay (commission) for completing the sale is a percentage of the actual selling price they extract from your pockets. Therefore, it's to their advantage to sell the house at a higher rather than a lower price.

Also, since the traditional agent represents the seller, if you were to mention to an agent as he showed you a lovely domicile that you'll offer $130,000 and will pay no more than $140,000, don't be surprised if that information gets to the seller. (Of course, there *are* indeed plenty of agents who'll knock themselves out for you and get you a great house at a good price. Just understand how the industry is set up and what you may be up against.)

All that said, one way to circumvent dealing with agents who pledge allegiance to the seller is to work with a "buyer broker." It's becoming more and more common for people to use the services of a buyer broker. With a buyer broker, you agree from the outset on what her fee will be (some restrictions may apply, depending on the state). It will usually come out of the proceeds from the sale, so you won't have to actually cough anything up to cover it. There's still an incentive for the broker to favor a higher sale price, but there are ways to work around that.

When negotiating a fee, start with the amount you expect to pay for your home. Then apply half the standard agent commission in your state to it. For example, if you're looking to pay $150,000 and the standard commission is 6%, then you might offer 3%, or $4,500. To ensure that the agent will work to get you the lowest price, offer to pay him $100 extra for each $1,000 he saves you under $150,000. In other words, if the selling price ends up being $147,000, you'd pay $300 extra to the broker. Fees are negotiable. If you don't negotiate a fixed price, you can very possibly negotiate a lower percentage commission. Remember that these brokers want your business and you can always take it elsewhere.

Finally, make sure you're familiar with exactly what you're spelling out in the contract. Understand the terms. Are you expected to pay anything if a satisfactory purchase doesn't happen? Are there any hidden fees or expenses? Have you agreed to mow the agent's lawn for a year or pay for his daughter's braces if a deal doesn't go through?

---

## 96 How should I go about choosing a broker or agent?

Here are a few ways:
- Ask your friends and neighbors for referrals, if they're in the neighborhood where you're searching.
- If you don't know anyone in the region where you're looking, contact the Better Business Bureau or Chamber of Commerce and ask for the names of several agents who are members. It's good to call at least five of these agents, and to meet with at least three.
- Interview agents. Ask each one about her background, training, and experience. Ask about homes in the region. See what questions she asks you and how well she listens. See if you trust her. You're looking for a strong agent, with experience and good negotiating skills. Make sure she'll be able to recommend a few settlement lawyers and building inspectors, if you anticipate needing them.
- Ask to be shown one house. See how the agent shows it to you and how comfortable your rapport is. Is she showing you the kind of home you're looking for?
- Evaluate what kind of information the agent is able to give you. You don't necessarily have to be the one digging up the scoop on local schools and neighborhoods. A good agent might have handouts at

the ready, or at least a lot of information stored in her noggin.

- Keep looking. If you don't find someone you like at first, take the time to continue looking. The more agents you check out, the greater the odds that you'll find one you really like who serves you well.

## 97 Do you have any tips for working with an agent?

Yup. Be very clear about what you're looking for in a home. Make a list for yourself and for the agent of what your new home *must* have (4 bedrooms, a big yard, at least two bathrooms, etc.) and what would be *nice* to have (a swimming pool, a nearby polka hall).

Also, honor any agreements. If you're not to use other agents, don't. If agents get wind that you're not playing by the rules, they may put a lot less effort into serving you. This goes beyond rules, too. Just be honest. If you're using two agents, let them know. (Don't feel that you have to sign any exclusive representation agreement. You might find it best to use several agents at first, until you settle on one you like best.)

## 98 How should I go about deciding what price to offer for a home?

First off, you might look up the going prices for similar homes in the same area. You can do this fairly easily at http://Fool.home-pricecheck.com, if you're online. If you're not, then call up the local government offices, such as city hall. The sale prices of homes should be a matter of public record. (Tax assessors' offices can tell you the appraised value of local homes, but while these are sometimes very close to reasonable selling prices, they're also sometimes too high or too low.) Your agent can be a valuable resource here, too. He should be able to provide information on comparable sales prices for the area.

Next, determine how "hot" the local market is. If demand for housing is high (sometimes referred to as a "seller's market"), you won't have too much bargaining power. Homes priced reasonably will sell quickly, for a price close to the asking price. In some super-hot markets, homes may even sell *above* the asking price, as buyers compete with other buyers. In a slow-paced market (sometimes referred to as a "buyer's market"), though, you may be able to buy a home 5% (or more) *below* the asking price.

Check out the market history of the home. Has it been for sale for a long time? Has the price been reduced over time? If so, when was the last asking-price reduction? (If reductions are a pattern, and it's been a while since the last one, the sellers may be mulling over another reduction.) Have there been any offers on the house? If so, for how much? Find out if others who made an offer are still interested, or if they were rejected (and why!).

Some other considerations:
- Be pre-approved for a mortgage before you bid. You'll be a more-attractive prospect because you'll be seen as seriously interested and ready to buy.
- Know where your boundaries are. Don't bid more than you can pay. Don't become so enamored with a house that you find yourself paying more than you should.
- Think twice before making an extremely low offer. It might work... but, then, it also might turn off the sellers, perhaps turning them into stiffer negotiators. Worse, you might lose out to another bidder making a more reasonable offer.
- Become very familiar with the house and its condition. Find out if any repairs need to be made and if they'll be made prior to closing the sale. If $10,000 needs to be spent on the roof and the sellers might or might not get it taken care of before selling, that's a big deal. Examine other issues, too, such as radon and lead levels, and termites. If the sellers promise to make any repairs, make sure that's part of the formal written agreement. Understand too, that sellers might not have your taste or willingness to spend money on a home they're selling. For cosmetic things — a worn carpet that needs to be replaced or the paint peeling on the walls, etc. — you probably want to ask for a monetary allowance so you can pick what you like, even if you have to do the repairs yourself or hire someone. Monetary allowances should also be spelled out in writing.

## 99  How should I go about making an offer?

When you make an offer, if you're not pre-approved for a mortgage, make sure that the offer is "contingent" on your securing financing. It should also be contingent on the property being cleared by the home inspector you hire.

Setting a time limit can also be a good idea. You can make your offer good for 24 or 48 hours, preventing the seller from stalling and waiting for a higher offer.

If you're serious about the offer, you can make it more enticing by giving your agent an "earnest money" deposit toward the price of the house. It can be a few thousand dollars, or even as much as 10% of the price, depending on what you're comfortable with. Your agent should apply it toward the house purchase if the sale goes through, and convert the check into confetti if it doesn't.

---

## 100 What do I need to know about the home inspector?

First off, *don't* use one referred by a traditional agent, as the agent is aligned with the seller of the house. If you're using a buyer broker, it's fine to go with a referral from him. But, also get references from the inspector. (If he's reluctant to provide them, say *sayonara*.)

Check out whomever you plan to use with the American Society of Home Inspectors (ASHI) (gesundheit!) to make sure he's got sufficient training and experience. Find out what will be covered in the inspection — in detail.

Make sure that you can accompany him on the inspection, and *do* accompany him, observing what he does. In addition, you want him to carry "errors and omissions" insurance, which will cover you in the event that he goofs and misses something costly.

Today, often for just a few dollars, you can purchase or ask the seller to provide a "home warranty" — insurance that covers unforeseen repairs for the first year or so after you buy the house. Most of these policies are contingent on a home inspection being performed by an inspector the insurance company trusts, but they offer great peace of mind. Many real estate agents and sellers are offering these policies as part of the sale to reduce liability for missed problems and to entice buyers. If they don't mention this, ask about it.

## 101 What are all the fees involved in buying a home?

Take a deep breath and read on.

- **Points or origination fees**: Remember that each point is one percent of the mortgage value, and that the more points you pay, the lower the interest rate should be. Sometimes a seller might pay the points for you — ask your buyer broker to look into that possibility for you.

- **Escrow fees**: Escrow is where the payment for your home will reside while you and the seller get everything settled. There are fees for this service, though. Think of them as room rates at the Escrow Hotel.

- **Homeowner's insurance**: This is generally required before you can take possession of your new home.

- **Legal fees**: Not everyone needs the services of a lawyer, but if your transaction is too complicated for boilerplate forms, you'll want an attorney preparing some paperwork.

- **Private mortgage insurance**: This is required if you're going to offer a smaller-than-usual down payment. You may need to pay upfront for as much as a full year's worth of premiums.

- **Document preparation fees**: These are lender or broker fees.

- **Title insurance**: This covers you in case the unlikely happens and the person who sold you the house didn't really own it.

- **Appraisal fees**: This will slap a fair market value on your home — important for tax purposes and for the mortgage company to approve your loan.

- **Credit report fees**: A verified credit report will be required.

- **Tax service fees:** These are to make sure that your taxes get paid.

- **Survey fee:** A survey will determine the exact boundaries of your property. (If an existing survey can be used, then you won't need to pay this fee.)

- **Property taxes:** You may owe some property taxes immediately, if the seller has paid them covering a time period when you'll own the home.

- **Pest inspection fee:** New homes don't normally require this, but older homes do.

- **State recording fees:** These depend on state requirements.

- **Notary public charge:** You'll need a notary to verify your identity.

Sadly, these aren't necessarily the only fees you'll pay. But, they're most of them.

## 102 What causes mortgage rates to rise and fall?

They fluctuate along with other interest rates. Interest rates are affected chiefly by inflation and the market for debt (notes, bills, and bonds, among other instruments). With inflation extremely low in recent years, we've enjoyed low interest rates. But, if signs of inflation begin to pop up, it's expected that the Federal Reserve, will hike up short-term interest rates via an adjustment in the rate of interest on "federal funds." The "fed funds" rate is the interest rate a bank can charge another bank for use of its excess money. The Fed can also change the "discount rate," or the rate paid by a bank to borrow short-term funds from the Fed. The prime rate and other rates (such as mortgage rates) are based primarily on these two interest rates.

The Fed raises these interest rates when the economy appears to be growing too briskly, which can spur inflation. When the economy is sluggish, the Fed might cut these rates to give American enterprise a boost. Lower rates give companies and people (including homebuyers) an incentive to borrow money or refinance existing loans at lower rates. However, remember that the money markets themselves (basic supply and demand for money at each price point) exert the biggest influence over interest rates, though the Fed is a big influence on market expectations.

## 103 Is refinancing a mortgage worth it?

Sometimes very much so. You may think of your house as an investment. Unfortunately, you probably won't see the return on that investment until you're loading up the white Cadillac for the big move to Sarasota. There's a more-immediate way you can make some money off your house, though: refinance your mortgage.

Refinancing is when you take out a new mortgage on your home, at a lower interest rate, decreasing the amount of your monthly payments. In some creative refinancings, you can actually increase the amount of the loan for such Foolish pursuits as paying down credit card debt or making long-term investments in stocks.

Mortgage interest is tax-deductible, so to calculate the effective yield of a mortgage, multiply the interest rate by your tax bracket. Then subtract that from your interest rate. Investors in the 33% bracket with a 7.5% mortgage interest rate, for example, are effectively paying a 5% mortgage interest rate. (7.5 x .33 = 2.5; 7.5 - 2.5 = 5.0.)

Your first step is to assess the myriad mortgage costs involved — such as the origination fee, discount points, the appraisal, the credit report, processing, title insurance, and the escrow fee.

Next, check out available loans and interest rates (made easy at websites like www.homeshark.com). Consider what "points," if any, you might have to pay. A point is equal to 1% of the value of your loan. It's paid upfront when you close the loan.

Interest rates lower by one or even half a percentage point can result in whopping interest savings over 15 to 30 years, depending on how much you borrow.

For example, $100,000 borrowed at 7% instead of 8% for 30 years will save about $25,000 over the length of the loan. If you invest the extra $69 a month in the S&P 500, at the S&P's historical 11% annual return, in 30 years you would have roughly $180,000. You owe it to yourself to crunch some numbers and see if refinancing makes sense for you.

## 104 If I'm saving money to buy my first home within three years, how should I invest my money so that I get decent returns on my investments?

To ensure that you can afford more than a corrugated aluminum shack when the time comes to buy a home, any money that you expect to need within five years or so should not be invested in the stock market. You should take great comfort and encouragement from the fact that the stock market has averaged an annual 11% return for most of this century. But, that rate of return is an average over the *long* haul. From year to year, anything can happen.

Short-term scratch should be kept in a safe place, such as certificates of deposit or money market funds, to protect your principal.

## 105 Okay. Howzabout some websites I can turn to for further home-buying information?

There are many online sites where you can brief yourself on the home-buying process and find useful resources. Here are a few helpful sites:
- www.homebuying.about.com/realestate/homebuying
- www.realtor.com
- www.Fool.com/house

These sites can guide you to finding lenders or real estate agents:
- www.Fool.com/house/mortgage
- www.homestore.com
- www.eloan.com
- www.realtor.com
- www.lendingtree.com
- www.MortgageIT.com

This site is very nifty, permitting you to look up the selling prices of homes in your target neighborhood (or heck, in your *own* neighborhood, or any of your friends' or relatives' neighborhoods!).
• http://Fool.homepricecheck.com

Here you can check out various regions, as well as their crime rates, quality of life, etc.:
• www.homefair.com
• www.bestplaces.net
• http://local.yahoo.com
• www.bestsmalltowns.com

If you're not online, several national magazines, such as *Money*, regularly offer surveys of the best places to live in the country. Regional magazines frequently do the same thing, focusing on their region, of course.

This is where you can hook up with any local Chamber of Commerce. If you're not online, call the Chamber of Commerce in any area of interest and they will often be willing to send you information on the services and characteristics of their city or town:
• www.uschamber.com/mall

At Fooldom, we've got a bunch of handy worksheets and calculators to help you crunch various numbers related to home buying:
• www.Fool.com/house/worksheets/worksheets.htm

---

## 106 What books are there related to choosing, buying, maintaining, and selling a home?

There are far too many to list. Here are a bunch that should prove helpful to you, though:
• *The Home Buyer's Kit* by Edith Lank
• *The Home Seller's Kit* by Edith Lank
• *Buy Your First Home* by Robert Irwin
• *All About Escrow and Real Estate Closings* by Sandy Gadow
• *How to Sell Your Home Without a Broker* by Bill Carey, Suzanne Kiffman, and Chantal Howell Carey
• *House Selling For Dummies* by Eric Tyson and Ray Brown

- *Home Buying for Dummies* by Eric Tyson and Ray Brown
- *Mortgages for Dummies* by Eric Tyson and Ray Brown
- *Retirement Places Rated* by David Savageau

# Paying for College

*It can be expensive to pay for a college education, but it will cost your child more if he doesn't go to college. The prospect of forking over many tens of thousands of dollars over a few years can be frightening, especially if you've got several whippersnappers. But, don't let yourself be paralyzed by fear. With a little reading up and strategizing, you can put together a sound plan. This chapter covers some of the highlights of paying for college and gives you leads to many online resources where you can learn even more.*

**107** **How can I convince my child that she *should* go to college? She's going to go regardless, but I want her to buy into the idea.**

You might point out the differences between high school and college. Some kids may assume that college is very much like their regimented high school. Point out the freedoms at college: She'll have much more latitude in choosing courses to take and she can focus primarily on subjects that interest her. Her schedule will vary widely, too. Some days she may have no courses until noon. Most courses may only meet three times a week. These are interesting details that not every youngster is aware of.

Play up the social angle, as well. She'll meet many, many new friends. She'll be in a community where almost everyone is roughly her age.

Colleges typically feature scores of clubs, sports, and other activities. She's not likely to be bored. Instead of being out in the working world, she'll be among new friends, taking many courses that interest her and enjoying a rich social life.

Finally, another compelling tidbit is financial. Point out how much difference a college education will make to her earning power for the rest of her life. Explain how most good jobs today require at least a college education. Share this eye-opening table with her, and you may find that she's suddenly thinking of law school!

| THE EARNING POWER OF EDUCATION | | |
|---|---|---|
| Education Level Achieved | Yearly Salary | Weekly Salary |
| Not a High School Graduate | $14,131 | $272 |
| High School Graduate only | $21,680 | $417 |
| Some College but No Degree | $24,916 | $479 |
| Associate's Degree | $29,749 | $572 |
| Bachelor's Degree | $40,695 | $783 |
| Master's Degree | $52,771 | $1,015 |
| Ph.D. | $79,346 | $1,526 |
| Professional Degree (medical doctor, lawyer, etc.) | $93,714 | $1,802 |

(*Source: U.S. Bureau of the Census, 1998*)

## 108 Are private or public colleges better?

It's worth thinking twice about private universities, which can cost several times what public schools cost. Some private schools have prestigious names, which can open some doors, or at least give a bit of shine to a resume. But, a hard-working, clever student at a public university can achieve just as much. Besides a college's name, graduate schools or employers will be looking at courses taken, grades, recommendations from faculty members, initiative taken, achievements, and so on.

An interesting exercise is to have your child interview five to 10 adults he admires, asking where they went to college, and how they think their college choice made a difference in landing jobs and in their career.

Your child might also look over these lists of people and the schools they attended, to see that successful people have gone to all kinds of schools:

| Public Schools | |
|---|---|
| Warren Buffett (investor extraordinaire) | University of Nebraska |
| Roger Ebert (movie critic) | University of Illinois |
| David Gardner (Fool co-founder) | University of North Carolina |
| Jim Henson (Muppets creator) | University of Maryland |
| Stephen King (writer) | University of Maine |
| David Letterman (TV personality) | Ball State University |
| Steven Spielberg (director) | California State College, Long Beach |
| Oprah Winfrey (media personality) | Tennessee State University |
| **Private Schools** | |
| Madeleine Albright (former Secretary of State) | Wellesley College |
| Bill Cosby (comedian) | Temple University |
| Carly Fiorina (Hewlett-Packard CEO) | Stanford University |
| Tom Gardner (Fool co-founder) | Brown University |
| Ruth Bader Ginsberg (Supreme Court justice) | Cornell University |
| Steve Jobs (Apple co-founder) | Reed College |
| Denzel Washington (actor) | Fordham University |
| Tiger Woods (golfer) | Stanford University |

Different personalities thrive in different environments. Public schools are attractive because (among other things) they can cost a lot less. But, with proper planning and perhaps some scholarships thrown in, private schools can be very affordable, too

---

## 109 How many colleges should my child apply to?

Well, within reason (because many have application fees), the more the merrier. If she only applies to five, she may just get into one or two. That's okay, as long as she's sure those are ones that she really likes. But, between the time she submits applications and hears back from schools, she may have changed her mind a little.

Applying to perhaps 10 or even more colleges will maximize the odds of getting into a bunch of schools she's excited about. She'll also be more likely to end up with a selection of schools to choose from. Also worth thinking about is that if she's applying for financial aid, each school will offer a different package. More schools applied to will probably yield more packages to consider.

Most colleges today have comprehensive websites that cover a broad range of topics, such as campus life, faculty, courses, financial aid, housing, information about the surrounding community, useful addresses and phone numbers for more information.

## 110 Tuition costs seem to be rising awfully fast. How much will college cost in the years ahead?

You're not imagining things. The cost of a college education has been increasing faster than the rate of inflation lately. (The growth rate does seem to finally be tapering off, though.) Here's one set of estimates of future costs, courtesy of The College Board:

| AVERAGE PROJECTED COLLEGE COSTS PER YEAR | | |
| --- | --- | --- |
| Four-Year Public College — Undergraduates | | |
| **Years** | **Tuition & Fees** | **Room & Board** |
| 1998-99 | $ 3,243 | $ 4,530 |
| 2000-01 | $ 3,601 | $ 5,048 |
| 2003-04 | $ 4,169 | $ 5,844 |
| 2006-07 | $ 4,826 | $ 6,765 |
| 2009-10 | $ 5,587 | $ 7,832 |
| Four-Year Private College — Undergraduates | | |
| **Years** | **Tuition & Fees** | **Room & Board** |
| 1998-99 | $ 14,508 | $ 5,765 |
| 2000-01 | $ 15,818 | $ 6,424 |
| 2003-04 | $ 18,311 | $ 7,436 |
| 2006-07 | $ 21,197 | $ 8,608 |
| 2009-10 | $ 24,539 | $ 9,965 |

Some experts estimate that, for children born today, an undergraduate college education at a private university will cost upwards of $225,000.

## 111 How can I figure out how much to save for college expenses?

First, get an idea of how much money you're going to need and how long you have until you need it. The table in the last Q&A should help with that. Then you'll have an idea of how much money you're going to need to save and how much you'll need it to grow.

Start saving early — as early as possible. The more time your money *has* to grow, the more it *will* grow. (In other words, to reach a certain dollar-amount goal, by investing earlier you'll have to invest fewer of your own dollars.) Here are some scenarios to consider:

* Invest $2,000 per year beginning when your child is 8 and, if you earn 11% annually, you'll end up with $45,000 by the time he's 18.
* Invest $5,000 per year beginning when your child is 10 (earning 11% annually) and you'll have more than $80,000 by the time he's 18.
* Invest $3,000 per year in the stock market, from the time of your child's birth. If it grows at the market's long-term average annual rate of around 11% per year, by the time he's ready for college, you'll have a little more than $140,000.

These are just rough guidelines. During the years that you're investing, the market might do significantly better or worse than average. In addition, if you're investing in individual stocks instead of market index funds, you'll more certainly fare differently than the market average. Companies selected carefully can do much better than average.

To help you figure out your own particular situation, take advantage of online calculators that will do the math for you. You'll just need to plug in some numbers. Here's where you'll find some of these calculators:

* www.finaid.org/calculators
* www.salliemae.com/calculators

## 112 What should I invest college money in? Stocks? Bonds?

The longer the time period until you'll need the money, the more risk you can take. Here's a typical set of guidelines that some financial planners might offer you:

* **Birth to School Age**: 100% growth stocks. You have more time,

you can take more risk.

- **Age 6 to 13**: You might want to think about making a few more "prudent" selections. 70% stocks, 30% bonds.

- **Age 14-18**: You want things to continue to grow, but you also want to protect yourself from market volatility. Consider 30% bonds, 20% stocks, and 50% money market funds.

- **College Age**: You want to be able to access the money easily and not have it drop in value. Consider putting the vast majority of it into a safe, interest-bearing account like a money market fund. For funds earmarked to be spent a year or two down the road, certificates of deposit are a good idea.

---

### 113 Do you have any general tips regarding saving and planning for college?

Yup. Here are a few:

- **Don't assume your youngster will follow a traditional route.**
  He may have no interest in a traditional college or university education and plans to make a career out of a trade. He may change his mind and attend college later — or perhaps he's already planning to work for a few years between high school and college. If so, that's not necessarily a bad idea. Students who attend college slightly later than usual may take their studies more seriously.

- **Involve your child in the financial planning process, as well as the college selection process.**
  From a fairly early age, he might help by contributing to his college fund. If he's interested in expensive schools, plan a financing strategy together. Knowing how much college costs might provide some motivation to work harder in high school, increasing odds of earning scholarships.

- **Don't neglect your own retirement needs.**
  If you're saving for college expenses, it doesn't mean you should put off saving for your retirement for 10 or more years. If you neglect your retirement needs to provide for your children, they may end

up providing for you, much more than you'd planned. Another related concern is that, when it comes time to apply for financial aid, any money that you've sheltered in IRS-sanctioned retirement funds (such as IRAs) isn't taken into account as assets tap-able for college. At least that's how the rules work at the moment.

- **Don't rule out financial aid.**
  Many people assume that their incomes and or assets will make their children ineligible for financial aid. Even children of people earning six-figure salaries can receive some financial aid. Financial aid is big business, with roughly $50 billion being awarded annually.

---

## 114 My kid is very close to college age, and I've got very little saved. What do you suggest?

Fret not. Junior isn't doomed to a life of flipping burgers. There are several things you can do to improve your situation.

For starters, Junior might delay going to college for one or more years. If the idea of working for a bit right out of high school appeals to him, it can be a smart move. Both he and you can save money for college as he works.

Next, have Junior focus on less-expensive schools, such as in-state public universities, which tend to charge much less for tuition. Local schools have additional benefits, such as additional scholarship opportunities and reduced travel costs to and from school. Another option is for Junior to attend a community college for the first year, before transferring to a bigger and more-expensive school for his last years. Another new possibility is online courses, many of which are now offered over the Internet.

Finally, consider loans. As long as you don't end up borrowing too much, this is an effective way to finance schooling. For more info on loans for college, click over to:
www.mapping-your-future.org/tours/borrow.htm.

We offer more tips on this topic in Fooldom online, in step four of our Paying for College collection at:
www.Fool.com/money/payingforcollege/payingforcollege.htm.

## 115 What's a FAFSA form?

FAFSA stands for Free Application for Federal Financial Aid. If you're only going to bother with one financial aid form, this is the one to bother with. It's required by all colleges that offer financial aid, and is also mandatory for most federal student aid programs. For some federal plans, though, you'll need to file additional forms. These exceptions include the Federal Family Education Loan, (FFEL), the Stafford Loan, and the Direct or FFEL Plus Loan.

You can get FAFSA forms in the fall at your youngster's high school. However, you're not to submit them until after January 1. (Aim to submit them just after January 1, as some funds are first-come, first-served.) Get the form as early as you can, so that you can begin gathering the required information.

Once you submit the forms, you'll receive a Student Aid Report (SAR) that should be checked for accuracy. It will state your "Expected Family Contribution" (EFC), which is how much money you're expected to contribute toward your child's education. The schools you apply to will get copies of the results and will base some or all of their financial aid decisions on the information it contains.

You can fill out the FAFSA form online, if you want. For details on how and why you might do it, visit: www.fafsa.ed.gov

## 116 What other forms are there to fill out besides the FAFSA?

Well, the Financial Aid PROFILE form (formerly known as the "FAF") is required by some colleges. In addition, many colleges have their own financial aid application forms. See what's required at every school your young one is applying to. (Or, better yet, have *her* check!)

## 117 What are all the components of a financial plan for college?

The money to pay for all those biology books, dorm rooms, and late-

night cheeseburgers will come from many places. Here are the biggies:
- Your savings
- Your child's savings
- Federal financial aid grants and/or loans
- Financial aid grants and/or loans from your child's college
- Other loans
- Campus work/study jobs
- Other part-time work
- Scholarships
- Change found under sofa cushions

---

## 118 Where can I learn more about college planning in general and financial aid in particular?

Here's a bunch of websites:
- www.ed.gov (the U.S. Department of Education)
- www.ed.gov/prog_info/SFA/StudentGuide
- www.finaid.org
- www.collegeboard.org
- www.petersons.com
- www.campustours.com
- http://smartmoney.lycos.com/ac/collegeplanning
- www.mapping-your-future.org

Oh, and of course, drop by www.Fool.com/money, too! We've got a collection of articles there on saving for college that should prove useful.

Here are some websites where you can look up scholarships that are available:
- www.finaid.org/scholarships
- www.collegeboard.org/fundfinder/html/ssrchtop.html
- www.fastweb.com
- www.uncf.org (the United Negro College Fund)
- www.hispanicfund.org (the Hispanic College Fund)
- www.collegescholarships.com
- www.college-scholarships.com (this is different from the site above)
- http://search.cashe.com

And here are some (of countless) books on paying for college and the college planning process:

- *Fiske Guide to Getting into the Right College: The Complete Guide to Everything You Need to Know to Get into and Pay for College* by Edward B. Fiske and Bruce G. Hammond
- *The College Admissions Mystique* by Bill Mayher
- *Get into Any College: Secrets of Harvard Students* by Jim Good and Lisa Lee
- *How to Go to College Almost for Free* by Benjamin R. Kaplan
- *The Government Financial Aid Book: The Insider's Guide to State and Federal Government Grants and Loans* by Student Financial Services
- *The Scholarship Book* by Daniel Cassidy
- *The A's and B's of Academic Scholarships* by Anna Leider and Ann Schimke
- *The Minority and Women's Complete Scholarship Book* by Student Services Inc.
- *Financing Your College Degree: A Guide for Adult Students* by David F. Finney
- *Peterson's Scholarships and Loans for Adult Students*
- *The Athletic Recruiting & Scholarship Guide* by Wayne Mazzoni
- *Barron's Guide to Distance Learning* by Pat Criscito

In these few pages, we've only *touched* on the many facets of planning for college. Spend some time with the above resources and you'll learn a lot more. The more you learn, the more you'll likely save.

**CHAPTER SEVEN**
**ANSWERS TO YOUR QUESTIONS ABOUT**
# Banking Foolishly

*One way to save money is to eat lobster only twice a week, instead of five times. Another way is to rent a movie to enjoy at home instead of forking over half your paycheck to the Googleplex down the road just to see one movie and enjoy a medium tub of popcorn. You may not have realized, though, that you can also save money by banking Foolishly. This chapter will offer a few tips to help you rethink your banking habits.*

## 119 Is this topic really such a big deal? Can't I just focus on investing?

If you minimize the money you spend on banking and maximize the money you get from your bank, you'll have more money to invest.

Banking is big business. Think of Las Vegas, with all its lights and cheap buffets — it's all subsidized by people losing lots of money, forking over chips and nickels endlessly. There's a bit of a parallel there to the banking world.

Drop in on many banking offices and you'll see expensive marble and fancy furnishings. Think about this for a second and you'll realize that, if the bank were trying to offer you the absolute best value, there would probably be just a canvas tent with some folding chairs serving as your local branch office.

That may seem extreme, but some new banks today are *surpassing* that extreme, establishing banks in the ether, on the Internet only. We'll talk about them soon. Until then, consider that:

- According to a 1999 Bankrate.com survey, savings account interest rates averaged a paltry 1.7%, compared to around 2% or more for money market accounts and 4.4% for 6-month CDs.
- According to 1999 FDIC data, savings accounts are just about the nation's favorite place to park money, as they hold a whopping $1.61 *trillion*. Money market accounts, which offer higher rates, held just $913 million — that's only 1/1,763 of what savings accounts hold. Jeepers!
- In 1997, as Congress considered "Fair ATM Fees" legislation, senators noted that the average American was spending $155 on ATM fees each year, sometimes paying as much as $3 to withdraw $20. Bankrate.com forecasts that consumers will pay $2 billion to use ATMs in 2000.

These facts certainly suggest that a great many of us should be making some changes in the way we use our banks.

## 120 How can I avoid paying ridiculous ATM fees?

There are a number of strategies you can employ:
- The simplest is to only use ATMs that belong to your bank. If you have an account with an institution such as Ubiquitous Behemoth Bank Inc., this is a very workable strategy.
- If you bank with an obscure three-branch bank, look into whether it's a member of any networks that offer in-network ATM access without surcharges. Many small banks and credit unions have formed such networks to better serve their customers.
- Plan your withdrawals. Don't just withdraw $20 every time you need $20. By planning ahead a little, you can withdraw larger sums of money on fewer occasions, reducing the number of times you're socked with ATM fees. (Just don't immediately spend those larger sums on skee-ball and aromatherapy — they're advances, not windfalls.)
- Get thee to a supermarket! At many (if not most) supermarkets these days, you can pay for your purchases with your ATM card. Better still, in most cases you can ask the cashier for some extra

cash, as well, which will come out of your account fee-free. (Just make sure, first, that your bank or the grocer doesn't charge for this.)

## 121 Is there any place online where I can look up the locations of surcharge-free ATMs?

There are several websites where you can search for the machines closest to you. Here are some:
- www.surchargefreeatm.com
- www.theco-op.org/index-ns.html
- www.know-where.com/intercept
- www.sum-atm.com

## 122 If I see a bank offering free checking, I should jump in and sign up, right?

Not necessarily. Banks are often coming up with ways to tease customers into the front door. They may offer extra-low introductory interest rates, or free checking, or a number of other things. In many cases, some other fees or higher interest rates make up for the free checking. When comparing banks, you need to closely examine *all* the services you'll be using.

## 123 How can I figure out how good or bad my bank is for me?

A checklist and a short expedition into your recent records should do the trick. Gather together all your banking statements and records for the past three months. (If you've been tossing these out, make a point of *keeping* them for the next few months before commencing this exercise.) On the following worksheet, fill in the monthly columns with all the data you can find.

| WHAT'S YOUR BANK COSTING YOU? | | | |
|---|---|---|---|
| **Fee** | **Month 1** | **Month 2** | **Month 3** |
| ATM surcharges | | | |
| "Foreign" ATM fees | | | |
| Other ATM fees | | | |
| Overdraft fees | | | |
| Monthly maintenance fees | | | |
| Check printing fees | | | |
| Deposit/other slips | | | |
| Call center charges | | | |
| Debit card fees | | | |
| Low-balance penalties | | | |
| Per-check charges | | | |
| Return check/NSF fees | | | |
| Money order fees | | | |
| Traveler's check fees | | | |
| Other bank fees | | | |

Once you're done, total everything and see how much of your money is going to your bank. There's a good chance that you'll look at this worksheet and gasp in unhappy surprise. If so, there are two things you can do to improve the situation:

a. Make some changes in your behavior.

b. Make some changes in your banking — perhaps by changing banks.

Perhaps you'll want to do both.

## 124 If I'm going to shop for a new bank, what services do I need to look for?

Different banks are best for different people for different reasons. What's best for you depends on what services you need and what your habits are. Use the worksheet below to help you. Cross out any items you don't need, so that you focus only on what's important to you. Add any items relevant to you that aren't on the list. (If you plan to compare many banks, you might want to make a few photocopies of this list first, or just reproduce it by hand on some note paper.)

| COMPARING BANKS | | | |
|---|---|---|---|
| | **Bank 1** | **Bank 2** | **Bank 3** |
| High-Interest Checking Account | | | |
| Online Bill Payment | | | |
| ATMs | | | |
| Debit and Credit Cards | | | |
| Money Market Accounts | | | |
| CDs | | | |
| Brokerage Services | | | |
| Mortgage Loans | | | |
| Convenience | | | |
| Overdraft Protection | | | |
| Express Checking Accounts | | | |
| FDIC Insured | | | |
| Insurance Products | | | |
| Loan Products | | | |
| Telephone or Online Banking | | | |
| Direct Deposit | | | |
| Personalized Checks | | | |
| Other | | | |
| Other | | | |

This worksheet will help you explore your options, enabling you to compare a bunch of contenders in one handy place. You'll see that bank charges for different things vary considerably. Prioritize the things that are most important to you (the services you need most often, in the order of their importance) and find the bank that charges the least for those services.

Also, consider other providers for some services. Use a discount broker for brokerage services. Buy money orders at the local convenience store rather than using pricey cashier's checks. Use your AAA membership to buy traveler's checks there instead of at the bank. Shop around for the lowest-cost credit card. These are just a few ways to save.

## 125 When I'm checking out a bank, what questions should I seek answers to?

Here are a few:
- What's the interest rate on various accounts?
- What's the minimum deposit necessary to open various accounts? And, how about the minimum balance necessary to avoid fees once the accounts are open?
- What is the per-check charge? What is the charge for ordering new checks? Will the bank accept industry standard checks printed elsewhere?
- What is the charge for a bounced check?
- Are canceled checks returned with the monthly statements? If not, what are the charges for having a canceled check returned?
- What ATM fees are charged to withdraw cash or make a point-of-purchase transaction (e.g., pay for groceries, pay for gasoline, etc.) with my ATM card? Am I charged a fee to speak to a teller rather than use the ATM for a transaction? Am I charged if I use another bank's ATM, even if they are in the same "ATM network"?

## 126 What are some common mistakes that people make with banking?

Many common mistakes result from not looking at the big picture, and just focusing on one attractive aspect of a banking service.

For example, imagine Lester, who keeps the required minimum of $2,000 in his interest-bearing checking account at his bank. The bank rewards him with the princely interest rate of 1%. (Lester is pleased with this, because other checking accounts at the bank offer even lower rates or no interest at all, although the minimums are lower.) So Lester earns about $20 per year. Meanwhile, though, this account charges him $9.95 per month as a "service charge." This amounts to roughly $120 per year in costs, leaving poor Lester with a loss of $100 for the year. Ouch!

Another big mistake is keeping too much money at your local bank, especially in savings accounts and other accounts that pay paltry interest rates. That money could be put to work for you much more effectively.

For example, let's say that Sonia has managed to save $6,000 in her savings account. (Way to go, Sonia!) She's not yet ready to invest in stocks, so she's content earning a little interest. But, her savings account is paying her just 1.75% per year. For $6,000, that amounts to just $105. She should consider some other options.

If she assumes that she won't need $2,000 of that money for at least two years, she could park it in a 2-year CD earning, let's say, 6.5%. That will amount to $130 in the first year. If she won't need another $2,000 for at least one year, it could earn 6.25% in a 1-year CD, amounting to $125 in the first year. She might park another $1,000 in a 3-month CD (renewing it every quarter), earning 5% or $50. So, the $5,000 she shuffled out of her savings account will bring her a total of $305 that first year, instead of $105. Not bad! (Oh, and let's not forget an additional $17.50 on the $1,000 still in her savings account.)

## 127 What's the difference between APY (annual percentage yield) and APR (annual percentage rate)?

You'll see both numbers used when banks advertise their offerings. The APR is simply the rate of interest paid on something. The APY is more informative for Fools, because it tells you what to expect from the rate. They're different because the APY takes into account *how often* interest is applied.

Here's a very rough and simplified example. Let's say that an account where you keep $10,000 pays you an APR of 6%. If the interest is compounded/applied just once a year, you'd earn $600 at the end of the year.

But, most interest compounds much more often than once a year. Typically, it's more like monthly, weekly, or daily. Let's imagine that your account compounds interest monthly. If so, at the end of the year you'll end up with more than $600. That's because when the first month's interest was added (perhaps it was something in the neighborhood of 0.5%), you immediately had more than $10,000 in your account, after just one month. And, more was added each month. So, each time the interest was calculated, it was on a slightly bigger principal. The more often interest is compounded, the more money you'll end up with (although the difference isn't always enormous).

The APY reflects how much your investment will grow over the whole year. If you're looking at two different accounts with the same APR, they may reward you differently, according to how often the interest is compounded. But, when you're looking at APYs, you've got apples and apples. If a bank is advertising something without disclosing its APY, ask what it is.

## 128 Do you recommend credit unions?

Credit unions have advantages and disadvantages. Let's review them:

### Advantages
- They're owned by their members, and are non-profit.
- They offer competitive interest rates, usually beating the best rates from local banks.
- Their service is often better, too. If you turn to a traditional bank for guidance, you might not be told everything you should know, as that's not always in the bank's best interest. But, credit unions have no reason not to help you as much as they can.
- Credit unions offer more and more services these days. Many offer credit cards, debit cards, mortgages, new and used car loans, checking, and more.
- At many credit unions, you need just $1 to open an account, qualifying you to take advantage of their many services.

### Disadvantages
- Credit unions typically have few branch offices and few, if any, ATMs. To circumvent the ATM problem, many credit unions have formed networks of surcharge-free ATMs that members can use.
- Not all are insured. The National Credit Union Administration insures roughly 97% of credit union member deposits up to $100,000, but a few credit unions remain uninsured. Before signing up with a credit union, ensure that it's insured.
- Some credit unions don't return cancelled checks to you. But then, these days, many traditional banks have stopped doing this, too.

- Your local credit union may not offer you as many services as you can get from the neighborhood bank. Check to see what's offered. You may end up deciding to keep accounts at each, for different purposes. (On average, though, credit unions have been adding services over the years.)

Learn more about credit unions at the website of the Credit Union National Association: www.cuna.org. That's also where you can search for credit unions in your neighborhood. Not everyone is eligible to join one, but tens of millions of Americans *are* — so don't assume you're out of luck. You may be able to join one through your employer, community, religious group, or some other association. If your employer isn't affiliated with a credit union, consider asking your benefits office to look into developing an affiliation.

## 129 What alternatives are there to traditional banks and credit unions?

There's always Uncle Mort, who'll be happy to keep your money for you under his porch. But, he has raccoon problems, so he's probably not your best bet. You're not out of luck, though. You can get many or all of your banking needs serviced at places other than traditional banks.

One new development is Internet banks, which have no physical, bricks-and-mortar presence at all. These have become more and more popular in recent years. In addition, many traditional banks are now offering online banking services. These allow you to pay bills, check on your account, and do much more, from the comfort of your computer. Some deposits are mailed in, while many are made via direct deposit. Withdrawals are usually made through other banks' ATMs, with Internet banks often allowing each customer a certain number of free ATM transactions per month.

Also, not everyone realizes it, but many brokerages today offer banking services. TD Waterhouse is one example. If you have a brokerage account there, any money not invested in securities is "swept" regularly into a money market account, where it will earn more than it would at a bank. In addition, as these brokerages are also banks, you can enjoy check-writing privileges, credit cards, electronic banking, mortgages, and home equity loans, among other things.

Another nifty advantage of brokerages serving as banks is the availability of margin. Margin, as you'll learn later in the book, is when you borrow money from your brokerage against the value of securities in your brokerage account. This is usually used to buy additional securities, but it needn't be. If you need to borrow a few thousand dollars, you might spend a lot of time getting a loan from your bank... or, through a brokerage-bank, you can simply ask for a check drawn on margin on your account. Easy as that. (There's a little more to margin, though, and it should be used in moderation. Make sure you learn all about it before you use it — or worse, over-use it.)

## 130 What does online banking entail?

First, it goes by many names, such as: online banking, Internet banking, PC banking, home banking, and electronic banking.

Online banking permits you to pay bills online, transfer money between accounts, and access account information at any time. Another perk is that if you use an Internet-only bank, you can access it wherever you are. You can move from Anchorage to Tampa and not have to change banks.

Since online banks don't have all the expenses that traditional banks do (such as marble columns and red carpets), they can typically offer more-competitive interest rates. These days, as online banks try to attract more customers, they're frequently offering extra-special rates and deals. Keep an eye out.

There are various degrees of online banking. You may have a traditional checking account at a traditional, hundred-year-old bank, but if it offers some online services, you might find that you can begin checking your account balances online. If so, you'll be doing some online banking. At the other end of the spectrum, you might move all your money to an Internet-only bank, and take care of *all* your banking needs online. There's a range of possibilities.

## 131 How would I know if online banking is for me?

It's most beneficial if:

- You are "wired" — meaning you own a computer with online access.
- You pay a lot of bills each month. Online banking can save you not only the stamp you'd stick on each envelope, but also the trouble of writing your account number on each check, the cost of envelopes, and more. (No paper cuts, either!)
- You use software such as Intuit's *Quicken* or Microsoft *Money*. Using either of these means you've got half the work done. You've likely already entered information on your usual expenses, and you may be able to have your bank automatically update your check register online.

Online banking isn't for everyone — yet. But it might be for you. Take some time to research it a bit. You can read more on it at: www.Fool.com/money/banking/online/one.htm.

## 132 Is online banking safe?

Online banks (and online wings of traditional banks) take security very seriously and use encryption technology to protect customers. But, don't take my word for it. With any online bank you're considering, poke around its website and look for a link to information on its security provisions. Each website should list this somewhere. If you don't find it, ask about it.

## 133 Where can I learn more about banking online?

The following sites will dazzle you with an array of very useful guidance and lots of information on various banks and their offerings. These include online and traditional banks.

- www.bankrate.com
- www.banking.about.com
- www.gomez.com

- www.ivillagemoneylife.com/money/departments/banking
- www.Fool.com/money/banking/banking.htm

## 134 Got any last tips on banking?

Of course. Use direct deposit with your paycheck. It saves time and some banks will give you free checking if you use it.

Don't order checks from your bank, which might charge as much as $25 for 200 checks. You can get the same thing for a fraction of the price through services such as www.currentchecks.com (800-204-2244) or www.checksinthemail.com (877-397-1541). Many of these services guarantee that your bank will accept their checks, since many banks use the same companies for printing checks.

# Living Below Your Means

*The title of this chapter might depress you, as you imagine people scrimping and saving by taking baths together as a family and making salads from lawn clippings. Fear not, though. In the following pages you'll stumble across many suggestions that will help you save money fairly painlessly. Read through them and act on the ones that appeal to you. Some are silly and extreme, and others will make you wonder, "Why didn't I think of that?" You may even find that you enjoy saving money in a few categories because you can spend more on things that matter more to you. In addition, the more you save, the more you can invest.*

## 135 How much of a difference will all these tips really make?

They add up. If you save just $50 per month (only about $1.75 per day), that will amount to $600 per year, and $6,000 in 10 years — nothing to sneeze at.

*Invest* that same $50 each month, and you'll do even better. If it grows at the historical stock market average of about 11% per year, it'll amount to nearly $80,000 in 25 years. All that from a brown bag lunch here, and some coupons clipped there.

So, take some time to read through this chapter — perhaps jotting down or circling the tips that appeal most to you. You certainly don't have to act on all of them.

## 136 How can I save money on my car?

Some of all of the tips below might prove useful:
- Minimize your speeding, and follow parking rules. Tickets are cost-ly, and if you end up getting your insurance premiums increased, you'll suffer a double financial whammy. (Speeding also consumes more gas.)
- Be insurance-smart. Shop around and make sure you're paying as little for your desired level of coverage as you need to. Look into discounts for alarms, short commutes, or safety features.
- Spend some time comparing local gas stations and use the ones that offer the lowest rates. Take advantage of special deals that offer you a few cents off on certain days. If your car doesn't need premium gas, don't use it. You can also save gas by keeping your RPMs at lower, rather than higher, levels. (Below 3,000 is a good target.)
- Spend some time finding a good and honest mechanic. Ask friends for referrals. Using one who inflates his rates or worse, recommends unnecessary work, will cost you.
- Keep tires properly inflated and rotate them on schedule.
- Take public transportation when you can. Or walk, when that's prac-tical. Or carpool.
- Follow your car's recommended maintenance plan. Skipping oil changes and the like might save you a few dollars now, but might cost you many more later.
- Before you rent a car, verify from your car insurance agent whether your policy covers rental cars. If it does, you can say "no thanks" when the car rental agent asks if you want to buy insurance coverage.
- Look into getting new cars at a discount store such as Costco. The prices are often lower than elsewhere.

## 137 How can I save money on food?

Dieting isn't your only option. Here are a bunch of good ideas:
- Use coupons at the supermarket, or at least focus your purchases on items that are on sale.
- Cook twice as much as you need, and freeze half. Then, when you

don't have much time, instead of going out or ordering food delivered, you can simply heat up something from the freezer.
- Discover homemade soup. It's cheap to make, tasty to eat, filling, and economical.
- Cook from scratch now and then. It's often cheaper than using prepared foods. (For example, spaghetti sauce is easy to make and you can make and freeze a lot of it.)
- Cover your pots when you cook. Doing so consumes less energy.
- Re-engineer leftovers into new meals.
- Make banana bread with aging bananas. (You can pop these bananas into the freezer until you have time to thaw and use them.)
- Use special plastic bags with holes in them to prolong the life of your veggies.
- Use powdered milk in baked goods — there's little taste difference and a great dollar difference.
- Rework your recipes. If one calls for 1 pound of beef and you only have half a pound, you might prepare the recipe with what you have, instead of running out to buy more. With many recipes, you might save money by strategically substituting or eliminating some ingredients.
- Don't waste food.
- Take up gardening. You can grow some of your own food.
- Become a little more vegetarian in your eating. Meat is often the most expensive part of a meal. Enjoy meatless meals more often, or reduce the amount of meat in each meal.

## 138 What are some money-saving tips related to eating and drinking?

Obviously, opting for canned tuna now and then instead of Chilean sea bass will save you a few pennies. But there are other possibilities, too:
- Take your own water to work instead of buying bottled water regularly. Better yet, encourage your employer to look into providing filtered water for everyone.
- Take your own coffee to work, too, in a thermos.
- When you're hungry for a snack, consider drinking a glass of water first. That should decrease or even eliminate your hunger.
- Take brown-bag lunches to work. Leftovers from dinner the night before make great lunches.
- Have friends over for dinner instead of going out to a restaurant.

- Host potlucks — and picnics.
- Use restaurant coupons.

---

## 139 What are some housekeeping tips?

Fear not — these ideas have little to do with dusting or vacuuming.

- Keep your thermostat turned down (or up in the summer) when you're away.
- Insulate your water heater and turn its thermostat down when you're away.
- Consider compact fluorescent light bulbs, as they're cheaper in the long run than ordinary light bulbs.
- Install dimmer switches. They allow you to use softer lighting when you don't need full-power lighting, and they'll save you money in the process.
- Close the blinds. This will keep your home cooler during the day and might keep some heat in at night.
- Turn off lights and appliances when not in use.
- When your liquid soaps are half finished, add some water to make them last a little longer.
- Consider using "Dryel" or similar at-home dry-cleaning products for items that require dry-cleaning.
- When using cleaning agents, use less than you're directed to. You'll usually get just-as-good results and you'll spend less. Also, take a look at the ingredients in name-brand cleaning agents you use and consider making your own. A gallon of bleach costs just a few dollars and goes a long way. A little bleach mixed with water in a squirt bottle makes a great anti-bacterial cleaning spray for the kitchen and any hard, colorfast surfaces (be careful and label it clearly to avoid accidents with carpet and fabrics). The bleach solution also kills mold and mildew on bathroom surfaces, just like the pricier Tilex-type products. (In fact, Clorox makes Tilex!) White vinegar mixed with water makes a great glass cleaner for pennies. Use it with old newspaper for streak- and lint-free sparkling windows and glass.
- If you need a desk, you can make one with a door resting on two 2-drawer filing cabinets. Buy the door before the doorknob hole is cut, and stain it if you wish. Office supply stores also carry sturdy folding tables meant for office environments that make great, portable desks — usually for less than $50.

- Don't toss out that tube of toothpaste until it's really empty.
- Measure things. If you're supposed to use two tablespoons of dishwasher detergent, don't guess at what that is — because you'll very possibly use more than you need to.
- Reuse Ziplock bags. You can wash them and turn them inside out to help them dry.
- Learn to do more of your home maintenance yourself.

## 140 What are some health-related money-saving tips?

The biggest tip is probably to go to the dentist and doctor regularly. You can save on possible future medical and dental costs by taking care of yourself. And, you may save up some extra years, in the process — not a bad deal! So, brush, floss, and get those check-ups. Some more suggestions:
- Don't smoke.
- Don't drink alcohol, or reduce your alcohol consumption.
- Spend more time exercising and less time shopping.
- Instead of buying exercise videos, consider taping some exercise programs on TV.
- If you have significant routine health-related expenses, look into using a flexible spending account, which can save you a lot of money by exempting some expenses from your taxable income. Ask your benefits administrator at work about this possibility.

## 141 Are there any good ways to save money on cigarettes?

Well, you can plan ahead and buy your cigarettes in cartons when they're on sale, rather than one pack at a time. But, you'll save a *lot* more money by quitting. Consider what the real cost of smoking is: Imagine that you're 35 years old, you smoke one pack a day, and each pack costs you, on average, about $3. Multiply $3 by 365 days, and you're looking at an annual cost of $1,095.

Let's see what would happen if you took this $1,095 and invested it in the stock market, earning the historical average return of 11% per year. In 30 years, you'd have $25,067. If you invested $1,095 in the market *each year* for 30 years, you'd end up with a whopping $218,000. Yowza.

If you'd like to quit, there are more resources available to you today than ever before. Online, we recently opened a "Quitting Smoking" discussion board and in its first year, it received about 15,000 messages from people who have quit or are interested in quitting. These folks are continually supporting and encouraging each other, and many end their posts with this unique kind of signature:

Madeline Houston
Three months, three weeks, four days, 11 hours, 8 minutes and 5 seconds. 3288 cigarettes not smoked, saving $557.29. Life saved: 1 week, 4 days, 10 hours, 0 minutes.

Rebecca Wolfe
Ten months, two weeks, two days, 1 hour, 30 minutes and 58 seconds. 9601 cigarettes not smoked, saving $1,248.24. Life saved: 4 weeks, 5 days, 8 hours, 5 minutes.

Imagine this future signature that might end your own posts:

Me
5 years, one month, one week, 1 day, 2 hours, 4 minutes and 13 seconds. 56,406 cigarettes not smoked, saving $7,344. Life saved: 24 weeks, 28 days, 1 hour, 9 minutes.

For more information and support to quit smoking, visit www.silkquit.com and check out the nifty SilkQuit tracker at: www.1tmc.com/~sfc/silkquit.htm. Other resources:
- www.silkquit.org
- www.quitnet.org
- www.quit-smoking.com
- www.quitsmokingsupport.com
- www.quitsmoking.Fool.com

---

## 142 What are some habits I can change to save money?

Well, for starters, you might stop giving your gerbils dollar bills to chew on. There are many other profitable tweaks you can make to your lifestyle, too. The long list below is just a beginning.
- Take stock of your common activities and note which ones cost you

money and which ones don't. Be aware of what you're spending on various activities. Change those habits a little. Perhaps shop less and play board games more.

- Develop new hobbies and interests that don't eat up too much money. You might take up hiking, for example, or gardening. Start a book club. Or go with a friend to an orchard and pick fruit there instead of buying it at a supermarket. Some activities that seem costly, such as golf, don't have to be, as long as you spend carefully. If you buy a few inexpensive clubs and play on affordable public courses, you might save money.
- Consider developing hobbies that can actually produce some income, such as woodworking or freelance writing.
- Use your local library more, instead of bookstores. Start a book exchange at work, where colleagues bring in and trade books.
- Rent movies instead of seeing them at expensive first-run theaters. Go to first-run theaters for matinee showings, which are usually discounted.
- Reduce, reuse, and recycle. You can often get some money back when you recycle some things. Reducing and reusing can also save money.
- Evaluate your TV viewing habits and, if you don't watch cable TV too much, consider dropping your cable TV subscription. At the very least, you might drop one or more premium channels.
- Read more.
- Think about every dollar you spend. Make yourself wait a month before you make most purchases. A month later, you might not want some things quite as much. Maintain a wish list of things you want. Delay purchasing to see if the urge passes.
- Create and stick to a budget. (It doesn't have to be a punishing one. Budgeting is mostly just about planning where your money goes.)
- Try bartering. You may be able to negotiate free haircuts in exchange for building a website for your local hair salon. See what your friends can do for you and what you can do for them. Perhaps a lawyer friend can draft your will in exchange for some massages. Maybe you can do some typing for someone in exchange for some time at her beach house. Think about what you can offer and what you can use.
- Reduce some of the complexities in your life. Do you really need call waiting, caller-ID, and that pager? These all add up. For some people, they're not necessities and even cause extra stress.
- Toss out those advertising supplements that pad your Sunday paper, unless you really need to buy something. Otherwise you may end

up buying things you don't really need.

- Don't buy magazines regularly at the newsstand. Subscriptions are much cheaper. Better still, read magazines at libraries.
- Eat before you go to the movies, so you're not tempted to mortgage your house to pay for a tub of popcorn.
- Convert some phone calls into e-mail. You can sometimes reach out and touch more people with e-mail than by phone. And it's cheaper.
- Negotiate. Foolish shoppers have asked salespeople, "Do you have any discounts or sales on this item?" and have received many discounts — such as 10% off. This can work on things as common as stereos and car washes. One Fool was buying sheets that were due to go on sale in a few days. She explained that she needed them today, and wondered if she could get them at the sale price. The salesperson talked to her manager, and a deal was struck.
- Shop around and find the long-distance company that offers the best plan to match your calling habits. You should be able to get most long-distance carriers to meet or beat the best deals offered by competing long-distance carriers.
- Call your credit card company and negotiate a lower interest rate. If they balk, tell them you'll be happy to take your business elsewhere.
- With shampoo, lather up, rinse, and then don't repeat.

---

## 143 What are some ways my family can save money?

One fun thing to do is to establish a family game night, where you just play board and card games with each other. If you don't have a family, plan game nights with friends. Here are some other ideas:

- Have some regular reading time, when all of you read some books or magazines or newspapers. It's good for the kids and good for you. And, it doesn't cost much, either.
- Buy a family pass to the local zoo or amusement park, if you plan to go there frequently.
- Spend time at public parks.
- This may sound off-the-wall, but if you have the space outside and the interest, consider getting some chickens. It can be fun for the kids, and you'll have fresh eggs.
- Make your own baby food. In a food processor or blender, puree canned fruits and vegetables (preferably separately) with a little water or juice from the can. (Make sure you're not using products

with a lot of unwanted sugar or salt, though.)

- Teach your children about the value of money by giving them allowances and expecting them to save and pay for some things they want. If you can get them to save and invest some of their money, you might even institute a matching program, where you'll chip in a dollar for every one or two dollars they save.
- At restaurants, you might offer to pay your child fifty cents or a dollar if she orders water instead of soda. You'll save a little money. She'll enjoy a healthier drink and earn a little money at the same time.
- Learn to cut your kids' hair yourself. You and your spouse might even learn to cut each other's hair. There are instructional videos and kits available. With a little practice, you'll likely be pleased with the results and will be saving considerable money.

## 144 What are some tips for shopping?

Clipping and using coupons is perhaps the most obvious suggestion. If you do this, consider keeping them organized in some kind of small file system — perhaps a series of small envelopes. Here are some additional ideas:

- Plan your shopping according to what's on sale.
- Most things will be on sale at some point. Wait for your favorite brands of items, especially non-perishables such as toilet paper or canned goods, to come on sale — then stock up.
- Don't food shop on an empty stomach.
- Don't shop without a list of what you need to buy.
- Compare prices per unit on what you buy. Sometimes a bigger or smaller container is the better bargain.
- Cereal is expensive. Buy it when it's on sale, or buy cereal in bags, which tends to be less expensive.
- Buy some items online, when it's less expensive to do so. Pet food can be found inexpensively online.
- Shop at outlets.
- Research purchases with *Consumer Reports* magazine (and website, at www.consumerreports.com) and other resources. They'll help you buy the better quality products at reasonable prices.
- Buy high-quality items. They tend to last longer and serve you better.
- Ask yourself if you really need whatever you're about to buy. Maybe you do really want it, but you can put off the purchase for a while.

- Examine restaurant and store receipts closely, as they often contain errors. (Sometimes intentionally!)
- Examine the change you get from cashiers.
- Shop at discount clubs such as Costco or BJ's. You'll find some amazing bargains at these stores. Just don't assume that everything there is a bargain. Compare prices.
- Buy store brands when possible, not name brands.
- Look for rebate forms at stores and send in for rebates.
- Buy used when you can — for items such as books, CDs, and furniture.
- If you like having fresh cut flowers in your home, grow them yourself.
- Plant a raspberry bush. Each time you pick a cup of raspberries, you'll be saving yourself a few dollars.

## 145 How can I save money on gifts?

Do your holiday and birthday gift shopping throughout the year. You may find some perfect presents at good prices four months away from the gift-giving time, and that will save you from having to buy a less-perfect, more-expensive gift later. Here are some more tips:
- Wrap gifts in the comics from your Sunday paper or aluminum foil.
- If you're sending flowers to someone, contact a florist near them and order a bouquet directly. This is usually considerably cheaper than using a national service such as FTD. If you're ordering flowers for someone in a hospital far away, try calling the hospital gift shop — they can often send a nice bouquet or plant to the patient upstairs for less than you'd pay ordering from a national florist.
- Some very special gifts can be quite affordable. Consider having a T-shirt, mug, or calendar made for a friend or relative from a favorite photo. Photos themselves make wonderful gifts. Grandparents, for example, will likely treasure a collection of family photos more than a new waffle iron.
- Make your own customized calendar gifts for others by buying a calendar of the upcoming year and pasting your own photos over the ones it comes with.
- For people who have everything, consider giving a gift to a charity in their name.
- Assemble a booklet of your favorite and most successful recipes

— it costs little and can mean a lot to the recipient.

- Create and give someone a scrapbook filled with memories — or a collection of letters and thoughts from the recipient's friends and loved ones.
- If you know what you want to buy for someone, look for the best price on it. Check out online sales, too.
- Consider doing some gift shopping using "pre-owned" items. (Just call them "vintage" or "classic" or "collectors' items," instead of "used.") Sites such as eBay.com, uBid.com, Half.com, as well as Amazon.com and Yahoo! auction sites can yield some treasures.
- Give coupons for services you'll render. Your parents can redeem a coupon worth six hours of your help fixing up the house. Give a friend a coupon offering two Saturdays of gardening help, or three nights of babysitting. You might even offer coupons for delivered meals. Just ask for a 48-hour lead-time to deliver a tasty homemade casserole and cake whenever they're needed.
- Chip in on a gift with friends and relatives. It can end up costing you less and resulting in a boffo gift for the recipient.

## 146 What are some clothing-related money-saving tips?

Care for the clothes you buy properly. Don't, and you'll end up with things like pants shrunk too small to wear or your spiffy red socks bleeding onto your nice new white shirt.

- When you're ready to get rid of old clothing, donate it to an organization such as the Salvation Army or Goodwill, where you can get an itemized receipt to file with your taxes. A pile of old clothing and shoes (not to mention other household goods) can represent a small windfall in charitable tax deductions.
- Consider buying some clothes for your kids slightly too large. They'll likely quickly grow into them and will get to wear them a little bit longer than if you'd bought something smaller.
- Seek out hand-me-down clothing for your younger children from friends, neighbors, and relatives.
- Convert old t-shirts and pajamas into useful rags by cutting them up.
- Shop for clothes at the end of the season, when you'll find the best discounts. Parkas will often be cheaper in February than in November. (Of course, you might find some exceptional sale prices during the season, as well.)

- Look for factory outlets, where you can often get extra-low prices on name brands. If you're looking for a Gap outlet, call a Gap store and ask where their outlets are located. If you're after Nike footwear, call and ask about their outlets.

## 147 Do you have any money-saving tips for weddings?

Yup. Here are a few:
- Elope! If you save pretty much the entire cost of the wedding, you can spend more on a nice honeymoon and still have some savings left over that can be applied to investments.
- Have your reception in a non-traditional place. Some public grounds, such as parks, can work — just contact your local recreation departments.
- Don't shoot for the fanciest of wedding dresses. You're only going to wear it once, after all, so why spend thousands on it? Consider buying a less-expensive one, borrowing one, or even renting one. Consider having bridesmaids wear inexpensive dresses, too.
- Have a morning wedding. Expenses for food, transportation, and hall rentals tend to be lower in the morning. In addition, guests might imbibe less at an earlier wedding, thereby reducing your liquor tab.
- Think twice before getting married on a Saturday or in June. As these are popular times, they tend to be when couples are charged the most.
- Consider having an expensive wedding and inexpensive honeymoon, or vice versa. By not splurging on both, you'll save a lot of money.
- Make the most of gift registries. Instead of registering for expensive luxuries, register for necessities such as everyday dishes and a bathroom scale. If you receive them as gifts, you won't have to buy them later.

## 148 Where can I find even more handy tips for saving money?

There are lots of places. Here are a few online addresses to visit:
- www.cheapskatemonthly.com
- www.stretcher.com

- www.blp.net
- www.valulinks.com
- www.juliemorgenstern.com

Here are some websites that feature special bargains or coupons:
- www.dealcatcher.com
- www.amazing-bargains.com
- www.bluefly.com
- www.gotapex.com
- www.edealfinder.com
- www.dealofday.com
- www.cyberrebate.com
- www.bargaindog.com
- www.kusner.com/nojunk/fstuff

There are a bunch of useful books you might read, as well. (Consider getting them at your local library, though, instead of a bookstore!)
- *The Complete Tightwad Gazette* by Amy Dacyzyn
- *The Wealthy Barber* by David Chilton
- *Your Money or Your Life* by Joe Dominguez and Vicki Robin
- *Getting a Life* by Jacqueline Blix and David Heitmiller
- *Living Cheaply with Style* by Ernest Callenbach
- *The More-With-Less Cookbook* by Doris Longacre and Mary E. Showalter
- *The Complete Cheapskate* by Mary Hunt
- *Frugal Families: Making the Most of Your Hard Earned Money* by Jonni McCoy
- *Penny Pinching 1999* by Lee Simmons and Barbara Simmons
- *The Frugal Almanac* by Melodie Moore
- *The Best of Living Cheap News* by Larry Roth
- *Wealth on Minimal Wage* by James W. Steamer
- *The Millionaire Next Door: The Surprising Secrets of America's Wealthy* by Thomas J. Stanley and William D. Danko

Last, but not least, drop by the Fool.com's "Living Below Your Means" discussion board, where our community of Fools is always coming up with new ideas.

**Are you some kind of genius or what, coming up with all these amazing money-saving tips?**

Well, I'm smarter than a doorknob, for sure, but I must confess that most of these tips come from members of the Fool's online community. We've got thousands of folks hanging out on our discussion boards online, where they ask and answer questions, share thoughts and tips, and amuse each other.

One of our boards is the exceedingly popular "Living Below Your Means" board. At the risk of leaving out some people, let me list some of the many people who contributed to the tips in this chapter by their Fool.com screen names:

> Absynthe, Actuarystdtjk, amshih1, AstridS, barbiannio, beteo, blainche, BookmFool, brake16, caponeman, CharlieBoy2, clbaker, compuser2, CPOCat, Crazyfred, Crazyinlovefool, Daveguy7, dduncan, DiabloQueen, DMD77, dmilne, easher, Edevere, eWineguy, flapdoodle, foolishcase, forumcap, funkychair, gangrelfool, greatscents, gwgross, haft2b, hlupak, hm001e, hondaman, hunnypot1, jenniebez, jjarmoc, jtesh, jthrelkeld, judy114, KentuckyLiz, khamber, kmshays, lanshark, levda, Litebeers, lsoowal, maddiemcwa, malakito, mcjanner, mdziama, mepe, mommabunny, mpkear, MrFun, pallahs, pamburns, phantomdiver, PolitIncorrec, reader99, RVGolding, SailDi, shfrank, smpitman, SouEu, soui, sphillipnew, spud1910, SquawIndian, Starrry, suzefan, swimdad, tamarab, TEXASGRAD92, theocat, ThePapii, TMF-Documama, tpesch, tvsotelo, UMsprite, Wilder514, wildgirl, wmhughes, yeilBagheera.

James Frye (WonderPup) and Jacki Stirn (Recovering Fool) in particular deserve special mention, for assembling many tips and helping organize the information shared on Living Below Your Means. Thanks!

# Taxes

*One of the main tax themes that we like to emphasize in Fooldom is that taxes shouldn't be attended to just in April. If you want to minimize what you fork over to Uncle Sam, you need to bone up a bit on tax issues and make some strategic decisions throughout the year. This modest chapter offers up just a few of the many tax issues about which you should be aware. It closes with some pointers on where you can learn even more.*

## 150 Can you explain the tax process? How is the final amount of tax I owe calculated?

It all begins with income — which, for most of us, is automatically reported to the IRS. Our employers report what was paid to us as salary. Our banks report interest we earned. Our brokerages report dividends paid to us and stocks that we sold (for which we'll need to calculate our gains or losses). You may need to report additional income sources, too — such as tips, gambling winnings, business income, rental income, alimony income... or the million dollars you won on that *DMV-Castaway* show after being locked up in a Department of Motor Vehicles office for three months with a dozen strangers and a registration to renew. (Just remember, we thought of it first.)

Total all your income for the year, and you'll be looking at what's called your "gross income." To this, you now make "adjustments."

- Subtract whatever amount you contributed to qualifying IRA or other retirement accounts.
- Subtract any alimony payments you made and any moving expenses that qualify.
- If you're self-employed, subtract half of the self-employment tax you paid.
- Subtract any qualified student loan interest paid, and any medical savings account deduction.

Once you've made all your adjustments, you'll be left with a very important sum: your "adjusted gross income," or AGI. The AGI is used throughout your tax return — expect it to pop up all over the place like the little critter in carnival "Whack-a-Mole" games. It's used to determine limitations on a number of tax issues, including exemptions, deductible IRA contributions, and itemized deductions.

From your AGI, you now claim your exemptions and make your deductions. You can take either an itemized deduction or a standard deduction — whichever is greater. The standard deduction ranges from about $3,500 to $7,000, depending on your filing status.

You're entitled to one exemption for yourself, plus one each for your spouse and/or dependents, if you have them. The exemption is a set amount that you're permitted to deduct from your income, reducing the sum on which you're taxed. Exemption levels are tied to inflation and change from year to year, usually increasing.

Once you've taken your exemptions and deductions, you're left with your "taxable income." It's this number that determines your tax. (You just flip to the tax charts, which tell you, for example, that if your taxable income is at least $35,300, but less than $35,350, and you are single, your tax is $6,596.)

Sound simple enough? It is. Except that we're not done yet. Although you may think this is the total amount of tax that Uncle Sam would like you to cough up, there are still a few steps to go.

You now take the tax due on your taxable income and subtract any credits. Then you add any other taxes. Credits are usually for children, the elderly, the disabled, adoptions, or foreign taxes paid. Other taxes include self-employment taxes and taxes on qualified retirement plans. The end result is your total tax. This is the sum that you must fork over to the government.

You're not going to sit down and write a check for this amount, though, because there's one step left. Remember all that money withheld from your paycheck every payday? Or the estimated tax payments you've already made? Items like these are subtracted from your total tax, leaving you with either a positive or negative number. If the number is positive, it's what you have to make a check out for. If it's negative, you can expect a tax refund in that amount.

That's it — you're done. It does take a while to do (it's estimated that upwards of 30 hours is required to complete Form 1040 and Schedules A, B, C, and D), but it isn't brain surgery.

## 151 What's the difference between a "marginal tax rate" and an "effective tax rate"?

Your marginal tax rate is the rate at which your last and your next dollar of taxable income are taxed. It's not the rate at which *all* your dollars are taxed. It's the maximum rate you're paying on any of your dollars of taxable income. If you're single, for example, according to the rules at the time of this writing, your marginal tax rate would be 15%, 28%, 31%, 36%, or 39.6%.

Remember that your marginal tax rate only deals with the specific tax on your income. As you know, there are other taxes that you may have to pay — such as self-employment taxes, alternative minimum tax, and even penalty taxes on retirement plan distributions. There are also credits that you may benefit from, such as the child tax credit, the dependent care credit, or the education credits.

So, after the jumble of other taxes and credits, your marginal tax rate may lose a bit of its importance. Which is why you'll want to take a peek at your *effective* tax rate. Your effective tax rate reveals the average rate of taxation for all your dollars. It's your total tax obligation (including your income tax and any other additional taxes and/or credits), divided by your total taxable income.

After all is said and done, it is very likely that your effective tax rate will be higher or lower than your marginal rate.

## 152 What do I do if I discover that I goofed and submitted a tax return with an error in it? Turn myself in to the IRS?

Not exactly. The tax form you prepare and mail in isn't the only one you're ever allowed to file for that year. After you've filed the regular return, if you need to, you can file an amended return, via form "1040X." In fact, you can even amend an amended return. You're permitted to amend your return until three years have passed since the date the original return was filed (or its due date). Also, if any of your changes affect your adjusted gross income, you'll probably want to amend your state return, too. Contact your state tax department for the appropriate forms.

For example, imagine that it's the year 2039 and the rules regarding amended return deadlines haven't changed. A woman named Hester files her return for the tax year 2038 on April 4, 2039 — 11 days before the filing deadline of April 15, 2039. She'll have three years in which to amend her return. The last day on which she can file an amendment will be April 15, 2042, three years after the initial due date.

## 153 What records should I keep to help me prepare my tax return?

You should keep a record of any and every investment-related expense, and anything that will relate to your tax return. The list below isn't comprehensive, but it'll give you an idea of what you'll need:
- Keep confirmation reports of stock purchases and sales, including the execution prices and trade dates.
- Keep all statements and reports sent to you by your brokerage, mutual fund company, or other investment services company, and from other sources. Perhaps most important are 1099 forms. They show your proceeds from sales of securities (1099-B) and other capital assets; interest income (1099-INT); state tax refunds and other government payments (1099-G); dividend income (1099-DIV); Social Security earnings (1099-SSA); and distributions from IRAs, pensions,

and annuities (1099-R).

- Keep records of how you acquired any securities (such as through purchase, inheritance, etc.), and your cost basis.
- If you participate in a dividend reinvestment plan (for stocks and/or mutual funds), keep track of the dividends you receive and how many shares they purchase at what price. This information is necessary to help you calculate the new cost basis for your shares.
- Keep records of contributions to IRAs and other retirement plans. If you make non-deductible contributions to an IRA, make sure you declare these on IRS Form 8606 so that you don't end up paying a second tax on them down the line. You should have year-end account statements as well as receipts for your contributions.
- If one of your securities becomes worthless, keep any documentation relating to that, especially something that includes the date on which it became worthless.
- Keep records relating to interest expense and how you used the loaned funds. This is an advanced topic, but it's an important one. For more information, consult IRS Publications 535 and 550 (available on the Internet at the IRS website: www.irs.ustreas.gov).
- Keep all your old sneakers and chicken bones. (Kidding! Just checking to see if you're still reading.)
- If you plan to deduct travel or meal expenses relating to investment-related travel, keep records of exactly what the trip involved. Know, though, that many investment-related trips are not deductible, such as travel to attend a shareholder meeting or an investment seminar. IRS Publications 463 and 550 will give you more details.
- Keep records of improvements made to your home. These can be added to your home's cost basis, decreasing your gain when you sell the home.
- Keep records of expenses related to selling your home. They can also be deducted from your capital gain.
- If you donate stock, keep records of what you donated, the day of the donation, your cost basis for the shares, and their fair market value. Keep track of cash donations, too.
- If you give stock away, also keep records of what you gave, the day of the gift, your cost basis for the shares, and their fair market value.
- Keep records of expenses for professional help, such as tax preparers and advisors, legal counsel, etc.

## 154 What documents do I need to keep after I've filed my return, and how long do I need to hang on to them?

Unless fraud, evasion, or a substantial understatement of income is involved in your tax return, you'll usually only need to keep the underlying documentation for about three years.

Keep your copy of the tax return forever. You never know when it'll come in handy. Remember that, in many cases, the IRS destroys the original returns after four or five years. It's always best to have *your* copy to fall back on.

Cancelled checks, deposit statements and receipts should generally be kept for at least three years — seven years is best, though. Note, though, that if a receipt is for something that won't appear on your tax return for several years (such as home improvements), then you'll want to hang on to it for at least three to seven years beyond when it appears on your return.

Stock trade confirmation receipts/statements should be kept for at least three years after both ends of the transaction (both buy and sell) have closed. Again, keeping them five or seven years is even better.

Keep proof of improvements to your property, until at least three years (preferably seven) after the sale of the property, to prove your basis in the property when it is sold. This is true for rental property, investment property, and even your own personal residence.

Remember when you put that new roof on your rental property in 1987? Well, you'd better still have that receipt — and keep it with receipts for the other improvements to that property for at least three years after you sell it. In cases like this, it is very possible that you'll have records 10, 20, 25 years old or older. It's not uncommon — if you're retaining your records appropriately.

Keep escrow closing documents a minimum of three years after the property is sold. You'll want to retain both the purchase escrow and sale escrow statements. Much like your stock confirmation statements, you'll need to show both sides of the transaction *and* be able to prove your improvements. And, as always, keeping the records for five or seven years past the sale is an even better bet.

---

## 155 Is it smart to use tax-preparation software such as TurboTax?

Many people think so. It's becoming more and more common for people to use inexpensive software to prepare their tax returns. Now you can even bypass the software and prepare returns on the Internet for a modest fee. With these programs, you end up printing filled-out tax forms, which you sign and then mail in, perhaps with a check attached.

The main contenders when it comes to tax-preparation software are Intuit's *TurboTax* and H&R Block's *TaxCut*. If you're the type who loves filling out questionnaires and answering questions, you might actually enjoy (gasp!) preparing your taxes this way.

They have many advantages:
- You don't have to gather any forms; they're all in the program already.
- You can revise and revise and revise, without making a mess with whiteout or an eraser. Enter your information, see what your tax liability is, and then you can make adjustments, playing out different scenarios to see which is most cost-effective. (You might see that it's smart to realize some capital gains this year, for example.)
- The software can assist you with decisions. It asks you questions and either makes decisions for you (regarding which forms to use, for example), or offers you some information and asks you to make a choice.
- You can pay less attention to details. Once the program has certain information, it will make sure that it's carried over to and entered in all the required places. You don't have to worry about that.
- Carryovers from year to year get taken care of automatically — if you used the same program to prepare your return last year.

There are, of course, some disadvantages. The main one is that you have to trust the software, even though you're still the one responsible for filing your return. There's always a small chance that the software caused an error — or that you provided an incorrect number and generated the error yourself. (Of course, even manually prepared returns may contain errors.)

Still, you might do well to at least try it once. Consider using it as a crosscheck for yourself one year — fill out your return the old-fashioned way, and then do it electronically. Compare the results and you'll get a much better feeling for how accurate and/or helpful the software is. You can choose whether you want to file your original return or the computer-generated one, and you'll probably have an idea of which approach you want to use the following year.

Perhaps the most powerful advantage of tax-preparation software is that it lets you play "what if" games. Once you've entered the necessary information, change one variable and see how the bottom line is affected. See what will happen if you get a big raise at work or if you sell some stocks for a sizable capital gain. This can be enormously valuable if you think you might have to pay estimated taxes. Let the *software* help you figure out whether you have to pay estimated taxes.

When buying tax-preparation software, make sure that the package includes state tax forms for your state — if you'd like it to prepare those forms, as well. Verify that it is compatible with your computer system. Make sure that it contains all the forms you'll need. If you buy the software early in the year, make sure you get an updated final version later in the year, so you're preparing your return incorporating the latest information and tax code revisions.

You can read more about available software at the company websites — and, in many cases, you can get demo versions there as well. Keep in mind that you can often prepare your return online without even buying the software — by paying a fee online instead.

You can check out the main tax-preparation programs at these sites:
- www.turbotax.com
- www.taxcut.com

---

**156** **If I don't use a software program and don't want to prepare my taxes myself, how should I go about finding a tax professional to do my taxes?**

Here are some tips:
- Ask for referrals from people whose business savvy you respect. Any

accountant can buy advertising, but she can't buy satisfied clients.

- Ask for an interview. The accountant should be willing to give you some time (at no charge) to discuss and assess your situation. At that time, ask the following questions:
- How big is your firm? (You want to determine how important your business will be and avoid ending up as a little frog in a big pond.)
- What are your fees and billing policies? (Ask for an estimate.)
- Who exactly will be preparing my taxes — you or somebody else? If I have problems or questions, do I speak with you?
- What are your continuing professional education (CPE) requirements, and how many CPE hours do you normally take each year? (If she exceeds the requirements, that's a good sign.)
- What research material do you use and subscribe to? (Answers such as "CCH," "Research Institute," and "BNA" are encouraging. If the answer is merely the current Federal Tax Handbook, run, don't walk, to the nearest exit. Sometimes complicated problems arise that require deep research. You don't want your tax geek just giving it her best shot. Being correct is always best when dealing with the IRS.)
- If my return is audited, will you represent me before the IRS? (She should go *instead* of you, not with you. If the accountant sources out the audit work, think twice before signing up. If she insists that you also be present at an audit, think a third time.)
- Can you get the return done in a few weeks? (It's late March, after all!)

Finally, select someone with whom you're comfortable. She might be the best tax technician in the world, but if you aren't comfortable with her, you will hesitate to call her and might not provide the information she needs to do a good job for you.

## 157 How much am I allowed to gain from the sale of stock before I must pay capital gains tax on it?

Uncle Sam's hand is out as soon as you make your first dollar. However, you can offset some of the gain with any losses from sales of stock.

## 158 What are the current capital gains rates?

As of the time of this writing, there are two holding periods for capital assets sold on or after January 1, 1998. Assets held for a year or less are considered short-term. Those held for more than one year are considered long-term.

If you're in the 15% tax bracket:
- Assets held for a year or less are taxed at your ordinary income tax rate.
- Assets held for more than a year are taxed at a 10% rate.

If your tax bracket is greater than 15%:
- Assets held for a year or less are taxed at your ordinary income tax rate.
- Assets held for more than a year are taxed at a 20% rate.

The difference can be enormous. If you hold a security for 12½ months and then sell, you'll likely pay just 20% tax on the gains. If you sell after holding only 11½ months, though, you'll be taxed at your ordinary income rate, which can be as high as 39.6%. So, you might pay almost twice as much in taxes.

Beginning January 1, 2001, the maximum capital gains rates for assets held more than five years are 8% and 18% (rather than 10% and 20%). If you're normally in the 28% (or higher) tax bracket, if you qualify, your capital gains rate could be reduced from 20% to 18%. Likewise, if you're in the 15% tax bracket, your long-term capital gains rate could fall as low as 8%. (Keep reading, though. As with most tax-related topics, this isn't as simple as it might appear. Sigh.)

Those in the 15% and higher-than-15% tax brackets are treated a little differently regarding when they can start taking advantage of the new rates.

The 18% rate only applies to assets with holding periods that begin on or after January 1, 2001 — no sooner. Using simple math, you can see that your long-term benefit will not kick in until 2006 at the earliest — when you actually sell the qualifying asset and meet your more-than-five-year holding period requirement.

For taxpayers in the 15% tax bracket, however, the five-year holding period begins on the date of actual purchase — and you are *not* required to wait and make your purchases in 2001 or later. It is very possible, if you're in the 15% bracket, that a stock you bought in 1996 will be subject to the lower capital gains rates if you hold it for more than five years and sell it after January 1, 2001.

## 159 How do I reconcile capital gains and losses on my tax return? Do I just add them all together?

It's a little more complicated than that. You'll have to "net" long-term gains and losses separately from short-term gains and losses. Then you'll net the long result with the short result. Consider this amusing example from an article that Fool community member Peter Thelander wrote on our website:

Long John Silver sold two stocks so far this year. Both were held for more than a year, so they are long-term items. Long John had a gain of $1,000 on his investment in BadCatch.com — an Internet startup selling trout and salmon online to unlucky fisherman — and a $600 loss on Fish-R-Us — a retailer of fish-shaped toys for kids. Subtract the loss from the gain and we find that he has a net $400 long-term gain.

Now, let's say that he sells two more stocks before year-end. His investment in Mackerel Industries has turned out to be a real stinker. So, he unloads it for a $300 short-term loss. And, Minnow, Inc. turned a small short-term gain of $50. Net these two items together, and Long John has a $250 short-term loss.

Finally, we net the short-term items with the long-term items and find that Long John has a net $150 long-term gain.

## 160 What are the most common results when you're netting long-term and short-term capital gains and losses, and do they all get the same treatment?

Here's concise explanation from our online *Tax Center*, written by Peter Thelander:

Everything will boil down to one of four situations:

- Long-term gain with short-term gain
- Long-term loss with short-term gain
- Long-term gain with short-term loss
- Long-term loss with short-term loss

### Long-Term Gain With Short-Term Gain

Ahhh — investment nirvana! Everything nets out to a winner. The long-term gain gets the preferential rate of 10% or 20%, depending on your tax bracket. The short-term gain is taxed with your other income at your marginal rate.

### Long-Term Loss With Short-Term Gain

We have to look at two situations here. If the gain is bigger than the loss, you have a net short-term gain — taxed at your marginal rate. If the loss is bigger, you have a net long-term loss. Up to $3,000 of loss can be used to offset other kinds of income. Any unused amount will carry forward to the following year as a long-term loss.

### Long-Term Gain With Short-Term Loss

Again we have to consider two scenarios. If the gain is bigger than the loss, you have a net long-term gain and get to take advantage of the favorable rates for the net gain. If the loss is larger, it is a net short-term loss and, just like the previous situation, you use up to $3,000 of the loss against other types of income, with any balance carrying forward to the next year as a short-term loss.

### Long-Term Loss With Short-Term Loss

You might want to consider changing your investment strategy! This scenario looks simple, but there is a twist. By now, you know that a maximum of $3,000 in losses will offset ordinary income. So, if the total of the two losses is less than $3,000, you're done. But, what if the total loss is more than $3,000 and some must be carried over to next year — is the carryover short-term or long-term? Well, it can be just long-term, or a combination of long- and short-term. It will never be just short-term, though, because you must use the short-term losses first. If your short-term losses are more than $3,000, you use the first $3,000 to offset ordinary income, then carry the remaining short-term loss, along with all of the long-term loss, over to next year. If the short-term loss is less than $3,000, you can just total the two losses together, take the $3,000 off, and the balance is a long-term loss carryover to the following year.

**161** **What's the difference between the "trade date" and "settlement date" on my brokerage transaction records? Which one do I use for tax purposes?**

Whenever you place an order to buy or sell a security with your broker, there will be a "trade date" and "settlement date" recorded. The trade date, which is the date that the order was executed, is the one that counts for tax purposes. The settlement date is just the date when the cash or securities from the transaction are plunked into your account.

**162** **How do I calculate my capital gains on a stock?**

You can only calculate your gain (or loss) once you sell the stock. First you'll need to figure out your "cost basis," though. Let's say you bought 100 shares of Excelsior Hair Growth Enterprises (ticker: SPROUT) at $25 each, paying your broker a $20 commission. Your total cost was $2,520 ($2,500 plus $20). That means your cost basis per share was $25.20. If you sell 50 of the shares a little later at $30 each, the proceeds will be $1,500 less another $20 commission, for a total of $1,480, or $29.60 per share. Therefore, your capital gain per share is $29.60 minus $25.20, or $4.40.

Notice how incorporating commissions has knocked 60 cents off your per-share gain. People who ignore commissions are leaving money on the tax table.

Once you've determined your gain, you need to figure out how long you held the asset, to see if it will be taxed as a short-term or long-term gain.

**163** **I bought a stock at $1.00 per share. It dropped to a few cents and then went off the board altogether. How can I get rid of it now, so that I can claim it on my tax return as a loss?**

If the company was liquidated, you'll receive a 1099-DIV form at year-end showing a liquidating distribution. Treat this as if you sold the stock for the amount of the distribution. The date of "sale" is the date that the distribution took place. Using your original cost basis in the shares, you can now compute your loss.

If the company hasn't actually been liquidated, you'll need to make sure it's totally worthless before claiming a loss. If you have worthless stock that's difficult or not worth it to sell through your broker, you can sell it to a friend (or cousin, aunt or uncle) for pennies. (But not to a spouse, siblings, parents, grandparents, or lineal descendants.) Here's one way to do it:

1. Get the actual stock certificates from your broker.
2. Formally sell the shares to the purchaser, with a check for payment and a bill of sale.
3. Sign over the stock certificate (on its back) to the purchaser. Have the signatures verified by your banker and/or a local stockbroker.
4. Send the certificate to the stock transfer agent. Explain that the shares have been sold, and ask them to cancel the old shares and issue a new certificate to the new owner.

Some brokerages will offer you a quicker alternative, buying all your shares of the stock for a penny. They do it to help out their customers and because, over time, some of the shares may actually be worth more than the penny they paid for them.

By selling the shares, you have a closed transaction with the stock and can declare a tax loss. Your friend, relative, or broker, for a pittance, has just bought a place mat or birdcage liner.

## 164 How do capital gains work on stock received as a gift?

Let's say you bought 100 shares of Carrier Pigeon Communications (ticker: SQAWK) at $50 per share. A year later they're trading at $100 per share and you give them all to your son. A month after that, he sells them for $110 per share. What's his taxable gain?

It might seem that your son's profit is just $10 per share, but our friends at the IRS don't see it that way. A recipient's cost basis (and holding period) for a gift of stock is the same as the donor's. So, although your son received the stock at $100 per share and held it just one month, his cost basis is $50 per share, and his holding period is 13 months. He can expect to be taxed on a gain of $6,000. And, since he's held the shares for more than a year, he'll be taxed at the more-beneficial long-term rate, which is 20% for most people.

The gift is not tax deductible by you, as it's not a charitable contribution. You're currently allowed to give up to $10,000 to any person, per year, tax-free.

## 165 Could you explain the wash sale rule?

Under the wash sale rules, if you sell a stock for a loss and buy it back within 30 days, the loss cannot be claimed for tax purposes. Don't worry, though — the loss isn't lost forever. You *do* get to claim it, just not now. The disallowed loss is added to the cost of the repurchased stock, and it's claimed when the stock is finally disposed of in a non-wash-sale way. You can avoid the rules entirely, though, by always waiting 31 days before jumping back into any stock.

If you do a lot of in-and-out trading (and sometimes even if you don't), this rule can complicate your life. Learn more about it before acting on it.

## 166 What do I do if I'm selling some stock and don't have a record of what I paid for it many years ago? How do I pay tax on it?

You must prove the cost of your shares when you sell them. If you can't, the IRS may not allow you a "cost basis" with which to reduce your sale price and compute your gain on the shares. Your entire sales price may end up subject to capital gain taxes. (Gulp!)

The broker's records may be long gone now. But, if you purchased shares directly from a company, it may have a record of the transaction. If not, you might try to reconstruct a record by finding the canceled check and the stock's price when you bought it, to determine how many shares you originally bought. Document your process in case Uncle Sammy wants to have a discussion (read: audit) with you about it. If your arguments and analysis seem reasonable, you may be fine.

Ideally, though, always hang on to your purchase records of stock, property, and other assets.

## 167 Is it true that I can avoid paying taxes on $250,000 of capital gains when I sell my house?

If you meet a few requirements, yes indeedy. Anyone planning to sell a primary residence in the near future should read up on the exciting new home sale exclusion rules. While you used to be able to exclude up to $125,000 of gain just once in your life, you can now exclude up to a whopping $250,000 every few years.

If that isn't tantalizing enough, consider that married couples can exclude up to a *half-million dollars*. Here are *some* of the requirements:
- You (the seller) must have owned and lived in the home as your principal residence for at least two of the five years preceding the date of sale. The two years don't have to be consecutive, though.
- In most cases, you can only take advantage of this home sale exclusion once during any two-year period.
- A married couple may exclude up to $500,000 of their home sale gain if all of the following apply:
  1. They file a joint return for the year of the home sale;
  2. Either spouse owned the home for at least two years in the five-year period ending on the sale date;
  3. Both spouses used the home as a principal residence for at least two years in the five-year period ending on the sale date; and
  4. Neither spouse had used the new exclusion on the sale of another residence within the two-year period ending on the date of the current home's sale.

Since this is such a big tax break, make sure you plan your home sale carefully to ensure that you qualify. This includes living in it for the required amount of time. Proper planning can save tens of thousands of tax dollars. Improper planning can cost you just as much.

## 168 Are there any special year-end tax tips you can offer?

One thing you can do is take advantage of your credit card. If you have deductible expenses coming up, charge them at the end of the year, take the deductions in that year, and then pay the bill early in the following year. (Just don't charge more than you'll be able to pay off quickly.)

If your itemized deductions usually don't exceed your standard deduction, you can try "bunching" your itemized deductions every other year. When bunching, you try to cram two years' worth of expenses into one year, by paying for the following year in the current year. For example, if you donate $2,000 to charity each year, you might give $2,000 in January and then give next year's gift in December, thereby technically giving $4,000 in one year. This way, you might be able to alternate standard and itemized deductions every other year.

Expenses are only deductible in the year in which they're actually paid (or, in the case of credit cards, charged). Checks should be dated and mailed in the year that you claim the deduction. When they clear the bank doesn't matter.

Don't overlook many valuable credits that might be available to you. The Child Tax Credit can save you $500 per qualifying child under the age of 17. The Hope Credit offers savings of $1,500 per student for qualified tuition and fees paid by or for the student. The Lifetime Learning Credit is for $1,000. If you've recently adopted a child, you may be able to enjoy a credit of $5,000 or more.

## 169 Where can I learn more about tax issues?

You've got plenty of choices, both online and off.
- The horse's mouth is the IRS website, at: www.irs.ustreas.gov. There you can download tax forms and publications, as well as read up on various new developments.
- The www.fairmark.com site is where tax attorney Kaye Thomas offers a wealth of information. Thomas also penned a book called *Consider Your Options*, which is a must-read for anyone grappling with employee stock option issues.
- The Fool's Tax Center is at www.Fool.com/taxes. We offer a host of articles on various tax-related subjects there, as well as links to our Tax Strategies discussion board, where Fools are asking ques-

tions and getting answers 24 hours a day.

- The Fool also offers tax advice in print, in the form of our book, *The Motley Fool Investment Tax Guide*.

**CHAPTER TEN**
**ANSWERS TO YOUR QUESTIONS ABOUT**

# Retirement

*Retirement is a topic that bridges the personal finance and investing sections of this book. It's hard to reach a comfortable retirement without having engaged in some savvy investing. The second part of this book will help you tackle many investing topics. In the meantime, this short chapter will give you a little perspective on some issues to consider as you plan for retirement.*

## 170 How can I figure out how much I need to save and invest for my retirement?

There's no hard-and-fast guideline for everybody. We're each different, in different situations. Here are some questions for you as you prepare to plan:

1. How many years are left until you retire?
2. How old do you plan to be when you retire? (This influences how long your retirement is likely to last.)
3. How much do you have saved up for retirement now and how much more will you be able to sock away each year until retirement?
4. How well do you want to live during retirement — or, more to the point, how much money will you want to live on during retirement? (Any plans for extravagant travel adventures? Do you plan to move to a region with a lower cost of living?)
5. How are you investing your nest egg money? What kinds of returns do you expect to earn? (If your money is all in Treasury

bonds and you're expecting it to grow 20% per year, you'll probably end up with a nasty surprise.)
6. What's your risk tolerance? Are you comfortable investing your
long-term money in stocks? Stocks are riskier than bonds, but
offer the chance of higher returns.

These are just some of the considerations you'll need to ponder. Once
you've thought about them for a bit, spend some time reading up on
retirement issues and perhaps plugging some numbers into online
retirement calculators.

## 171 I'm nearing retirement. Where should I invest my money so it's safe?

The traditional answer has long been to invest retirement proceeds
in utilities, preferred stock, REITs, bonds, and other dividend-pro-
ducing, interest-paying securities. You would take the interest and
dividends as income for the year and let the principal ride. The focus
was on income, and little attention was usually paid to increasing the
value of the underlying investments. It was often assumed that too
much risk was involved in seeking appreciation of your investments.
And risk, according to many retirement investors, was to be avoided at all costs.

Times have changed, though. Fewer companies pay significant dividends, utilities have been deregulated, the bond markets can be volatile,
interest rates have been low for quite a while, and to top it all off, people are living longer! In this kind of environment, a "low-risk, income-
only" investment strategy may not serve retirees too well. The worst-
case scenario is that retirees could run out of money earlier than they
expected. So, ironically, it can actually be very risky to not take some
risk with your retirement savings.

Consider this scenario from Dave Braze, the Fool's retirement expert:

An all-bond portfolio with an average return of 6% might throw off
enough income for a retiree today. But, with a modest annual inflation
rate of, say, 3%, every $1,000 produced by that portfolio will be worth
only $554 in 20 years. Worse, the principal available then for rein-

vestment wouldn't have grown through the years. As purchasing power declines, a retiree using such a strategy almost certainly will have to dip into principal to sustain her lifestyle, and the use of that principal will definitely shorten the life of her portfolio.

Conversely, an all-stock portfolio may produce growth from which one may take income. Yet stocks can plunge in value overnight, and they can stay down for five years or longer. To a retiree, that too can be a devastating result.

So, what's the answer? There's one solution that might work. It's called asset allocation.

---

## 172 How should retirees allocate their money?

You've got three main options when it comes to parking your moolah: stocks, bonds, and cash. The theory is that when one market segment is down, another may be up, and vice versa. So, by dividing your money (not necessarily in equal parts) among all three segments, you shouldn't see all your money shrink at once. You'll have decreased your downside risk, while still maintaining some upside risk.

The "cash" category doesn't necessarily mean just cash — especially cash stuffed into a cigar box under your bed. Instead, think of it as simply very liquid investments — those that can be converted into cash quickly and easily. Many of these actually pay interest, too, such as money market accounts and short-term CDs.

How much money should you have in each category? Well, one age-old guideline recommended that you should subtract your age from 100 and devote that portion to stocks. Therefore, a 50-year-old would have 50% of her portfolio in stocks and a 70-year-old only 30%. As people started living longer, the number to subtract from became 110. This isn't a baseless approach, but it's wrong to assume that we're all alike in everything except age. This rule's results won't be right for everyone. It's best to take some time and assess your particular situation carefully, to determine the right allocation mix — one that should generate the income and portfolio growth required for the rest of your life.

A helpful way to approach the problem is to jot down how much you have, how much you want to withdraw each year, how quickly you expect your nest egg to grow invested in your various options, and how long your money needs to last. The stock market, on average over the past few decades, has gained about 11% or so annually. Meanwhile, fairly conservative bonds have offered between 3% and 6% annually, while in real terms cash can actually lose value over time if it does not outperform the rate of inflation.

However you decide to divide your money, you'll need to re-assess your allocation periodically. Let's say that you allocated 50% of your savings to stocks, 30% to bonds, and 20% to cash. If, after 12 months, you notice that your stocks have grown to become 55% to 60% of your portfolio, you might want to rebalance and reallocate a little.

A Foolish retirement allocation is really determined no differently than it is for any other investor at any other age. Figure out which mix fits your risk tolerance for losing money, yet still achieves your objectives, which should be growth and income. Adjust for risk by controlling the ratio of stocks within that portfolio. A major factor in your decision-making is your desired withdrawal rate from your portfolio.

## 173 What's a good percentage of money to withdraw each year from my nest egg after I retire?

This is a critical question. You want to live comfortably, but not so comfortably now that you end up eating government surplus cheese in your last years.

Many formulas will help you plan, but they rely on average rates of return and inflation. Over the long term, an average rate should work, especially when you're still saving for retirement. Unfortunately, actual year-to-year results won't be the same as the average and, for retirees in some time periods, those yearly variations may prove devastating. In other words, one 15-year period might average a 14% annual return, while another 15-year period might average just 2%. The longer the time period you're dealing with, the less the overall average return rate should fluctuate.

*When* you start withdrawals is just as important as how much you take. Whether the market is surging or slumping in your first years can make a big difference. Since we can't predict the future, what's the right percentage to withdraw?

Three Trinity University professors — Philip Cooley, Carl Hubbard, and Daniel Walz — examined this issue by looking at historical annual returns for stocks and bonds from 1926 through 1995. Not surprisingly, their study revealed withdrawal periods longer than 15 years dramatically reduced the probability of success at withdrawal rates exceeding 5%.

They also concluded that:
1. Younger retirees who anticipate longer payout periods should plan on lower withdrawal rates.
2. Owning bonds decreases the likelihood of going broke for lower to mid-level withdrawal rates, but most retirees would benefit with at least a 50% allocation to stocks.
3. Retirees who desire inflation-adjusted withdrawals must accept a substantially reduced withdrawal rate from the initial portfolio.
4. Withdrawing 4% or less from a stock-dominated portfolio is probably too conservative.
5. For short payout periods of 15 years or less, a withdrawal rate of 8% to 9% from a stock-dominated portfolio appears sustainable.

According to many studies, a "safe" withdrawal rate would amount to between 4% and 6% of a retiree's starting portfolio. Withdrawal rates above 5% increase the probability that a retiree will go broke in her lifetime. Many studies also agree that the presence of bonds provides a measure of stability absent in an all-stock portfolio.

Additionally, it appears that inflation-adjusted withdrawals fare best at lower to mid-level withdrawal rates.

You can read more about the Trinity professors' study here:
- www.scottburns.com/wwtrinity.htm
- www.Fool.com/retirement (check out the "Managing Retirement" section)

**What is an IRA?**

IRA stands for Individual Retirement Account. A traditional IRA is an account where you're permitted (if you qualify) to sock away a certain amount each year, tax-deferred. The amount is currently $2,000, but it may be raised in the near future.

The tax deferral is an important aspect of this kind of account. If you earn $30,000 per year and you contribute $2,000 to an IRA, that $2,000 is deducted from your income and you're not taxed on it — that year. Traditional IRA contributions are taxed upon withdrawal. This means that in the year that you contribute $2,000, if you're in the 28% tax bracket, you don't have to pay $560 (28% of $2,000). If that $560 were plunked into the stock market and grew at the historical average rate of 11%, it would grow to $4,515 in 20 years ($12,820 in 30 years).

A new option, introduced in 1997, is the Roth IRA, which works a little differently and offers different benefits.

---

**175** **How do Roth IRAs work, and should I use them?**

Many hail the Roth IRA as the greatest tax break ever invented, but there are some important issues to consider before jumping on board.

Like other IRAs, the Roth allows you to accumulate funds for retirement and to enjoy some tax advantages at the same time. While traditional IRAs are tax-deferred, Roth IRAs are designed to be tax-*exempt*. Traditional IRAs permit you to contribute pre-tax dollars; Roth IRAs accept only already-taxed dollars.

Let's say you're 35 years old and you invest $2,000 of your post-tax income into a Roth IRA each year, starting today. You earn a 12% annual return for the next 30 years until you retire at 65. By then, your contributions would have grown to about $600,000. With a Roth, that's your take-home pay. With a regular IRA, you would pay taxes on any withdrawals, netting just $510,000, assuming a 15% tax bracket during retirement, or merely $432,000 if you are still in the 28% bracket. So far, this is very convincing. But, remember that if the $2,000 had gone directly into a traditional IRA, you would have reaped about $560 in tax savings each year. If that had also been invested, the total difference between the Roth and the regular IRA becomes slimmer.

The Roth is fully available to individuals who earn up to a certain amount. At the time of this writing, it was $95,000 for single people and $150,000 for married couples filing jointly. You can roll over, or convert, your traditional IRA into a Roth one by paying taxes on it, counting the entire value of the account as income.

The Roth IRA isn't an unequivocal godsend. It makes the most sense if you've maxed out all your other tax-deferred options, such as your 401(k). There are more benefits and limitations to consider before you decide whether the Roth is for you. You can get details on these from your local tax professional, from the IRS at 800-829-1040, and also at Fooldom online (www.Fool.com/taxes).

## 176 Can IRAs hold investments other than mutual funds, such as individual stocks?

They sure can. An IRA itself isn't an investment. Think of it instead as a container that helps you avoid income taxes on earnings (and sometimes on your contributions, too) until you begin withdrawing money years later. In your IRA, you're free to invest in a broad array of securities to be held in the account by a custodian. The custodian may be a bank, a broker, a mutual fund, or an insurance company.

If you want to invest in stocks yourself (and how commendably Foolish of you if you do!), establish your IRA with a brokerage in something called a "self-directed account." Then you can deposit your annual contributions, directing your broker when and what shares to buy or sell within that account. In this self-directed account, you can also trade in just about every security offered by the broker, such as CDs, bonds, T-bills, notes, and mutual funds.

There's actually a benefit to holding and trading stocks in an IRA account — you get to avoid current taxation on any capital gains. Trade stocks in a traditional IRA account and the tax is deferred. Trade in a Roth IRA and, assuming you're following the rules, you'll be trading tax-free!

## 177 If my IRA is invested in mutual funds and I want to shift that into an index fund or stocks, can I do that?

If your IRA is maintained by a brokerage, you should be able to shift around your investments from one mutual fund to another, or to and from individual stocks. You won't have to pay taxes on any gains, but you probably will have to pay your brokerage the applicable commissions for the transactions.

If your IRA is with a mutual fund family, you can probably switch between its own funds with minimal charge. You might pay steeper fees to switch to other funds, and may not be permitted to invest in individual stocks at all.

## 178 What is a 401(k) plan?

A 401(k) is a retirement plan where your employer permits you to defer part of your pay into a special kind of account. The funds are contributed on a pre-tax basis, and the contributions and all earnings remain untaxed until withdrawn from the plan. The 401(k) may also permit voluntary, after-tax contributions. Earnings on after-tax contributions accumulate tax-free until withdrawn.

Your pre-tax contributions are limited to the lesser of a maximum percentage of pay or $10,500 (that's the amount for 2000). The percentage limitation varies from employer to employer depending on a number of factors, but it generally ranges from 12% to 25% of your salary. Many employers also match a certain percentage of employee contributions.

A 401(k) plan permits you to invest money for your retirement in a range of ways. These may include institutional or mutual funds investing in the money market, bond market, or stock market; annuities; guaranteed investment contracts; company stock; and self-directed brokerage accounts. A typical plan will offer a selection of a money market fund, a bond fund, and a stock fund.

In general, money can be withdrawn penalty-free from a 401(k) plan on these five occasions: termination from employment, disability, reaching the age of 59 (or age 55 in some cases), retirement, and death. Additionally, a plan may include provisions for loans and/or hardship withdrawals.

## 179 My company matches a certain percentage of my contributions to a 401(k) plan. Should I contribute enough to this 401(k) to get the maximum amount that the company will match?

In most cases, it's definitely smart to take advantage of as much company matching as possible. Let's say that for every $1 you sock away in your 401(k), your employer chips in 50 cents. That's an immediate *50% return*. It would be extremely difficult to beat that with any investment method.

The only time it might not be so great is if the matching money is going into something you're not comfortable with. If it's going into stock in the company, and you're very uncomfortable about the company's future, then perhaps you're getting a 50% return that will soon become a 0% return. That's an extreme example, though. And, even in that case, the money that *you* socked away can be in a safer place, growing.

## 180 My company's 401(k) plan makes my eyes glaze over. It's full of unfamiliar words such as aggressive growth, bond, gold, emerging growth, international, value, and money market funds. I haven't a clue what to do about it, so I've been doing nothing. Any advice?

You're not alone. It isn't as complex as it looks, though.

Here are some tips:

Begin participating in your company's plan as soon as possible, contributing as much as you can. It not only builds your nest egg, but also reduces your taxable income.

Keep emergency money separate. Invest only what you don't expect to need for at least five years. (Note: There's a penalty on withdrawals before age 59½ ).

If your employer matches your contributions to any degree, take *full advantage* of the available matching — it's *free money*.

Stocks might be scary but, over the long run, they perform best, by far. Unfortunately, more than two-thirds of 401(k) money is in low-yielding bond or money market funds, where it grows very slowly.

Your best stock-fund bet is a stock market index fund, which continually beats the majority of mutual funds and has lower annual fees, to boot. If your 401(k) plan doesn't include such a fund as an option, urge your payroll professional to have one added. Every 401(k) plan in the nation should include a stock market index fund.

Leave your money in the plan for as long as possible. This delays the ultimate tax bite and permits maximum growth. Don't borrow from your account unless it's an emergency.

Taking advantage of your 401(k) means you shouldn't end up having to rely on government programs like Social Insecurity — er, Security.

---

## 181 I see you prefer index funds to all other mutual funds. But, there's no index fund among the funds I can invest in through my 401(k) plan. Am I stuck?

Not necessarily. Visit your company's 401(k) administrator. Explain why it's so important that employees be able to invest in an index fund. Point out that, according to Lipper Analytical Services, only about 17% of all open-end equity funds outperformed the market average (as measured by the S&P 500 Index) over the past 15 and 20 years. Tell your co-workers, too. If enough people ask for an index fund, you might get it.

---

## 182 How can I learn what to expect from Social Security?

Well, given the concerns about whether and when Social Security funds will run out and how the program might be changed, it's not entirely unreasonable to think of it as Social Insecurity. Nevertheless, the program currently remains intact, and you'd be smart to look into what you might expect from it in retirement.

The best source of information is the horse's mouth, the Social Security Administration (SSA) and the best way to get information from the SSA is arguably at its website: www.ssa.gov.

Even if you're not too close to retiring, you can get a record of your Social Security earnings history detailed year-by-year, as well as estimates of the benefits that you may qualify for, now or later. You'll simply need to fill out Form SSA-7004, which also goes by the name "Request for Social Security Statement." You can access an electronic version of this form online at the SSA website, or you can call the SSA at 800-772-1213.

---

### 183 What are some resources for learning more about retirement issues?

Here are a bunch of websites:
- www.Fool.com/retirement
- www.Fool.com/calcs/calculators.htm
- http://retireplan.about.com
- www.retireearlyhomepage.com (This is a very rich website devoted to teaching people about retiring early.)
- www.ssa.gov (the Social Security Administration)
- www.quicken.com/retirement
- http://moneycentral.msn.com/retire/home.asp

And some books:
- *Last Chance Financial Planning Guide* by Anthony Spare with Paul Ciotti
- *Last Minute Retirement Planning* by Stephen M. Rosenberg
- *The Retirement Sourcebook* by Mary Helen and Shuford Smith
- *Ernst & Young's Retirement Planning Guide* by Robert J. Garner
- *Retire Rich: The Baby Boomer's Guide to a Secure Future* by Bambi Holzer

# Divesting—
# Giving to Charity

*If you manage your finances well and invest successfully, you'll be on track to enjoy a comfortable retirement. If you start early enough and raise your children to be savvy about money and investing, they'll likely be financially independent for the rest of their lives. This is all the more reason to look into how you can best give some of your wealth away to those less fortunate.*

## 184 What's the best way to go about donating to charity?

Here are a few tips:

- Take the time to think about what causes are most important to you. Then concentrate your giving on those issues. Otherwise, you run the risk of sending a little money this way, and a little money that way, and never really being able to keep up with all the activities you're supporting.

- Get really involved with the organization you're most interested in. You might serve on its board, or volunteer some time working in its office or in the field. If you have some special expertise, such as public relations, marketing, or fundraising, you might offer those services. This is a good way to learn more about the issues, too.

- If you have children, involve them in giving, beginning when they're young. Share with them what you're donating and why, and what your gift will do. Encourage them to develop causes that they care about and that they donate to, as well.

- If you're not yet blessed with riches (and even if you are), consider all the non-monetary gifts you could give. You might volunteer, for example. Or donate things such as used clothing, computers, and cars to charities that can use them. (If you do, make sure to get a receipt for tax purposes.)

- Don't give money to some organization that cold-calls you. Always investigate them first. There are many hucksters out there calling people and wheedling donations out of them. Some shifty outfits beg for donations of cars, too.
- If you end up donating your car to an enterprise that isn't formally tax-exempt (qualifying under IRS section 501(c)(3)), your deduction won't be valid. So, look into how legitimate a charity is before giving away your clunker. Also, it's up to you, the donor, to place a value on the vehicle. You want it to be accurate, so you might look it up in the Kelly Blue Book at the time of donation. (Look it up many months later, and the vehicle will probably be worth less.) If it's worth more than $500, you'll have to file an additional tax form Form 8283. If it's worth more than $5,000, you'll need to include a qualified written appraisal.
- If you donate $250 or more to any charity, you'll need to receive and keep a receipt for tax purposes.
- Keep records of your donations. If you fail to do this, you might end up at year end totaling donations in your check register and realizing that you gave to some organizations much more often than you thought you did.
- Realize that "tax-exempt" is not the same as "tax-deductible." A tax-exempt organization doesn't have to pay taxes. But, donations to it may still not be tax-deductible. You can ask to see a copy of a charity's tax-exemption paperwork, and some proof that deductions are tax-deductible.

## 185 What should I look for in a charity and how should I evaluate one?

First, learn what exactly it *does* with the donations it receives. What problems is it addressing, and how does it aim to solve or lessen them? If possible, learn about the successes the organization has had in the past and the lessons it's gleaned from mistakes. Find out what plans it has for the future — what are its goals, its new initiatives?

Examine its financial record. Ideally, the charity will have a website where it lays out its finances transparently. You should be able to see what percentage of dollars donated go toward actual program work rather than administrative or fund-raising efforts. The higher that percentage, the better, for the most part. Many sources recommend that 60% or more be spent on program work, but a little digging will yield outstanding organizations that apply 80% or 90% or more to program work.

Still, don't automatically begrudge a charity, especially a small one, its necessary overhead expenses. It does need to maintain a photocopier, pay some salaries, and fund some travel. You just don't want to see these numbers be extraordinarily high.

In addition, you can dig deeper. Even if an organization says that 75% of its income goes toward its good works, see if you can get an itemized breakdown of that. The organization might be including a sheet of educational facts in its fund-raising mailings, and counting that as program work instead of marketing. A term to look out for is "public education" — that's often used for items that are essentially fund-raising in nature.

Ask for or look up the organization's most recent annual report and IRS Form 990 filing. These should offer important details about where money comes from and goes. Inquire whether the charity is registered with federal, state, or local authorities.

You can look up the charity's record with one or more of the watchdog organizations that evaluate charities. You might also contact the Better Business Bureau or the local Attorney General's office, to see if there have been any complaints about the organization.

## 186 What organizations offer reports on charities? I'd like to learn more about some organizations.

Here are the main industry watchdogs:

**The American Institute of Philanthropy**
(www.charitywatch.org, 301-913-5200)
This outfit rates several hundred charitable organizations, focusing on their finances. You can order their *Charity Rating Guide & Watchdog Report* for $3.

**The National Charities Information Bureau**
(www.give.org, 212-929-6300)
This organization rates hundreds of charities and can help you learn which ones may be spending too much of the money they receive on things like fund-raising or office parties. It offers a free *Wise Giving Guide* and will send you a free in-depth report on any single charity, as well.

**The Philanthropic Advisory Service of the Council of Better Business Bureaus**
(www.bbb.org, 703-276-0100)
Contact these folks to ask or complain about a charity, or to order their Philanthropic Advisory Service (PAS) report on a particular charity. They also publish a free guide called *Give, but Give Wisely*, which you can read online.

---

## 187 What are some warning signs about a charity?

For starters, be wary of any aggressiveness or high-pressure tactics. The organization shouldn't be harassing you and urging you for donations. (If they're holding you upside down by your feet and shaking you, that's a bad sign.) Look closely at their name — some unscrupulous outfits will choose a name extremely close to that of a well-known charity, and some careless readers will be conned. (For example, here are some organizations I just made up: National Lung Association, Habitat for Humanitey, and Uniting Way.)

If they're evading questions you ask, that's also a bad sign. If they've called you, ask for some printed material or their web address. If they're not forthcoming, and insist on communicating by phone, again this is not auspicious.

Sometimes you'll get called and asked for donations to a charity you know well. You might still be careful, though. Sometimes these organizations hire telemarketing companies to raise money, in which case the telemarketers might be taking a third or more of whatever you donate for themselves, before passing on what's left to the charity. Ouch.

If you're suspicious about a call, you might hang up and then look up the charity's number separately. Call and ask whether they authorized the call.

More red flags:
- The charity's address is a P.O. Box, not a street address.
- You're thanked (by phone or mail) for a donation you don't remember making.
- Extremely emotional appeals, such as sob stories.

Just say no if you're told:
- You're guaranteed to win a prize if you donate.
- You'll need to make out the check to a person, not an organization. Or you're to just use the organization's initials.
- The caller is eager to pick up your donation instead of having you mail it in.

## 188 Can you tell me about the merits of giving stock instead of cash to charity?

The tax advantages can make donating stock instead of cash very worthwhile. Here's how it works, if you're ready to donate stock.

First, note whether you've held the stock for one year or less (short-term), or for more than a year (long-term). Then, figure out its fair market value (FMV). This is what you would receive from the sale of the stock on the day you make the charitable contribution. It doesn't mean you have to sell the stock then — just figure out its value on that date.

With stock held for the short-term, you can claim as a contribution and deduct the FMV less the amount it has appreciated since you've held it. In most cases, this means that your deduction is basically your initial cost basis for the stock. So, stock bought for $800, held for the short-term, and donated when it's worth $1,000 amounts to an $800 charitable deduction.

If the sale of the stock on the day of the contribution would result in a *long-term* capital gain, you can generally deduct the full FMV of the stock. For example, if you've held 150 shares for more than one year and they're worth $10 each on the day you donate them, you can probably deduct $1,500.

Your main decision is whether to sell the stock and donate the proceeds, or whether to donate the stock itself. By selling it first, your gain counts as income and it might affect your total taxes. By donating it, you don't recognize any income. If you do want to contribute stock to a charity, give the organization a jingle. They'll likely be thrilled and should help you make arrangements.

As with all tax-related issues, there are always details to consider that relate to your particular situation. You'd be well advised to consult a tax professional in addition to a Fool.

## 189 Is it safe to donate money online?

For the most part, yes, very much so. You just want to make sure before you send any confidential information through a website that it's using some sort of secure encryption. You can usually tell with most web browsers, because there will be a little icon that changes, such as an unlocked padlock suddenly becoming a locked padlock, or a broken key becoming a whole key.

Take some time to poke around the website first. There will likely be a link to information on its security technology, or perhaps the security issue will be tackled in a "Frequently Asked Questions" document.

## 190 Is The Motley Fool very involved with charitable giving?

Oh, yes! For several years running, we've held online annual charity drives — with our readers and the company together contributing more than a million dollars to fight hunger, poverty, and disease.

You can learn more about our "Foolanthropy" efforts at www.Fool.com/foolanthropy.

## 191 What's Foolanthropy?

Foolanthropy (n): The form of charity advocated and practiced by The Motley Fool.

It has five tenets:

**Foolanthropy seeks to fulfill the same mission as The Motley Fool: to educate, amuse, and enrich.**
Great charities are deeply involved in education, offering it to beneficiaries and/or the volunteers and the public at large. Amusement can come in the form of creative fund-raising campaigns or infectious excitement and enthusiasm. Enrichment occurs for beneficiaries, volunteers and society — and it's not just financial enrichment, either.

**Foolanthropy expects.**
Foolish charities are not paternalistic. When possible, they don't give expecting nothing in return. Instead, they aim to confer a sense of ownership on those whom they serve, expecting beneficiaries to be participate in their own assistance. They foster a sense of personal responsibility.

**Foolanthropy make its finances transparent.**
Anyone giving to a Foolish charity should be able to clearly see exactly where his money has gone, starting with a simple look at the financial statements.

**Foolanthropy creates sustainable solutions.**
Foolish charities aim to not offer stopgap, short-term aid, but instead to support self-sustaining long-term solutions. Ideally, a Foolanthropic charity tackles epic problems and offers powerful solutions.

**Foolanthropy involves the public at large.**
The most Foolish charities are tackling major problems so effectively that they tend to capture the public's imagination and support.

---

## 192 Can you recommend any Foolanthropic charities?

We don't want to recommend any charity, as it should completely be your decision. (And, there are *so many* wonderful organizations doing amazing work.) But, since it *is* useful to learn about a bunch of different approaches to solving big problems, here are some charities and models we think are very interesting. Learning about them should help you think about and evaluate other charitable organizations.

Social entrepreneurs:
- www.socialentrepreneurs.org
- www.ashoka.org
- www.sea-change.org
- www.socialent.org

Microcredit and microenterprise:
- www.microcreditsummit.org
- www.grameenfoundation.org
- www.heifer.org
- www.count-me-in.org

Participatory relief:
- www.habitat.org
- www.secondharvest.org

## 193 If I can't give much money or time, what else can I do to help those in need?

There are a bunch of clever new websites which collect large sums of money for great causes in innovative ways. Some of the best examples are:
- www.thehungersite.com
- www.therainforestsite.com
- http://rainforest.care2.com

At these sites, you simply click on a button and a few cups of food will be delivered to a hungry person, or a few square feet of the rainforest will be saved. You send no money — it's all paid for by advertisers. All they want is for you to click one button with your mouse, after which you'll see a few small ads. (You'll make their day by clicking on and investigating any of the ads, but that's not required.)

You can also look into donating some of your expertise to causes you care about. Perhaps you can help a small organization build a database or create a website. Maybe you're a marketing maven with some fundraising advice to share.

## 194 Where can I learn more about philanthropy and about various charities to which I might donate?

There are a bunch of resources. First, some websites:

Research charities and volunteer opportunities:
- www.guidestar.org
- www.give.org
- www.charitywatch.org
- www.helping.org
- www.charitableway.com
- www.donationdepot.com
- www.volunteermatch.org
- www.pointsoflight.org
- www.singlevolunteers.org
- www.voa.org

Learn about philanthropy in general:
- www.fdncenter.org
- www.philanthropy.com
- www.pnnonline.org
- www.philanthropy.org
- www.women-philanthropy.org
- www.ncrp.org
- www.philanthropyroundtable.org
- www.womenphil.org

Give while you shop:
- www.greatergood.com
- www.4charity.com
- www.igive.com

Here are some books that might be of interest:
- *Robin Hood Was Right: A Guide to Giving Your Money for Social Change* by Chuck Collins and Pam Rogers with Joan P. Garner
- *Don't Just Give It Away: How to Make the Most of Your Charitable Giving* by Renata J. Rafferty
- *Wealthy and Wise: How You and America Can Get the Most Out of Your Giving* by Claude Rosenberg Jr.

- *The Halo Effect: How Volunteering Can Lead to a More Fulfilling Life-And a Better Career* by John Raynolds
- *Volunteering: 101 Ways You Can Improve the World and Your Life* by Douglas M. Lawson
- *The International Directory of Voluntary Work* by Louise Whetter and Victoria Pybus

Finally, these days most major charitable organizations have an online presence. Many have sophisticated and informative websites where you can learn all about the organization and where you can often donate online, as well. For example, the Red Cross is at www.redcross.org and the Nature Conservancy is at www.tnc.org. If the "www.[insert-namehere].org formula doesn't work, just use a search engine such as www.google.com to find the charity you're interested in.

CHAPTER TWELVE
ANSWERS TO YOUR QUESTIONS ABOUT

# Death, Funerals,
# & Estate Planning

*This is a dreary topic, but if you want to be financially responsible to yourself and your loved ones, it needs your attention. Consider that, after your home and vehicle, a funeral is likely to be your next most-costly expense. It doesn't have to be, though, if you're informed and prepared. Similarly, estate planning is something we often fail to attend to, and our survivors suffer for it. A failure to plan and prepare can cost your loved ones much stress, time, and even hundreds of thousands of dollars. This chapter offers many useful tips on funerals, but it just scratches the surface of the estate-planning iceberg.*

## 195 Do I really need to learn about estate planning?

Well, according to the Prudential website's estate planning section, you do only if one or more of the following is true for you:

- You want any say in who receives your assets after you're gone.
- You want your kids or grandkids to receive their share of assets when they are mature enough to handle the responsibility — and not all at once.
- You want someone you know, not a court-appointed administrator, to handle the distribution of your assets.
- You think it's important to maximize the amount of money you provide to your beneficiaries, and minimize court costs and taxes.
- You want to select the appropriate guardian for your child.
- You want your business to continue after your death.

If you're thinking to yourself, "Jeepers... that includes just about everyone," you're right.

## 196 What does a will really do?

Many things:
- It lets you designate who will inherit which of your assets.
- It lets you name a guardian for your children and an executor of your estate. (The executor can be an individual you know or a trust company.)
- It lets you specify *when* your children will receive what. Otherwise, an 18-year-old may end up receiving his entire inheritance before he's mature enough to keep from spending it all on stereos and cars.
- It lets you save money by waiving the probate bond, which will otherwise be required.
- It can let you authorize the sale of some of your assets during probate administration. This can be important, because sometimes such a sale is necessary to raise money needed to pay taxes and expenses related to death.
- It can permit your business to continue operating.
- It can save you some money in taxes.

## 197 What is "probate"?

Probate is the legal process of administering an estate. The nolo.com website explains it well, saying:

"Probate is a legal process that takes place after someone dies. It includes:
- Proving in court that a deceased person's will is valid (usually a routine matter)
- Identifying and inventorying the deceased person's property
- Having the property appraised
- Paying debts and taxes, and
- Distributing the remaining property as the will directs."

Part of the process also includes transferring title and ownership of various assets to the inheritors.

If this all sounds like a complicated hassle, it is. It can be a costly one, too, involving lots of paperwork and fees to people such as lawyers, accountants, appraisers, and executors, as well as court costs. All these costs would otherwise have gone to beneficiaries. Probate costs amount to roughly 5% to 10% of the value of the estate. So, with an estate worth $200,000, probate would eat up $10,000 to $20,000 — a sizable chunk. In addition, property remains in a kind of limbo while in probate — and that can last months or even years.

Probate has some good points, though. For example, it tends to be a methodical and unbiased system, since a judge oversees it.

For most people, the downside of probate overshadows the upside, so it's best avoided. And, it *can* be avoided, if you take the time to learn more about it and take some actions.

## 198 How can I avoid probate?

There are many ways to avoid probate, and you'd be best served by reading up on the topic and then consulting a professional. In brief, though, one way to avoid probate is through a living trust or a life estate trust. With a trust, you're actually formally transferring the title of various properties to your heirs *before* you die. You retain control over it while you're alive, but it technically belongs to the trust. Once you die, a trustee passes it on to your specified heirs. This tends to be a fairly quick and simple process.

Also, many states permit a certain amount of property to be inherited without going through probate. In some states the limit is $100,000, for example.

Other possibilities include "payable on death" designations on bank accounts (where the contents of the account pass immediately to the designated beneficiary on your death) and retirement accounts such as IRAs and 401(k)s (where you also specify beneficiaries). Thanks to the Uniform Transfer-on-Death Securities Registration Act, most states now permit securities held by the likes of brokerages to pass to beneficiaries without going through probate.

## 199 What does "intestate" mean?

It's a state that you don't want to die in. Dying intestate means that you've passed on to the great beyond without leaving behind a will or trust. In such cases, your friendly state government takes over and follows strict procedures. You might have preferred to leave everything to certain relatives, but the state will follow prescribed inheritance formulas. These formulas are designed to do what's right for the average person, but they're not always right for every person.

Dying intestate often means that, not only does your estate end up in probate, but it may spend years there, as various heirs litigate. This is clearly an undesirable situation (unless you never really liked your family). To make matters worse, probate proceedings are usually a matter of public record, so any family fighting may become a matter of public knowledge. Yuck.

## 200 What do I need to take into consideration when deciding who should get what?

According to the National Association of Financial and Estate Planning, here are the kinds of heir-planning issues to consider:
- Do you want to bequeath equal or unequal shares?
- At what age should each heir inherit? (You can set it up so that they receive specified chunks at specified ages.)
- How to distribute non-divisible property (such as a house or the bowling ball with which you won a tournament).
- Whether to leave out or disinherit any heirs.
- What to do in complicated family situations, where spouses have children from other marriages.
- What to do when you have a reckless child that spends with abandon.
- How to deal with mentally or physically disabled heirs.
- Ensuring that heirs will use their share to pay for college, or whatever you had in mind.
- What happens if an heir "predeceases" you.
- What special gifts you might want to give—such as to favorite nieces or charities.

## 201 What are some resources for learning more about estate planning?

Here are some websites:
- www.nolo.com
- www.lifenet.com
- www.nafep.com
- www.estateplanninglinks.com
- www.suite101.com/welcome.cfm/estate_planning
- www.netplanning.com
- www.prudential.com/estateplan

And books:
- *J.K. Lasser's Estate Planning for Baby Boomers and Retirees: A Comprehensive Guide to Estate Planning* by Stewart H. Welch
- *Plan Your Estate: Absolutely Everything You Need to Know to Protect Your Loved Ones* by Denis Clifford, Cora Jordan
- *Pass It on: A Practical Approach to the Fears and Facts of Planning Your Estate* by Nancy Randolph Greenway and Barbara J. Shotwell
- *The Complete Book of Wills, Estates & Trusts* by Alexander A. Bove
- *The Complete Idiot's Guide to Wills and Estates* by Stephen M. Maple
- *The Artful Dodger's Guide to Planning Your Estate* by Thomas Hart Hawley
- *Death & Taxes: The Complete Guide to Family Inheritance Planning* by Randell C. Doane and Rebecca G. Doane

## 202 Do you recommend "pre-need" funeral insurance?

Pre-need arrangements are typically made with mortuaries, cemeteries, and/or insurance companies, and more and more people are making them. The benefit of such arrangements is that when you move on to the great beyond, your loved ones won't have many arrangements to make. They'll be able to focus mainly on mourning, because plots will have been chosen and paid for, as will the funeral and burial. That's all very good.

The downside, and a reason to think twice before plunking down pre-need money, is that it tends to be a lot of money. And, it could be out of your hands and earning interest — for the people you paid. Let's say you're 75 and you pay $5,000 for a cemetery plot and $10,000 to a funeral home to cover your casket and various services. That's well and good, but what if you're blessed and live another 20 years? You've lost the benefit of that $15,000 for a long time. If you'd invested it and earned 10% per year on it, you'd have $101,000! That would probably be enough to cover death expenses and would leave some to your loved ones, as well. Another consideration is that you might actually need that $15,000 at some point before you die.

At the talks.com site referenced below, Nancy Dunnan warns readers to be careful, because:
- Pre-need plans are often nonrefundable.
- Plans are often nontransferable, meaning you cannot change your mind or switch mortuaries.
- Plans often have hidden fees, meaning your survivors could wind up paying even more when you die.
- Plans can be mishandled.

---

### 203 If I decide I *do* want to pursue pre-need arrangements, what do you recommend I do?

Here are some tips:
- Read all the fine print in whatever you sign.
- Find out what happens if the establishments where you've prepaid go out of business. (Do you get your money back? With interest?)
- Find out what the cancellation policy is and to what degree you can change your mind along the way.
- Learn exactly what you're buying with your money — what's covered and what isn't. Get an itemized list, with prices broken out.
- Compare those prices with others. A big benefit of pre-planning is that you have a chance to comparison-shop with a clear head, not troubled with grief.
- Ask where exactly the money will be kept — in a trust? In the third drawer from the bottom of a filing cabinet? Ask for the name of the bank or insurance company serving as the trustee.
- Don't make any decision about this hastily. If a salesperson is using any high-pressure tactics, walk away.
- Take one or more friends or family members with you when you

talk to a salesperson.

- Don't think of pre-need arrangements as investments. They're *conveniences*. If you're looking for an investment, you can do much better elsewhere.
- Consider that, as an alternative, you might just take the amount of money you'd spend on pre-need arrangements and park it in a special separate fund, for the purpose of covering death expenses. You could invest that money in CDs or money market funds, perhaps — and you may well end up faring better than if you'd bought the pre-need plan.

## 204 Where can I learn more about pre-need plans?

Here are some resources on pre-need plans:

Websites:
- www.xroads.com/~funerals
- www.talks.com/library/nd100198.html
- www.clearfieldshops.com/chmc/preplan.html
- www.post-gazette.com/regionstate/19990525deathplanning2.asp

Books:
- *Before It's Too Late — Don't Leave Your Loved Ones Unprepared* by Sue L. Thompson and Emily J. Oishi
- *In the Checklist of Life: A Working Book to Help You Live & Leave This Life!* by Lynn McPhelimy
- *At Journey's End: The Complete Guide to Funerals and Funeral Planning* by Abdullah Fatteh with Naaz Fatteh

## 205 How can I prepare my family for my death?

You can save them a lot of trouble by putting down in writing for them the following information:
- Your financial portfolios: List what you own and specify names of brokerages or institutions and account numbers. If your spouse isn't a joint owner, you can simplify estate issues by making him or her a co-owner.
- Details on bank accounts and safety deposit boxes.

- Details on insurance, pension, annuity, and retirement policies and accounts.
- Real estate: What do you own and where are the deeds?
- Where you keep valuable papers and items.
- Your will: Where is it? It's smart to have a living will, also.
- Your after-death preferences: Do you want to be buried or cremated? A fancy, plain, or very plain casket? A memorial service or a funeral? Flowers or donations to a charity? *Amazing Grace* or *Muskrat Love*? Who should be invited to various services?

If you fear that your survivors (likely your children) won't agree on who gets what when you're gone, you can elect to be very specific in your will. Alternatively, you might have some family discussions and decide together who gets what. Make a list of family valuables and heirlooms and come to a mutual agreement regarding who gets what.

On a less financial note, there are some things you can do now that will probably make your family and descendents very happy:
- Preserve your life story. Take some time to write down the story of your life. You might fill a notebook with it or type it into a word processor. You can also record it on audiocassettes or a videocassette.
- If you're one of the few people who can put names to faces in old photographs, take some time to label these photos.
- Buy or rent a video recorder and record at least several hours of your family talking and sharing. One day one or more of you will be gone and the tape(s) will be treasured. (Camcorders aren't just for filming babies — they great for filming grandma, too!)

## 206 How can I save money on funeral arrangements?

This is a great question. You can save a *lot* of money if you do a little research. Over the last few years, the death-care industry has become dominated by a few companies that buy local funeral homes. (You may not realize it, but your local funeral home may be owned by one of these giants.) As competition has decreased, prices have increased.

To make matters worse, consumers who need death-care services are usually in very vulnerable and distracted states of mind, not wanting to skimp when it comes to honoring their loved ones.

Here are some smart ways to go about funeral planning:

- Take the time to get informed about the industry *now*, when you're not in a state of emotional upheaval. Learn how much various things cost and think about what might be best for you and your loved ones.
- Make decisions before you need to, if possible. Get down in writing what your loved ones' wishes are, too. Once you know, for example, that grandma prefers cremation and grandpa wants a simple pine casket, you'll have fewer decisions (or *guesses*) to make later.
- Consider getting an inexpensive casket. Bodies will decay wherever they are, and the cost difference is great between various caskets. Some cost many thousands of dollars, others cost several hundred dollars. (And, many $3,500 caskets may have cost the funeral home just $700 wholesale.) Simple and dignified cardboard caskets are a possibility, too. Don't believe anyone who tries to sell you something that will "preserve a body forever."
- In most cases, you don't have to buy the casket from the funeral home. You can often buy the same caskets from a discount vendor (at *substantial* discounts) and have them delivered to the funeral home. Homes are generally required to accept them.
- In most cases, embalming is not required, unless an open casket is desired. Many funeral homes will try to talk you into paying for it, though — at an average cost of $400.
- Beware the recommended rubber gasket (a.k.a. "protective sealer") which, according to some sources, costs just dollars to make but is sold for several hundred dollars. It's pitched as "protecting the body from decay," but nothing can stop a body from decaying.
- Don't tell a funeral director more than you need to, such as how much the deceased was worth, or what insurance benefits may be forthcoming.
- Take a friend with you when you talk to death-care providers.
- You can save some money and honor a death in a more personal fashion in several ways. You don't have to buy a casket — you can build and decorate one yourself, or have one built. You don't have to use a funeral home's viewing room, either — a loved one can "lie-in-honor" in someone's home, a community hall, or a church.

## 207 How much does an average funeral cost?

Here's a breakdown of average costs, nationwide, according to a 1999 National Association of Funeral Directors (www.nafd.org) survey. Some parts of the country will be more expensive, though, and others will be less expensive. In addition, you can spend a lot more or a lot less, depending on some decisions you make.

| Most Commonly Selected Services | Average Cost |
|---|---|
| Professional service charges | $1,182.31 |
| Embalming | $400.51 |
| Other preparations (Cosmetology, hair, etc) | $150.35 |
| Visitation/Viewing | $314.42 |
| Funeral at Funeral Home | $356.68 |
| Transfer of remains to funeral home | $158.66 |
| Hearse (local) | $179.08 |
| Service car/van | $87.42 |
| Acknowledgement cards | $14.47 |
| Casket | $2,176.46 |
| Vault | $757.80 |
| **Total** | $5,778.16 |

Of course, this isn't all that's involved. It's just what a funeral director would typically be involved in. Here are some additional expenses:

| Possible Additional Expenses | Estimated Cost |
|---|---|
| Cemetery plot | $500 to several thousand dollars |
| Opening and closing the grave | $350 to $1,500, depending on the time and day of the week |
| Headstones, statues, or markers | $500 to several thousand dollars |

By contrast, a cremation can cost just $1,500 or less.

If you don't want cremation, with careful planning and purchasing, you can pay just $2,500 or less for a funeral and traditional metal casket. (More details at www.xroads.com/~funerals and some of the websites referenced later on.)

## 208 What should I know about cremation?

Consider it. It's a lot less costly than traditional burials, and is more

environmentally sound, too, using less land. Cremation has been growing in popularity over the past years. Today, roughly a quarter of all
deaths in the United States are followed by cremation, with the Cremation Association of North America estimating that 40% of all deaths
will be cremated by 2010. In some states, such as Florida, Washington, Alaska, and Arizona, it's estimated that cremation will be used in
more than 65% of deaths.

One benefit is that you (or your loved one) won't end up in a cemetery,
but instead the remains can be buried or scattered in places that have
special meaning, such as your church's memorial garden or a favorite
mountain.

With cremation, don't be talked into getting an expensive casket. A
simple wood or cardboard one should do — it will be quickly de-
stroyed, anyway. Some states permit there to be no casket at all. (You
can rent a casket if you want to, also, for a funeral service.) When
the cremation is over, you'll receive a few pounds of ashes and bone
fragments. You can purchase a memorial urn for between $25 and sev-
eral hundred dollars, if you want, which can be buried or displayed.

A simple cremation can cost several hundred dollars, while a funeral
service with cremation can cost up to $2,000 or $3,000, depending on
some choices you make.

## 209 What should I know about organ donation?

This is a wonderful and vital thing to do. You or a loved one might
be gone, but by donating organs and tissues, something good can result from the death. Someone with a desperate need for a heart, or
cornea, or liver (among many things) can have a dream come true. In
many cases, it's an actual matter of life or death. There are long lists of
critically ill people waiting for organs, and there aren't enough organs
to go around.
- Acceptable donors range in age from newborns to senior citizens.
- If you want to donate your organs, you'll need to: (a) indicate that
  on your driver's license, (b) carry an organ donor card, and (c) tell
  your family. Informing your family of your wishes is vital, because
  sometimes there can be confusion at the time of death.

- Donation doesn't disfigure a body. An open casket will still be a possibility.
- If you're an organ donor, doctors and hospitals shouldn't be treating you any differently. Don't expect to receive less care.
- There is often an extra need for organs and tissues of minorities, as transplants often are more successful when made between members of the same ethnic or racial group.
- The donation of organs and tissues does not cost the donor anything.

A final option you might consider is donating your entire body to science. There are several benefits to total body donation. For starters, it can lead to medical progress. At the very least, a body can be used to train future doctors. It can also be used in research. Both healthy and sick bodies can be used. Another benefit is financial. By donating a body, there's usually no need to buy a casket or cemetery plot, or to pay for cremation. Some schools or institutions will cremate or bury the body for you after the research is concluded. If you're interested in donating your body to a particular institution, contact it.

Learn more about organ (and body) donation here:
- www.organdonor.gov
- www.shareyourlife.org
- www.transweb.org
- www.bodydonation.com

---

**210** **Where can I learn more about planning for funerals and death?**

Here are some informative resources:

Websites:
- www.funerals.org
- www.nfda.org/resources/index.html
- www.efmoody.com/miscellaneous/funeral.html
- www.dragonet.com/funeral/index2.htm
- www.cremation.org
- www.webcaskets.com
- www.discountcasket.com/headlines.html

- www.naturaldeathcare.org
- www.FinalThoughts.com
- www.compassionatefriends.org (for help with deaths of children)
- http://dying.about.com

Books:
- *Profits of Death: An Insider Exposes the Death Care Industries* by Darryl J. Roberts
- *The Affordable Funeral: Going in Style, Not in Debt: A Consumer's Guide to Funeral Arrangements & the Funeral Industry* by R. E. Markin
- *Before It's Too Late — Don't Leave Your Loved Ones Unprepared* by Sue L. Thompson and Emily J. Oishi
- *In the Checklist of Life: A Working Book to Help You Live & Leave This Life!* by Lynn McPhelimy
- *At Journey's End: The Complete Guide to Funerals and Funeral Planning* by Abdullah Fatteh with Naaz Fatteh
- *Final Celebrations: A Guide for Personal and Family Funeral Planning* by Kathleen Sublette and Martin Flagg
- *Dealing Creatively With Death: A Manual of Death Education and Simple Burial* by Ernest Morgan
- *Coming to Rest: A Guide to Caring for Our Own Dead, an Alternative to the Commercial Funeral* by Julie Wiskind and Richard Spiegel

# PART TWO
# Investing

**CHAPTER THIRTEEN**
**ANSWERS TO YOUR QUESTIONS ABOUT**

# The Basics

*Once you have your personal finance house in order, it's time to think about investing. Part One of this book is focused on helping you minimize how much you spend and maximize your savings. Part Two aims to help you increase your wealth.*

*You have to start somewhere. If investing is a completely new topic to you, or if you've never really studied it in any depth, you probably have lots of basic questions. Don't worry, though. At least you're learning these things now! This chapter covers a range of basic investing questions, from "What is a stock?" to "What is a dividend yield?"*

## 211 How should I go about starting to invest?

The most important thing is to approach it at your own pace. Don't rush into anything before you're comfortable with what you're doing. Take the time to read a lot and think a lot and ask questions and get answers. Once you have some ideas of what you'd like to do, you can ease into it by starting a "mock portfolio," where you pretend to buy or sell various stocks and track your performance over time.

Another school of thought is that as you begin learning you might want to jump into a stock or two with just a little money, just to begin feeling (and thinking) like an investor. You should only invest money at this point that you can afford to lose.

It's hard for me to avoid steering you to Fool.com, as that's where you'll find a wealth of educational fare, all written in an easy-to-understand style and with a sense of humor. (We don't want people nodding off mid-article, you see.) Other good ways to learn about investing and the business world are through books and magazines. Start with a book or two by Peter Lynch (a former superstar Fidelity mutual fund manager) and/or by David and Tom Gardner, Fool co-founders.

Business magazines and newspapers can be a great way to learn about investing and the business world. For example, if you get into the habit of regularly reading *Forbes*, *Fortune*, *BusinessWeek*, and *The Wall Street Journal*, you'll learn about ways that companies succeed or fail. These and other publications can make you a better evaluator of a company's quality and prospects.

## 212 What is a stock?

A share of stock represents actual ownership in a company. Consider this very simplified example: Imagine that Home Surgery Kits, Inc. (ticker: OUCHH) has 10,000 shares outstanding. If you own 100 shares of OUCHH, you own 1% of the company. (Divide 10,000 by 100 and you'll get 100. So, you own 1/100th of the firm.)

Ownership entitles you to a share of the company's earnings. These are sometimes partially paid out to shareholders in the form of dividends. Earnings may also be reinvested into the company, to fuel growth and generate more value.

Along with ownership of most shares of common stock comes voting rights. That's right — when a company you hold shares in has a big decision to make, it will ask you what you think. Individual investors typically buy "common stock" in a company. Another form of stock is "preferred," which usually carries some extra conditions and often excludes voting rights.

## 213 What is "preferred stock"?

Like common stock, a share of preferred stock confers partial ownership of a company to its holder. But, unlike common stock, holders of preferred stock usually have no voting rights. Shares of preferred stock often pay a guaranteed fixed dividend that is higher than the common stock dividend.

Preferred stock isn't really for individual investors, though. The shares are usually purchased by other corporations, which are attracted by the dividends that give them income taxed at a lower rate. Corporations also like the fact that preferred stockholders' claims on company earnings and assets have a higher priority than those of common stockholders. Imagine that the One-Legged Chair Co. (ticker: WOOPS) goes out of business. Many people or firms with claims on the company will want their due. Creditors will be paid before preferred stockholders, but preferred stockholders have a higher priority than common stockholders.

## 214 What is a bond?

Bonds are essentially long-term loans. If a company issues bonds, it's borrowing cash and promising to pay it back at a certain rate of interest.

Bonds sold by the U.S. government's Treasury Department are called "Treasuries." State and local governments issue "municipal bonds," while businesses issue "corporate bonds" (sometimes called corporate "paper"). Companies that may be perceived as low quality are forced to offer high-interest-rate "junk" bonds to attract buyers. There's a higher risk that someday they won't have the cash to cover interest payments and the bonds could default.

Bond investors receive regular interest payments from the issuer at what is called the "coupon rate." For example, a $1,000 bond with a coupon rate of 10% generates payments of $100 per year. When the bond matures — after perhaps 5, 10, or 30 years — investors get back their initial loan, called "par value." Most corporate bonds have a par value of $1,000, while government bonds can run much higher.

Sometimes a company will "call" its bond, paying back the principal early. All bonds specify whether and how soon they can be called. Federal government bonds are never called.

To calculate a bond's yield, divide the amount of interest it will pay over the course of a year by its current price. If a $1,000 bond pays $75 a year in interest, its current yield is $75 divided by $1,000, or 7.5%.

Once issued, bonds can be traded among investors, with their prices rising and falling in reaction to changing interest rates. For example, when rates fall, people bid up bond prices. If banks are offering 6%, an 8% bond starts looking good.

In the long run, stocks have outperformed bonds handily. According to Jeremy Siegel's *Stocks for the Long Run*, from 1802 to 1997 (yes, you read that right — 195 years), the stock market offered an average nominal annual return of 8.4% per year, compared to 4.8% for long-term government bonds.

Stocks outperform bonds even when you eliminate the 19th century data. According to Ibbotson & Associates, from 1926 to 1996 (notice that includes the Great Depression years), U.S. Treasury bills returned an average of 3.7% per year, compared with 5.6% for long-term corporate bonds, 10.7% for large-company stocks, and 12.6% for small-company stocks. If you had invested $5,000 in T-bills 50 years ago, it would now be worth $30,754. Growing at 10.7% in stocks, it would be worth $806,030.

For long-term investors, stocks offer the best potential for growth. Still, it's smart to understand how bonds work before you dismiss them.

## 215 What is a "zero coupon bond"?

Most people are familiar with zero coupon bonds in the form of U.S. Savings Bonds. You buy them at a discount to the face value, hold them for a specified time period, and then cash them in at face value. In a nutshell, that's how zero coupon bonds (or "zeroes") work.

Imagine a regular 5% $10,000 bond, where you lend $10,000 to a company or government. You receive interest payments of 5% per year until the bond matures, when you get your $10,000 back. (You used to have to send in coupons to get these payments.)

With a zero coupon bond, you don't receive any interest payments, but the amount you lend is smaller than the amount you'll receive at maturity. Thus, a zero coupon bond could pay you the equivalent of 5% per year by having you pay $6,139 today to receive $10,000 in 10 years.

## 216 What is a "long bond"?

Bonds come with a variety of maturity periods. The long bond is the U.S. government's 30-year bond. Its yield is the one often cited by the media when interest rates are being discussed. Treasury notes are shorter-term, maturing in two, five, or ten years. Treasury bills (or T-bills) mature in 13, 26, or 52 weeks. The minimum purchase amount for most of these instruments is $1,000.

## 217 Isn't investing in the stock market risky?

Yes, it does have some risk. Shares of stock are valued based on the value of the companies that issued them. If you buy stock in the Whoa Nellie Brake Co. (ticker: HALTT) and it declares bankruptcy, you're probably going to lose money. Most well-known companies don't suddenly go out of business, though. (Think of Coca-Cola, IBM, Wal-Mart, and the like.) Look at a graph of the stock market average over many years and you'll see that it's a zig-zaggy line. The zigging and zagging is volatility, and those downward zags can create risk. But step back and look at the graph and you'll see that the jagged line slopes upward over the long haul. Despite the risk, it gradually gains in value.

You can probably afford to take on some risk by investing in stocks — as long as the money invested won't be withdrawn within the next five or more years. If you'll need the money you're investing for college or a house down payment in two years, stocks aren't a good idea — the market could drop in the short term. But, if you're investing for the long haul, you can patiently ride out downturns. Short-term investors should stick to safer plays, such as money market funds.

Even if you're nearing retirement, odds are that you won't be tapping most of your nest egg for at least five years. So, much of it — the long-term portion — can still remain in stocks. Don't assume that just because you're in or near retirement, you need to completely withdraw from the stock market.

Investing in stocks is certainly not risk-free, but it can be riskier to just conservatively park all your money in an ultra-safe spot such as a money market fund. The more you learn, the more you can manage risk.

## 218  Are there ways to reduce risk when investing?

You betcha. Here are a few.

- **Avoid futures, commodities, options, penny stocks, shorting, and margin** — at least until you've learned a heck of a lot about them. These are all extra-risky ways of investing. Only experienced investors should use some; others are best avoided by all.

- **Be a long-term investor, not a day-trader.** Holding a stock for only a few weeks, days, or hours is not investing — it's gambling. Real investors think of themselves as committed part-owners of businesses. Convinced of a company's value, they plan to hang on for many years.

    The longer your investing horizon, the more likely the stock market is to rise, and the less risk there is of losing money. In the short term, anything can happen — including market corrections and crashes. One or all of your holdings could fall by 20% tomorrow. If you're holding on for years, you can ride out downturns. If you plan to sell in 15 or 20 years, what happens this year isn't a big risk to you.

- **Increase your knowledge.** The more you know, the less chance you have of making mistakes. Too many people buy companies merely on "hot" stock tips from friends or strangers. Sometimes they don't even know what the company does.

- **Learn about investing.** Read all you can. Start with books by Peter Lynch. Read Berkshire Hathaway Chairman Warren Buffett's letters to shareholders, which are written very clearly and impart many commonsense investing lessons. (They're online at www.berkshire-hathaway.com.) Hang out at Fool.com online, reading and asking questions. Invest only in companies you know and understand well, ideally companies whose products or services you use yourself.

- **Limit your downside.** Read up on the risks companies disclose in their financial statements. Consider valuation. A company that seems undervalued (according to measures such as market capitalization, price-to-sales and price-to-earnings ratios, and expected future earnings) should offer less downside risk than an exciting highflier. You can do well with some highfliers; just understand that they're riskier.

By reducing your risk, you'll increase your chances of doing very well.

## 219 How exactly do you profit by owning stocks?

There are two main ways: dividends and price appreciation.

Imagine that you buy 100 shares of International Alphabet Corp. (ticker: ABCDE) for $50 per share. You spend $5,000 total (plus perhaps $12 commission to your discount broker). Let's say that ABCDE is paying a $2 per share dividend when you buy it. That means that as long as you hold on to your shares, you'll be paid $2 for each share annually — that's $200 per year. Over time, companies typically increase their dividends. So 10 years from now, you might be receiving $5 per share, or $500 per year. Each year that you hold the stock, you'll be paid a dividend. Not every company pays a dividend. This is fine — some companies are growing quickly and need that money, and they may more than make it up to you via price appreciation.

Let's look at price appreciation now. Recall that you bought your shares of International Alphabet for $50 per share. Well, 10 years from now they may be trading at $130 per share (that's about 10% growth per year). If so, then they would be worth $13,000. You spent $5,000 for them originally, so if you were to sell, you'd make a profit of $8,000 (on which you'd pay capital gains tax). And if there had been dividend payments all along, that's icing on the cake.

## 220 If I put some money in stocks, can I lose more than I invest?

As long as you invest in common stocks without borrowing any money (using "margin"), your maximum potential loss is no more than 100%. Once you get into borrowing money, playing options, or shorting stocks on margin, you could lose *more* than you invest. Beginning investors shouldn't even *think* of investing on margin or shorting stocks — and even advanced investors might consider steering clear of options.

Don't let the 100% loss possibility frighten you too much, though. If you're researching companies before investing, selecting financially healthy firms with track records of growth, and are keeping up with their developments, you're unlikely to lose large chunks of your investment. Remember also that losses only occur when you sell. Even good companies go through occasional slumps, so it's often best to patiently ride them out.

## 221 When a stock price falls, we lose money. But, to whom or to what? Where does the money go?

Investing isn't like gambling; you're not playing against the house. Out in Las Vegas, if you lose a bet that money goes right into casino coffers. But, on Wall Street, when a company's stock price declines, nobody necessarily directly benefits from the loss. Let's say you own shares of the Velvet Elvis Art Factory Inc. (ticker: KINGG). If the stock drops 20% one day, you haven't technically *lost* any money — unless you sell the stock. You still have the same number of shares you owned yesterday. The shares are each worth a little less today, though. When a stock tumbles, its value isn't redistributed. It merely shrinks.

That said, there *are* people who profit when certain stocks fall. These folks do something called "shorting" a stock, where they profit if a stock price drops. Shorting will be discussed later in this book.

## 222 How do you choose stocks to invest in?

Think of them as companies and businesses instead of stocks. Then, don't make the mistake that many people make — basing a decision to buy stock in a company on just one or two factors. For example, some people see what they think is a low price-to-earnings (P/E) ratio, and think that's enough. Or, maybe they read an article about a company that made it seem irresistible.

Instead, take the time to learn how to evaluate companies. Learn how to read financial statements. Assess P/E ratios along with *many other* numbers. Read widely about companies that interest you, ideally in industries that you're familiar with and would enjoy keeping up with. In the rest of this book, you'll come across many things to consider when evaluating a company. You'll also be pointed to many resources (check the resources in the Appendix, too).

The more you learn, the better your investment decisions and performance are likely to be.

---

### 223 Is it just me, or is it weird that the media always refer to moves in the market by total points, and not by percentages? Wouldn't percentages be better?

It's not just you. At Fool HQ, we often shake our heads in bemusement at reporters who exclaim, "The Dow was up 100 points today!" We're dismayed because the media usually refers to market moves in points, when it's the percentages that really matter.

For much of 2000, the Dow Jones Industrial Average (which comprises the stocks of 30 blue-chip companies) hovered around 10,000. On March 16, it rocketed up 499 points, which was a 5% move. Compare this with 1987, though, when the Dow stood around 2,247 before plunging 508 points in a single day. That represented a whopping 23% move. As the Dow heads into ever-higher territory in the future, 500-point drops or pops will become more common and less meaningful. Be prepared for bigger numbers, too. When the Dow is at 20,000, a 5% rise or fall will mean 1,000 points.

Next time you see a TV anchorman report (with a grave expression) that "The Dow fell 50 points in heavy trading today," put that number in perspective. If the Dow is around 10,000 at the time, divide

50 by 10,000 and you'll get 0.005, or just half a percentage point. Back in 1956, when the Dow was at 500, it would have been a 10% move. In 1906, with the Dow at a mere 100, it would have been an eye-popping 50% free-fall. But today, 0.5% isn't really news.

A sudden drop can certainly be the beginning of a long slump, such as in 1929. But its effect is frequently reversed within a matter of months. As of this writing, the biggest point drop in Dow history occurred in 1997, when the Dow fell 554 points on Oct. 27. It regained lost ground within a matter of days.

A final point to remember is that occasional big drops are to be expected, but you needn't reach for the antacid if you're Foolishly hanging on for decades. Trust in the long-term upward trend of the market, look for bargains amid downturns, and focus on percentages rather than points.

## 224 What does it mean when I hear, "AT&T is up 2 1/2 today"? Is that dollars per share, or what?

Stock prices are listed in dollars per share. They're not always in whole numbers, though. The world of stock prices is full of fractions, all the way down to 64ths, and occasionally even smaller. So, if the film-editing firm Splice Girls Inc. (ticker: SPLIC) is listed at 28, that means it last traded at $28 per share. Similarly, 15 17/32 means 15.53125 or $15.53 per share. (The stock market is in the process of switching from fractions to decimals, but the decimals will still reflect prices per share in dollars.)

Another way to think of a price move is to consider how much total market value the company has gained or lost with each move. Find out the number of shares outstanding the company has. (Do this via online stock research tools or the firm's financial statements.) Multiply the number of shares outstanding by the share price. If SPLIC has 200 million shares outstanding and drops by $2 per share, the company has lost $400 million in market value.

## 225 When watching a company's stock price go up and down, I wonder what percentage or number of shares is necessary

## to move a stock's price. Who determines this number?

There is no required number or percentage of shares. The stock market is really very much like an old-world public market where each buyer haggles with the sellers. Shares end up trading at different prices to different people because they trade at prices that individual buyers are willing to pay and sellers are willing to take.

Imagine that shares of Spackle World (ticker: SPACK) close around $30 each at the end of trading one day. Then Spackle announces that it has recently experienced amazing growth in sales and that it expects to report record earnings next month. All of a sudden, there may be a surge in demand for Spackle World shares. The very next shares to trade may go for $35 each or more. The price won't necessarily inch its way up.

Similarly, if Spackle World announces that it's going to file for bankruptcy, then there will likely be many more sellers than buyers, and the price will quickly drop considerably lower. If the stock is immediately perceived to be worth just pennies per share, it's not going to sell for $29 per share, then $28, then $27, etc. It'll immediately be worth a lot less.

It's all a balance between supply and demand, between what people are willing to pay or accept.

## 226 If people are selling a stock in droves, where do those shares go?

Believe it or not, when a stock is plunging as many people sell, some people are actually buying it. For each seller there's a buyer, and vice versa. (If there were no buyers at any price, the stock would drop to zero or trades would not execute — you have to have someone on both ends of the deal for a trade to occur.)

As a stock is sold off, its price falls. While those who are selling don't want to own it at the current price, there are always others who think differently, seeing it as a bargain. Consider a stock racing upward on a wave of enthusiasm. For every buyer with great expectations, someone is selling, deciding that the stock price is too rich to be sustainable.

## 227 | What exactly do companies do with their earnings?

Imagine that the NHL Demolition Co. (ticker: PUCKS), specializing in property destruction, earns $15 million on sales of $120 million this year. There are four main things it can do with that moolah:
- Pay out all or some of its profits to shareholders as a cash dividend.
- Repurchase some of its own shares on the open market. (This boosts the value of the remaining shares, as the company's worth ends up being divided among fewer shares outstanding.)
- Plow that money into its ongoing operations, renting more property to destroy or hiring more employees.
- Invest in other business ventures, perhaps buying a smaller demolition company or a related company, such as a recycling enterprise.

A publicly traded company's main priority should be to build value for shareholders. To do that, it must determine which strategies will generate the biggest bang for the puck... er, buck.

## 228 | What is a dividend?

A dividend is a portion of a company's earnings that the firm pays out to its shareholders. If the Tattoo Advertising Co. (ticker: YOWCH) is earning roughly $4 in profit per share each year, it might decide to issue $1 annually to shareholders and use the rest of the money to help build the business. If so, it will probably pay out 25 cents per share every three months.

This may seem like a pittance, but it adds up. If you own 200 shares of a company that's paying $2.50 per share in annual dividends, you'll receive $500 per year from the company.

## 229 | I know that companies pay dividends — but what's a dividend yield?

A company's dividend yield simply expresses the relationship of two numbers: a company's stock price and the amount of its annual dividend.

For example, look at Ford Motor Co. At the time of this writing, it was trading around $51 per share and paying out $2 per year (in quarterly installments) as a dividend. Take $2 and divide it by $51 and you'll get 0.039. Multiply that by 100 and you have a dividend yield of 3.9%. This means that if you pay $51 for a share of Ford, you'll earn 3.9% per year on your investment just from dividends alone.

Companies rarely decrease or eliminate their dividends, as that would make investors unhappy. But, dividends do tend to rise over time, delivering more value to shareholders. Every now and then, a company will announce an increase. If, in 20 years, Ford's annual dividend is $8, that would represent a 15.7% dividend yield on those shares you bought for $51. You'd be earning a 15.7% return each year, just from dividends. There would probably be some stock price appreciation on top of that, as well.

Note that, for months or years at a time, a dividend will hold steady. But, the yield can fluctuate daily. That's because a stock's price fluctuates. As a stock price rises, the dividend yield falls, and vice versa. If Ford shares, for example, suddenly doubled in price to $102, the yield would be halved, to 2% ($2 divided by $102 is 0.02). If Ford stock fell to $30 per share, its yield for those buying it at $30 would be 6.7%.

You can find some hefty dividend yields among companies whose stock prices have tumbled. At the time of this writing, for example, R. J. Reynolds Tobacco Holdings pays about $3 per share in annual dividends. With its stock trading around $30 per share, that's a whopping 10% dividend yield! Be careful, though. If you're attracted to an unusually high dividend yield, you should probably study the company carefully to make sure it's not in so much trouble that a dividend cut is around the corner.

Lastly, know that not all companies pay dividends. Younger and quickly growing companies in particular prefer to plow extra cash back into operations.

## 230 Is dividend growth something I should pay attention to?

A little attention paid to dividends can really pay off. You may think of venerable blue-chip companies such as Ford, General Electric, and Chevron as stodgy and old-fangled, but think again. They pay generous dividends.

If you bought Ford when its annual dividend was $2, you're very likely to get that $2 payout every year, regardless of what happens to the stock price. (Struggling companies may decrease or eliminate their dividends, but they try like heck not to, because it looks really bad. Firms aim to maintain or increase their dividends over time.) Couple stock appreciation with dividends, and you've got an appealing combination.

Here's something investors rarely consider. Let's say you bought 10 shares of Stained Glass Windshield Co. (ticker: STAIN) for $100 each, and it pays a respectable 3% dividend. With a $1,000 investment, that amounts to an annual payout of $30. Not bad.

But wait — remember that dividends aren't static and permanent. Companies raise them regularly. A few years down the line, perhaps STAIN is trading at $220 per share. If the dividend yield is still 3%, the company is paying out $6.60 per share (0.03 times $220 equals $6.60). Note: $6.60 is a 3% yield for anyone buying the stock at $220, but since you bought it at $100, to you it's a 6.6% yield. You paid $100 for each share and each one is kicking out $6.60 to you.

Decades pass. Your initial 10 shares have split into 80 shares, each currently priced at $120. Your initial $1,000 investment is now valued at $9,600. The yield is still 3%, paying $3.60 per share ($3.60 divided by $120 equals 0.03, or 3%). Since you own 80 shares, you receive a whopping $288 per year. Think about this. You're earning $288 in dividends in one year on a $1,000 investment. That's 29% return per year (and *growing*) — without even factoring in any stock price appreciation. The dividend yield for you has gone from 3% to 29%, all because you just hung on to those shares of a growing company. That's security! Even if the stock price drops, you're still likely to get that 29% payout.

With many great dividend paying companies, by holding on, your dividend yield keeps rising. Consider this: One share of Coca-Cola bought in its first year has become more than 97,860 shares through stock splits and dividend reinvestments, and that investment is now earning an annual dividend of more than $58,000.

## 231 What is the smallest number of shares of stock that I can buy?

Would you believe *fractions* of a share? If you buy stock directly from a company, such as through a dividend reinvestment plan, your money often buys fractions of shares at a time. For example, a $50 investment would buy you 0.67 shares of a $75 stock. When buying stock through a broker, you can buy as little as one share at a time. Just pay attention to commissions — if you buy one $40 share of stock and pay a $25 commission, you're not doing yourself a favor.

## 232 What is the least amount of money that I can invest? I don't have enough money to buy 100 shares of a company I'm interested in. Am I out of luck?

It's tragic that many people put off investing for years, thinking they're not rich enough to benefit from the stock market. You don't need to have $1,000 or more before you start investing. You don't have to buy 100 shares at a time. You can buy 17 shares or 9 shares — or even fractions of shares, using some services.

Why the misunderstanding? Well, the notion is just a little out of date, that's all. See, historically, full-service brokers charged very high commissions, with extra charges for purchases that weren't made in "round lots," or multiples of 100. So 100 was viewed as the minimum number of shares you *had* to buy to avoid incredibly high commissions. Today, however, commissions at discount brokers are much more reasonable and people can affordably purchase any amount of shares they'd like... including just one.

## 233 If I can only save a few dollars a week, can I still invest? Is investing worth it for those of us with limited means?

Many people think they'll never join the investing set. They assume they don't have enough money to start, but investing isn't just for the rich. If you have just $20 or $30 per month to invest in stocks, you can do so, thanks to dividend reinvestment plans ("Drips").

Drips permit you to buy shares of a company's stock directly from the company or its agent, bypassing brokers (and brokerage commissions!). They've grown in popularity in recent years, and hundreds of major corporations now offer them, with more companies introducing them every day.

With traditional Drips, the company expects you to already own at least one share of its stock before you enroll in the program. The share must also be in your name, so if you're not already a shareholder, you'll have to buy at least one share through a broker, paying the commission. In addition, you'll have to specify that you want the share(s) registered in *your* name — not the brokerage's name (also called "street name"), as is typically done. Once you own at least one share, then you can open a Drip account with the company and buy additional shares directly through the company (or its agent).

A new variety of Drips, direct stock purchase plans (DSPs), operate in much the same way, except they don't require you to own at least one share before enrolling. You can buy your very first shares through the company.

With Drips, you can "dollar-cost average" — accumulating shares in a company by regularly investing a set amount of money. (Dollar-cost averaging involves spending the same amount at regular intervals on a certain investment.) Drips will even purchase partial shares for you. For example, if PepsiCo is trading around $45 per share and you send in a $50 contribution, that will buy a little more than a share of stock. If, next month, PepsiCo is at $30 per share and you send in $50, you'll get roughly 1.7 shares. When the price is low, your money buys more shares, and vice versa.

---

**234** **I see that "Drips" let you reinvest dividends to buy additional shares of stock. What's the big deal about reinvesting dividends? Why not just take those few dollars as cash, and enjoy them?**

One of the best things about Drips is that they allow you to have all or part of your dividends reinvested into additional shares of company stock, even if the dividends just buy fractions of shares. This might not seem like much, but it's actually extremely powerful in the long run.

Consider Ford Motor Co. If you bought some shares of it at the end of 1980 and hung on for 18 years, to the end of 1998, they would have appreciated nearly 3,900% (22.7% annually). That's amazing enough. But, get this — if you'd been reinvesting dividends to purchase more shares, your total return would skyrocket to 12,300%, or 30.7% per year! An initial $1,000 investment would have grown to $39,000 without reinvesting dividends and $124,000 with reinvested dividends. (This doesn't even take into account Ford's spin-offs during that period.)

Over the same 18-year period, Pfizer advanced 22.3% annually without reinvestment and 25.3% with it. J.P. Morgan shares grew 12.3% without reinvestment and 17% with it. Coca-Cola appreciated 24% without reinvestment, and 27% with it. Over a decade or two, these differences can make a big difference in your investment returns.

With some discount broker commissions recently falling to under $10 per trade, it's become possible to gradually accumulate shares of a company without using a formal Drip plan. You can now invest just several hundred dollars at a time through your brokerage without paying too much in commissions. And, just as important, some brokerages now offer dividend reinvestment options, as well.

---

## 235 Where can I learn more about Drips and DSPs?

Here are some websites:
- www.netstockdirect.com
- www.Fool.com/DRIPPort/WhatAreDRIPs.htm
- www.dripadvisor.com
- www.dripinvestor.com
- www.moneypaper.com
- www.dripcentral.com

And some books:
- *The Motley Fool's Investing Without a Silver Spoon* by Jeff Fischer
- *Buying Stocks Without a Broker* by Charles B. Carlson
- *No-Load Stocks: How to Buy Your First Share & Every Share Directly from the Company —With No Broker's Fee* by Charles B. Carlson

Note that the National Association of Investors Corp. (NAIC) offers its own version of Drips, called the Low Cost Investment Plan. For more info, give them a call at (877) 275-6242.

---

**236** **I've just noticed a new breed of online investing service that works a little like a brokerage, but with extra-low trading fees, such as $2.99 per trade. (For example, www.BUYandHOLD.com and www.ShareBuilder.com.) Is there any downside to these?**

Not much. These are attractive options that Foolish investors should consider. They permit you to get started investing with as little as $20, and they have some advantages over traditional dividend reinvestment and direct investment plans. With Drips, it frequently takes weeks and some paperwork before you can buy or sell stock. Last time we checked, BUYandHOLD was executing trades twice daily and Share-Builder once or twice a week. That's a big difference.

These services operate very much like regular brokerages, but with a few notable differences. For starters, they don't buy and sell shares of a stock throughout the day. Instead, they accumulate orders and place large consolidated orders according to a schedule. This means that buyers and sellers can't expect to trade at any exact price that they may want to specify. This shouldn't be a big deal, though. As long as you're planning to hang on to your shares for years, paying a smidgen more than you expected shouldn't be the end of the world. And, in many cases, you'll pay a smidgen less.

To learn more about these companies' services, fees, risks, and advantages, poke around their websites and ask them any questions you have. As with everything important, read all the fine print.

---

**237** **Is it better to invest in stocks or bonds?**

Money you won't need for five or more years will likely grow fastest in stocks. According to Ibbotson & Associates, from 1926 to 1996, U.S. Treasury bills returned an average of 3.7% per year, long-term corporate bonds returned 5.6%, and stocks averaged about 11% per year.

At that rate, $5,000 invested for 50 years in T-bills would grow to $30,754 (pre-tax). Invested in the stock market, it would reach $922,824 (pre-tax). That's quite a difference!

Of course, note that returns are far from guaranteed in the stock market, while Treasury bill interest rates *are* guaranteed. The more risk you take with investments, the higher the returns can be.

## 238 What do the terms "bull" and "bear" mean in relation to the stock market?

An investor "bullish" on a particular stock or the market is one who expects it to go up. Conversely, a "bear" is more pessimistic, perhaps expecting a market drop in the near future. We Fools won't guess what the market will do in the short term, but we're long-term bulls. Over many decades, stocks have returned an average of 11% per year — and that's despite market crashes, world wars, the Great Depression, and the disco years.

## 239 What's the difference between a private and public company?

A private company is one that's privately owned. Its owners don't have to reveal much about their business. And, most of us investors can't invest in it.

A public company is one that has sold a portion of itself to the public, via an initial public offering (IPO) of shares of its stock. If it's an American company trading on an American stock exchange, it's required to file quarterly financial reports with the Securities and Exchange Commission (SEC). These reports are also made available to shareholders and the public. A public company can't keep mum about how much it made in sales last year. It must report information like that — its revenues, cost of sales, tax expenses, administration costs, debt load, cash levels, and so on.

## 240 What major companies are private?

Take a gander at these biggies: Levi Strauss, Cargill, M&M Mars, Bertelsmann AG, Bechtel, Publix Supermarkets, IKEA International, (Fidelity Investments parent) FMR Corp., Seiko Epson, Amway, DHL Worldwide Express, Virgin Group, Rosenbluth International, Penske, S.C. Johnson & Sons, Packard Bell NEC, Enterprise Rent-A-Car, Hallmark Cards, Borden, McCain Foods, Hyatt, Subway, National Amusements, PurdueFarms, McKinsey & Co., LEGO Company, and Domino's Pizza. Some of these firms offer shares to employees, but individual investors are out of luck.

United Parcel Service was private until recently, as was Goldman Sachs. So, just because an established firm is private doesn't mean it'll always be private.

---

## 241 Can you explain all those terms that describe different kinds of companies, such as "cyclical"?

Sure can. Here are some key groups.

- "Cyclical" companies react strongly to economic change. Think of it this way: People spend money more conservatively during recessions, putting off major purchases such as cars and refrigerators. Thus, manufacturers of automobiles and large appliances are considered to be cyclical. Meanwhile, companies that aren't so affected by the economy are "defensive." An example would be pharmaceutical firms. If you're taking heart medication, you're not going to stop because of an economic downturn.
- "Seasonal" companies experience significantly different levels of business at various times of the year. Department stores, for example, see sales surge during the Christmas holiday season. Swimming pool companies see large sales and profits mainly in the summer.
- "Blue chip" companies have been around a long time and are perceived as being of higher-than-average quality and lower-than-average risk. They're usually steady growers and often pay dividends. (The term "blue chip" is derived from poker chips, where the blue chips are the most valuable.) "Red chip" companies are smaller, younger, less proven, and usually riskier. Some examples of blue chip companies: General Electric, ExxonMobil, Johnson & Johnson, Procter & Gamble, Coca-Cola, and Boeing.
- "Growth" companies are growing faster than the market average. They usually pay little or no dividend, as they need any extra cash

to fuel their growth. Their stock prices often go up — and sometimes down — quickly. Aggressive investors favor growth stocks. Some examples of growth stocks: Microsoft, America Online, Cisco, and eBay. (Railroad and telegraph businesses were growth companies once — but things change over time.)

- "Value" stocks are favored by investors looking to buy the proverbial "dollar for fifty cents." These are often companies that are temporarily out of favor or whose underlying value and prospects have not been recognized by investors.
- "Income" stocks may not grow too quickly, but they pay fat dividends. They're sort of like bonds, which pay interest. Traditionally, utility companies have paid high dividends. Today, some real estate companies do, as well. People in or near retirement, who rely on the dividends to supplement pensions or savings, often favor income stocks.

When evaluating companies, it helps to think of what categories they fall into. Learn these terms and concepts (and drop them in conversation), and you'll be the savviest Fool on your block.

## 242 What exactly are "tech stocks"? Companies that make computer stuff?

People often use the term to refer to computer-related companies and software companies. But, these days, it is hard to think of companies that *don't* employ a fair amount of technology.

Think of pharmaceutical firms, for instance. Drug chemistry and drug delivery processes involve technology. Golf club manufacturers apply technology to their new product development. Pretty much any airplane-related enterprise uses technology — from building jets to booking flights. Likewise, FedEx and other delivery specialists rely heavily on technology. Of course, some companies do so more than others. Sun Microsystems, for example, is much more of a technology company than Hershey.

When we hear that "Tech stocks were up today," we have to wonder what exactly is being said. A good way to think about the term might be to use it for companies that draw most of their revenue from directly using or creating technology.

## 243 What is a "holding company"?

Holding companies are conglomerates that own other firms or shares in other firms. They usually maintain voting control of these companies, as well. A good example is Warren Buffett's Berkshire Hathaway, which owns GEICO, See's Candies, Executive Jet, and Dexter Shoe Company, among many other businesses.

Another major holding company is Fortune Brands, which owns companies making distilled spirits (Jim Beam, DeKuyper, Ronrico), golf equipment (Titleist, Cobra, FootJoy, Pinnacle), home products (Moen faucets, Aristokraft and Schrock cabinets, and Master Lock padlocks), and office products (ACCO, Day-Timers, Swingline).

While many companies routinely acquire other companies, they frequently aim to blend these acquisitions into their operations. Holding companies keep the businesses they buy more separate.

## 244 What is a company's "market capitalization"?

It's a quick way of placing an approximate price tag on a company. Just multiply the stock price by the number of shares outstanding. For example, if Excelsior Hair Growth (ticker: SPROUT) has 10 million shares outstanding priced at $50 each, its "market cap" is $500 million.

People often refer to several categories of market capitalization. There are no strict guides as to what defines each one, but here's our rough take: If a company's market capitalization is $5 billion or higher, it's a large-cap; between $1 billion and $5 billion, a mid-cap; $250 million to $1 billion, a small-cap; and less than $250 million, a micro-cap. If small-cap SPROUT were to be acquired by another company, that company would have to cough up $500 million — or more, as buyouts generally occur above market prices.

## 245 Do you have any special advice for women on investing?

Investing and personal finance principles are largely the same for women and men. However, women do need to take the time to learn about investing and money management. Statistics show that women, in general, outlive men — so anyone counting on a husband to tend to the family finances forever is on dangerous ground. In addition, many women are more risk-averse than they need to be and invest too conservatively. Stocks shouldn't be shunned, as long as your investment horizon is five to ten years (or more) away.

## 246 Are investment clubs good ideas? How do they work?

A dozen heads can often be better than one. In investment clubs, folks pool their money, their brains, and their time, and make investments together.

There are thousands of clubs across America, with more than 38,000 alone registered with the National Association of Investors Corp. (NAIC). Clubs typically have 10 to 20 members and meet once a month. Members each contribute about $20 to $75 monthly to a pooled account, research stocks individually or in small groups, present their findings to the group, and vote on investments.

Clubs are ideal for beginning investors, as members can learn together in a comfortable group setting. But even savvy investors can benefit from clubs, as they leverage valuable resources like time. Imagine that you're an experienced investor and you only have enough time to research one company each month — 12 per year. If you band together with a dozen similar investors and each of you researches and presents a dozen companies per year, you'll each learn about 144 companies, not just 12. That's leverage!

Many folks who go about investing on their own fall prey to un-Foolish ways. They may act on an acquaintance's hot stock tip or try to time the market, jumping in and out of stocks on hunches. Investment club members, meanwhile, are more circumspect. They're usually bound by their partnership agreement to study a stock carefully before voting on whether to invest in it. Clubs tend to own such solid, leading enterprises as General Electric, ExxonMobil, PepsiCo, and Intel, hanging on for years, not months or weeks. These kinds of habits can lead to market-beating performances.

## 247 Can you offer any tips for people forming an investment club?

Sure. Start by gathering around 6 to 15 interested people. Begin by discussing your goals and expectations, making sure they're compatible. Don't actually form the club until you're sure you're all committed to it.

Agree on the amount of the monthly contribution per person and where and when you'll meet. Choose a name for your club, elect officers, and file for a Tax Identification Number via IRS Form SS-4 (which you can download direct from the IRS website at: www.irs.ustreas.gov/forms_pubs/forms.html).

Draft a partnership agreement and bylaws. Open a brokerage account. (Alternatively, you might create a less-formal club, which learns and researches together, but stops short of investing actual money together.)

Start meetings on time and stick to your agenda. If learning about investing is one of your club's goals, you might elect an education officer to organize lessons for the group. Members can each read a book or article on investing or business and then report back to the group. Or distribute some required reading at each meeting to be discussed at the next. One member might learn how to calculate some stock valuation ratios and then teach fellow club members. You can all go on a field trip to a local company or stock exchange. Or visit a local library together and ask the librarian to show you useful reference materials, such as *Value Line* stock reports. Consider inviting some guest speakers, as well, such as a veteran investor, a member of a more-experienced investment club, or someone who works in an industry you're thinking of investing in. These activities help keep interest high among members.

Research stocks Foolishly, studying companies' financial statements, competitive positioning, and business strategy. Just about all the information you need to evaluate a company is available online. Visit www.Fool.com/investmentclub and let us open a Fool discussion board exclusively for your club. Being able to take care of some business online between meetings can help make your face-to-face time more productive.

There are a few perils you'll want to avoid. Don't under-delegate. Each member should be an active participant. Don't be impatient. Focus on long-term rewards. Don't be "all business." Have fun, offer refreshments, and socialize — perhaps even with another local club.

## 248 Are investment clubs a good idea for teenagers?

They're a terrific idea. The only problem is that minors can't trade stocks on their own. Still, teens can form clubs to learn together and can form and maintain a mock portfolio on their own. Once they find and research companies they want to own, they can do so individually, with a parent acting as custodian of their account.

## 249 I recently joined an investment club. Do you have any advice, or a suggestion for something I can talk about at my next meeting?

Remain focused on learning about investing and studying companies, not just tracking stocks the club has bought. And be patient. Amazing portfolio performances aren't built in a year.

Consider sharing and discussing copies of interesting articles you've read on various websites or in print, or read a book on investing or about an interesting company or business strategy and then report on it to the group.

Some good books to consider:
- *Built to Last* by James Collins and Jerry Porras
- *Selling the Invisible* by Harry Beckwith
- *The Gorilla Game* by Geoffrey Moore, Paul Johnson, and Tom Kippola

## 250 Where can I learn more about investment clubs?

Here are some websites:
- www.better-investing.org
- www.bivio.com

- www.investorama.com/guides/clubs
- investmentclub.about.com
- www.Fool.com/investmentclub

And some books:
- *Starting and Running a Profitable Investment Club: The Official Guide from the National Association of Investment Clubs* by Thomas O'Hara and Kenneth S. Janke
- *Investment Clubs: How to Start and Run One The Motley Fool Way* by Selena Maranjian

## 251 I've heard that it's possible to accumulate more than $50,000 in 20 years by investing small amounts. How?

Well, the stock market's historical growth rate in this century is about 11% per year. So, if you save $75 per month and invest $450 every six months in the S&P 500, history suggests it will grow to roughly $60,000 in 20 years.

You can invest in the S&P 500 through an S&P 500 index fund. That's a type of mutual fund offered by many fund companies, such as Vanguard. Another way is through "Spiders." Spiders work more like a stock, have the ticker symbol (SPY), and you can buy small amounts. Each is valued at approximately 1/10 of the S&P 500 index. If you're investing small amounts in Spiders, make sure you use a discount brokerage with low commissions — you don't want to pay $40 in fees to invest $450. Some commissions are now as low as $7 or less.

## 252 If my child saves $500 per year starting when he's 18, can he turn it into a million dollars in his lifetime? I want to explain to him how money can grow.

It all depends on what he does with the money. If he parks it in a bank, earning 4% per annum, he'll be a 112-year-old millionaire. But, with an S&P 500 index fund, which has matched the stock market's average 11% return, he'll have seven figures around age 71 (assuming the market continues to average an 11% annual return).

Keep in mind, though, that he should be able to beat the stock market and get there a lot sooner, if he takes the time to learn more about investing. If he gets good at evaluating and selecting companies in which to invest, he might earn an annual average of 20% or so. At that rate, he'd be a millionaire by age 50. And, this assumes he won't save more than $500 a year — which of course he will, right?

By investing intelligently, anyone can get to a million in a few decades — starting with just a few hundred bucks. And, no matter your age, there's no better time to start than now.

---

**253** **I'm middle-aged and don't earn much money. Can I really invest? And would my investments really ever amount to much?**

It's never too late (or early!) to begin investing. For a little inspiration, look to the amazing story of Anne Scheiber. Most people haven't heard of her, but she's one of the world's greatest investors. In 1932, Ms. Scheiber was a 38-year-old IRS auditor. Intrigued by the stock market, she forked over most of her life savings to her brother, a young stockbroker on Wall Street, who lost it.

Determined to try again, but this time relying on herself, she saved $5,000 and invested it back into stocks in 1944. By the time she died in 1995 (at the age of 101), her money had grown to $20 million. How'd she do it?

Well, for starters, she was a long-term, involved investor. She didn't buy a stock today and sell it tomorrow. She attended shareholder meetings and followed her companies closely. She bought big consumer-brand companies like PepsiCo, Schering-Plough, Chrysler (now DaimlerChrysler AG), and Coca-Cola, and she reinvested her dividends. She placed her faith — and her money — in these growing companies and watched their earnings grow higher over decades. And when she died, Anne donated it all to Yeshiva University in New York.

Anne wasn't totally Foolish, though, as she didn't stop to smell the roses enough. Those who knew her say she was a recluse in her small, rent-controlled apartment. Never married and painfully frugal, she wore the same coat year after year and skipped meals to save money. Fools generally enjoy not just investing and compounding enormous long-term profits, but also family picnics, beating friends in board games, reading occasional trashy mystery books, and the messiness of children spilling cranberry juice on expensive furnishings.

Anne Scheiber's investment legacy provides a powerful example of what we can achieve if we are methodical and patient with our money.

---

## 254 I don't want to pay too much in commissions when I buy or sell stock. But, how much is "too much"?

Let's go through the math and see. (Don't be alarmed — I'm talking simple multiplication and division here.)

Think of a stock you're interested in buying. Let's say it's Exotica Foods (Ticker: ICK), famous for its popular Tripe Tarts. Now, let's answer a few questions.
1. What is Exotica's share price? $50
2. How many shares do you want to buy? 20
3. What's the value of that purchase? $50 x 20 shares = $1,000
4. How much does your broker charge? Let's say $25 per trade
5. What percentage of the investment is the commission? $25/$1,000 = 0.025, or 2.5%

You'll be paying 2.5% in commissions. That's a little steep. It's best to avoid paying more than 2% in transaction fees on any stock investment. If you're paying much more than that, you're hurting yourself.

Let's take another example. Say that you want to buy $400 of Par Domes Inc. (ticker: UNDRPR), a chain of indoor golf courses — and your broker charges a $30 commission. That comes out to 7.5% ($30/$400 = 0.075 or 7.5%). Ouch! If your original goal for your Par Domes investment was a 15% return, you'd now have to earn more than 22% after commissions to get there because you're starting out 7.5% in the hole! (Pardon the pun.)

What's the solution? Well, you should either move to a deeper-discount broker that charges $12 or less per online or phone trade, or you should put more money into the investment. Save up and invest $1,500 all in one shot into Par Domes, and a $30 commission will amount to just 2% of that investment.

You can find lists of discount brokers in financial magazines at your local library. *SmartMoney* magazine, for example, reviews discount brokers every year in its July issue. Online at the Fool, we've got a special Discount Broker Center, too, with guidance on how to choose a brokerage, as well as information on a bunch of brokerages: www.Fool.com/dbc.

If your funds are limited, check whether the company offers a direct stock purchase plan, allowing you to bypass brokers entirely. Not all companies have them, but an increasing number do. Aim to pay no more than 2% in commissions.

---

### 255 I keep reading that the Wall Street bull run is over and we're heading into a recession. What's the long-term small investor to do? I've got 20 years until retirement. Do I pretend to be smart and sell? Or do I hang in there?

We don't time or attempt to predict the market. We go on historical long-term trends. As long as you won't need your money for five (or ideally 10 or more) years, we think it's best to just leave it in the stock market. It's true that the market does crash now and then, but it also recovers. And, since no one knows exactly *when* crashes will occur, by selling prematurely you'd be likely to miss out on gains while trying to avoid losses.

According to a 1994 University of Michigan study, 95% of the stock market's cumulative gain between 1963 and 1993 occurred in just 1.2% of the trading days (about 90 days out of 7,500). Investors trying to time the market and sitting out any of those few days would have sacrificed significant portfolio performance.

As long as your money isn't needed in the near future, you're probably best off remaining in stocks for the long haul. If the market crashes, you'll have time to ride out the recovery.

## 256 I've heard that online chat boards are full of stock hypesters. Should I really avoid them? Don't you have these boards at Fool.com?

Let's define our terms first. Chat rooms are where people can "talk" online in real time, typing interactive "conversations." Only people who are there at the same time are communicating with each other. With chats, there often isn't any record of who said what once the chat is finished. It's a somewhat ephemeral form of communication.

Discussion boards (or message boards), meanwhile, are where people post messages that can be read later. At boards.Fool.com, for example, we have hundreds of boards for individual companies and for various investment topics and issues. These messages remain available indefinitely. You can post a question and come back an hour or a week later to see who has responded to it. If you find a board you like, you can read posts on it going back several years.

Although some discussion boards do get unruly and harbor hypesters, they're not all like that. In Fooldom, we've got staffers strolling through our boards, keeping the peace (and cracking jokes). We remove posts that violate our rules, as we want our corner of cyberspace to be friendly and welcoming. Discussion boards can be great places to get answers to your questions and to learn about companies that interest you. Give 'em a whirl.

## 257 How does online trading work? Is it something your average Joe can do?

Millions of average Joes and Josephines across America are successfully trading online. Pretty much all you need is a computer, a modem, and access to the World Wide Web. Most brokerages offering online trading do so through their websites. You simply open an account by filling out some paperwork and mailing in a check to the brokerage of your choice. Then click over to its website, log on via a password, and proceed to check the status of your account or place a trade order. All reputable online brokerages have security measures in place. Read up on them first at the website, to ease your mind.

Many investors comfortable with making their own decisions find online trading preferable to old-fashioned alternatives. It's cheaper, with some rates as low as $7 or less per trade versus full-service broker fees of up to hundreds of dollars. A few brokerages now even offer free trades to customers who meet certain criteria. Online, you can examine orders carefully before placing them, and you don't have to listen to 101 Strings play "Stairway to Heaven" while waiting for the next available broker.

## 258 What are some common mistakes that investors make?

Here are a few common mistakes:
- **Racking up credit card debt**. It feels like free money, but it isn't. High interest rates increase your debt, making it harder and harder to pay off. That's reverse investing!

- **Not investing soon enough**. You're rarely too young or too old to invest. Kids have the most to gain from many decades of stock appreciation, but even retirees can benefit from leaving in stocks whatever money they won't need for five or ten years.

- **Investing too conservatively**. Any long-term investment is likely to grow most rapidly in stocks.

- **Over- or under-diversifying**. If all your eggs are in two or three baskets, you're exposed to too much risk. If you have too many baskets to count, then you probably aren't able to keep up with each company. Between five and 15 stocks is a manageable number for most people.

- **Focusing inordinately on a stock's price**. Contrary to popular opinion, a "cheap" stock isn't a bargain. Penny stocks — those trading for less than $5 per share — are often risky and dangerous. A $150 stock can actually be a bargain and, if your funds are limited, you can always just buy a few shares.

- **Investing in what you don't understand**. The more familiar you are with how companies you invest in work and how well they're performing, the fewer unpleasant surprises you're likely to encounter.

- **Relying on the advice of others.** It's great to learn from others, but ultimately you should learn enough to make your own decisions. You're the one who cares the most about your finances.

- **Not tracking your returns.** Shrug off this duty at your own peril. You always want your investment returns to be (in the long run) beating a benchmark or market average such as the S&P 500. Otherwise, you might as well match it by investing in an index fund.

- **Impatience.** Building great wealth takes time.

Perhaps the worst mistake is never taking the time to learn about investing. You're not making that one, though, if you're reading and thinking about the topics in this book!

# Wall Street's Ways

*Wall Street's ways are mysterious, and this has served the fi-nancial services industry rather well over the years. The less you know and understand about how stock markets, broker-ages, and investment banks work, the more likely you'll be to let professionals manage your money. You don't have to be in the dark anymore, though. This chapter will explain some of the workings of the financial establishment.*

## 259 What is the origin of Wall Street?

It all started in the early 1600s when the Dutch had a colony called "New Amsterdam" on what is now Manhattan. It was even then a region devoted to commercial enterprises, with much trading going on. When the Dutch began to fear trouble from English colonies to the north, they built a wall to protect themselves. Unfortunately for the Dutch though, the attack did come, but by sea. New Amsterdam be-came New York, and in New York City you'll now find Wall Street where the wall used to stand.

New York's commercial spirit flourished, as did the city itself. Philadel-phia was also thriving, and that's where America's first stock mar-ket was established, in 1790. The New York Stock Exchange (NYSE) came soon after. The NYSE traces its origins to some traders meet-ing regularly under a buttonwood tree in 1792. It was formally or-ganized in 1817.

Today the term "Wall Street" often refers to the financial establishment. Many of America's (and the world's) financial institutions are based in New York City on and around Wall Street, but you'll find many that are located elsewhere.

## 260 How do stockbrokers get paid?

Brokers are generally paid by salary, commissions on sales, or a mix of both. It depends on the brokerage they work for. If the bulk of your broker's compensation depends on commissions, look out; that system motivates him to help himself to heavy commission rewards from you by actively and needlessly trading your account. That's called "churning." A better arrangement is for brokers to get paid flat salaries with bonuses for results that outperform the market averages.

## 261 What do stockbrokers do in their jobs?

Brokers are agents who take and fill your orders to buy and sell stocks and other securities. They charge commissions for these services, and in some cases they also offer you advice and make recommendations.

A former broker recently revealed to us how he was trained and under what conditions brokers typically work. He explained that it was hard to land the job of broker, as his educational background (BS in Business and an MBA) and training counted far less than his lack of prior sales experience. His on-the-job training included a course actually called "Gorilla Cold Calling," covering how to call and sell to as many prospects as possible. Prospects were found by looking in the Yellow Pages for doctors, lawyers, and the like.

Every morning there was a "Squawk Box" call from the home office on Wall Street, listing stocks upgraded or downgraded by analysts that day. These represented reasons to call clients and urge them to buy or sell (generating all-important commissions). The brokers were updated weekly on new investments to push, such as complicated options strategies or limited partnerships that could be pitched as tax shelters. They were also given lists of stocks that the firm held in inventory and needed to get rid of. These were to be aggressively sold to clients, "commission-free." Calls were often made during dinner hours, and clients were urged to decide immediately. ("Commission-free if you buy tonight!") Contests were even held, with prizes awarded to those who generated the most sales.

This is just one broker's experience, but from what we've heard, it's a fairly common one. It's true that many brokers are good people who do well for their clients. But, sadly, many are simply salespeople, ringing up commissions to get ahead. We think this represents an unacceptable conflict of interest. Financial professionals should be compensated based on how well they manage your money, not how often they churn it.

---

## 262 Is there any way I can check on my stockbroker to see if he's gotten into hot water in the past?

You bet. The National Association of Securities Dealers (NASD) recently unveiled a new public disclosure program. It's designed to help investors gather information on brokers and brokerages to help them steer clear of the Snidely Whiplashes of the brokerage world.

Information available includes employment history, criminal felony charges and convictions, bankruptcies, consumer complaints, formal investigations, terminations of employment, outstanding liens or judgments, and much more. The program isn't perfect, though. At the moment, not all the information investors might want is available, and not all information is accessible online. Still, this is a big step toward protecting investors.

Visit the program online at www.nasdr.com/2000.htm or call the Public Disclosure hotline at 1-800-289-9999.

---

## 263 If I open an account with a discount broker for $10,000 and only invest $5,000 of it at first, is the remaining $5,000 earning anything while it sits there?

It usually is. Most brokerages park your extra wampum in money market funds, where you'll earn monthly returns that are a little better than those from a savings account.

## 264 What is a "cold call"?

You've got a cold call on your hands when a broker you don't know calls you out of the blue, usually interrupting your dinner, to urge you to buy some security.

If you're going to do business with any cold-calling broker, first do a little digging. Check out their regulatory background by calling NASD Regulation's Public Disclosure Hotline at 1-800-289-9999 or visit the website at www.nasdr.com/2000.htm.

If you've already had a run-in with a cold caller from the dark side, report the incident. You can do so by calling the SEC at 202-942-9634 or going to their website at www.sec.gov. Or you can contact the North American Securities Administrators Association (NASAA) and ask for the contact information for your local securities regulator. NASAA can be reached at 1-888-846-2722 and at www.nasaa.org.

You can learn more about how to deal with cold callers by visiting www.nasdr.com/2560.htm — and you can complain about unscrupulous ones there, too. The Securities and Exchange Commission (SEC) also offers some good guidance on the topic. Pop over to the SEC website at www.sec.gov/consumer/search.htm and search for the term "cold call."

Here's some info on cold calls, drawn from both of those sites:
- You don't have to accept these calls. You can just say you're not interested and hang up. You can also ask to be put on any firm's "Do Not Call" list.
- Cold callers should introduce themselves, promptly offering their name, the name of the firm they represent, their firm's address and phone number, and that they're calling to sell you something.
- Cold callers should not threaten or frighten you, and shouldn't be annoying you by calling again and again. They should be polite.
- Be very concerned if they're using high-pressure sales maneuvers on you. Don't believe that you "Must act today!" Be extremely skeptical of any "once-in-a-lifetime opportunity" and any "guaranteed" returns, especially very high returns.
- A cold caller should be happy to send you written information on any investment that they recommend.

If you think all this is a lot to remember about cold callers, you can just remember these two words instead: *Hang up.*

That's right. If a cold-calling broker really has a valuable stock to offer, he or she wouldn't have to sell it by persuading strangers to buy it. People would be snapping up shares on the open market. Stocks that cold callers try to sell are often ones that no one else wants, that their firm is trying to unload.

---

## 265 I just learned that my broker is holding my stocks in "street name." What does this mean?

Stocks registered in street name are listed as belonging to your broker, not you. Don't be alarmed, though — this is a routine, accepted practice. Shares registered under your broker's name can be traded electronically by phone or computer. Since the brokerage is in possession of the shares, they can be traded in a matter of minutes. The alternative involves requesting to receive your shares in your own name when you place a buy order or asking your broker to transfer street-name-held shares to your name (for which there may be a fee). If the shares are in your name and you hold the certificates, you'll have to keep them in a secure place, and when you want to sell them you'll have to mail them in or hand-deliver them to your broker. It's more convenient to simply let the shares be held in street name.

If your stocks are held in street name, that does not mean they aren't owned by you and aren't insured. It's merely an artificial classification designed to facilitate trading. Consider that, as of the end of 1999, fewer than half of IBM's 1.4 million shareholders had shares registered in their own name. The rest owned shares through brokerages, banks, and other financial institutions.

---

## 266 What is an "index"?

An index is a group of stocks, the performance of which is measured as a whole. Some are large, containing hundreds or thousands of companies. These are often used to gauge the performance of the overall market, as with an index such as the S&P 500. Other indexes are smaller, or more focused, perhaps containing just small companies or pharmaceutical companies or Latin American companies.

Indexes aren't things you invest in, though. To meet the needs of people interested in investing in various indexes, index mutual funds were created. If you want to invest in a certain index, for example, you would invest in an index fund based on it.

## 267 What is the Dow Jones Industrial Average?

Created in 1896 by Charles Dow, who also established *The Wall Street Journal*, the "Dow" is an index of 30 major American companies chosen to represent U.S. industry. It's probably the world's best-known index.

The 30 companies that make up the Dow don't change much from year to year. In fact, typically, many years go by with no change at all. Still, every now and then a few companies are ejected from the Dow to make room for some upstarts. Of the original component companies, General Electric is probably the only name familiar to most investors today. Laclede Gas, Distilling & Cattle Feeding, Tennessee Coal & Iron, and American Cotton Oil are no longer the blue chips they once were.

The most recent big shake-up in Dow component companies occurred in October of 1999, when Sears, Union Carbide, Goodyear Tire & Rubber Co., and Chevron were removed so that Home Depot, Microsoft, Intel, and SBC Communications could be added. This was a milestone, as Microsoft and Intel were the first additions coming from the Nasdaq Stock Market and not the more venerable New York Stock Exchange.

The Dow is a familiar name to most Americans, because it has been used as a market proxy by the media for decades. Until recently, a newscaster might have reported on the state of the entire stock market simply by saying, "The Dow was up 40 points today." It's more common these days for the media to report on other market measures as well, such as the S&P 500 (an index of *500* of the biggest companies around) and the Nasdaq (with about 5,000 companies).

## 268 Which 30 companies make up the Dow Jones Industrial Average?

Here's a list, as of early 2001:

| | |
|---|---|
| Alcoa | IBM |
| American Express | Intel |
| AT&T | International Paper |
| Boeing | Johnson & Johnson |
| Caterpillar | McDonald's |
| Citigroup | Merck |
| Coca-Cola | Microsoft |
| Disney | Minnesota Mining & |
| DuPont | Manufacturing (3M) |
| Eastman Kodak | Morgan, J.P., Chase and Co. |
| ExxonMobil | Phillip Morris |
| General Electric | Procter & Gamble |
| General Motors | SBC Communications |
| Hewlett-Packard | United Technologies |
| Home Depot | Wal-Mart Stores |
| Honeywell | |

The list could change at any time, but it doesn't change too often. This list may remain correct for years. For the latest on the Dow's component companies, head to: http://averages.dowjones.com/home.html (note: no "www").

## 269 How is the Dow Jones Industrial Average calculated?

The Dow is essentially the average price of its 30 component stocks. This may seem strange, though, with the Dow recently around 10,000 and none of the 30 stocks trading anywhere near $10,000 per share.

On average, though, the shares really *would* trade in the neighborhood of $10,000 — *if* they had never been split, issued dividends, or undergone major changes such as spin-offs or mergers during the time they were listed in the index.

For example, consider a share of Microsoft. If you bought one share of the company when it came public in 1986, it would have been worth less than $100. But, as of the time of this writing, the stock has split eight times and that single share has become 144 shares, each worth about $50 today. Total it up, and that single initial share has grown to be worth roughly $7,200.

Today, though, most stocks don't trade at such lofty levels — thanks to events such as stock splits. To get from current stock price levels to the larger index number, a number called the "divisor" is used. Here's how it works. If General Electric falls four points, you just divide four by the divisor (which is adjusted frequently, and was 0.17677618 last time we checked). This shows that this drop will decrease the DJIA by 22.6 points (4 divided by 0.17677618 equals 22.6). The overall average is calculated by adding up the current stock prices of the 30 stocks, and then dividing by the divisor.

## 270 What are some of the other indexes?

There's a bunch, with each one representing a particular group of companies. I'll highlight just a few. The most famous one is the Dow Jones Industrial Average ("the Dow"), which includes 30 flagship American giants, such as ExxonMobil, Wal-Mart, Merck, Coca-Cola, and DuPont. Similarly, the S&P 500 also focuses on large companies, including 500 of America's biggest and best. Here are a few other major indexes:

**Russell 1000 Index**
A market-cap-weighted index made up of the 1,000 biggest U.S. companies in the Russell 3000 Index, representing about 92% of the value of all companies in the U.S. market.

**Russell 2000 Index**
A market-cap-weighted index made up of the 2,000 smallest U.S. companies in the Russell 3000 Index. This index is commonly used to measure the performance of the universe of small American companies.

**Russell 3000 Index**
A market-cap weighted index made up of the 3,000 largest U.S. companies, representing about 98% of the value of all companies in the U.S. market.

### Standard & Poor's MidCap 400 Index

A market-capitalization-weighted index composed of 400 companies with market values between roughly $200 million and $25 billion. This index measures the performance of mid-size American firms.

### Wilshire 4500 Equity Index

A benchmark index made up of the Wilshire 5000 Equity Index, excluding the companies in the Standard & Poor's 500 Index. For those who own only or primarily S&P 500 index funds, purchasing shares of the Wilshire 4500 would provide exposure to all of the rest of the market. This index contains and measures about 6,500 mid-cap and small companies.

### Wilshire 5000 Equity Index

A benchmark index made up of all U.S. stocks regularly traded in the U.S. market. The name Wilshire 5000 is somewhat of a misnomer — although it was more or less accurate at the time of the naming, there are now more than 7,000 companies included. This is a "total market" index.

There are many more indexes. Some are for international regions such as Latin America or the Far East. Others address sectors such as utilities, semiconductors, the Internet, and fried chicken. (Just kidding about the chicken.)

---

## 271 What is the New York Stock Exchange?

The NYSE, as it's commonly referred to, is the oldest stock exchange in the United States, tracing its roots back to a partnership agreement in 1792. It's the seemingly chaotic place you often see in the background behind reporters on CNBC. Roughly a billion shares of stock trade hands on the NYSE each day.

---

## 272 What is the Nasdaq?

The Nasdaq was created in 1971 as the world's first electronic stock market. It was originally an acronym for the National Association of Securities Dealers Automated Quotation system. Today, it considers "Nasdaq" a word, and refers to itself as the Nasdaq Stock Market. You can learn about it at the Nasdaq website, www.nasdaq.com.

Some factoids from the site:

- Nasdaq ranks second among the world's securities markets in terms of dollar volume. It lists roughly 5,000 companies, considerably more than the 3,000-some listed on the New York Stock Exchange.
- Trading volume often exceeds one billion shares per day and has surpassed two billion on occasion.
- More than 2,000 Nasdaq-listed companies have market values above $100 million. More than 600 have values topping $1 billion.
- The combined market value of all Nasdaq companies is more than $5 trillion.

## 273 What are OTC stocks?

OTC officially stands for "over-the-counter," but "over-the-computer" is more appropriate today. Long ago, to buy or sell a stock that didn't trade on a stock exchange, you would call your broker. He would call another broker and make the trade over the phone — not a terribly efficient system. Then, in 1971, the Nasdaq was established, offering an automated stock quotation and trading system. Suddenly, it was much easier to get a good price on your transaction, and trading activity could be monitored.

Stocks listed on exchanges are traded face-to-face at one location, in "trading pits." All others are OTC stocks, traded electronically via a network of dealers across the country. The Nasdaq market is the main OTC system in America, listing some 5,000 companies. It encompasses a range of firms, from young, relatively unknown enterprises to behemoths such as Microsoft and Intel. Thousands of more obscure OTC companies that don't meet Nasdaq's listing requirements trade separately, often with their prices listed only once daily, on "pink sheets." Often, little information is available about these companies, and they're frequently penny stocks.

## 274 What does "triple-witching hour" mean? Should I be scared?

Triple witching occurs on the third Friday of March, June, September, and December. On that day, stock options, stock-index options, and stock-index futures all simultaneously expire. The witching "hour" is the one before the market closes on that day (currently from 3:00 to 4:00 p.m. ET), when traders often rock the boat, trading for profits before the final bell.

If you're a good Fool, though, you won't pay much attention to the hubbub, since options and futures represent contracts based on short-term pricing rather than long-term business growth. You'll find the Fool's favorite triple witches gathered around a boiling cauldron — in *Macbeth*.

---

## 275 What are ADRs?

American Depositary Receipts, or ADRs and the similar American Depositary Shares (ADS) make it possible for folks in America to easily buy and sell shares of foreign companies that don't normally trade on U.S. exchanges. Without them, if you wanted to buy stock in Volkswagen AG, you'd have to convert your dollars into euros, and then somehow buy shares on the German DAX stock exchange. Through ADRs, shares of Volkswagen are held by an American financial institution overseas and you can trade shares with U.S. dollars. ADR holders are entitled to dividends and capital gains, but they have no voting rights.

---

## 276 What are these buy-side and sell-side analysts I occasionally hear about?

First, much of the stock trading each day occurs between large institutions, such as pension funds and mutual funds. To determine which stocks to buy and which stocks to sell, these institutions rely on the research and opinions of analysts.

Analysts who work for brokerages, dispensing recommendations to clients, are sell-side analysts. Buy-side analysts don't sell their research to outsiders. They work for mutual fund companies or other financial institutions and give recommendations internally, almost exclusively to portfolio managers and other money managers.

It might make more sense if you imagine a retail situation, where you're shopping for a new broom at Sweep City (ticker: BRUM). The guy who works there, describing and recommending various brooms to you, would be the sell-side clerk. He's out to drum up business and make sales. Meanwhile, a friend of yours who's giving you advice on why you should or shouldn't buy brooms at these prices would be on the buy-side, aligned with you, the buyer.

## 277 What does it mean when a brokerage announces that it is initiating coverage of a particular stock? Should I pay attention to this?

Full-service brokerages and investment banks typically employ analysts to follow and study various companies. The analysts issue recommendations that are passed on to broker clients and others. When a brokerage initiates coverage of a company, it means that the company is now being followed by the firm and that the brokerage has an opinion on it.

Examples of recommendations are "hold," "near-term attractive," "long-term buy," and "market outperform." You'll rarely see a "sell" recommendation, though. Because these recommendations usually come from organizations with investment banking operations, the analysts probably don't want to burn any bridges with current or potential investment banking clients by being too negative. So rather than cry "sell," most firms issue nothing worse than a "hold" rating — and sometimes a "market underperform" rating.

A *Fortune* magazine article from July 2000 pointed out, "Of the 33,169 buy, sell and hold recommendations made by stock analysts last year, only 125 were pure sells. That's 0.3%." Also amazing is that 23,551 of the recommendations were "buy" or "strong buy" — fully 71%. Clearly, analysts tend to wax positive in their ratings.

It's smart to not put much stock in these ratings. Still, though, many analysts do offer excellent research. In preparing their reports, analysts typically speak with corporate executives, model expected performance, and make estimates of future earnings per share (EPS). Although analyst reports are often reserved for company clients, you can sometimes get copies from your brokerage, from the company that was analyzed, or from online services such as www.multexinvestor.com.

## 278 Am I imagining it, or is there some conflict of interest when a brokerage keeps upgrading and downgrading a stock, and its brokers are recommending buying and selling it?

We've also noticed that. When brokerage analysts announce rating changes, such as from "buy" to "outperform," it creates an opportunity for brokers to call clients and recommend purchases or sales. And, the more buying and selling there is, the more commissions will be generated for the firm and the brokers.

The ratings changes often strike us as weird, too. Consider the difference between "buy" and "outperform." If a company will outperform, shouldn't you buy? And what about "accumulate"? How can you accumulate without buying? The difference between "buy" and "strong buy" is similarly confusing — either way, the advice appears to be that you should pick up some shares.

## 279 What is "churning"?

Look up the word "churn" in the *Merriam-Webster Dictionary* and you'll find three definitions. The first two should be familiar: 1) "to agitate (milk or cream) in a churn to make butter" and 2) "to stir or agitate violently, to make (as foam) by so doing." The third is one that we at the Fool like to point out to people: 3) "to make (the account of a client) excessively active by frequent purchases and sales, primarily to generate commissions."

In other words, take a stroll down Wall Street and listen intently, and you might hear the sound of stockbrokers and money managers shaking and shuffling your portfolio. The system is flawed, both for stockbrokers and mutual fund managers, and as a result the portfolios of individual investors can suffer. Billions of dollars are lost each year due to churning.

You see, many stockbrokers are paid based on the number of trades they make in your account, not on how well that account performs. Even if your broker is good and has your money invested in growing companies, she might still frequently be moving you out of one good company and into another. Each transaction results in a profit for the brokerage — regardless of how it fares for you.

Churning is also a problem in the mutual fund industry. Fund managers are so pressured to beat the market each year that they can't simply be patient with solid investments that are temporarily doing poorly. Mutual funds that buy and sell often have what is called a high "turnover rate." It shouldn't surprise you that the funds with the highest turnover rates are often those that consistently lose to the market averages.

Commissions aren't the only things hurting the churned investor. Consider taxes. Any stocks you've held for more than a year get taxed at the preferable long-term capital gains rate, which is 20% for most people. Short-term gains are taxed at your ordinary income tax rate, which can be as high as 39%, almost twice as much as long-term capital gains taxes. If your account or fund is being churned, you're probably paying more in taxes than you'd want to.

## 280  What is "front running"?

Front running occurs when a financial expert talks up a company after having bought into it himself.

Imagine that a mutual fund manager is bullish on a company called Magazine Aromatics (ticker: WHIFF). If she buys some shares for her personal portfolio and then begins buying many shares for her fund, that will drive the price up and she'll profit. Similarly, she might buy many shares of a company for her fund and then appear on television singing the company's praises. These are instances of front running.

## 281  What does "pump and dump" mean?

It's the illegal act of buying shares in a company, hyping it to pump up the share price so that you profit, and then dumping your shares quickly before they fall in value. Since this practice is usually done with small and volatile stocks, your selling will likely contribute to the stock's rapid downfall.

Steer clear of penny stocks (those trading under $5 per share), as they are more easily manipulated, and be wary of any hype that you might run across about small obscure companies you've never heard of.

## 282 What are "hedge funds"?

Hedge funds grew quickly in popularity in the '90s, more than doubling in number. While the word "hedge" might conjure up images of investors cautiously hedging their bets, hedge funds are often extra-risky, extra-volatile investment vehicles that demand huge upfront investments, sometimes in the millions. You're unlikely ever to invest in one, but it's good to understand what they are and aren't — if only to impress colleagues at the water cooler.

Let's leaf through some of their qualities. Like mutual funds, hedge funds comprise the pooled money of multiple investors, which is then invested by a professional money manager. However, unlike mutual funds, hedge funds are not regulated by the Securities and Exchange Commission, are not permitted to advertise, and their managers don't have to be registered investment advisers. In addition, they're not open to any investor: Only "accredited investors" need apply. These are folks earning upwards of $200,000 per year and who are worth more than a million smackers.

Since hedge fund managers are relatively unfettered by restrictions, they can and do take many more risks than ordinary investors or mutual fund managers. They frequently invest aggressively in options and futures, short stocks, buy on margin (use borrowed money), and make currency bets. Because of their frequent trading, hedge funds can also rack up considerable amounts in taxable capital gains.

In the right hands, hedge funds can work. Billionaire philanthropist George Soros' Quantum Fund, for example, reportedly returned an average of 33% per year over some three decades, before stumbling a bit in early 2000. More often, though, hedge funds don't fare nearly as well. According to Van Hedge Fund Advisors, the Van U.S. Hedge Fund Index underperformed the Standard & Poor's 500 between 1995 and 1999. Poorly performing managers still have reason to smile, though, as they typically take a big chunk of fund profits — as much as 25%.

Regardless of fund performance, they also command an annual management fee of roughly 1% to 3% of assets under management.

## 283 I've heard of warrants in law enforcement, but what's a warrant on Wall Street?

Like the part-man, part-beast Minotaur of Greek mythology, warrants share characteristics of both stocks and options. They trade like stocks, but unlike stocks, don't represent real chunks of companies. Instead, like an option, a warrant gives you the right to buy a stock at a preset price during a pre-set time period.

Most options expire within a few months. Warrants, however, are usually good for a few years, until the company "calls" them. Calling essentially forces holders to exercise the warrants by buying the stock at the pre-set price.

Like options, warrants are more volatile than their underlying stocks. Their appeal is that your money can buy you many more warrants than shares of stocks. This leverage can help you make more moolah than if you simply bought the stock, but it's also a lot riskier, as your warrants can end up close to worthless if the market doesn't go your way.

## 284 Can you tell me what an "institutional investor" is?

Institutional investors include mutual funds, pension funds, banks, and insurance companies. Trading in large volumes, they can account for more than two-thirds of daily market activity.

## 285 What are these "whisper numbers" I've heard about?

When a company is about to report its quarterly earnings, investors are usually eager to see if it will meet, beat, or miss the consensus estimate of Wall Street analysts. Apparently, though, some people have tired of this game. They now focus on *rumored* estimates called whisper numbers. We wondered just who was doing this whispering until, much to our surprise, we received a phone call at Fool HQ asking for *our* whisper number for a particular company. (We declined.)

So, next time you hear of a whisper number, know that those seeking it out are asking just about anyone for their guess — even Fools!

---

**286** **What does it mean when a financial guru on television says that a stock is "overbought"?**

The term "overbought" suggests that too many people were trying to buy the stock, sending the share price higher than it should be. The guru is essentially making a short-term call on a stock price, which is most likely futile.

---

**287** **Why would a stock close at one price on one day, but then commence trading the next day a few dollars lower?**

Stocks often open higher or lower if there's been some major news released after the market close the day before. For example, if the underwater dress shoe company Wet Loafer Inc. (ticker: SQSHY) announced it was recalling all its wingtips, many more sell orders than buy orders might accumulate overnight. Before trading begins, the share price would probably be adjusted southward, to better match buys with sells.

---

**288** **How should I make sense of stock quotes I see online or in a newspaper?**

You just need to familiarize yourself with the information they present. Let's review a typical online stock quote. Here's one for General Electric supplied by America Online in January of 2001:

GE - GENL ELECTRIC
Exchange:.........................NYSE comp
Delay:................................at least 20 minutes
Last Price:.........................44.375 at 12:51 EST
Change: ............................Down 1.1875 (-2.61%)
High:................................46.25 at 9:34 EST
Low:................................43.75 at 12:10 EST

```
Open: ...............................45.9375
Previous Close: .................45.5625 on 1/8
Volume: ............................12,155,300
30-Day Avg. Volume: ..........18,461,000
Shares Outstanding: ...........9,908,802,000
Market Cap.: .....................439,703,088,750
52-Week High:...................60.50
52-Week Low:....................41.64
Beta: ................................1.23
Yield:................................1.40%
P/E Ratio: ........................36.37
EPS: .................................1.22
```

Here's the same listing, with some explanatory comments after each line item:

GE - GENL ELECTRIC
   This is the company's ticker symbol and its name.

Exchange:...........................NYSE comp
   GE trades on the NYSE (vs. Nasdaq or somewhere else).

Delay:.................................at least 20 minutes
   This information is at least 20 minutes old.

Last Price:...........................44.375 at 12:51 EST
   This is the last price GE shares traded at.

Change: .............................Down 1.1875 (-2.61%)
   This is 1.1875 (or -2.61%) lower than the previous closing price.

High:...................................46.25 at 9:34 EST
   The high price so far today has been $46.25 per share.

Low:....................................43.75 at 12:10 EST
   The low price so far today has been $43.75 per share

Open: ................................45.9375
   The shares began trading at $45.9375 each today.

Previous Close: ..................45.5625 on 1/8
  The stock last traded at $45.5625 in the last trading session.

Volume: .............................12,155,300
  So far 12,155,300 shares have changed hands today.

30-Day Avg. Volume: ...........18,461,000
  Over the last month, an average of 18.461 million shares of GE traded daily.

Shares Outstanding: ............9,908,802,000
  GE has 9.9 billion shares "outstanding" — in existence.

Market Cap.: ......................439,703,088,750
  GE's market capitalization (shares outstanding times current price)
  is $439.7 billion.

52-Week High:....................60.50
  In the last year, the highest GE stock has traded was $60.50.

52-Week Low:....................41.64.
  In the last year, GE's lowest stock price was $41.64.

Yield:.................................1.40%
  GE's current dividend yield (annual dividend divided by current
  stock price) is 1.40%.

P/E Ratio: ..........................36.37
  GE's price divided by its trailing 12-month earnings per share is
  36.37

EPS: ..................................1.22
  GE's earnings per share over the last year have totaled $1.22.

Newspaper stock listings are very similar. They'll usually contain many,
but not all, of the above items. Newspapers also list stock information as of the previous day's close, whereas online quotes are updated continually throughout each trading session.

**289** On TV stock tickers, I've often wondered what the "10.000s" is when I see something like "BLAH10.000s15 3/8."

The "10.000s" means 10,000 shares of BLAH have traded. For trades of 10,000 or more, the comma is changed to a period. If fewer than 10,000 shares are traded, the number is rounded to the nearest hundred and the last two zeros are removed. So BLAH 9s15 3/8 means 900 shares traded at a price of $15 3/8 per share. If no number of shares is indicated, it means that it's a "round lot" of 100 shares or an "odd lot" rounded to 100. (Please remember that I didn't make up this logic — I'm just trying to explain it.)

**290** What is a "block trade"?

It's a large order that has been placed in the stock market. The New York Stock Exchange defines it as an order involving at least 10,000 shares or amounting to at least $200,000 in total market value. The Nasdaq defines it as generally 10,000 shares or more.

**291** I keep hearing about "after-hours" trading, and I'm beginning to wonder if I'm at some great disadvantage to Wall Street on this score. Would you please tell me who gets to trade after hours and why?

Here's an explanation in the form of a short tale.

Imagine that you arrive at a Blockbuster video store to rent an action film just minutes after the store closes. Darn! But then, in the parking lot, you bump into another latecomer, looking to return a movie whose box depicts a tank-topped Woody Allen smooching a starlet while toting a high-powered rifle. What luck! You can rent the movie directly from him.

This is essentially what's going on with after-hours trading. Computerized systems such as Reuters's "Instinet" allow institutional investors to match buy and sell orders after the market closes. After-hours trading is perfectly legal... but it has, in the past, shut out individual investors.

The times have changed, though. As of 1999, a bunch of brokerages have set up after-hours trading systems that serve small investors. In addition, the New York Stock Exchange and Nasdaq Stock Market have both announced plans to offer extended trading hours in the near future.

It's nice that the proverbial "little guy" will have the same trading opportunities as the big banks, but these new opportunities shouldn't get any Fool's heart beating faster. As super-investor Warren Buffett has explained, he'd be perfectly happy with a market that just opened one day per year. Solid investment portfolios are very often the result of infrequent trading.

## 292 What is an "order imbalance"?

Order imbalances happen on stock exchanges such as the New York Stock Exchange when there are too many buy orders and not enough sell orders — or vice versa. When they occur, the exchange might halt trading temporarily, to allow more of the other kind of order to come in. This permits better matching of buyers and sellers, and makes prices less volatile.

You might see order imbalances happen whenever there's very good or bad news related to a company, and suddenly many people want in or out of its stock.

The Nasdaq stock market operates on more of a supply-and-demand basis, with its trading conducted between many market participants. It doesn't halt trading for order imbalances.

## 293 What's up with "circuit breakers" on Wall Street? What are they supposed to accomplish?

Instituted after the 1987 stock market crash, circuit breakers were designed to slow down market activity during major declines and surges. For example, when the Dow Jones Industrial Average moves a certain number of points in either direction, restrictions are placed on some computer-guided orders. In addition, trading of all U.S. stocks and futures are halted for various periods of time whenever the Dow Jones Industrial Average drops 10%, 20%, or 30% (based on the previous month's closing value).

As an example, at the time of this writing the Dow is hovering around 10,500, and a 1,050-point drop occurring before 2:00 p.m. would halt trading for one hour. A 3,150-point drop would bring all trading to a stop for the rest of the day.

Opinion is divided on the effectiveness of these restrictions. Some feel a cooling-off period is necessary, while others say it merely postpones the inevitable or even encourages selling. As long as you're a long-term investor, not trading hour-by-hour, circuit breakers shouldn't matter to you.

## 294 When a stock report mentions a "fair value" followed by a price, is that what the analyst thinks the stock is really worth, regardless of the actual current price?

Exactimundo. Analysts work with earnings estimates, growth rates, and other factors to determine fair values. Based on these target prices, they conclude whether a stock is under- or overvalued, in their opinion. These opinions vary between analysts and don't necessarily reflect the intrinsic value of the company.

Some Fools don't pay much attention to valuation and fair values. They figure that if they're buying truly high-quality companies and are planning to hold on to the stock for decades, then it shouldn't matter if they bought at a price that was ahead of itself. They point out that many wonderful companies appeared overvalued according to conventional measures, and people who avoided these companies based on valuation ended up missing great investment opportunities.

Other Fools disagree, believing that it can only help if you take the time to learn various valuation measures and if you focus your investments on stocks that appear undervalued. It's true that this approach should minimize your downside risk. These Fools would have you learn enough to determine your *own* fair values for stocks, rather than relying on the estimates of others, though.

## 295 What is a "market maker"?

You might think that when you buy stock you're getting those shares directly from a shareholder who's selling, but that isn't quite the case. Nasdaq-traded stocks are bought and sold through market makers. Maintaining a fluid market, they earn their keep by pocketing some or all of the spread between the purchase and sale price ("bid and ask price"). Market makers typically keep some shares in inventory, too. That way, if someone wants to buy shares and no one wants to sell at that time, the market maker can sell from inventory.

## 296 In my brokerage statement, I noticed that my broker is a "specialist" in one of the stocks that I hold. It seems odd that the brokerage would recommend this stock to me as a "good buy." Is something sneaky going on here?

The New York Stock Exchange assigns securities to various members of the exchange. These members are called "specialists"— it's their job to "make a market" in the security, by processing buy and sell orders fairly and efficiently. To keep orders flowing smoothly, they'll even buy and sell the security for their own account.

The fact that your brokerage is a specialist for the stock merely means that it buys and sells the stock for people. It may even result in better prices for you. When a brokerage has to rely on someone else to execute a trade, it often costs the customer more.

That said, brokerages frequently find themselves with too much of a certain stock on hand and may try to push it to customers. This happens more often than it should. When a firm is a specialist in a stock it recommends, you should be extra diligent in your research. You don't want less-than-first-class stock inventory dumped into your account. Better still, don't rely on the recommendations of others, but do your own research and make your own decisions as to what *you* want to buy.

## 297 Can you explain what "arbitrage" is?

Arbitrage is the practice of profiting from short-term differences in price. Imagine that you can buy stock in Rent-to-Own Underwear Inc. (ticker: EWWW) for $25 per share — in the United States. Meanwhile, you see that it's currently selling for $25.50 per share in England. If you simultaneously buy shares in America and sell the same number of shares in England, you've earned a profit of 50 cents per share (not counting commissions). This may not seem like much, but it adds up quickly if you're dealing with massive numbers of shares. That's why those who practice arbitrage are usually institutional investors with millions of dollars to invest.

# Understanding Stocks

*Once you have a handle on what a stock is and a rudimentary understanding of how the stock market works, you're ready to learn more about how stocks behave. This chapter addresses stocks in more detail, explaining how you should think about them and some basic ways to measure them.*

## 298 Why do stock prices go up and down?

If a company's profits keep growing, its stock price will follow suit — eventually. Corporate earnings drive stocks in the long run. In the short run, though, there are many different reasons stock prices flitter up and down. Some of these reasons matter and some don't. It does help, though, to understand the factors that can move a stock.

Some things that move stocks that matter to us Fools:
- The company's latest earnings report. Strong and growing earnings and profit margins may push a stock up, while rising debt or inventory may depress it.
- New products or services. Positive media coverage and strong market acceptance are cause for stock appreciation, while sluggish sales foreshadow depreciation.
- Earnings report pre-announcement. If the firm expects to underperform Wall Street's quarterly earnings estimates significantly, expect the stock to fall. If the firm hints of outperformance, expect a rise.

- News about the company's ongoing business operations. Landing a monstrous new, long-term contract bodes well, as does news that the company's methodical global expansion is proceeding at a rate 15% ahead of plans.

Some things that move stocks that we Fools ignore, or even chuckle at:
- Gurus on television or in financial magazines speculating that a company might be bought out at a premium price.
- Company insiders selling some shares.
- Soothsayers divining future stock prices by looking at charts of price movements.
- Crowds of people snapping up shares of "hot" stocks without understanding the industries involved.

Remember also that stock prices often rise or drop on rumors or hype — or for no reason at all. Perhaps a bird flapped its wings extra hard flying over the Zambezi River in Zambia and that set off a domino-like chain of events, eventually leading to people buying more shares than usual of a stock this morning. (This is a rather remote possibility, but hey — you never know.)

Sometimes stocks will also rise or drop just because other stocks in the same industry are rising or dropping. And if most of the market is slumping or surging, it will take many stocks along with it for the ride.

Don't sweat these small day-to-day moves. Focus on quarterly and annual earnings performance and the growth of the business over the next few years. Short-term pricing on the stock market can be irrational, but long-term values are driven by business growth.

---

**299** **I've noticed that stocks jump in price when they're added to the S&P 500 Index. Why is this, and is there any way to learn which companies will be added in the future?**

You've noticed correctly. When it was announced a few years ago that America Online would be added to the S&P 500, its shares quickly rose about 12%. More recently, news that handheld computer maker Palm Inc. had been tapped for an S&P 500 berth caused the stock to pop 13% in after-hours trading.

Companies get added to indexes regularly, replacing ones deemed no longer worthy or "representative" of the index, or ones that have merged with other companies and are no longer traded as a separate entity. These announcements draw the attention of investors, sending share prices up. And once the companies are added, index funds that mirror the holdings of the respective indexes will have to own these stocks — so they snap up shares, too.

Unfortunately, the stocks begin moving as soon as the announcements are made, before they're even officially added, so there's little time to sneak in and benefit. But, if you've invested in high-quality, growing companies, chances are you may eventually see some of them added to important indexes.

**300** **I often notice that when a company is downgraded by a big brokerage firm for underperforming earnings estimates, its stock plunges. If a company's financials are still solid, but it earns $87 million in a quarter instead of the expected $94 million, why should a brokerage have such power to depress the stock price?**

An earnings disappointment matters because the expectations that brokerages have are usually based on guidance from the company itself. Disappointments aren't the end of the world — many great companies have had regrettable quarters — but they certainly need to be explained.

Imagine that Pelczarski's Traveling Penguin Circus Inc. (ticker: FLIPR) steers analysts on Wall Street to project earnings of $52 million and $0.19 per share for its third quarter. If the company then reports only $41 million in profits and $0.15 per share, the investing community may feel they've been duped and worry that something is seriously wrong at Penguin HQ. Because of this, analysts may downgrade their ratings, perhaps from "buy" to "hold," further inspiring investors to bail.

Don't be that hasty, though. Wall Street's research can be very sound, but acting on recommendations such as "buy" or "sell" often isn't a good idea. Instead, pore through the earnings report and, if you still think the company has solid growth ahead, keep those penguins on ice.

## 301 Why would a company be downgraded and then see its stock price fall after it announces that it is purchasing another company?

It all depends on the particulars. Let's say you own shares in Office Automation Services Co. (ticker: ZIPZIP), which is growing quickly and doing very well. Both you and Wall Street expect continued rapid increases in sales and earnings.

Then one day the company announces that it's buying a typewriter retailer called Typewriter Land Inc. (ticker: QWERTY). Clearly, Typewriter Land is a less dynamic business. It's likely to slow down Office Automation's progress. This is why some analysts will downgrade Office Automation — because it's now a less attractive company. You might not be as eager to hang on to your shares, as well.

If, however, Office Automation announced that it was buying a company that could help it grow even faster, the news would likely draw investor interest, and might send shares up. It all depends on how effectively investors expect the merging parties to work together. Some mergers make great sense, while others are less promising.

## 302 Do stocks move more on rumors or news?

Well, they should move just on news, but history has shown us that rumors or vague announcements can also have major effects. Consider, for example, Amazon.com, which reported in 1999 that the next day it would make a big announcement. Immediately, its shares rocketed ahead more than 20%. Then, the next day, after the actual announcement that it would begin selling home improvement items, video games, software, and gifts, the shares quickly lost half that gain.

Well, you'd think the stock price would move only after the facts were out, wouldn't you? But stocks often move on nothing more than rumors, and once the stock price begins moving northward, more people tend to jump into the fray, pushing it higher. By the time the news is revealed or the rumor confirmed, a re-evaluation of its likely impact on the company often results in an adjustment downward in the stock price. This is the source of a well-known Wall Street maxim: "Buy on the rumor, sell on the news." As Fools, we don't follow that maxim, but if you ever hear someone say it, now you'll know what they mean.

## 303 Why is it that some good news from a company will launch its stock price higher, while other good news from it will have no effect at all?

It largely depends on what investors have been expecting. Sometimes news isn't really news to most people.

For example, imagine that people following McDonald Farms Inc. (ticker: EIEIO) have determined that sales really picked up in recent months. The stock price may have been steadily moving up as more people piled into it, excited by the company's growth prospects. Let's say McDonald suddenly reports that earnings rose 40% in the last quarter, more than the company had forecast. If that's what investors were expecting, the stock might not move much on the news. But, if investors were expecting a significantly higher or lower growth rate, you might see the stock jump up or down.

## 304 Is there any silver lining to falling stock prices?

There sure is. When you buy shares of stock or even a mutual fund, it's natural to start cheering the market on. After all, the old maxim says to buy low and sell high. It's not that simple, though.

Consider the words of Warren Buffett in his 1997 letter to Berkshire Hathaway shareholders: "A short quiz: If you plan to eat hamburgers throughout your life and are not a cattle producer, should you wish for higher or lower prices for beef? Likewise, if you are going to buy a car from time to time, but are not an auto manufacturer, should you prefer higher or lower car prices? These questions, of course, answer themselves."

Buffett continues, "But, now for the final exam: If you expect to be a net saver during the next five years, should you hope for a higher or lower stock market during that period? Many investors get this one wrong. Even though they are going to be net buyers of stocks for many years to come, they are elated when stock prices rise and depressed when they fall. In effect, they rejoice because prices have risen for the 'hamburgers' they will soon be buying. This reaction makes no sense. Only those who will be sellers of equities in the near future should be happy at seeing stocks rise. Prospective purchasers should much prefer sinking prices."

These words should ring true for anyone investing for the long haul — especially those just starting out. If you've just plunked your first thousand dollars into the stock market and plan to keep adding to it over the next decades, you'll benefit from falling prices in the short term. And by investing for more than 10 years, you smooth out the risk of owning common stocks.

This counter-intuitive perspective is also important if you're someone who regularly invests in stocks. Since you're buying stock perhaps every few months, you'll be able to get more shares with each payment if the prices are falling. Remember: It's not timing the market that matters, but your time *in* the market.

You can learn a lot from Buffett's engaging letters to shareholders. Read them online at http://www.berkshirehathaway.com.

## 305 Is it better to buy a stock before or after it splits?

That's like asking, "Should I eat this peanut butter and jelly sandwich before or after Mom cuts it in half?"

Stocks don't become more inexpensive when they split. True, you get more shares. But, each is worth less. Imagine that you own 100 shares of Sisyphus Transport Corp. (ticker: UPDWN). They're trading at $60 each for a total value of $6,000. When Sisyphus splits 2-for-1, you'll own 200 shares, worth about $30 each. Total value: (drum roll, please) $6,000. Yawn.

Some people drool over stocks about to split, thinking the price will surge. Stock prices sometimes do pop a little on news of splits, but these are artificial moves, sustainable only if the businesses grow to justify them. The real reason to smile at a split announcement is because it signals that management is bullish. They're not likely to split the stock if they expect the price to go down.

Splits come in many varieties, such as 3-for-2 or 4-for-1. There's even a "reverse split," when you end up with *fewer* shares, each worth more. Companies in trouble usually employ reverse splits to avoid looking like the penny stocks they are. If a stock is trading at a red-flag-raising $2 per share and it does a reverse 1-for-10 split, the price will rise to $20 and those who held 100 shares will suddenly own just 10 shares.

## 306 Why do companies split their stock?

Well, one reason is so that the price will remain psychologically appealing. Reducing a stock's price makes some investors think (incorrectly) that it's a better value.

Sometimes, not splitting would mean that few people could afford even a single share. If, in its 80-odd-year history as a public company, Coca-Cola had never once split its stock, one share would be priced at more than $300,000 today. Not too many people could afford even a single share. In fact, Coke has split so many times in its history that if you had bought just one share when it went public in 1919, you'd have more than 4,600 shares today.

Some companies split their stock fairly frequently, while it's a rare event for others. It largely depends on how rapidly the stock price is rising. Warren Buffett's Berkshire Hathaway has *never* split its stock. Accordingly, a share of Berkshire stock was trading for around $57,000 at the time of this writing. Buffett did spin off a lower-priced class of shares at one point, though — called "Class B shares" and sporting the ticker symbol BRK.B — to help investors of more modest means buy in.

With stocks, just as with any purchase, examine what you're getting for the price. Study the company and compare the stock price to other numbers, such as earnings. A low price might be inviting, but a $200 stock can be a better bargain than a $20 stock — and can be an even better buy than a $2 stock. If your funds are limited, you can just buy fewer shares of whatever company you'd like to buy into.

It's always fun to suddenly own more shares, but splits are like getting four quarters for a dollar. They're not cause for celebration.

---

### 307 When do stocks split? Would a stock priced at $40 split, or do most wait until they get near the $100 level?

There's no fast rule. Some companies split their stock at relatively low prices, such as $30, while others split after the price passes the $100 mark. Some rarely split, and trade well into three digits. Stock might be split merely to increase the number of shares outstanding, perhaps to meet a stock exchange requirement.

---

### 308 How does stock splitting affect a company's earnings, dividend, and fair value?

Stock splits are minor mathematical events that change numbers, but not value.

Let's say that the Dodgeball Supply Co. (ticker: WHAPP), trading at $50 per share, has reported $2.50 per share in earnings for the last year, and pays a $1.50 annual dividend. If it splits 2-for-1, the number of shares outstanding will double and will trade around $25 each. (Shareholders will own twice as many shares valued at about half their pre-split price.) Its previous earnings per share (EPS) will also be halved, to $1.25, and its annual dividend will be $0.75 per share.

If the stock's fair value had been $60 pre-split, it will be about $30 post-split. Its price-to-earnings ratio shouldn't change, as both the price and the EPS components have decreased in the same proportion. Its total market value is also unchanged.

---

### 309 Where can I find out about a company's recent stock splits? I'd also like to see a chart that shows me how the stock performed after its splits.

One good source is the horse's mouth. Call the company's investor relations department and ask. If you're online, head to http://quote.Fool.com. In the data section, type in a company's ticker symbol and choose "charts." When specifying what kind of chart you want to see, select "show splits." For lists of past and upcoming splits, visit www.streetwatch.com and the split calendar we offer at http://quote.Fool.com.

---

### 310 What happens if you buy a stock that is splitting between the record date and the actual pay date? Do you not get the additional shares?

You still get them if you buy between the two dates. The record date is mainly for accounting purposes and has no direct effect on the individual investor. Those who own shares on the day of the actual split, the pay date, get the benefit of the split shares. As long as you hold shares when the stock splits, you'll get your due.

---

### 311 I know the Fool avoids penny stocks, yet I see that your Rule Breaker Portfolio bought shares of America Online at 46 cents each. What gives?

You're looking not at hypocrisy, but at the effect of stock splits. The Rule Breaker Portfolio bought the stock at roughly $58 per share in 1994. Since then, it has split 2-for-1 seven times. Divide $58 by two seven times, and you get... just about 46 cents. Next time AOL splits 2-for-1, the cost basis will be just over 22 cents per share.

---

### 312 Why do dividend yields rise when stock prices fall?

It's because of a little simple math. Imagine the dividend yield as the fraction it is — the dollar amount of the annual dividend on top (the numerator) and the current share price on the bottom (the denominator).

Let's say the Light Saber Defense Systems Co. (ticker: ZHOOM ) pays out $3 per year in dividends and trades today at $100 per share. The yield is 3% (3 divided by 100 equals 0.03 or 3%). Drop the share price to $75 and the yield jumps to 4% (3 divided by 75 equals 0.04 or 4%). Raise the share price to $120 and the yield falls to 2.5%.

3/100 = 0.03 = 3%
3/75 = 0.04 = 4%
3/120 = 0.025 = 2.5%

Notice what happens if we keep the stock price steady at $100 per share and change the annual dividend amount from $2 to $3, and then to $4:

2/100 = 2%
3/100 = 3%
4/100 = 4%

The higher the dividend dollar amount in relation to the stock price, the higher the dividend yield, and vice versa. The higher the stock price in relation to the dividend dollar amount, the lower the dividend yield, and vice versa.

---

### 313 I read somewhere that dividends are taxed twice. Is this really true?

It's true. Consider Spray-On Socks Inc. (ticker: PFFFT). Let's say it rakes in $100 million in sales one year and, after subtracting expenses, retains $20 million as its operating profit. Well, Uncle Sam doesn't just pat the company on the back. He demands his share in taxes. Corporate income tax rates can reach 35% or higher. So, perhaps $13 million will remain after taxes as net profit.

If the company pays out some of these earnings as dividends to shareholders, the shareholders will recognize the dividends as income. Which means Uncle Sam will claim a chunk of that personal income in taxes. Ugh, that money has now been taxed twice — once on the company's tax return and once on the shareholder's tax return.

This is one reason why investors might prefer to see a company using its money to build more value for shareholders without paying out dividends. It's also why some companies are reducing dividends, opting instead to repurchase shares and reward shareholders in a tax-free way.

---

## 314 What does "ex-dividend" mean?

A company's dividend is not simply paid to whoever is holding the stock on the day the dividend is paid. Instead, an "ex-dividend" date is set, often several weeks before payday. If you buy shares of a dividend-paying stock on or after the ex-dividend date, you won't receive the upcoming dividend payment. The person who owned the stock when it went ex-dividend gets that chunk of change. Stocks trading ex-dividend often have an "x" next to their listing in newspapers.

You might think it would be a neat trick to buy such stocks just before they go ex-dividend, so that you can quickly profit from the dividend amount. But stock prices get adjusted downward around the ex-dividend date to compensate for the upcoming dividend payout. As Snidely Whiplash would mutter, "Curses! Foiled again!"

---

## 315 If I own shares in a company, and the company is bought out or merges with another company, what happens to my shares?

Several things could happen. If the firm is bought out for cash, you might receive a check for your shares. If it's bought with stock or there's a merger involving a stock swap, your shares might be replaced with shares of another company. The number of shares you get will be prescribed by an announced formula. Some deals involve both stock and cash.

When a deal you're interested in is announced, track down its press releases for details. If you can't find the press release, look for it or for the terms of the merger on the company's website —or just call the company's investor relations department ask them for the scoop.

---

## 316 If a company buys another company, not with cash but by issuing a bunch of new stock, doesn't that dilute the value

## of existing shares, hurting shareholders?

As long as the purchase price is fair and the deal makes strategic sense, shareholders shouldn't suffer. If, for example, Chocolate Inc. (ticker: CHOCO), valued at $500 million, buys Peanut Butter Inc. (ticker: PNUT-TY) by issuing $100 million in stock, then an investor would want the acquisition to increase the combined company's earnings by at least 20%. That's the amount of new stock Chocolate Inc. is issuing. In transactions like this, companies typically pay a premium for the acquired company up front, hoping that mixing peanut butter with chocolate will create even greater earnings down the road.

Many investors still prefer companies to pay for acquisitions in cash, especially if their stock is undervalued. Buying with overvalued stock can be a smart move, as a company can potentially buy a firm that is undervalued with stock that is richly valued.

## 317 What does it mean when a company's stock gets diluted?

Stock dilution happens when a company issues additional shares — decreasing, or diluting, the value of existing shares. For example, imagine In-Your-Face Telemarketing Inc. (ticker: RINGG), which has 100 million shares outstanding, trading at about $50 each. Its current market value is $5 billion (100 million times $50 equals $5 billion). Let's say that, to raise money, it issues an additional 10 million shares. The company is still valued at about $5 billion, but now that's divided among 110 million shares — so each share is worth roughly $45. The shares have been diluted in market value.

If the money raised is used to generate additional sales and earnings, long-term economic dilution might not occur. The money might end up generating enough to more than make up for the short-term dilution. But, if shares are issued to finance value-destroying projects or overly generous stock-option awards, then dilution is certain.

Companies are now required to report earnings per share (EPS) in two formats: basic and diluted. Focus on diluted numbers, as they take into account stock options, warrants, preferred stock, and convertible debt securities. These can be converted into common stock, diluting the value of existing shares.

## 318 Should I think favorably of a company buying back shares of its own stock?

In many cases, yes. Repurchasing shares with excess cash is an excellent way for a company to boost its stock price and please shareholders. It's also a sign of management's confidence in the firm. By announcing that it's buying back shares of its own stock, a company can signal that it thinks its stock is a good buy at current prices. Of course, it might also be the case that the firm can't think of anything more productive to do with the money. Buybacks aren't unilaterally good or bad.

## 319 Where can I find out what percentage of a company's stock is held by management?

Check the newspaper *Investor's Business Daily*. Insider holding percentages appear on Thursdays for New York Stock Exchange companies and on Mondays for Nasdaq companies. Many financial websites also have this data, including www.insite.dbc.com/tour/insider.html.

## 320 Should I pay attention to what percentage of a company's shares is owned by insiders or institutional investors?

When investigating small companies as possible investments, it's always good to learn who else owns shares.

Insider holdings are generally a good thing. Executives who own 30% of a company, for example, are motivated to make it succeed. The best employees and executives work harder when they work for themselves. As shareholders, they can see a one-to-one correlation between their efforts on the job and their compensation. Insiders buying shares is also usually a good sign, as it means they expect the shares to rise. Don't be alarmed by insider sales, though, unless there's a lot of them.

Institutions, such as mutual funds and pension funds, are major players. They buy or sell in large chunks, and whether a stock is in or out of their favor can have a big effect on its price.

Small firms usually have relatively few shares outstanding, and their total worth is modest. Imagine Scruffy's Chicken Shack (ticker: BUKBUK). It has 20 million shares outstanding, valued at $5 each. (Total market value: $100 million.) Institutions that might typically buy $10 million worth of shares cannot do so with Scruffy's without buying fully 10% of the entire company, something they're often prohibited from doing.

Here's where opportunity creeps in for Fools who discover Scruffy's and snap up shares early on. If Scruffy's is indeed a gem in the making, it will keep growing. In time, Wall Street will take notice. Institutions will begin buying shares, in their usual big way. All that demand will push up the price of the stock — and Fools can clap their hands in glee.

Discovering a small-but-growing company with significant insider ownership (perhaps 15% or more) and low institutional ownership is a promising prelude to finding a rewarding investment — provided all the financial measures are sound. You can call any public company and ask its investor relations department about insider and institutional ownership. Just remember that small companies are best suited to investors with a few years of experience under their belt.

## 321 Shouldn't I be worried about insider selling at a company in which I own shares?

Not necessarily. Imagine that you're a shareholder in Carrier Pigeon Communications (ticker: SQAWK) and its CEO, Frederick Shmedrick, has filed to sell 20,000 of his shares of company stock. This is insider selling. Does it mean that Carrier Pigeon is in trouble? Does Fred know something the rest of us don't know? Should we all sell our shares of SQAWK?

Some investors might worry about this, thinking that it's a bad sign. But the truth is that insider selling isn't necessarily something to fret about. Let's think about why Fred might be selling.

Maybe he really does think the company is in trouble. Or maybe he believes another investment holds better promise. Or possibly he just needs the money — to buy a house, to pay for his son Oswald's college education, or to bid at Sotheby's for Theodore Roosevelt's gilded ashtray.

Another reason many executives sell their shares is that stock options are the major component of their compensation package. This is particularly true at upstart technology companies. Some of these managers have worked for the company for a long time and have been fed stock options by the board of directors instead of big salaries. In many cases, they have most of their wealth tied up in stock, without much cash lying around. For them, cashing in some options is a fairly routine thing to do.

Executives sell for a variety of reasons. If you see an insider selling shares, it doesn't necessarily mean the company is going down in flames. There's always a chance that the insider does know some bad news, but it's just as likely that he simply needs some cash. You should definitely take a look at how many shares he is selling relative to his total ownership position. Insider sale reports should include that statistic — if they don't, consider calling the company and asking for that information.

Insider buying is a much better sign. After all, managers don't buy shares of stock unless they're believers. But, next time someone shouts that insiders are selling a stock you own, don't jump ship without doing a little research first.

## 322 What's the difference between a company's outstanding shares and its "float"?

All the shares a company has issued are its "shares outstanding." Company insiders may hold some, while the public owns the rest. Insider shares are usually held for a long time and are not traded too often, while shares in public hands trade more frequently. The shares owned by the public represent the "float."

Consider Holy Karaoke Co. (ticker: HYMNS), which has 50 million shares outstanding. If the CEO and other insiders own 40% of them, then the float is the remaining 60%, or 30 million shares.

It's good to pay attention to this number with smaller companies, as stocks with small floats (referred to as "thinly traded") can be extra volatile. Any demand will send the stock price soaring, as supply is so limited, and vice versa.

## 323 What is a company's "liquidity"?

There are two meanings. With companies, liquidity refers to their cash, as well as assets that can be quickly converted into cash (such as certificates of deposit, money market funds, and investments in stocks and bonds). Companies with high liquidity are less risky, but they might also grow slowly, as assets that could be put to work increasing sales are instead kept easily available.

When you're discussing a stock, liquidity refers to the market's ability to handle a large volume of trading without significant price swings. Major investors, such as mutual fund managers, care about this because if they want to buy a million shares, they don't want their purchases to drive up the stock price too much. For example, if Acme Explosives (ticker: KABOOM) has only two million shares outstanding at $10 per share, there's only $20 million worth that the market can buy or sell. Compared to companies like Microsoft that trade more than two billion dollars worth of shares per day, KBOOM is tiny and volatile. It's illiquid.

## 324 What is a stock's "spread"?

When you go to your local used car dealer to unload your beloved 1991 Schnauzer 900ZX, the dealer will probably buy your trusty heap for fewer dollars than he plans to sell it for on the used car market. That's understood — the difference is his profit. Wall Street has a similar dynamic, and it's called the "spread."

The spread is the difference between "bid" and "ask" prices. The "bid" is the price that someone is willing to pay to buy a security, while the "ask" is the price at which a security is offered for sale. On exchanges such as the New York Stock Exchange (NYSE), spreads are relatively uniform, roughly one-eighth to one-sixteenth of a point (or dollar). So, while you might be able to buy Lord-of-the-Trance Hypnotics (ticker: GLAZE) for $32 per share, its sale price might be $31 7/8. That might not seem like a big deal, but for every 1,000 shares traded, it amounts to $125. On an average day, more than one billion shares are traded in the United States. If the spread for each were one-eighth of a point, that would total more than $125 million — per day.

Spreads serve as payments to those who keep the markets liquid — brokerages and the market makers from whom we buy and to whom we sell shares of stock.

Nasdaq spreads have often been on the wide side, historically. Recently, though, regulations and pressure have nudged them down. Nevertheless, it's still smart to check what the spread is when buying or selling any stock.

Be wary of wide spreads, as they usually flag volatile, infrequently traded stocks. If a bid is $10 per share and the ask is $11, you're looking at a $1 spread, in this case equal to 10% of the bid. That means you start out 10% in the hole. Another way to think of it is this: If you bought that stock for $11 per share and immediately wanted to sell it, you'd be selling it for around $10 per share — an immediate and significant loss.

Spreads are unavoidable, but you can keep them from eating too much of your long-term savings. Limit their bite by not trading too frequently and by shunning infrequently traded stocks.

---

**325** **I've seen shares of a stock jump when the company announces massive layoffs. Why would that happen?**

Layoff announcements usually accompany restructuring plans. If investors expect the changes to improve the company's performance, they may buy shares, driving the price up. This was the case with sewing-machine maker Singer, which announced a few years ago that it was laying off 28% of its workforce and that it would be closing some plants to integrate its production units with those of a recent acquisition. Shares shot up 17% that day.

News like this doesn't always pump up share prices, though. When East-man Kodak made a similar announcement, its stock fell nearly 6%. (A little later, Kodak stock rose on news of further layoffs.) It all depends whether the market believes the layoffs are a promise of greater operational efficiency or a sign of a long-term downturn in the business.

---

**326** **Please explain how the rise or fall of their stock prices affects companies. A company issuing stock gets its money when the stock is issued. After that, when its shares are sold, the money goes from the buyer to the seller, not to the company, right?**

Yup. The stock price still matters, though. Executives and employees holding stock or options benefit when the stock rises. If the company wants to issue more stock, it will want to do so when the price is higher rather than lower, to generate more capital for fewer shares. If the company is buying another company with its stock, the higher the price of its stock, the more bang it gets for each share.

Meanwhile, a company's falling stock price might make it more attractive to companies thinking of buying it.

CHAPTER SIXTEEN
ANSWERS TO YOUR QUESTIONS ABOUT

# Researching and Evaluating Companies

*When it comes time to buckle down and examine a company closely to see if it deserves any of your hard-earned investment dollars, there are lots of measures to consider. This chapter will help you make sense of many terms, numbers, and ratios. It should prove useful as you wend your way through various financial statements. It will also help you zero in on companies that deserve a close examination.*

## 327 What are some characteristics of great companies?

When examining a company, too often people get bogged down in details prematurely. It's vital to evaluate the big picture, to make sure that the company you're looking at is a first-class operation and one you'd be proud to own in your portfolio. Here are some marks of great companies.

- **Powerful brands.** Think of well-known brand names in the United States or, better yet, around the world. Brands like McDonald's, Gucci, Campbell Soup, and IBM fit the bill. If most people don't yet know a company's name, then it still has a lot of work to do.

- **Significant products or services.** Look for a company that's selling its customers something they really need or really want. Pharmaceutical companies, for example, manufacture products that people will buy whether they're flush with funds or strapped for cash. Firms like Ben & Jerry's and Starbucks offer consumers things they love. Look for repeat-purchase products that people buy over and over again, such as cheeseburgers and shampoo, instead of items bought only sporadically, like cars or garbage disposals.

- **Consistent, reliable earnings and sales growth** — and robust margins. Track how sales and earnings have increased over past years. An upward-sloping line suggests that management is planning and executing well. Stack your company's gross, operating, and net profit margins up against those of its competitors to see which one is wringing the most value out of each dollar of sales.

- **Lots of potential.** What are the company's growth prospects? Is it expanding abroad? Is it coming out with exciting new products or services? Are its offerings taking the country by storm? Is it trouncing its competition? (Does it even *have* competition?)

A final consideration when qualifying companies for further research is how well you know the company and industry, and how much you'd enjoy keeping up with its developments. A company might have enormous potential, but if reading about it puts you to sleep, it might not be the best addition to your portfolio.

## 328 What are the most valuable brands in the world?

A brand consulting outfit called Interbrand Group tracks and lists the most valuable brands in the world each year. You can read more about its surveys at its website: www.interbrand.com.

Here are the top 20 international brands for 2000, along with what Interbrand estimates to be the market value of each brand:
 1. Coca-Cola..............................$73 billion
 2. Microsoft Windows..............$70 billion
 3. IBM.......................................$53 billion
 4. Intel .....................................$39 billion
 5. Nokia ...................................$39 billion
 6. General Electric ...................$38 billion
 7. Ford .....................................$36 billion
 8. Disney...................................$34 billion
 9. McDonald's...........................$28 billion
10. AT&T ...................................$26 billion

| 11. | Marlboro | $22 billion |
| 12. | Mercedes | $21 billion |
| 13. | Hewlett-Packard | $21 billion |
| 14. | Cisco Systems | $20 billion |
| 15. | Toyota | $19 billion |
| 16. | Citibank | $19 billion |
| 17. | Gillette | $17 billion |
| 18. | Sony | $16 billion |
| 19. | American Express | $16 billion |
| 20. | Honda | $15 billion |

It's interesting to keep up with changes in this list from year to year, as it can offer clues about how aggressively various companies and industries are growing. Nokia, for example, is a relative newcomer, yet its ranking is extremely high. It's clear that it has firmly established itself in the minds of people the world over. Intel's position is interesting, because people rarely knew what company made the component parts of the computers they bought. Yet, through its "Intel Inside" ad campaign, Intel made itself a household name and, more importantly, got people looking for its name when buying a computer.

## 329 What does it mean when someone refers to a company's "business model"?

A firm's business model is simply the method by which it makes its money. Some examples: Wal-Mart's business model was initially to establish profitable stores in small communities that other discount chains had dismissed. Coca-Cola's business model involves using its secret formula to manufacture syrup that it supplies to bottlers. By distributing its beverages through stores, restaurants, vending machines, and more, it is attempting to make its drinks easily available to anyone.

Online auction site eBay's business model is to connect individual buyers and sellers through a website, and to profit by charging fees and taking a percentage of each sale — all without carrying any inventory. Fellow online commerce enterprise Amazon.com has a different model, which requires it to keep many products in stock, so that they can be quickly shipped out to customers.

**330** I know that sometimes numbers can be misleading. When I'm looking at a company's press release, what are some things to look out for?

It's smart to not take what you read at face value. Be skeptical. We often do this when reading words — but we should think critically when reading about numbers, too. Here are some examples of how things are not always what they seem.

Consider that many companies will report "record earnings." This isn't always as impressive as it sounds. Feline Footwear (ticker: MEOWW), for example, might earn a record $3 per share in 1996. If it earns $3.01 in 1997, $3.02 in 1998, and $3.03 in 1999, each of those will also be "record earnings," but they'll represent meager growth. You need to examine how *quickly* a company's earnings are growing. But, this alone isn't enough, either.

Imagine Yamburgers Inc. (ticker: YAMBS), which reports that its revenues advanced 200% over the past year. That's more telling than "record growth," and would intrigue most investors. Check to see what the actual revenue numbers are, though. Perhaps Yamburgers has been struggling, and took in only $300,000 in 1998. Growth of 200% would put it at $900,000 in 1999. That's still mighty tiny. It's important to consider companies in the proper context. A behemoth such as Wal-Mart can't double earnings as quickly as a small upstart can. It's usually easier to double $10 million than $10 billion. As companies grow larger, their growth rates tend to slow down. You can't keep tripling each year forever.

Another potential danger is the "annualized" growth rate. When a company (or mutual fund) takes its total return over a number of years and "annualizes" it, it's telling you how much it roughly earned, on average, per year. This is handy, but check what period of growth is covered. For example, if the Dodgeball Supply Co. (ticker: WHAPP) increased its earnings from $0.12 per share in one year to $0.37 per share five years later, its annualized growth is about 25%. If Spray-on-Socks Co. (ticker: PFFFT) doubled its earnings in three months, its annualized rate would be more like 1,500%. Does that mean we can expect 1,500% each year? Not likely. Annualizing a short period's returns can magnify the numbers and distort things. Those might have been extraordinary months. Minding the numbers can pay off.

## 331 How can I avoid making errors with numbers as I research companies and calculate various measures?

You should always check your work by doing it a second time. You might approach it from a different direction, too, to decrease your chances of repeating an error. So, if you were adding a list of five numbers, you might start from the bottom of the list the second time.

When working with formulas and plugging in numbers, it's critical to be consistent with the numbers you're using. If you enter a number in the millions for one part of a formula, make sure that the other numbers you use aren't in billions or thousands. This is important because sometimes the various sources of data you'll use will differ in how they present numbers. One balance sheet might list numbers in thousands (where 10,000 is shown as "10"), another data source might offer figures in millions (where 10,000,000 is shown as "10"). See the problem? Since it can be clunky to add, subtract, multiply, and divide really big numbers, they're shortened temporarily for convenience.

If you're not used to working with math and big numbers too often, check out the following ways of writing the same number:
$6,344,175,000
$6,344,175      (in 000s, or thousands)
$6,344         (in millions)
$6.344         (in billions)

So, if you read on a financial statement that a certain item is valued at $13,885 and you note (probably at the bottom or top of the statement) that all numbers are "in 000s," that means you need to tack on three zeroes and the number is really $13,885,000. If the statement says that all numbers are in millions, you'll need to tack on six zeroes, for $13,885,000,000.

Keep all numbers in the same format and the formulas should work smoothly.

## 332 What are "Rule Breaker" companies, and how can I find some?

Online at Fool.com, we run several real-money portfolios in full view, so that people can learn from our successes and mistakes. One is our Rule Breaker Portfolio, which can offer some useful tips on how to find fast-growing young companies that are creating or redefining emerging industries.

In David and Tom Gardner's book, *The Motley Fool's Rule Breakers, Rule Makers*, they discuss two powerful kinds of investments: companies that *break* all the rules, changing the status quo — and the kind of company they sometimes grow into, one that *makes* the rules for others to follow. Here's a look at some Rule Breaker characteristics:

First, the company should be a "top dog" and first-mover in an important, emerging field. In other words, being top dog in the left-handed scissors industry isn't enough. A company like Amazon.com fits the bill, though, as it has long led the online consumer retailing industry.

Next, the company needs to demonstrate a sustainable advantage gained through business momentum, patent protection, visionary leadership, or inept competitors. Examples of these include Wal-Mart (with business momentum that featured net income gains of 25% during much of the 1980s), Amgen (enjoying patent protection of its drug formulas for many years), and Microsoft (with visionary leadership that benefited from Apple Computer's regrettable decision not to license its operating system technology).

Look for good management, like the steel company Nucor (yes, steel!), led by Ken Iverson, which became a world-class powerhouse by revolutionizing steel production processes.

Also important is having a strong consumer brand. Consider Starbucks, and how its name recognition is so much stronger than competitors such as... um... (get the point?).

It's also a good sign when the financial media, not seeing the big picture, calls a firm "overvalued." (*Barron's* asks about America Online: "Short on Value?" Great!)

Those who invest in Rule Breakers consciously take on lots of risk, believing that for the experienced and Foolish, high risk will lead to high reward.

Rule Breaker stocks should make up only a part of any portfolio, though, not all of it, as it *is* a risky approach. If you invest in several Rule Breakers, one or two might do very well, but several others might have problems. The expectation is that winners will more than make up for losers.

## 333 What is "Rule Maker" investing all about?

Rule Breaker companies succeed by breaking all the rules. The most successful among them grow up to become dominant Rule Makers, able to call the shots in their industry and generate great value for shareholders.

To identify Rule Makers, look for the No. 1 brand name in an industry. What companies come to mind when you think of chocolate, ketchup, diamond rings, and microprocessors? We suspect that most people will name Hershey, Heinz, Tiffany, and Intel.

Repeat mass-market purchases also characterize Rule Makers. Most people don't buy many automobiles or washing machines each year, so General Motors and Whirlpool are out. Think instead of things you routinely use, either because you like to or you have to: soda, e-mail access, blood-pressure pills, and shampoo. Think Coca-Cola, America Online, Merck, and Procter & Gamble.

When crunching financial numbers looking for possible Rule Makers, check several measures. You ideally want to see gross margins (gross profits divided by revenues) above 60%, net margins (net income divided by revenues) topping 10%, and sales growing faster than 10% per year.

Cash is king with Rule Makers. You want to see plenty of it (and little debt) on the balance sheet. A low "Flow Ratio" is also key, revealing that the company is managing cash flow effectively by demanding payment quickly, but paying its obligations slowly. (The Flow Ratio is explained in more detail later in this book.)

Just as important as how the company fares on the above measures is the direction it's moving in. You want to see margins rising, the company buying back its own shares, cash outgrowing debt, and the Flow Ratio falling. When compared with industry peers, the Rule Maker candidate should clearly be at the head of the class.

There's more involved in identifying Rule Makers, but these are some of the core principles. They'll help you zero in on companies worth a closer look. Visit us online at www.rulemaker.Fool.com and read the nightly reports for our real-money Rule Maker Portfolio.

## 334 What are Merchant Kings?

Merchant Kings are companies that share many characteristics with Rule Maker companies, yet never entirely qualify as Rule Makers — usually because their gross and net margins fall short of the required levels. This is to be expected, though, because retailers traditionally *do* sport lower margins. What they lack in margins, though, they tend to make up for in volume.

Whereas Rule Makers tend to be manufacturers, Merchant Kings are distributors. Examples of Merchant Kings include Wal-Mart, Home Depot, Dell Computer, eBay, and Amazon.com.

## 335 What is a "pure-play" company?

A pure-play company has a single business focus. When investors are drawn to a particular kind of business, they may seek out a company that's a pure play, so that their invested dollars won't be spread out over other, less desirable business segments.

Coca-Cola is a beverage pure-play, while PepsiCo isn't because it owns Frito-Lay snacks. Until recently, Ben & Jerry's was an ice cream pure-play compared to the conglomerate Diageo, which owns Haagen-Dazs, Green Giant, and Burger King. But Unilever recently snapped up Ben & Jerry's.

## 336 What are "roll-ups"?

If you've ever marveled at a company that appears to be on an acquisition spree, you may be looking at a "roll-up." Roll-ups are companies that grow not by ramping up operations and increasing sales internally, but by acquiring many smaller competitors, usually in a fragmented industry. This can be a risky business, as each acquisition has its own ways of doing things and each has to be integrated into the roll-up.

Some roll-up companies include Loewen Group (funeral homes), Metals USA (metals), U.S. Office Products (office products and services), and USA Floral Products. U.S. Office Products is the result of more than 230 acquisitions. Yowza.

Whereas many diversified firms begin as small companies and grow organically, gradually buying other companies, a classic roll-up has a more unusual *modus operandi*. The company may not even exist until its founder/promoter finds about five to 15 companies willing to join forces with him in exchange for cash and stock. This cash and stock may not materialize until the company goes public (which it quickly does), enticing investors with its rosy projections and plans. In a sense, the roll-up acquires companies on credit!

This process likely continues, with the company issuing more stock as it acquires more companies. Let's say that an acquisition target company's stock price is valued by the market at about 10 times earnings. If it generates $5 million in annual earnings, the roll-up might buy it for about $50 million in cash and stock. Meanwhile, the roll-up itself might be enjoying a valuation on the stock market of about 20 or 30 times earnings. In this way, the roll-up is immediately recognizing a higher value for its purchase than it paid.

One problem with roll-ups is that they're often run by people more adept at sales and promotion than at running large and growing businesses. Management may have little experience in the industry or with managing full-scale operations of dozens of companies. Integrating the businesses can be extremely difficult.

Not all roll-ups are to be avoided, but study them closely before jumping in.

---

## 337 What are "tracking stocks"?

Bought and sold like regular stocks, tracking stocks are usually issued by companies with several different lines of business. They serve as an attractive alternative to spinning off divisions.

Imagine Buzz-n-Boom Corp. (ticker: BZBM). It runs a chain of hair salons and also manufactures fireworks, which are more profitable. A high interest level in fireworks might spur the company to issue a tracking stock for the fireworks business. This will help investors see the value of the fireworks operations, separate from coiffures.

When a company issues a tracking stock, it has to prepare three sets of financial statements (such as balance sheets and income statements) instead of one. One set will reflect the company as a whole. A second set will reflect the business line being tracked. A third will reflect the company's operations, excluding those belonging to the tracking stock. The company hasn't really split up; but for reporting purposes, its assets, expenses, income, and cash flow are allocated between the company and its tracking stock.

The appeal of tracking stocks is that they can help investors see a company's full value. For example, perhaps AT&T thought that investors were just thinking of it as a fuddy-duddy giant telephone company. It recently issued a tracking stock for its wireless unit, AT&T Wireless Group, drawing attention to its dynamic wireless operations. The reasoning is that these operations may be accorded a higher value than if they remained embedded in regular AT&T stock. Higher-valued shares can be used as currency when the company wants to buy another firm or forge an alliance.

The downside to tracking stocks is that they're not backed by corporate assets in the same way as regular stocks. With regular common stock, shareholders own a chunk of the underlying company. With tracking stocks, the company retains ownership, but shareholders get to enjoy returns that track a specific part of the company's business.

There are several high-profile tracking stocks. General Motors issued a Hughes Electronics tracking stock; Ziff-Davis issued stock for its ZDNet unit; AT&T's Liberty Media cable programming business is a tracking stock; and Sprint issued a tracking stock for Sprint PCS Group.

If you dare type in the following long Web address, you can learn more about tracking stocks here:
www.Fool.com/EveningNews/foth/1999/foth990316.htm.

## 338 Okay, so once I've found a company I'm interested in, how do I go about researching it?

Let's say you're intrigued by Wookie Cookies Inc. (ticker: CHEWY). Give the firm a jingle and ask the investor relations department to send you an investor information package. (They're free!) Say you'd like to receive the most recent annual report, the latest 10-K and 10-Q reports, any recent press releases, and any available analyst reports. Alternatively, you can save a few trees (and a few days) by gathering the information online at the company's website and sites such as www.freeEdgar.com.

The annual report will probably feature glossy photos of smiling customers (or assorted alien life forms) chomping on cookies. Enjoy the feel-good glossy pages, but wend your way to the back of the report, where the numbers will tell you the real story about the business.

The financial statements there will tell you how quickly sales are growing, how the company is financing its growth, how much profit it's making, and much more. Pay attention to trends, to see if the firm's financial health is improving or declining. Compare the company with its industry peers, too, to see how it stacks up.

Remember that you can improve your chances for success if you're actually a consumer of Wookie Cookies and are familiar with the company's offerings. Also, talk about the business with other investors, perhaps in an investment club.

Don't neglect online resources. Most major companies these days have websites that feature an investor information section, with press releases, financial statements, annual reports, and answers to frequently asked questions (sometimes abbreviated "FAQ"). Investor information sites like ours also offer a wealth of information on companies and communities of investors sharing information. (Visit http://quote.Fool.com for company research tools and www.Fool.com for everything else.)

## 339 When do companies issue earnings reports?

Most publicly traded American businesses are required to publish their financial performance four times a year. Once a year, companies issue an annual report and, along with it, a more-detailed 10-K report. In the intervening quarters, companies issue 10-Q reports.

The 10-Q summarizes quarterly performance. While it's fairly abbreviated, it can still be extremely enlightening. The 10-K reviews the year's results and features a lengthy discussion of the firm's operations and challenges, as well.

Public companies also often hold a quarterly conference call between management and Wall Street analysts. Many open these calls to the public, and websites such as www.broadcast.com and www.ccbn.com provide online access to numerous corporate conference calls. Online, we offer a calendar of conference calls, with access to listen to them, at: http://quote.Fool.com/calendars/monthly.asp?calendar=1

(Usually you'll be listening to a recording of the call, not the live call.) This is a terrific way to stay in touch with your holdings. If your company hasn't opened up access to its quarterly call, give it a call, express your displeasure, and remind it that the Securities and Exchange Commission (SEC) frowns on selective disclosure of material information.

## 340 How do I find the phone number of a company to request financial information?

To get phone numbers of companies trading on the New York Stock Exchange (NYSE), call the exchange at 212-656-3000. The Nasdaq can be reached at 202-728-8039 and the American Stock Exchange (AMEX) at 212-306-1490. At many local libraries, *Value Line* also has phone numbers. You can also visit http://quote.Fool.com and look up a company's "snapshot" — which will include its phone number. A visit to other sites, such as www.marketguide.com, will also turn up the phone number.

Remember also that if you're online, you can bypass calling the company and just gather all the information you need there.

**341** **Where online can I access earnings reports that companies file with the SEC?**

Many websites, such as Fool.com, include access to these filings in their stock data offerings. But you can also go right to the source and search the EDGAR database at www.sec.gov or www.freeEdgar.com. (EDGAR is an acronym for the Electronic Data Gathering, Analysis, and Retrieval system.)

**342** **How can I find out when particular companies are expected to unveil their quarterly earnings reports?**

One good way is to call the company and ask, or call your brokerage and let them find out for you. If you're online, click over to the Fool's quotes and data area at http://quote.Fool.com, where we've got an earnings calendar that tracks recent and upcoming earnings reports.

You can also pop over to www1.firstcall.com or www.zacks.com for summaries of earnings estimates. Or ask for details on online discussion boards for individual companies.

**343** **How can I research the risks facing various companies?**

Grab a company's 10-K report, which is issued once a year along with its annual report. These documents detail a company's financial and operational progress and also address risks facing the business.

For example, Internet company Yahoo!'s recent 10-K cites many risk factors. The stock price is volatile, and the company's operating history is limited. The firm's growth strategy depends on things beyond its control, such as the market's adoption of the World Wide Web as an advertising medium. Most revenues come from advertising, which is seasonal and has short-term contracts. The firm "depends substantially on third parties for several critical elements of its business, including technology and infrastructure, content development, and distribution activities."

PepsiCo's 10-K mentions international market risks as well as interest rate and currency exchange rate fluctuation. Ford Motor Company's 10-K cites greater price competition, declining sales resulting from slowing economic growth, currency or commodity price fluctuations, higher fuel prices, lower-than-anticipated residual values for leased vehicles, increased safety or emissions regulations, the discovery of defects resulting in recalls, and more. There's a wealth of valuable information in the 10-K.

All companies have risks. Don't let them scare you away, but do consider them.

## 344 I want to learn to read annual reports, so can you describe the different financial reports they contain in a nutshell?

There are three important financial statements in every annual report, beginning with the income statement, which is sometimes called the statement of operations. It shows how much was raked in through sales and how much was kept as profit over a certain period of time, such as a quarter or a fiscal year. The balance sheet reflects a company's financial health as of a particular date, showing what the firm owns and owes in terms of assets and liabilities. (Little cash or high debt might be worrisome.) The statement of cash flows notes how much cash was generated (or lost) during the period and where it came from and went to. Pay attention to how much is coming from ongoing operations — the stuff produced and sold. If asset sales or stocks and bonds issued are generating most of a company's cash rather than operations, that might be a cause for concern.

## 345 What should I know about the balance sheet?

The balance sheet is essentially a snapshot of a company's financial condition at a single point in time (often the end of a fiscal quarter). This is different from several other statements, which reflect how a company did over a period of time. Balance sheets focus on just one moment.

For your own personal balance sheet, you'd list all your assets, subtract your debts and obligations, and end up with your net worth. Companies essentially do the same thing, and Fools can gain valuable insights into a firm's financial strength by studying this document.

The balance sheet has three main parts: assets, liabilities, and shareholder equity. Assets are set equal to — or in *balance* with — liabilities and shareholder equity. The funny thing is, though, some assets can be bad and some liabilities can be good. Here's why.

Take a gander at assets. In this category, you'll find items such as "cash and cash equivalents" and "short-term investments." That's how much unused gunpowder the company has. These assets are good, but most other assets are not as good. Consider "accounts receivable." That's money from sales the company hasn't yet received and can't use. "Inventory" reports how much product is in various stages of preparation. It's cash tied up in materials and products that haven't yet been sold. Not so good.

Other balance sheet assets may include investments, "prepaid expenses" (such as insurance that's paid ahead of time), and "property, plant, and equipment" (PP&E).

Liabilities are likely to include short-term (also called "current") debt and long-term debt. Debt is not necessarily a bad thing, although we generally don't like to see much long-term debt. In a sense, debt can be considered an asset, as it often represents cash that the company is putting to work.

"Accounts payable," essentially short-term debt, represents invoices not yet paid. This can also be a good thing. They may reflect a company delaying payment until it's due and using the money in the interim.

Finally, shareholder equity is the portion of the company that stockholders can claim. Simply put, it's the difference between assets and liabilities. By studying a balance sheet, you can evaluate a company's current condition and also see whether its financial health is improving or failing.

---

## 346 How should I begin to evaluate information on a balance sheet? Can you take me through an example?

Let's examine the increasingly ubiquitous coffee purveyor, Starbucks.

To make this a little bit more of a learning exercise, we'll review the results for its fiscal year that ended on September 27, 1998. Then you can dig up the company's most recent balance sheet and see whether the company has improved.

Glancing at the balance sheet, we see $101.7 million in cash and cash equivalents, up 45% from the previous year. A growing pile of cash is generally promising.

You usually want to see little or no debt. Between 1997 and 1998, Starbucks' long-term debt plummeted from $169 million to $1.8 million. That's good. If debt was substantial, we might peek at the footnotes to check out the interest rates. Low rates would indicate that the firm is financing operations effectively.

Next up, inventory. Valued at $120 million in 1997, it ended 1998 at $143 million, up about 19%. Rising inventories can indicate unsold products languishing on shelves, but since sales rose 34% year-over-year, the rise in inventory appears well under control. (Ideally, sales growth should outpace inventory growth.)

It's also good to measure inventory turnover, which reflects how many times per year the firm sells out its inventory. Take 1998's cost of goods sold (sometimes abbreviated COGS) (from the income statement) of $578 million, and divide it by the average of 1997 and 1998 inventory ($120 million and $143 million averaged is $131.5 million). This gives us a turnover of 4.4, up a smidgen from last year's 4.3. The higher the better, so no worries here.

Accounts receivable are less rosy. They rose 63%, outpacing sales growth. Normally, this might be a concern, but Starbucks has been expanding its range of activities. New non-retail business lines have been added, altering its usual receivables pattern.

Finally, look at the "quick ratio." Subtract inventory from current assets and then divide by current liabilities. Starbucks' result, 1.08, is above 1.0. That means there's enough cash (and assets readily convertible to cash) on hand to cover bills. Cool beans.

Many investors focus only on sales and earnings growth. While that's important, long-term investors should also study the balance sheet to see how sturdy the underlying business is.

## 347 Can you explain when debt on a company's balance sheet is good and when it's bad?

First, the bad. If a company is saddled with a lot of debt, it's locked into making interest payments. If it doesn't have the cash to cover these payments, it's in deep doodoo. Many individuals can probably relate to this, having experienced the dark side of debt when racking up charges on credit cards.

Now, the good. Consider that most people would never be able to buy their homes without taking on debt with a mortgage. Without car and school loans, many of us would probably be driving clunkers and taking correspondence courses we found on matchbook covers.

Debt can be helpful for businesses, too. Many great companies, such as Federal Express and the Walt Disney Co., came to life because of early loans to their founders. Established companies also can make good use of debt, borrowing to expand operations and grow their business. Interest payments also decrease a company's taxable income, as they're deductible. Investors willing to consider companies with debt need to evaluate whether the debt taken on is manageable and whether the capital raised and invested is earning more than it costs.

Perhaps you're worried about the debt load of Fingernail-on-Blackboard Car Alarm Co. (ticker: AIEEE). Glance at the notes in the annual report and you find that the effective interest rate for its debt is just 5%. If AIEEE is putting the borrowed funds to work earning say, 8%, then things aren't so bad.

When companies need money, they typically have two main choices: They can issue more stock or take on debt. Issuing stock can dilute the value of existing shares. Debt can sometimes be more efficient, as its after-tax cost can be much cheaper than equity.

All things being equal, though, we prefer to see little debt on a balance sheet. Companies that can grow without using debt or issuing extra stock are in a more powerful position than other firms. Still, you needn't balk at the first sight of debt. Just evaluate it carefully.

## 348 What are the advantages and disadvantages of companies carrying a lot of cash on their balance sheet?

Companies with piles of cash have a lot of flexibility to act quickly when various opportunities arise, but many successful companies manage down their cash balances to near zero. They use the money to buy back shares and acquire other companies, among other things. If they suddenly need some cash, they draw on lines of credit available to them.

You might be surprised at just how much cash some companies have on hand. As of June 2000, Microsoft had nearly $24 *billion* in cash and cash equivalents sitting in its coffers. Fellow giant Wal-Mart, meanwhile, had just $1.4 billion in April of 2000, while America Online had $2.5 billion as of June 2000. At the other end of the spectrum are companies such as Gillette, which had just $101 million on hand as of March 2000. Different companies manage their cash in different ways, with varying degrees of success.

## 349 What's this "goodwill" that I see on company balance sheets?

Goodwill usually appears on a balance sheet if a company has acquired another firm and paid more than the acquired company's appraised net worth, which is very close to its book value.

Imagine that Roadrunner Industries (ticker: BEEEP) acquires the Acme Explosives Co. (ticker: KBOOM). Let's say that Acme is considered a gem among explosives manufacturers and that other companies would be happy to acquire it. If so, Roadrunner probably can't get away with paying just what the company is worth — an offer like that might trigger counter bids for Acme. So Roadrunner pays a premium. This difference between the price paid and the book value of the acquired company is entered on the acquiring company's balance sheet as "goodwill."

Let's say that Acme was calculated to be worth $20 million, but Roadrunner paid a premium for it, offering $25 million in cash. Roadrunner won't have that $25 million in cash it paid for Acme as an asset on its balance sheet anymore, but the cash doesn't simply disappear. It was used to purchase a new asset. So the $25 million in cash is replaced by the $20 million value of Acme and a new $5 million value designated as "goodwill." Goodwill is amortized over a period of years. In other words, just as capital assets like factory equipment are depreciated, with their value on the balance sheet decreased eventually to zero, goodwill is also incrementally reduced to zero.

## 350 What should a company's income statement tell me?

If you're new to investing, you've probably stared at an income statement (sometimes called a "statement of operations" or "profit and loss statement") and scratched your head, wondering what it's telling you. Be puzzled no longer.

The income statement summarizes sales and profits over a specific period. It might cover three months or a year, for example. It will usually offer information for the year-ago period as well, so you can compare the two and spot trends.

Let's look at the income statement for fiscal year 1999 for Coca-Cola. We'll compare our findings with some numbers from PepsiCo's 1999 income statement. Just remember that the two companies are not in identical businesses — while Coca-Cola is pretty much just a beverage company, PepsiCo's business includes substantial snack food operations (from Frito-Lay, for example).

At the top, as with every income statement, you'll find net sales (sometimes called revenues). Coca-Cola's "net operating revenues" are $19.8 billion. From now on, as we work down the income statement, various costs will be subtracted from the revenues, leaving different levels of profit. These are called "margins" and are an important item for investors to evaluate.

The item you'll find just under revenues is "cost of goods sold" (sometimes abbreviated as COGS or called cost of sales), which represents the cost of producing the products or services sold. For Coca-Cola, it's

$6 billion. Subtract the COGS from revenues, and you'll get a gross profit of $13.8 billion.

To find the gross profit margin, simply divide the gross profit by revenues. $13.8 billion divided by $19.8 billion yields a gross profit margin of 70%. (Compare results with industry peers. For example, gross margin is 60% for PepsiCo.)

Next, the remaining costs involved in operating the business, such as support staff salaries, utility bills, and advertising expenses are subtracted, leaving the operating profit. Coca-Cola's operating profit is $4 billion. Divide this by revenues, and you get a healthy operating margin of 20%. This reveals the profitability of the company's principal business. (PepsiCo: 14%.)

Finally, after items such as taxes and interest payments are accounted for, we come to net income, near the bottom of the statement. Coca-Cola's is $2.4 billion. Divide that by revenues and you get a net profit margin of 12%. (PepsiCo: 10%.) The last part of the income statement is where the company divides its net income by shares outstanding, to arrive at earnings per share (EPS).

Compare all these margins with those from previous years. Increasing margins indicate increasing efficiency and profitability. Check out the margins of the company's competitors. Is the firm more efficient than its peers? Look for significant changes in revenues, SG&A (selling, general, and administrative) expenses, and costs of goods sold.

And, finally, note that margins vary widely by industry. Software companies, for example, tend to have high margins, while retailers tend to have low ones.

---

### 351 Should I avoid companies with low profit margins, or are some of them okay?

In general, higher margins are better than lower margins.

But a glance at inventory turnover can reveal some exceptions. (Inventory turnover is represented by the cost of goods sold divided by the average dollar value of inventory.) Imagine two companies: the Acme Piano Co. (ticker: GRAND) has a whopping profit margin of 28%, while the Krazy Kazoo Co. (ticker: BZZZ) has only a 2% margin. If Acme only sells three pianos a year while Krazy sells out of kazoos each week, Krazy may well be the better buy, generating more cash in total than Acme.

Some industries, such as software, typically have high profit margins. Discount stores and supermarkets typically have very low profit margins — but if they turn over inventory fast enough, they might still be decent investments.

## 352  Can you explain what a company's statement of cash flows should tell me?

The cash flow statement shows how much money a company is really making as it works through operations, makes investments, and borrows money.

The statement breaks cash inflows and outflows into three categories: operations, investments, and financing. Some operating activities include purchases or sales of supplies, and changes in payments expected and payments due. Investing activities include the purchase or sale of equipment, buildings, property, companies, and securities such as stocks or bonds. Financing activities include issuing or repurchasing stock and issuing or reducing debt.

If the bottom-line number is positive, the company is "cash-flow positive." That's a good thing, but it's not the only thing you should look at on this statement. Check to see where most of the moolah is coming from. You'd rather see more greenbacks generated from operations than financing. Cash flow from operations is arguably the most important line on this statement.

Examine the various line items, though, and see how they have changed compared to past years. You may notice, for example, that "payments of debt" double or triple from one year to another. This shows the firm increasingly paying off debt. "Purchase of company stock" would reflect a company buying back some of its own shares, to increase the value of the remaining shares — something shareholders generally smile at. If you're thinking of investing in any company, the more you know about it, the better... and scouring the cash flow statement can be a very profitable thing to do.

## 353 I gather that some things are referred to by different names on different companies' financial statements. Is there any list of these alternate names?

You're right. Within the financial statements, names for some items vary from one company to another. Don't let this confuse you. If you're looking for "Revenues," for example, just know that the same thing might also be called "Sales." See the list on the next page. (This list is by no means comprehensive. It'll just give you an idea of the variation you'll likely run across.)

## 354 What does the word "consolidated" mean on financial statements?

Major corporations (and even many minor ones) typically have various subsidiaries and lines of business. Some companies are more formally considered "holding companies," if they own the securities of other firms. (A classic example of a holding company is Warren Buffett's Berkshire Hathaway, which owns GEICO Direct Auto Insurance, See's Candies, and the Dexter Shoe Company, among other companies.) When a company reports "consolidated" numbers, it has simply combined the results from all its various operations into one report.

## 355 What does "pro forma" mean when I read it on a financial statement?

It means that you're looking at some what-if numbers. Imagine that Joanie Inc.'s fiscal year runs from January through December. Let's say that Joanie Inc. merges with Chachi Co. in April. At the end of the year, you might see some pro forma financial statements in JoanieChachi's annual report. These would show you the financial state of the firm as if it had been a combined company all year long.

# Financial Statement
# Words and Phrases

Within the financial statements, names for some items vary from one company to another. Don't let this confuse you. If you're looking for "Revenues," for example, just know that the same thing might also be called "Sales." This list is by no means comprehensive. It'll just give you an idea of the variation you'll likely run across.

| Word or Phrase | Alternate Wording |
| --- | --- |
| Accounts Payable | Payables |
| Accounts Receivable | Trade Receivables |
| | Receivables |
| Additional Paid-in Capital | Capital in Excess of Stated Value |
| | Capital Surplus |
| | Paid-in Capital |
| Balance Sheet | Statement of Financial Condition |
| | Consolidated Balance Sheets |
| Cost of Goods Sold | Costs of Sales |
| | Cost of Revenue |
| | Cost of Products Sold |
| | Costs, Materials, and Production |
| Inventories | Merchandise Inventories |
| Earnings | Net Income |
| | Net Profit |
| Income Statement | Earnings Statement |
| | Profit & Loss Statement |
| | Statement of Operations |
| | Consolidated Statement of Income |
| Earnings Before Income Taxes | Income (Loss) Before Income Taxes |
| | Earnings Before Provision for Income Taxes |
| Earnings Per Share | Net Income Per Share |
| | Net Income Per Common Share |
| Net Income | Net Profit |
| | Net Earnings |
| Revenues | Sales |
| | Net Sales |
| Shareholder Equity | Shareholders' Investment |
| | Stockholders' Equity |
| Short-term Debt | Debt Payable Within One Year |
| | Current Portion of Long-term Debt |
| | Notes Payable |

Pro forma results are useful. If you were researching JoanieChachi Inc., you'd want to be able to compare apples to apples. It wouldn't be too insightful to contrast one period's results, pre-merger, with post-merger results. By examining combined results, you get a clearer idea of the company's financial health.

---

## 356 What is a "run rate"?

Imagine that you're studying the financial statements of Peter's Pipedreams (ticker: HOPE). It's growing very rapidly from quarter to quarter. Perhaps, for some calculation, you want to estimate its *current* annual rate of sales. You could add up the last four quarters' worth, but that would clearly understate sales, as each quarter's numbers have been rising.

Enter the run rate. Take the most recent quarter's sales. Let's say they're $30 million (up from $25 million the quarter before and $21 million before that). Multiply that by four and you'll have the company's current run rate for sales: $120 million. It's not a forecast or a measure of past sales — it's a reflection of the current level of annualized sales.

---

## 357 How do I calculate growth rates — of earnings, for example, or revenues, or anything else?

Many people get intimidated by the math involved in company analysis. But, truthfully, the math isn't that hard, once you figure out the formulas and practice a little. It rarely involves anything more than some multiplication and division, and an understanding of percentages.

Let's consider an example. Imagine the Wicker Sink Co. (ticker: SIEVE), with sales of $12 million in 1996 and $48 million in 1999. If you have a slightly fancy calculator, it might actually sport a feature that calculates growth percentages for you. If not, here's what to do to figure out the revenue growth rate in this example:

Divide $48 million by $12 million and you'll get 4. This means that sales quadrupled, or increased by a growth multiple of 4. That doesn't translate to a gain of 400%, though. (After all, doubling is a gain of 100%, not 200%.) To get the percentage, you need to take the growth multiple, subtract 1, multiply by 100, and then tack on a percentage sign. So, 4 minus 1 is 3. And 3 times 100 is 300%. So, from 1996 to 1999, Wicker's sales increased 300%.

1996: $12 million
1998: $48 million
   $48 million / $12 million = 4
   4 - 1 = 3
   3 x 100 = 300
   300 + a percentage sign = 300%

Another way to approach it is to take the $48 million and subtract the $12 million to get $36 million, which represents the growth. Divide it by $12 million and you'll get 3. Multiply that by 100 and you've got 300%. Same answer.

$48 million - $12 million = $36 million
$36 million / $12 million = 3
3 x 100 = 300
300 + a percentage sign = 300%

One last valuable step is to annualize the growth rate. In other words, to figure out roughly by how much Wicker Sink's sales are growing each year. To do this, we first need to figure out the time period involved. From 1996 to 1999 is three years, so we'll be taking the third, or cube, root of the growth multiple. (If the time period were five years, you'd raise the multiple to the 1/5 power. For 8.4 years, it would be the 1/8.4 power. Two-year periods are easy — you just take the square root.)

You'll need either a computer with a spreadsheet program or a calculator with a "^" button — one that raises numbers to various powers. Raise the growth multiple of 4 to the 1/3 power, and you'll get 1.59. Now subtract 1, multiply by 100, and you've got 59% as the approximate average annual growth rate.

It is tricky stuff, until you get used to it. Practice it a little and you'll be happy you did. And don't feel bad if you can't get the hang of it too quickly. It doesn't always come easily to everyone. Join many other Fools online at our discussion boards, where you can ask for help when you're confused. (Head to http://boards.Fool.com and pop into "The Information Desk" or "Investors' Roundtable.")

## 358 Where can I find historical stock prices? I want to learn how much it traded for on a particular day some years ago.

Sometimes the company itself can tell you. Try giving its investor relations department a call. Another good resource is your public library, where librarians should be able to help you look up the price in newspaper archives or elsewhere. Online, hop over to www.financialweb.com/market or use the Fool's data service, at http://quote.Fool.com.

## 359 There are so many different measures to look at when studying a company — can you help me put them all in perspective?

You're right — there are a *lot* of measures. If you're foolish (with a small "f"), you might only look at the price-to-earnings (P/E) ratio. Fools (with a capital "F") will consider many measures, such as profit margins, cash from operations, earnings growth rates, and return on equity.

The more measures you learn about, though, the more confused you may become. Try thinking about it this way: As you study a company, there are two key questions that need to be answered by the information you gather:

1. Is this a high-quality company that I'd love to own a piece of?
2. Is the price right to buy it now?

Fools generally agree that it's best to invest in high-quality companies, but they put different emphases on the second question. To some, as long as you've got a terrific company, the price isn't that important. They reason that the company will keep growing — and if it's overvalued now, it'll eventually grow into and surpass its price. To others, buying at a good price is critical to reduce risk and maximize gain. To just about all Fools, though, it's vital to understand a company's business and get a handle on its quality.

Conveniently, most company evaluation measures are related to either quality or price. Here's where some measures fall.

**Company Quality**: Sales and earnings growth, margins and margin growth, return on equity (ROE), return on invested capital (ROIC), leverage, inventory turnover, Flow Ratio, return on assets (ROA), product and service offerings, market share, competitive positioning, revenues per subscriber, proprietary technology or knowledge, brand strength, management savvy.

**Stock Price (or Valuation)**: Market capitalization, enterprise value, price-to-earnings (P/E) ratio, price-to-sales ratio (PSR), price-to-cash-flow ratio, price-to-book-value ratio, market-value-per-subscriber measures, and dividend yield.

Quality-related measures will help you understand how efficiently and profitably the company is run, how robust its financial condition is, and how quickly it's growing. Price-related measures will help you determine whether the stock is priced attractively or not.

---

## 360 Can you explain how to calculate a price-to-earnings (P/E) ratio? I see it everywhere, but I'm not sure what it is.

It's probably simpler than you think. The P/E ratio is a measure that compares a company's stock price to its earnings per share (EPS), usually for the previous 12 months. You can think of it as a fraction, with the stock price on top and the EPS on the bottom. Alternatively, tap the price into your calculator, divide by EPS, and *voila* — the P/E.

Consider Wanton Punctuation (ticker: ?#$@!), trading at $30 per share. If its EPS for the last year (adding up the last four quarters reported) is $1.50, you just divide $30 by $1.50 and get a P/E ratio of 20. Note that, if the EPS rises and the stock price stays steady, the P/E will fall — and vice versa. For example, a stock price of $30 and an EPS of $3 give a P/E of 10. You can calculate P/E ratios based on EPS for last year, this year, or future years.

Since published P/E ratios generally represent a stock's current price divided by its last four quarters of earnings, they reflect *past* performance. Intelligent investors should really be focusing on future prospects. You can do that by calculating forward-looking P/E ratios. Simply divide the current stock price by coming years' expected earnings.

Many investors seek companies with low P/E ratios, as this can indicate beaten-down companies likely to rebound. (Of course, a low P/E may also indicate a beaten-down company that's just begun its beating.) Low P/Es might be attractive, but understand that P/Es vary by industry. Car manufacturers and banks typically sport low P/Es, while software and Internet-related companies command higher ones. Don't compare kumquats to kiwis and don't stop with the P/E ratio — there are many other numbers to examine when studying a stock.

## 361 A low P/E ratio for a company is a good sign, though, right?

It can be a good sign (highlighting an overlooked gem) or a bad one (flagging a company that's ailing).

In pre-digital days, low P/Es often signaled a temporarily mispriced stock, but computers have made the market more efficient. Despite this, you can still find some promising low-P/E stocks that, for some reason, the market has simply overlooked. Just don't let the P/E ratio be your only evaluation tool; crunch some other numbers, such as the earnings growth rate. For example, a company with a P/E of 40 that will grow earnings by 80% next year is most likely a better value than a company with a P/E of 20 growing earnings 4% annually.

## 362 I've seen some sky-high P/E ratios. How can a company have a price-to-earnings ratio of 1,000?

Remember that the P/E ratio is a simple fraction — the company's stock price divided by its earnings per share (EPS). As long as there are no earnings (such as with start-ups, or companies temporarily or permanently in trouble), the bottom of the fraction is zero and a P/E can't be calculated. But, as soon as a tiny bit of profit occurs, the fraction suddenly comes alive. With a bigger number on top (the stock price) and a very small bottom number (the EPS), the P/E is large.

Imagine a rapidly growing igloo construction start-up called IceBoxes (ticker: BRRRR). For its first five years, it reports losses and has no P/E ratio. In year six, it finally generates a profit of $0.01 per share. With its stock price at $20, its P/E is a whopping 2,000 (20 divided by

$0.01). The following year, if its EPS is $0.05 (up 400%!) and its stock price remains $20, its P/E will be 400. If its stock price hits $35 when its EPS is $0.40, the P/E will be 88.

---

## 363 How could a company have a price-to-earnings (P/E) ratio of 77 and a projected P/E of 22? How is it expected to change so quickly?

If the company's stock currently trades at $77 per share and has $1 per share in annual earnings, its P/E is 77. Let's say it is growing rapidly, though, and is expected to earn $3.50 next year. If so, the projected P/E for that year is 22 ($77 divided by $3.50 is 22).

With a growing company, if the earnings grow more quickly than the stock price, the P/E ratio will decrease.

---

## 364 What are "multiples" and what role do they play in evaluating a company?

Imagine you're researching Downsizers Diet Centers (ticker: SLIMM), and you read that "it deserves to trade at 28 times trailing earnings, or about $56 today. If it maintains 18% earnings per share (EPS) growth, it appears to be a bargain right now." You were doing fine until this sentence, but now you're flummoxed. The concepts involved are simple and valuable, though, so let's clear them up.

The word "multiple" usually refers to a company's P/E ratio, which as you know by now is its current stock price divided by its earnings per share. If a company has a P/E of 28, people will say that it's trading at "28 times earnings" or at "a multiple of 28."

Savvy Fools often examine a company's multiple and compare it with what seems to be a fair multiple, given its industry and competitive position. Let's say that Downsizers' peers all have multiples in the high 30s, and its own multiple is in the low 20s. A low multiple can be promising, suggesting that the stock is undervalued and that the price will increase as the multiple catches up to its peers. (It can also indicate a firm that's losing in the marketplace, though.)

Also auspicious are briskly growing earnings. Earnings growth drives stock price growth. Rapid growth can even make up for a relatively high multiple. How fast earnings grow is also a good indicator of how high a company's P/E should be. In other words, a company doubling its earnings each year deserves a higher P/E than a firm growing gradually.

Expected earnings growth coupled with P/E multiple growth can offer a powerful one-two punch. Imagine a stock trading at $10 per share — 10 times its EPS of $1. As earnings grow, the stock price will likely increase to maintain the multiple. For example, when earnings are $2 per share, the stock price should be near $20. But, if the multiple is also growing, the price is likely to increase even more. If a reasonable multiple is perceived to be more like 15 and the earnings are $2 per share, the stock should eventually approach $30 per share.

Companies generating above-average earnings growth and trading at below-average P/E ratios can make for great investments.

---

### 365 Are there any other types of multiples?

You bet. If you read analyses of various companies, you'll see references to price-to-sales multiples, book value multiples, cash flow multiples, and more. It's instructive to compare a company's various multiples with those of its competitors.

---

### 366 How can a firm's earnings per share rise when its earnings are flat?

This can seem puzzling, but it happens when the number of shares falls. Imagine that the Free-Range Onion Co. (ticker: BULBS) has 10 million shares outstanding and earns $20 million in a quarter, making earnings per share (EPS) $2. If it spends some of its cash to buy back a million shares and then earns $20 million again in the next quarter, its EPS has suddenly risen to $2.22 (20 million divided by 9 million equals 2.22.).

This is why many shareholders rejoice when a company aggressively buys back some of its own stock. It's a sign of management confidence — plus the remaining shares can be worth more.

**367** **How can you tell if a company's increased earnings per share isn't just due to the company buying back shares of its stock?**

While share buybacks are generally good, as they boost the value of each remaining share of stock, ideally they shouldn't be the *only* driver of EPS growth.

The solution is a simple one. Focus on net income. Share buybacks reduce the number of shares outstanding. When the number of shares decreases, the earnings *per share* rise. To get a handle on what's happening without regard to buybacks, just examine the total net income.

**368** **In financial statements, I see references to "diluted" and "basic" earnings per share. What's the difference?**

This reflects some interesting recent changes in how companies report their earnings. At the end of 1997, a new rule went into effect, instituted by the Financial Accounting Standards Board (FASB). It requires companies to report their quarterly earnings per share (EPS) in two ways: basic and diluted.

This is important stuff for investors to understand, as corporate per-share profits are, in many ways, at the core of all things financial. Per-share profits show an investor her share of a company's total profits. Fools should pay attention to the diluted, not basic, numbers.

Basic EPS is net income, less any preferred stock dividends, divided by the weighted average number of common stock shares outstanding during the reporting period. Diluted EPS takes into account stock options, warrants, preferred stock, and convertible debt securities, all of which can be converted into common stock. These common stock equivalents represent the potential claims of other owners on earnings, and show the investor how much of the company's earnings she's entitled to, at a minimum.

Any increase in the number of shares of stock dilutes the earnings attributed to each share. The difference can be dramatic. For example,

Dell Computer reported $0.66 per share in basic earnings for its fiscal year 1999, while fully diluted earnings were 7.6% lower, at $0.61 per share. Options and other securities would have added 192 million shares to the 2,536 million shares outstanding. Options are not all bad, though. Employee compensation in the form of options permits companies to attract and keep talented employees and also to reduce current salary expenses, leaving more money to help the firm grow.

Since many firms issue gobs of stock options, the new rules will help investors more accurately determine how much of the company's earnings they're entitled to, and will impart a sense of what stock options actually cost a shareholder. The change will also align U.S. accounting standards with international standards being developed, ultimately helping investors compare companies around the globe.

---

**369 I understand that investors typically evaluate companies based on earnings. But what if there are no earnings, such as with young upstart companies or firms in temporarily tough times?**

That's when you should focus on other measures instead. (And, besides, you should always be looking at other measures, anyway.) Check out revenues, for example, and revenue growth rates, and margins, and debt levels, and competitive positioning, and brand strength, among many other things. You essentially want to evaluate whether the company is on the path to profitability, and how well it's executing its strategy.

---

**370 Is it smart to look for stocks whose share prices are trading near their 52-week lows and to consider selling ones trading near their highs?**

A company whose stock is trading near its 52-week low might make a profitable investment... or not. The price alone doesn't offer enough information. The company might be a great one temporarily facing some trouble, in which case it could be well worth your while to research it further. Alternatively, it might be careening to its demise and about to burst into flames. A company going down in flames will hit

52-week lows one after another for quite a while.

Selling a stock at its all-year high isn't generally a good idea. Think of wonderful companies that have rewarded shareholders for many years. They set new highs all the time, despite occasional bumps in the road. Sell now and you might miss out on future gains.

## 371 Could you explain what a "quick ratio" is?

The "quick ratio," sometimes called the "acid-test ratio," measures a company's liquidity. It helps investors see how comfortably a company can meet its short-term obligations. Let's run through a quick ratio based on Kmart's balance sheet for fiscal 1999.

Take the current assets of $8.2 billion and subtract the current inventory of $7.1 billion. Divide the result, $1.1 billion, by current liabilities of $4.1 billion and you get 0.27. Yikes. Low ratios, such as those below 1.00, can be cause for concern, especially for smaller companies with less access to bank loans.

A year earlier, at the end of fiscal 1998, Kmart's ratio was 0.35, so its financial health, according to this measure, has been worsening. Looks like Martha Stewart and Jaclyn Smith have their work cut out for them!

## 372 What is "book value"? Is it a good measure of a company's worth?

Book value is an accounting concept, reflecting a company's value according to its balance sheet. It is equal to shareholders' equity, or the difference between assets and liabilities.

Book value once approximated a company's market value, as most assets, such as factories and land, were capital-intensive and appeared on the balance sheet. Today, however, as America's economy is becoming less industrial and more service-oriented, book value is a less-relevant measure for investors.

Consider Microsoft Corp., for example. Its recently reported book value was about $41 billion. This is far from a fair value for the company, as Microsoft's market value was upwards of $350 billion, and it had more than $24 billion in cash alone. Much of Microsoft's value stems from assets that don't register significantly on the balance sheet — its intellectual property, talented employees, strong brand, and phenomenal market share.

Book value can even be a poor indicator of fair value for a heavily industrial company. Imagine a firm that owns a lot of land and many buildings. Over the years, the value of these assets is depreciated on the balance sheet, eventually to zero. But these assets are rarely worthless and can even appreciate in value over time. Such a company might actually be worth a lot more than its book value (while other companies can be worth much less). For these reasons, it often makes sense to largely ignore book value.

## 373 How should I make sense of inventory on a company's balance sheet?

Inventory refers to all items in a company's production pipeline. There are three main categories of inventory: raw materials, work in progress, and finished goods. Imagine PlastiCrania Inc. (ticker: NOGGN), which makes Mr. Burrito Head toys. Making the toys involves ordering, receiving, storing, and using raw materials, such as chemicals, cardboard, and paint. These are assembled into finished products. At any time, PlastiCrania's inventory is likely to include vats of plastic, half-assembled burrito molds, finished products waiting to be shipped to distributors, and returned products from retailers.

If a company carries too little inventory, any shortages that occur will hold up production. Too much inventory will generate high storage costs and tie up capital that could be used elsewhere. Finished goods sitting on shelves a long time also pose a risk of not being sold due to obsolescence. In recent years, many American companies adopted "just-in-time" inventory systems pioneered by the Japanese. These systems have firms holding precisely the minimum necessary inventory, replenishing supplies continually as needed.

Compare a company's inventory levels with those from the year before, and with revenue growth. If inventory is rising faster than revenue, it could signal a sales slowdown. If inventory growth lags sales, either the company is not meeting demand or it's successfully tightening controls on production processes and distribution.

## **374** What is "inventory turnover"?

It's a measure that will give you a sense of how quickly a company's products are flying off the shelves. Here's how you'd crunch this number:

From the company's income statement, find the "cost of goods sold" (or COGS). You'll want the last 12 months' worth. If the fiscal year has just ended, you can use the figures in the annual report or 10-K report. If it's mid-year, just re-create the last year's results by adding together the numbers from the last four quarters' reports. Once you have this number, jot it down.

Next, you calculate the average value of inventory for the 12-month period you're looking at. If, for example, you're using the cost of goods sold for the 1999 fiscal year, you want to take the inventory value from the end of fiscal 1998 and average it with the inventory value from the end of 1999. This way, your numbers address the same time period — the duration of fiscal 1999.

Once you have the cost of goods sold, divide it by the average inventory, and you'll get the inventory turnover rate. A company with high and growing inventory turnover rates would appear to be well managed, freeing up its working capital for other uses.

## **375** Can you explain why you generally think low inventory levels are good and high ones are bad? This doesn't make sense to me.

While a high inventory level might make a company appear well positioned to meet demand, it can be risky: demand may suddenly plunge. Indeed, a large inventory may signal that demand has already slackened.

Products end up sitting on the shelves all the time. Fashion trends change, technological advances make current products obsolete, and the functional utility of some products is gone after a certain time. A PC manufacturer with a large stock of older computers probably can't sell many of them because buyers want newer models. (A warehouse full of Christmas ornaments in January faces similarly bleak prospects.)

Anything left sitting on a warehouse shelf costs money to hold and risks not being sold. Efficient companies generally try to maintain low levels of inventory. These levels permit quick reaction to market changes and minimize the chances the company will get stuck with extra goods.

## 376 What does "shrinkage" mean in the business world?

It refers to the loss of inventory that happens through unusual ways, such as accidental breakage, theft, weather damage, etc.

## 377 What does it mean when a company is said to be "stuffing the channel"?

When a company stuffs the channel, it ships inventory ahead of schedule, filling its distribution channels with more product than is needed. Since companies often record sales as soon as they ship products, channel stuffing can make it appear that business is booming. In reality, the products not sold may well be returned eventually to the manufacturer. This means sales already claimed may never occur. In a sense, sales are made at the expense of sales in future quarters.

To determine whether a company is stuffing the channel, see if its accounts receivable growth is outpacing sales growth. If so, that's a red flag. Alternatively, calculate "days sales outstanding" (DSO). First, divide the last four quarters' revenues by 365. Then divide accounts receivable by that number. This reveals how many days' worth of sales the current accounts receivable represents. Between 30 and 45 days is typical. You can also follow the same process for the last quarter, dividing last quarter's revenues by 91.25 (days in a quarter, on average). A company with a low DSO is getting its cash back quicker and, ideally, putting it immediately to use, getting an edge on the competition. Rising numbers might indicate channel stuffing. Remember that this isn't useful for all companies. Restaurants and cash-based business-es, for example, aren't going to have much, if any, receivables.

## 378 Can you explain the "accrual" method of recognizing sales?

With pleasure. It's an important concept to understand, because under this system, a company might not have actually received the "revenues" on its income statement.

Revenues don't necessarily represent the receipt of cash in a sale. Many firms "accrue" revenues — booking sales when goods are shipped, when services are rendered, or as a long-term contract proceeds through stages of completion.

Imagine the Beehive Wig Co. (ticker: WHOAA). With the accrual method, if it has shipped 1,000 crates of wigs, but hasn't yet received payment for them, those sales still appear on the income statement. The checks "in the mail" get reported as "accounts receivable" on the balance sheet.

Keep an eye on receivables to make sure a company isn't booking as sales that which it cannot collect. Also, make sure it's not packing sales into this quarter that really belong in the next quarter.

## 379 I know it's very important to make sure that a company you're investing in has high-quality management, but how can you assess such a thing?

Financial statements can help you discern whether a company's management is on the ball.

Dig out the company's annual report or its latest earnings report and look at the balance sheet. Is there more long-term debt than cash? Many companies carry a lot of debt successfully, but you could look into whether management is borrowing more than it can pay.

Look at the income statement and compare numbers over the past few years. Have sales and earnings been growing consistently? A smooth upward trend suggests that management has been planning well, encountering few surprises.

A growing operating margin is another sign of high quality, showing that the firm is working on wringing more and more profit from each dollar of sales. In a period of slowing sales growth, savvy managers can maintain earnings growth momentum by increasing margins. To boost margins, management has to run its business more efficiently, decreasing expenses such as the cost of supplies or employee salaries.

One of the best barometers of management excellence is a company's return on equity (ROE). It measures how well the company is using its reinvested earnings to generate additional income.

Invest in companies only after you make sure their highly compensated executives are earning their keep.

## 380 How is return on equity calculated, and what does it show?

A company's return on equity (ROE) reflects the productivity of the net assets (assets minus liabilities) a company's management has at its disposal.

Whenever a company generates profits, there are four main things it can do with that moolah. It can:
• Pay shareholders a dividend
• Pay down debt
• Buy back shares of company stock
• Reinvest in operations.

Return on equity reveals how effectively reinvested earnings and capital that shareholders originally invested in the company are used to generate additional earnings. For example, profits might be used to acquire another company. Or a new factory might be built, increasing the firm's output and sales.

To calculate return on equity, take one year's (or four quarters') worth of earnings (often referred to as "net income") from the income statement. Next, look at shareholders' equity on the balance sheet. Remember that net income reflects income generated over a period of time, whereas shareholder's equity listed on the balance sheet reflects a value at one point in time. You want to use a shareholders' equity figure that covers the same period of time as the net income figure. So, you should average two shareholders' equity numbers, from the beginning and end of that period, adding them and then dividing by two.

To finally arrive at the ROE, divide the year's earnings by the average shareholders' equity. (Whew!)

Consider Gillette. In fiscal 1999, it reported net income of $1.3 billion and average shareholder equity of $3.8 billion. Dividing 1.3 by 3.8 yields a return on equity of around 33%. That's an impressive number, but it's even more meaningful when compared to the company's past performance.

Gillette's ROE fell to 23% in 1998 from 31% in 1997. It appears that executives at this consumer-product conglomerate are improving the use of shareholders' capital. (Of course, taking the time to look farther back will reveal an ROE of 23% in 1996 and 30% in 1995, so while 33% is the best result in quite a while, it hasn't been rising in a straight line. Net income itself has also bounced up and down.)

Another way to add context is to compare a company with its peers. Based on a quick look at the 1999 annual reports of Gillette's peers in consumer personal-care products, here are some ROEs: Colgate-Palmolive (48%), Procter & Gamble (31%), and Dial (29%). Whenever you crunch any numbers for a company, it's valuable to compare them with previous quarters or years and also with those of industry peers.

## 381 What is a company's "payout ratio"?

It's the percentage of net income the firm pays out to shareholders as dividends. If Buzzy's Broccoli Beer (ticker: BROCB) pays $1.00 per year in dividends and sports earnings per share (EPS) of $4.00, its payout ratio is 25% ($1.00 divided by $4.00 equals 0.25, or 25%).

This shows what the company is doing with its money. If you see that a company is returning 75% of its earnings to shareholders, then little is being reinvested in operations. That can be okay, as sometimes reinvested earnings would return less than shareholders could get investing the payout on their own.

## 382 What kind of company research should I do in addition to scouring the financial statements?

A lot can be learned about a company or industry by asking some carefully chosen questions of carefully chosen people. In his 1958 masterpiece *Common Stocks and Uncommon Profits*, Philip Fisher advocated this practice, calling it "scuttlebutt":

> "Most people, particularly if they feel sure there is no danger of their being quoted, like to talk about the field of work in which they are engaged and will talk rather freely about their competitors. Go to five companies in an industry, ask each of them intelligent questions about the points of strength and weakness of the other four, and nine times out of 10 a surprisingly detailed and accurate picture of all five will emerge."

Imagine you're considering investing in Ethan Allen Interiors. It might look good on paper, but you should still check out the scuttlebutt. If you're in an investment club, you can work in teams to gather information. Give Ethan Allen's Investor Relations department a call and ask some questions. Find out who the company's top competitors are. Then call *them*. You might even track down a furniture trade association and see what information it can provide.

Computers are bringing scuttlebutt to your desktop, as you can now access valuable industry information online. Head to a search engine such as www.google.com or www.hotbot.com, for example, and you can discover some wonderful resources, such as trade journals, trade associations, websites, and articles, all focused on the industry you're researching. At websites such as Fool.com, you'll find individual discussion boards for thousands of companies like Ethan Allen.

Here's another site that should prove useful: www.Fool.com/community/resource. It's where we've collected many links to websites offering info on specific industries and companies — and many more topics.

Someone who lives near an Ethan Allen factory might visit it late at night and on the weekend, to count cars in the parking lot and see if workers are toiling overtime. They might report on discussions with local employees and suppliers. You and others across the country can don trench coats and visit retail outlets, checking to see how many customers are placing orders and how successful the product mix appears to be. You can interview store workers, too. Assembled together, this information should be quite revealing.

By mixing a careful reading of financial statements and scuttlebutt gathered from a variety of sources, you'll have a much better chance of beating the market. Keep up with scuttlebutt even after you buy and own shares of a company.

## 383 Can you explain what a company's "capital structure" is, and whether it's important?

When evaluating a company's merits as a possible investment, you should examine the components of its value and explore how it finances its workings. This is referred to as a company's "capital structure." It's usually a mix of cash, debt financing (borrowing from a bank or issuing bonds), and equity financing (selling a chunk of the company and/or issuing shares of stock).

Some (extreme) examples will shed more light. Imagine a company financed completely through debt. If the company is paying 5% interest on its debt, but growing earnings at 10% yearly, its payments can be met and the financing is effective. The lower the interest rate and the greater the difference between it and the company's earnings growth rate, the better. If a company is carrying a lot of debt at high interest rates, but is growing slowly, this is bad news. Fluctuating earnings can also be problematic, as interest payments may sometimes completely wipe out earnings.

Next, imagine a company that raises needed funds only by issuing more stock. This is an appealing option when the stock market is hopping; cash is generated with little effort. The downside to equity financing, though, is that the value of existing shareholders' stock is diluted every time new shares are issued. This is okay only if the moolah raised creates more value for the company than the value eroded by dilution. Eventually, many companies grow so profitable that they can methodically buy back shares, driving up value for existing shareholders.

Finally, imagine a firm that's financing its operations completely on its own. This means that it's fueling growth with the cash created from operations. The advantage of internally financed growth is that it forces a firm to plan and budget carefully, resulting in (sometimes gradual) value creation for the company's owners. The weakness is that it can be a slow, grueling process. Worse yet, competitors effectively issuing debt or stock can fund more rapid growth than this company.

## 384 What is the "Flow Ratio"? I know that it's used in Rule Maker investing, but I don't know how to calculate it or what it means.

It's a handy measure you can calculate using a company's balance sheet that reveals how effectively cash flow is managed. Here's the formula:

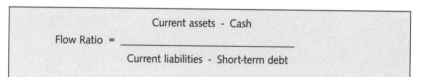

$$\text{Flow Ratio} = \frac{\text{Current assets} - \text{Cash}}{\text{Current liabilities} - \text{Short-term debt}}$$

Let's consider the Flow Ratio of Harley-Davidson as an example. For its second quarter ending in June 2000, it sported $1.07 billion in total current assets. Subtract its $298 million in cash and equivalents, and you get $802 million. Next, take current liabilities ($470 million) and subtract short-term debt ($48 million). Divide the first result ($802 million) by the second ($422 million) and you'll arrive at a Flow Ratio of about 1.83.

Any result below about 1.25 is admirable, so 1.83 is not ideal. (The lower the Flow Ratio the better.) Still, a little more number crunching will reveal that a year earlier, Harley-Davidson's Flow Ratio stood at 2.06, so it's clearly dropping, which is a good sign.

Think about the ratio's components and you'll better understand what it's showing you. When you subtract cash from current assets, you're mainly left with accounts receivable and inventories. Ideally, a powerful company will demand rapid payment from its customers, keeping its accounts receivable at low levels. Likewise, it will manage to keep only necessary minimum inventory on hand. So, a low number for this part of the Flow Ratio equation is a good thing.

Meanwhile, current liabilities, after you subtract debt, are usually dominated by accounts payable. That's money a company owes and can temporarily use — interest-free. Industry-dominating companies often wield enough clout to demand favorable payment terms. A high number for this part of the Flow Ratio is preferred.

Divide an ideally low asset number by an ideally high liability number, and you get a low Flow Ratio. This suggests a company aggressively collecting payment from others, while gradually making its own payments, resulting in more cash at its disposal. And, since cash is the lifeblood of a company, a low (and preferably declining) Flow Ratio is indicative of a strong and healthy business.

If you're wondering how low a Flow Ratio can go and how some well-known companies stack up, here are some recent numbers (as of mid-2000):

Yahoo!...........................0.34
Microsoft.......................0.49
America Online.............0.86
Intel..............................0.93
Coca-Cola......................1.03
Nokia.............................1.19
Gap................................1.34
Pfizer............................1.77

## 385 What is the "Cash King Margin"?

Like the Flow Ratio, the Cash King Margin is a key measure used in the Fool's Rule Maker investing strategy. It is essentially like the net profit margin, except that instead of using net income from the income statement as the measure of income, it uses operating cash flow from the statement of cash flows. This is done because operating cash flow is a more honest number, in many ways.

It's not that companies are maliciously lying on their income statements, but accounting rules do allow various kinds of manipulation. For example, a company might record as sales whatever product it has shipped. Half of these items may end up returned, though, or perhaps some customers will end up stiffing the company. In these cases, sales at the top line will be, in a sense, overstated — and the resulting bottom-line earnings will be skewed.

Cash from operations, as reported on the cash flow statement, isn't easily manipulated. It's based on actual cash inflows and outflows. It's a much purer number, and can make it easier for an investor to compare apples to apples when studying various companies.

Here's how the Cash King Margin is calculated:

$$\text{Cash King Margin} = \frac{\text{Operating Cash Flow - Capital Expenditures}}{\text{Sales}}$$

Some notes:
- Operating cash flow might go by a different name on a company's cash flow statement. It's often listed as "Net cash provided by [or used by] operating activities."
- Capital expenditures are often listed as "Additions to [or subtractions from] property and equipment" in the investing activities section of the cash flow statement. They include major equipment purchases, factory construction, and other big-ticket items.
- By subtracting capital expenditures, we can see how profitable the business is on its own, without regard to capital expenses.

When evaluating a company's Cash King Margin, you can smile at any result over 10% and grin widely at any that tops 15%. Here are a few results for some well-known companies, as of mid-2000, just to give you a little perspective:

Microsoft ....................60%

Intel............................28%
America Online ............16%
Campbell Soup Co.........16%
Dell Computer..............14%
Coca-Cola .....................14%
Nokia..........................7.7%
ExxonMobil.................6.9%
Procter & Gamble.........2.7%

That's still very little perspective, though. If you were really interested in one of these companies, you'd want to see what the trend has been for its Cash King Margin, as well as for many other measures. And you'd want to compare a company's numbers with those of its competitors.

Still, consider the amazing Microsoft figure above. It means that every dollar the company took in generated about 60 cents in cold, hard cash for the company's coffers.

## 386 I'm evaluating two companies with similarly strong sales and earnings growth. What else should I look at to see which company might make a better investment?

One good item to examine would be the balance sheet. If inventory levels or accounts receivable are outgrowing sales (in terms of percentage), that's a bad sign. Another red flag is when a company is taking on a load of long-term debt. Two companies performing similarly on the income statement can look very different on the balance sheet.

Examine the statement of cash flows, too, to see how the company's cash is being generated. Look at how much investment is required to create earnings. Generally, you want to see most cash coming from ongoing operations — the stuff produced and sold — and not from the issuance of debt or stock.

Also worth a closer look are the companies' margins. These include gross margins, operating margins, net margins, and the Cash King Margin. Higher gross margins might suggest that a firm has a more proprietary brand or technology. That usually indicates a higher-quality company, with pricing power in its markets and the ability to hold down manufacturing costs.

You could also examine return on equity and return on assets, comparing companies in the same industry. See which firm is generating more dollars of earnings for each dollar of capital invested in the business. Check previous years' numbers, to see whether the trend is positive.

Basically, the more angles you examine a company from, the better. The more information you gather, the more sure you'll likely be of your decision to invest or not to invest.

## 387 Should companies reporting increased losses per share be avoided?

Not necessarily. Companies sometimes do spend a lot more in one year than another. This might happen if they buy another company, or perhaps if they ramp up research or advertising expenditures to grow.

Imagine online retailer FreshFish.com (ticker: SCROD), which delivers fresh fish to America by mail. Let's say it lost about $30 million in 1997 and $125 million in 1998. Some investors see numbers like this and run the other way, preferring to invest only in companies reporting steadily increasing profits. Fair enough.

But, perhaps while net losses increased 317%, revenues grew *more* briskly, up 350%. If you're willing to consider companies that are not yet making money, this is a promising sign. Many investors believe that, for emerging start-ups like FreshFish.com, this is the time to plow money into advertising and into growing the business. They reason that the time for profits is later, once the company has amassed a huge seafood-by-mail-loving customer base.

## 388 Is researching companies online really that much better or easier than doing it the old-fashioned way, at a library?

It sure is. The Internet has revolutionized investing, giving folks on Main

Street many of the resources used by the folks on Wall Street. With a computer and a modem, you can access all the information you need to make financial decisions — information that a few years ago might have cost you thousands of dollars per year, but is now mostly free.

One of the first places to look is (humbly submitted) our website at www.Fool.com, featuring commentaries on company news, discussions of various investing strategies, and lots of data — such as dividend yields, historical financial information, stock charts, a stock-split calendar, and an earnings report calendar. In Fooldom, you can have your financial questions answered 24 hours a day by Fool staffers and contributors across the country.

Perhaps most valuable for investors are a company's financial reports, filed with the Securities and Exchange Commission (SEC) and available online at www.freeEDGAR.com and other sites. Because the SEC requires companies to include certain key information, reading a few 10-Qs and a 10-K is often the most efficient way to figure out a company in a few hours. The 10-K reports include detailed company descriptions, as well.

If you're looking for a company's history, financial information, and addresses, take a look at www.hoovers.com. (There's a fee for some of this info.) Also, don't neglect to visit a company's own website, where you'll often find information on its history, products and services, and stock.

Keep up with a company's happenings with keyword "Company News" on America Online. It features searchable archives of Associated Press, Reuters, Business Wire, and PR Newswire stories. On the Web, review company news at www.newsalert.com, www.businesswire.com, and www.prnewswire.com. Your local newspaper is likely to have its own website, too.

Head to www.bigcharts.com, for comprehensive historical stock charts. Five- or six-year financial trends are available at www.wsrn.com. If you're willing to cough up a little cash, you'll get lots of detailed information at www.marketguide.com.

All investors should explore these online resources. If you don't have a computer, you can usually get free access through your local library — or bum dinner off a buddy and surf the 'Net at his place while he's cooking!

---

**389** **I'm interested in taking a course or two at a local college to help me become a better investor. What would be the most valuable kind of course to take?**

One of the most useful subjects to understand as an investor is financial accounting. It's not the most exciting topic to study, but it can make reading financial statements a lot more fruitful. With accounting concepts under your belt, you may be able to spot red flags in balance sheets and income statements before most investors do. You can learn a lot about accounting from books, too. Consider John Tracy's *How To Read a Financial Report*. You'll learn a lot about financial statements in general in *Analysis of Financial Statements* by Leopold A. Bernstein.

# Advanced
# Research Topics

*If you hunger to learn more about researching companies, this chapter covers a few higher-level investing topics. It's a short chapter, though. If I addressed all the possible topics in this book in great depth, you'd have to haul it around with a forklift. So, permit this chapter to give you a taste of the kinds of things you can learn with a little more digging. I'll conclude it with a pointer to some good resources for learning more.*

## 390 How should I go about analyzing an industry?

You're smart to think about and evaluate an industry when you are assessing a company within it. In his book *Competitive Strategy*, Harvard Business School professor Michael Porter lays out five competitive forces that affect an industry.

- **Threat of entry**. This can be assessed by evaluating how much capital it takes to enter the industry — the economies of scale, switching costs, and brand value. It's easier to enter the lawn-service industry than the semiconductor equipment industry — one requires some relatively inexpensive equipment, while the other requires factories and much specialized knowledge. Switching costs protect some companies. For example, some customers will think twice about switching from America Online to another e-mail provider because they'll have to alert too many people of their new address.

- **Bargaining power of suppliers**. If you're running an airline, there are only a few airplane suppliers (such as Boeing and Airbus). It's more difficult in that situation to play one against the other, trying to strike a bargain. If there were many suppliers, they'd likely be competing more for your business, which might result in lower costs for you.

- **Bargaining power of buyers.** This is affected by brand power, switching costs, the relative volume of purchases, standardization of the product, and elasticity of demand (where demand increases as prices fall, and vice versa). In book retailing, buyers have many choices and can easily compare prices online. This gives them bargaining power.

- **Availability of substitutes.** If you're in the restaurant industry, your business will be affected by how easily people can buy take-out meals at supermarkets, how many people prepare meals at home, and the availability of other alternatives.

- **Competitive rivalry.** The more competitive an industry is, the more likely it is to have price wars and reduced profitability. The airline industry is a good example here. Over the years, it has not offered the best returns to investors.

Take these things into consideration and you may be able to zero in on the most attractive company in the industry. Alternatively, you might learn that the entire industry just isn't as attractive as you thought. Learn more about researching companies at www.multex.com and www.Fool.com/research.

## 391 What is a company's "earnings yield"?

One way to think about what you're paying for a company is to look at its price-to-earnings (P/E) ratio. Another way is to calculate the inverse of that, which is its earnings yield.

Consider the example of Fryyndar and Ulf Scandinavian Pharmaceuticals (ticker: FANDU), whose motto is "Varsågod och svälj!" (That's Swedish for "Here, swallow this pill!"). To calculate its P/E ratio, you divide the current stock price by the annual earnings per share (EPS).

If its current annual EPS is $3 and the stock is trading for $111 per share, the P/E is $111 divided by $3, or 37.

To calculate Fryyndar and Ulf's earnings yield, just reverse the P/E ratio, dividing the annual EPS by the current stock price ($3 divided by $111 equals 0.027, or 2.7%). Compared to risk-free Treasury bond interest rates (of roughly 6% at the time of this writing), this doesn't appear to be a bargain. But remember: Whereas bond rates are fixed, earnings typically grow. Imagine that FANDU is expected to increase earnings 10% per year. If so, in 10 years its EPS should grow to $7.78. Assuming we bought shares when they were at $111, the earnings yield for us has now become 7%, considerably better ($7.78 divided by $111 is 0.07, or 7%).

It can be instructive to see how long it takes for the growing earnings yield to pass the current 30-year bond rate. FANDU passes it within nine years.

If your desired rate of return on your invested dollars is 15%, it will take FANDU 18 years to reach that target — if earnings actually grow at the estimated pace, that is. Perhaps you can find another investment that will get you there more quickly. With riskier companies, you might look for them to pass your target rate sooner rather than later.

The earnings yield is just one of many investor tools. It shouldn't dictate any decision for you, but it can help you think more effectively about your expectations for investments.

---

## 392 Can you explain what "enterprise value" is?

Enterprise value (EV) represents a company's economic value — the minimum someone would have to pay to buy it outright. It's an important number to consider when you value a stock.

You may remember that earlier in this book I explained that market capitalization (the current stock price multiplied by the number of shares outstanding) can also serve as a price tag for a company. That's true, but market cap ignores debt, and with some companies debt is substantial and changes the picture significantly. Enterprise value is a modification of market cap, incorporating debt.

To understand the concept of enterprise value better, imagine that you're looking at two companies that have equal market caps. One has no debt on its balance sheet, while the other one is rather debt-heavy. The latter company will be making lots of interest payments on that debt over the years — so you probably wouldn't pay the same price for each company.

By the same token, imagine that you have two companies with equal market caps of $50 billion and no debt. One has negligible cash and cash equivalents onhand, and the other has $5 billion in cash in its coffers. If you bought the first company for $50 billion, you'd have a company worth, presumably, $50 billion. But if you bought the second company for $50 billion, it would have cost you just $45 billion, since you instantly have $5 billion in cash.

To calculate enterprise value, start with a company's market cap, add debt (found on a company's balance sheet), and subtract cash and investments (also on the balance sheet). To get total debt, add together long- and short-term debt.

Debt = Long-term debt + Short-term debt
Enterprise Value = Market capitalization − Cash & equivalents + Debt

Let's examine Kmart, using its quarterly earnings report from April 2000. Its 481 million shares, at a recent stock price of about $7, yield a market cap of $3.4 billion. To that, we add its $1.9 billion in debt and subtract its $0.35 billion in cash and cash equivalents. The result is $4.95 billion, a significantly higher number than the market cap.

Debt can make a big difference. If you paid $3.4 billion for Kmart, you would actually end up with a total bill of $4.95 billion, because the company comes with a lot of debt. The enterprise value reminds all investors, large and small, that debt is a cost to the business.

## 393 Can you explain the concept of "intrinsic value"?

Imagine you're looking at a newfangled invention called the "dollar machine." Once a year for 10 years, it spits out a brand-new dollar bill. How would you value this contraption? Obviously, a price tag higher than $10 is silly. Paying $9 might seem smart, as it locks in a $1 prof-it. But you can do better with your $9.

Think of it this way. If you invest $9 for 10 years and it turns into $10, you've achieved a total return of 11.1%. That might look good, but that's 11.1% over a 10-year period. It amounts to only about 1% per year. Sheesh — even a passbook savings account can beat that, and it's even insured. Investors should always consider where else they might invest their greenbacks, and what other kinds of returns they might expect.

Back to our dollar machine. Let's say you expect a rate of return equal to the stock market's historic rate of about 11% growth per year. If so, you might decide to pay just $3.52 for the machine. $3.52 invested for 10 years, earning 11% annually, becomes $10. (You would probably be outbid by someone else, though... someone who realized that she could reinvest those dollars elsewhere at the end of each year.)

The dollar machine is not just a fantasy. It's very much like companies in which you buy stock. The price you'd pay for the machine today is its "intrinsic value." Companies also have intrinsic value, or "fair value" (based primarily on earnings), and investors need to keep this in mind when buying stock in them. Pay attention to a company's earnings and dividend payout.

If you bought a share of General Electric 10 years ago, it would have cost you about $6. In the last 10 years (1990-2000), it has paid out more than $6 in dividends. Was the $6 a good price, then? Well, considering that GE stock split 2-for-1 in 1994 and again in 1997, went up to around $150 per share, split 3-for-1 in 2000, and now trades around $55 per share, you betcha.

Companies are valued on the profits they earn. When buying stock, you don't want to end up paying too much for a dollar machine.

---

## 394 What is the "price-to-sales ratio"?

The price-to-sales ratio (PSR) can be a handy measure to use instead of a price-to-earnings (P/E) ratio if you're dealing with a company that has no earnings. No earnings mean you can't calculate a P/E — but as long as a firm has sales, or revenues, you *can* calculate a PSR.

The PSR takes the market capitalization of a company and divides it by the last 12 months' revenues. Remember that the market cap is the current value that the market is giving the company, arrived at by multiplying the current share price by the number of shares outstanding.

Imagine Iditarod Express (ticker: MUSH), famous for its slogan, "When it absolutely has to get to a remote corner of Alaska in the next few weeks." If MUSH has 10 million shares outstanding priced at $10 a share, then its market capitalization is $100 million. If it had $200 million in sales over the last four quarters, its PSR would be 0.50 ($100 million divided by $200 million equals 0.50). Compare the PSR with sales growth. A high PSR isn't necessarily bad if sales are growing rapidly.

The price-to-sales ratio is especially handy with start-ups, small-cap companies, and unprofitable firms. Assume that Iditarod Express lost money in the past year, but has a PSR of 0.50 when its peers have PSRs of 2.0 or higher. If it can turn itself around and start making money, it's likely to have substantial upside potential if it can match competitors' profit margins. There are some years during recessions when none of the auto companies are profitable. This doesn't mean they're all worthless and there's no way to compare them. You can just use measures such as the PSR instead of the P/E ratio. Measure how much you're paying for a dollar of sales instead of a dollar of earnings.

Despite its usefulness, the PSR should never be the only number you crunch.

The PSR can sometimes give you a nice context for a company's value relative to its industry peers, but while sales growth is great, those sales must be transformed into meaningful and rising earnings to make shareholders happy. Some companies have massive and growing revenues, but little earnings to show for it. How much a company earns from its sales will eventually drive the value of the business and the stock.

**395** **I've heard that the PSR has limitations. What are they, and what might I use instead?**

You're right. For starters, it's based largely on sales (a.k.a. revenues), but all dollars taken in as sales are not equal. Some companies have hefty profit margins and keep much of their sales dollars as earnings. Other companies have small margins and keep very little as profit. In addition, the PSR ignores debt. A company's debt load should factor into your assessment of it.

One way to avoid these problems is to use a variation on the PSR — the enterprise value-to-sales ratio (EVSR). If you'll recall from the explanation of enterprise value above, while a company's market cap ignores debt, by making a few adjustments to it you can arrive at enterprise value, a more accurate measure of a company's value. With the EVSR, you simply use the company's enterprise value instead of its market cap, like this:

$$\text{Enterprise Value-to-Sales Ratio} = \frac{\text{Enterprise Value}}{\text{Trailing 12-Month Revenues}}$$

**396** **How do you calculate "return on assets," and what does it tell you?**

Return on assets (ROA) measures the profitability of a company's total assets, and is often used as a gauge of management effectiveness. There are a few steps involved in this, but they aren't too tough. (Got your pencil ready?) You'll find all the numbers you need on a company's recent balance sheet and income statement. We'll use Wal-Mart's fiscal 2000 results as an example.

Return on assets is determined by multiplying net profit margin by asset turnover. To get net profit margin, look near the bottom of the income statement for net income and divide that by net sales (also called "revenues") from the top of the statement. Dividing Wal-Mart's net income of $5.4 billion by its revenues of $165 billion (yowza!), we get a net profit margin of 0.0327, or 3.27%.

Asset turnover is calculated by dividing total revenues by the average of total assets for the period. (Total assets are listed on the balance sheet.) Since the revenues we're using cover all of fiscal 2000, we'll add the total assets from this earnings report to those from a year ago, and divide by two. Dividing Wal-Mart's revenue by its average total assets of $60.2 billion yields an asset turnover of 2.74. In other words, Wal-Mart generates nearly $3 in sales from each dollar of assets. Not bad.

Now that we have a net profit margin of 0.0327 and an asset turnover of 2.74, we multiply them to get a return on assets of 9%. This shows that Wal-Mart creates nine cents of earnings from each dollar of assets. By comparison, Kmart's ROA over the same time was 2.75%.

## 397 Is there an easier way of calculating ROA?

There is. You can simply divide net income (though sometimes operating income is used) for a period by the average total assets for the period.

The reason for making it more complicated, as I did above, is to get even more information out of the calculation. ROA can be broken down into two telling parts: net profit margin (net income divided by revenues) and asset turnover (revenues divided by average total assets). You'll learn more about a company by determining both parts and multiplying them together to arrive at ROA. This offers insights into two different business levers. At a glance, you can see whether a firm's ROA of 20% is determined by a profit margin of 5% and an asset turnover of 4, or a profit margin of 10% and an asset turnover of 2. By knowing what's typical for the industry, you can quickly see why a company is succeeding, which components might be improved, and the effect any improvement will have on earnings.

## 398 What is "working capital"?

Working capital is the financial fuel that keeps corporations chugging along. To calculate working capital, you subtract current liabilities from current assets.

Working Capital = Current Assets - Current Liabilities

Companies need working capital — they generally need to have more current assets than current liabilities. They can spend this excess capital to fund growth. It can pay for hiring new employees, building new plants, research and development of new products, additional advertising, and much more.

When evaluating a company, you want it to have positive working capital, as that represents discretionary spending money. As with other measures, though, know that a company with gobs of working capital isn't necessarily going to win its race. Some companies simply have a lot of cash on their books — almost perpetually. It means they have the flexibility to do all kinds of things, but if they never use it, then the opportunity is squandered. Working capital reveals a company's possibilities, but isn't a predictor of definite success.

## 399 What is a "burn rate"?

A company's burn rate refers to how quickly it is using up its cash. This isn't much of an issue for large established companies, but with small and quickly growing enterprises, it's valuable to look at their burn rate. The number to examine is free cash flow, which is income from operations less capital expenditures. If this number is negative, then the company is "burning" through its cash balance.

For example, take a gander at the women-oriented website iVillage. The company lost $93 million in 1999 on revenues of $45 million. In a recent quarterly report, the company reported negative $23 million in free cash flow, as its cash balance fell to $83 million from $106 million in the previous quarter. It's not unusual for firms to lose money in their early years, but it is important for investors to evaluate how much money those firms are taking in and using up. At its current burn rate, iVillage will use up its cash hoard in just a few quarters. To stay alive, the firm will have to either reduce spending (possibly resulting in slower growth), or find more money (perhaps taking on debt or issuing additional stock, diluting value for existing shareholders).

# Buying &
# Selling Stocks

*If you're relatively new to the investing scene, you may find yourself confused by brokerage terminology and procedures. This chapter will help you understand the ins and outs of brokerages and the various ways that you can buy and sell stock.*

## 400 Can you explain the difference between full-service and discount brokers?

Think of it this way: When dining out, your choice of restaurants ranges from Bob's Burger Pit to Chez Maurice. At Bob's, your meal is handed to you in a bag, along with change for your fiver. At Chez Maurice, your napkin is fluffed onto your lap and the bill bears a remarkable resemblance to your mortgage payment.

You have a similar choice with brokerages, deciding between the full-service broker and the increasingly popular discount broker.

Advocates of full-price (er, full-service) brokers assert that you get what you pay for. Full-service brokerages such as Merrill Lynch and Morgan Stanley Dean Witter offer, above all else, advice. Their teams of research analysts study industries and companies, recommending what should be bought or sold. In exchange for this advice, investors pay hefty commissions.

It's hard to determine commissions charged by full-service brokerages, as they don't like to publish rate schedules. It's safe to say, though, that for many of their customers, commissions run up to 5% or more of the value of a trade. For example, it might cost a couple of hundred dollars to buy or sell $8,000 of stock. (To be fair, though, some of them have introduced lower rates recently.)

At the other end of the spectrum, offering little in the way of advice or handholding, are discount brokers such as Charles Schwab and Ameritrade. They're the local steakhouses of the brokerage industry, charging roughly $8 to $30 per trade. Some charge even less.

Full-service brokerages offer everything from stocks and bonds to annuities and insurance. As their brokers profit largely from commissions, they're sometimes motivated to encourage a lot of buying and selling that isn't necessarily in your best interest. Other times, they might just toss your money into a mutual fund and forget about it. There *are* good brokers at full-service brokerages, though, who keep your best interests in mind and do a bang-up job for their clients. If you're taking the full-service route, you simply need to determine just how good a job your broker is doing for you, and if the cost is worth it.

Discount brokerages have traditionally offered a narrower range of services, but they've been adding to this range in recent years. Today many discounters offer mutual funds, banking services (such as checking accounts), IRAs, mortgages, and more. Charles Schwab recently added fee-based portfolio consultation and investment advisor services for its wealthier clients. The discount brokerages compensate their brokers mainly with salaries, not commissions, making their money through high-volume trading.

Assess what services you need from a broker and how much you're willing to spend. If you're a do-it-yourself investor, get thee to a discount broker. You'll probably save enough for a meal at Chez Maurice.

---

## 401 What are some things I should consider when comparing brokerages and choosing one?

Fees are one big factor to examine. Find out how much you'll be charged in commissions for various transactions and services. Since many discount brokers set up their fee structure to encourage high-volume trading, find out if you're required to make a minimum number of trades per year or per quarter and if additional fees are imposed for not meeting the trading requirements. Here are some other considerations:

- **The minimum initial deposit.** Some brokerages require at least several thousand dollars, while others have no minimum.

- **Usability and service.** If the brokerage offers online trading, check out its website's interface and see how easy it is to navigate and use. Ask some questions and see how responsive the customer service is. You might also check online sites such as Gomez.com that allow customers to rate brokers on customer service and product offerings.

- **Banking services.** Some brokerages now offer banking services, such as check writing, money market accounts, credit cards, ATM cards, direct deposit, and more — some with no fees. Look into these if you're interested. It might benefit you to consolidate bank, money market, mutual fund, IRA, and other accounts to take advantage of the attractive one-stop shopping options offered by some discount brokers today.

- **Research.** Some brokerages now offer free company research for their customers. This can be attractive, but know that there's quite a bit of research available for free all over the Web.

- **Mutual fund offerings.** Many brokerages offer a variety of mutual funds. If you're interested in some particular funds, check to see which brokerages offer them. Know, though, that you can usually purchase no-load mutual funds directly from their companies.

- **Non-stock offerings.** If you're interested in bonds, for example, see whether they're offered.

- **Convenience.** Would you rather place trade orders through an actual person, touch-tone phone, or the Internet? See which brokerages offer what you want.

Some of these factors are more important than others. For example, if you trade only twice a year, commission costs might not matter as much. To guide your decision, make a list of all the services you need and how vital they are — then evaluate each contender on each category. For more guidance on choosing a brokerage, visit www.brokerage.Fool.com.

## 402 Are brokerage accounts insured?

Reputable brokerages do offer insurance. Just as the FDIC insures bank accounts, the Securities Investor Protection Corporation (SIPC) insures brokerage accounts up to $500,000 per account (including up to $100,000 in cash). Note, though, that this insures your account against your brokerage going under, not your stocks losing value. (Sorry!)

Many brokerages even surpass SIPC levels of insurance. But there might be a shady brokerage or two out there that somehow isn't insured. Ask your brokerage (or prospective brokerage) for clarification on what insurance protection it offers.

## 403 If I sign up to use an online brokerage, can I deposit funds by just mailing in checks?

You certainly can. That's how most online brokerage account holders handle it. You mail in a check and it's credited to your account. Then you can place orders by phone, over the Internet, or in person. If your brokerage has a local office, you can drop by and deposit money in person, as well. Most brokerages also permit electronic transfer of funds.

## 404 I want to open a brokerage account, but the firms I called require between $1,000 and $5,000 upfront just to open an account. What can I do?

Many brokerages, such as Quick and Reilly, DLJDirect, and American Express, don't have minimums. Others, such as ScotTrade, have small minimums ($500). Note that by the time you're reading this, various brokerages may have changed their minimums. In addition, you might be able to get a good deal by shopping around. Sometimes brokerages offer special deals here and there.

Details on and ratings for many discount brokerages, both traditional and online, can be found in *SmartMoney* magazine (and at www.smartmoney.com/si/brokers), *The American Association of Individual Investors Journal*, and other periodicals. Online brokerages are also reviewed and rated at www.gomez.com and at www.brokerage.Fool.com.

## 405 When trading stocks on the Internet, how can you be sure that the price you see is the one you end up paying?

First, know that the stock prices listed in newspapers and online simply reflect the price at which the stock *last traded*. The next trade could occur at a higher or lower price — sometimes a significantly higher or lower price — depending on supply and demand. You're not out of luck, though. You can control the price you pay by placing a certain type of order, called a limit order. There are several main types of orders, each with advantages and disadvantages.

## 406 What are the different kinds of orders I can place with my broker?

You have many choices. Here are the main ones to understand:

**Market order:** This is for immediate execution at the best price available when the order reaches the marketplace. This is the most common type of order and is nearly always filled, since no price is specified. As an example, you might call your broker and bark into the phone, "Buy me 75 shares of Scrunchie Manufacturing (ticker: SCRNCH) at the market!"

**Limit order:** This is an order to buy or sell only at a specified price (the limit) or better. Investors who have a maximum or minimum price at which they're willing to trade use limit orders. As an example, imagine that Amalgamated Chorus Girls Inc. (ticker: KICKK) is trading at $35 and you want to buy, but not at the current price. You might click over to your brokerage's website and place an order to buy 50 shares of KICKK at a limit of $33 per share. This means that if KICKK hits $33 during the day and your order is next in line to be filled, it will be filled at that price. With a limit order, you'll only pay $33 or less per share, *if* your order is filled.

**Fill-or-Kill**: This order is submitted for immediate execution. If it cannot be filled immediately, it's automatically cancelled.

**Day Order**: This order terminates automatically at the end of the business day if it hasn't been filled.

**GTC (Good 'til Cancelled)**: This order remains in effect until cancelled by the customer or executed by the broker. It doesn't typically remain in effect forever, though; many brokerages cancel GTC orders after a month or two.

**All-or-None (AON)**: This is a limit order in which the broker is directed to attempt to fill the entire amount of the order or none of it. An all-or-none order differs from a fill-or-kill order in that, with an all-or-none order, immediate execution is not required.

**Stop Order**: This becomes a market order when a specified price is reached or passed. Buy stops are entered above the current market price; sell stops are entered below it. For example, you might place a stop order to have your shares of Stained Glass Windshield Co. (ticker: STAIN) automatically sold if the price falls below $40 per share. A stop order guarantees execution, but not price.

**Stop Limit Order**: This is similar to a stop order, but it becomes a limit order instead of a market order when the price is reached or passed. If you place a "sell 100 XYZ $55 stop limit" order, if XYZ drops to $55 per share or below, the order becomes a limit order to sell 100 shares at no less than $55.

Note that there are trade-offs with each option. Selling at the market means your shares will probably be sold quickly, but the price may be a little higher or lower than you expected (and on some occasions, considerably higher or lower). With a limit order, you specify the limit of what you're willing to pay or accept, but you risk not getting any takers at your price.

### 407 If I bought a stock at $20 that is now trading at $50, and I want to sell it if it drops to $40 (locking in a 100% gain), what kind of order should I place?

You're describing either a "stop loss" or "stop limit" order. The "stop" activates the order if shares sink to a certain price ($40 in your example). The stop *loss* order immediately sells the shares at the best price it can, while the stop *limit* will only sell if the shares are at $40 or above. Here are the risks: if, perhaps due to bad news, the shares suddenly fall below $40 overnight and don't rise above that, the stop-loss will sell your shares for less than $40, while the stop-limit order won't sell the shares at all.

### 408 Is it better to place market or limit orders?

If you're a long-term investor and plan to hang on to the shares you're buying for years, it shouldn't make much difference whether you buy your shares of Scruffy's Chicken Shack (ticker: BUKBUK) for $41 each or $41.50 (or even $43, for that matter). Market orders are usually all you need.

### 409 What is a CUSIP number?

It's a security's identifying number, not unlike a product's catalog or bar code number. Its nine digits are assigned by the Committee on Uniform Security Identification Procedures (CUSIP). The first six digits identify the issuer, such as a company, while the last three digits reveal exactly what kind of security it is, such as a particular kind of stock or bond. It's good to have CUSIP numbers handy when you're transferring shares of stock or if you've lost your certificates.

### 410 What does "shorting" a stock involve?

You're probably familiar with the maxim, "Buy low, sell high." You might not know it, but if you've spied a stock you're pretty sure will drop, there's an interesting way you might profit from its fall. You'd reverse the old saying — by selling high and then buying low. This is shorting a stock.

Here's how it works. Let's say that an Internet fan club, GroverCleveland.com (ticker: GROVY), has gone public. Despite much media hoopla, you have little faith in it and expect the stock to sink. You call your brokerage and say that you want to short GROVY. The brokerage will "borrow" shares from a GroverCleveland.com shareholder's account and proceed to *sell* them for you at the current high price. Then, once the share price drops, you'll "cover" your short by *buying* shares on the market at a lower price; to replace the ones you borrowed. If you shorted GROVY at $35 and covered when it fell to $20, you made $15 per share (less commissions).

This technique sounds weird, but it's perfectly acceptable and done often. Shorting can be beneficial because:

- With shorts in your portfolio, you might profit from both rising *and* falling stocks. If you see a great and growing company, you can buy shares in it. If you see a stinker, you can profit by betting against it.
- Shorting can bolster a portfolio. If the market takes a big drop, your shorts should boost your portfolio's performance.

Of course, shorting has its negative side, too, though:

- If the stock price rises, you lose. With shorts, you can only earn up to 100%, since a stock price can't fall lower than zero. But, if your short keeps rising, your downside is theoretically unlimited. Since you can actually lose more than 100% of your money, you need to keep a very close eye on any shorted stocks.
- Shorting is based on short-term expectations, and Foolish investors generally prefer to focus on the long term.
- It bucks the overall long-term upward trend of the market.
- If you short a company's stock, you'll have its management working against you to make the company succeed, perhaps with new financing, partnerships, or products.
- If the stock you shorted pays dividends, you'll be required to pay the dividend to the shareholder whose shares you borrowed. (Your broker should take care of this.)

Shorting can be effective, but it's only for seasoned investors. Even experienced investors may want to avoid it — unless they run across a business as unpromising as GroverCleveland.com, that is.

## 411 Can you short any stock, or just some stocks?

To be shorted, a stock needs to qualify as "marginable." That means investors can purchase shares on margin, with funds borrowed from their brokerages. Most stocks on the New York Stock Exchange are marginable and most Nasdaq stocks also qualify, while stocks trading for less than $5 per share often do not.

## 412 What is a "short squeeze"?

A short squeeze is when those who are short a stock bail out en masse, driving the stock price up as they buy shares to replace the ones they borrowed when shorting.

Imagine Chihuahua Channelers Inc. (ticker: YIPYIP), which helps people communicate with long-lost pets. Let's say it's very heavily shorted by investors who believe the company and stock are in for a beating. If, for some reason, the stock price begins to soar, these shortsellers will be in a tough position. They might hang on, watching their investment move farther and farther into the red. Or they can close their short position by buying shares to replace the ones they borrowed. As the stock price rises, more shortsellers will cut their losses and buy shares to close out their short position. This buying will push the stock price up even higher. And, *voila*, you've got a short squeeze.

## 413 Where can I learn more about shorting?

Here are some online resources:
- www.Fool.com/school/13steps/steptwelve.htm (scroll down)
- www.theonlineinvestor.com/selling_short.shtml
- www.suite101.com/article.cfm/women_and_investing/20834

And some books:

- *Tools of the Bear: How Any Investor Can Make Money When Stocks Go Down* by Charles J. Caes
- *When Stocks Crash Nicely: The Finer Art of Short Selling* by Kathryn F. Staley
- *Selling Short: Risks, Rewards and Strategies for Short Selling Stocks, Options and Futures* by Joseph A. Walker.

Be careful with some of these resources, though. They're likely to spend a significant amount of time on non-Foolish investing — such as short-term trading, technical analysis, options, etc.

## 414 Can I deduct commissions paid to brokerages from my net capital gain for tax purposes?

Yes, you can — and you must. The expenses incurred in purchasing or selling a capital asset (stock, in this example) are capital expenses, and are required to be added to or subtracted from the cost basis of the stock for tax purposes.

Let's say you buy $3,000 of stock and pay $50 in commission and other charges. Your actual cost is $3,050. You sell the stock later, when it's worth $4,000, paying another $50 to the brokerage. Your "net" sales price, or proceeds (generally, the amount reported to you by your broker at year-end on your Form 1099B), would be $3,950 ($4,000 less $50). On your tax return, you would report a gain of $900 ($3,950 less $3,050 equals $900.)

Note that you've not had to pay tax on that $100 in commissions — so you've probably saved at least $20.

## 415 How does buying stocks on margin work?

Using margin means borrowing money from your brokerage, usually to buy additional stocks. For that privilege, you pay interest, just like with other loans. If the market turns against you, you either sell for a loss — plus interest costs — or hold on until the market picks up, paying interest all the while. If you're borrowing on margin and paying 9% interest, you should be pretty confident your stocks will appreciate more than 9%.

When margined securities fall below a certain level, the borrower will receive a "margin call," requiring an infusion of additional cash. If she can't raise the cash, the brokerage will sell some of her holdings to generate the needed funds. This can sting, possibly resulting in short-term capital gains taxed at high rates.

Margin amplifies your investment performance. As an example, imagine that you hold $100,000 of stocks and you margin that to the max, borrowing $100,000 to invest in additional stock. If your holdings double in value, you'll have earned an extra $100,000 (less interest expense) thanks to margin. But, if your $200,000 holdings drop by 50%, they'll be worth $100,000 and you'll still owe $100,000 (plus interest). That will leave you with... nothing. Your holdings dropped by 50%, but margin amplified that to a total loss. Margin cuts both ways.

On the Fool's discussion boards, one of the most read and recommended posts is from a reader named "globalstreamer," detailing how he lost his entire portfolio, $60,000, in two weeks — by getting carried away with margin. Only experienced investors should use margin. Although you're currently allowed to borrow up to 50% of what your actual holdings are worth, it's smart to limit yourself to no more than around 20%, if you borrow on margin at all.

# Mutual Funds

*You've surely heard of mutual funds, and you very likely invest in them, but do you really understand what they are and how they operate? Do you know for sure whether they belong in your portfolio? Have you met the friend of the Fool, the index fund? This chapter will help you tackle these questions.*

## 416 What exactly is a mutual fund?

Imagine this scenario: You have only $500 to invest. You believe that it's risky to invest in only one stock, but you also know that you shouldn't spread yourself too thin with that amount of money. But what if you gathered 20 friends who each had $500? Together you'd have $10,000, enough to invest in several stocks without commission costs running too high. Nice job. Uh-oh, now who decides what to buy and when to sell? Ah, another problem.

Perhaps your group chooses to pay some guy in a bow tie and suspenders to manage it for you. If so, then you've essentially got a mutual fund on your hands. A mutual fund is thousands of people's money, pooled together by an investment company and invested in stocks, bonds, and other things, all managed for you by Wall Street professionals — for a sometimes hefty fee, of course.

**417** I'm confused by the many different kinds of mutual funds out there, such as "Growth and Income," "Equity Income," and "Fixed Income." How do these differ, and what other kinds of funds are there?

There are a few key words to understand. Fixed income means bonds. Equity means stocks. Income funds aim to generate regular payoffs for shareholders through dividends from stocks and/or bond interest. Growth funds don't try to generate income; instead, they tend to seek stock price appreciation. Sometimes you may see the term "Balanced" used, which means that the fund is about half stocks and half bonds, generally. There are many variations of these kinds of funds.

There are also other kinds of funds, such as industry-specific sector funds. One sector fund might focus on just biotechnology stocks. Another sector fund might concentrate on computer-related firms, while a third one invests solely in banking stocks.

Some mutual funds focus on particular geographic regions. One might invest in Indian companies, another might specialize in Russian companies, and a third might limit itself to Latin American enterprises.

Other funds restrict themselves to certain sizes of companies, such as the universe of small-cap companies or large-cap companies.

"Index funds" mimic indexes. An S&P 500 index fund, for example, will contain stocks in the 500 companies that make up the S&P 500 index — in the same proportion as the index. These are passively managed funds, as opposed to actively managed ones, because there's no manager subjectively evaluating and selecting stocks. Instead, it's just a matter of making sure that at all times the fund contains the appropriate stocks in the appropriate proportions.

**418** What is a money market fund?

A money market fund is a mutual fund that buys securities such as Treasury bills, short-term commercial debt, and certificates of deposit. It sticks to short-term, high-quality securities and is relatively safe and liquid. Money market yields vary according to short-term interest rates, but they fall dramatically short of the stock market's historical average return of 11% per year. They're ill suited for long-term savings, but they're great for short-term investments, such as for money you'll need in the near future.

## 419 What is a mutual fund's NAV? Is that its share price?

Just about. NAV stands for "net asset value." To understand what it is, know that mutual fund prices don't fluctuate during the day. Since funds are composed of many different securities, fund companies wait until the end of trading each day, and then they add up the current market value of all their holdings. They then subtract the fund's expenses for the day, such as commissions paid. The result is divided by the number of shares of the fund that exist — and that's the NAV.

## 420 What is a "prospectus"?

A prospectus is a booklet that describes a mutual fund's goals, fees, risks, policies, and investment style. It should show you how well the fund has performed in the past and how much money it will charge you in fees, while giving you an idea of how it will invest your money. If you're thinking of buying shares of a mutual fund, you should obtain and read its latest prospectus. Mutual funds are required to provide prospectuses to help investors make informed decisions. You can request them from the mutual fund company. Many such companies make prospectuses available electronically on their websites.

## 421 Is looking for funds with above average returns the best way to pick mutual funds?

Very likely not. Think about it this way. You're a smart cookie — you know that many mutual funds aren't too impressive. So, you look at lists of mutual funds and check their returns over the past few years. You invest only in the ones that have done well over the last year or several years, the ones that beat the market average. This sounds like a reasonable approach, but it's flawed. Here are some things to think about:

Funds that beat the market average one year are not likely to beat it the following year. To some degree, a terrific return isn't the result of the fund manager's brilliance, but of good luck. (At least over the short term. And many fund managers invest only for the short term.) Most funds have occasional very good years.

Funds with a great 3- or 5- or even 10-year average are likely to have that great average because of one amazing year. After all, a five-year average is just an average of five numbers. If one of them is unusually high, the average will be high. Let's consider an example. If in a five-year period, a fund earns respectively 8%, 11%, 4%, 12%, and 33%, its average annual return will be about 13%. That might look respectable, but note that in reality it exceeded 13% in only one of five years. That 33% return (an "outlier" in statistical terms) has skewed the average.

It might shock you to learn that, according to Lipper data, only 17% of all open-end equity funds outperformed the market average (as measured by the S&P 500 index) over the five years from March 1995 to March 2000. Over the last decade, only about 20% of funds outperformed it.

So, what to do? Well, consider investing in an index fund. If you can't otherwise beat the market average, you can *meet* it (and outperform the vast majority of mutual funds) by investing in a market index fund. Many companies, such as Vanguard, offer these. We like funds that track the S&P 500 or the broader "total market."

## 422 I've heard that it's not a good thing when a mutual fund gets really big. How does this hurt its performance?

Imagine you're suddenly given $30 billion. You'd probably be pleased. But, if the money were given to you as a stock mutual fund that you had to manage, you'd run into some problems. Mutual funds have strict rules that make effective investing difficult.

For starters, you'd have to keep 5% to 10% of the fund's value in cash, to cover withdrawals when people sell shares. You also wouldn't be able to invest more than 5% of the fund's value in any one stock, limiting you to no fewer than 20 stocks. Typically, mutual funds invest in 50-200 different companies, a far cry from the six to 15 stocks that Fools with the time and willingness to invest in individual stocks should shoot for.

To better appreciate the problem of overdiversification, take a look at Fidelity's mammoth Magellan Fund. As of March 31, 1999, its biggest holding was General Electric, representing 4.2% of the fund's value. If an investor had plunked $3,000 into Magellan then, she'd own only $126 worth of GE, not much more than a share or two. And that's the biggest holding. Of her $3,000, $42 would be divided among seven aerospace and defense companies — such as Boeing and General Dynamics — for an average of $6 each. Some $114 would be divided between 11 "electronics" companies — such as Intel and Motorola, amounting to an average of $10.36 each.

Being spread so thin is problematic, because when you're invested in hundreds of companies, if some of them do very well, their impact is diluted by the many less-stellar performances. If Boeing triples in value one year, for example, even though you may have $3,000 invested in Magellan, your stake in it might simply go from $6 to $18. If an individual investor had invested $3,000 in 10 companies in equal proportions, and one had been Boeing, the Boeing stake of $300 would have turned into $900, increasing the portfolio value by 20%. The more companies you own, the more dilution becomes a problem.

Even if your fund limits itself to owning the minimum number of stocks, other problems still arise. Let's return to your imaginary $30 billion fund. Imagine that you want to (and can) spend 10% of its value, $3 billion, on Polaroid. Oops. Polaroid's entire market value (at the time of this writing) is less than $1 billion. Your $3 billion would buy more than the entire company. Also, if you're limited — as many managers are — to not buying more than 10% of any one company, then you could spend only $90 million on Polaroid. It's hard to avoid spreading yourself too thin when $90 million is merely a drop in your mutual fund's bucket.

Pity the mutual fund managers. Working with much less freedom and a lot more money than we have, the odds are stacked against them. It's no surprise that most of them underperform the market average.

## 423 What are these "turnover ratios" I read about in mutual fund prospectuses?

Turnover ratios measure how much buying and selling a fund does each year. If a fund has a total value of $5 billion and buys and sells $5 billion of securities in one year, its turnover ratio is 100%. Steep turnover ratios hit investors with a double whammy: high commission charges for all those trades and taxable capital gains.

Published returns in glossy magazines typically incorporate commissions paid, but not taxable capital gains. In 1992, Stanford economists John Shoven and Joel Dickson found that a typical stock mutual fund can have up to 40% or more of its return eaten up by taxes.

A high turnover ratio doesn't necessarily mean you shouldn't buy a particular fund. According to recent Morningstar mutual fund data, the five top-performing mutual funds for the past five years sported turnover ratios ranging from 115% to 753%. Just know that, in theory, the higher the ratio, the higher the tax burden and commission costs.

## 424 Can you explain the various fees that mutual funds charge?

Virtually all fund fees fall in two categories: load and expense ratio. A load is a one-time sales charge. Front-end loads are levied when you deposit money into a mutual fund, and back-end loads, also called redemption fees, are exacted when you withdraw money. A typical load is around 3%. As an example, we tossed a dart at a bunch of funds and it landed on the Seligman Communications and Information Fund — Class A. (Classes B and D have different fee structures.) This fund has a 4.75% front-end load, so if you want to put $10,000 into it, $475 would be deducted from your money upfront.

Loads exist to support brokers and aggressive sales efforts that bring more money into the fund and into the fund company coffers. This isn't usually in your best interest as an investor, so Fools should favor no-load funds. These often fare better than load funds and have lower expense ratios, to boot.

With no-load funds, you just need to focus on the expense ratio. Chairs, computers, catered holiday parties, and other administrative costs that support the fund are included in this annual fee. Two of its components are often reported separately: 12b-1 and management fees. The

12b-1 fee is defined as covering marketing expenses, but it's essentially a continual load in the form of an annual sales charge. Management fees pay for fund manager salaries. The median total expense ratio is around 1.00% and the Seligman Fund comes in at 1.44%. Included in the 1.44% is a 0.25% 12b-1 fee and a 0.98% management fee.

Index funds, which the Fool recommends for investors who want to invest in mutual funds, typically sport very low fees and outperform most other funds. The Vanguard Total Stock Market Index Fund (ticker: VTSMX), for example, has no load and a piddly annual expense ratio of 0.20%. With a $10,000 investment, that amounts to just $20. Your money has a much better chance of growing if 99.8% of it is left to grow.

## 425 Why do you make such a fuss about mutual fund fees?

Because they really make a big difference. Imagine that you've invested $10,000 in a fund that charges a 2% management fee. In 30 years, if that investment grew at 12% per year on average, it would become $174,000. Not bad. But suppose you'd plunked that money into a fund with just a 1% fee. In 30 years at 12%, it would grow to $229,000. That's a $55,000 difference!

## 426 What is meant by "window dressing"?

It's an arguably shady practice employed by some mutual fund managers. Mutual fund managers typically report to the public on their funds' holdings once per quarter. Managers want to look savvy to impress their existing shareholders and attract new shareholders. Therefore, they'll sometimes sell lackluster investments they've held for a while and buy recent stellar performers — just so the fund's holdings on the day of record look good.

For example, the Kitten Kaboodle Fund (ticker: MEOWX) might have spent the last few months languishing. Rather than reveal that it holds large positions in poorly performing companies, the manager might sell off some regrettable holdings and load up on recent market darlings — to look good. This is window dressing.

You might be pleased to see Cisco Systems and Intel among your fund's holdings, but that just means they were held on one particular day. The fund hasn't necessarily owned those stocks for a long time, participating in their gains. The fund might have had most of its money sitting in the stock of companies such as Giddyup Buggy Whips, Inc. (ticker: WHOAA) for most of the quarter. But, as long as it sells most or all of those shares by the date that it reports on, you'll never know.

## 427 I know that you Fools recommend index funds, but what exactly are they and what's so great about them?

Wall Street mutual fund managers want you to believe you'd be lost without their savvy stock-picking skills. Just read some fund ads: "You may not have the time or expertise to choose and manage your investments... [let] our investment professionals do the rest."

In reality, most of these highly educated, highly compensated professionals have actively managed their mutual funds to below-average returns. That's right. According to Lipper Inc., for the five years ending in March 2000, only 17% of stock mutual funds outperformed the S&P 500, the most commonly used barometer of the stock market.

While Fools generally shun mutual funds, we make an exception for index funds, which match the market because they *represent* the market. Since the S&P 500 index fund, for example, contains the same massive American companies that make up the Standard & Poor's 500 — firms from American Express to Xerox — its managers don't have many decisions to make. As one index fund's prospectus notes, "Management typically does not judge the merits of any particular stock."

Over the last seven decades, through rallies and recessions, the stock market has gained an average of about 11% per year. A thousand dollars in an S&P 500 index fund that matched this performance would have grown to $13,585 in 25 years and to $184,565 in 50 years — just from a single initial $1,000 deposit. Another great thing about index funds is that, once you put your cash into them, you can ignore them and tend to your garden. (And, to think that someone said you don't have the time or expertise to choose and manage your investments!)

Know that there are many different kinds of index funds, mimicking the holdings of different indexes, and there are often many different funds available for each index. There are several dozen S&P 500 index funds alone, for example.

The index fund is the first rung on the Foolish investment ladder. If you're not yet comfortable picking stocks on your own, you really have to ask yourself why you would *not* begin with an index fund. It relies on the long-term growth of great American companies, rather than the long-term ability of most mutual fund managers to underperform the market.

You can invest directly in an index fund or you can participate via your 401(k) plan at work. If your plan doesn't offer an index fund, it should. Visit your plan administrator and show her this Q&A.

## 428 Where can I find some S&P 500 or whole-market index funds in which to invest? Which companies offer them?

Index funds have grown very popular, as more people have learned how they outperform more than three-quarters of their mutual fund brethren. Accordingly, many fund companies now offer them.

Here's just a smattering of the many funds available, with some info on them, as of the end of 2000:

| Ticker Symbol | Name of Fund | Minimum Initial Deposit | Annual Fees | Phone # |
|---|---|---|---|---|
| PEOPX | Dreyfus S&P 500 Index | $2,500 | 0.50% | 800-373-9387 |
| SWPIX | Schwab S&P 500 Inv. | $2,500 | 0.35% | 800-435-4000 |
| VFINX | Vanguard 500 Index | $3,000 | 0.18% | 800-662-7447 |
| SWTIX | Schwab Total Stock Market Index Inv. | $2,500 | 0.40% | 800-435-4000 |
| VTSMX | Vanguard Total Stock Market Index | $3,000 | 0.20% | 800-662-7447 |
| WFIVX | Wilshire 5000 Index Portfolio | $1,000 | 0.62% | 888-200-6796 |

## 429 What are "Spiders"?

Spiders, trading on the AMEX (American Stock Exchange) under the ticker symbol "SPY," are Standard & Poor's 500 Depositary Receipts. Just like S&P 500 index funds, they represent a bundle of 500 of America's biggest and brightest corporations. But, unlike index funds, which are mutual funds, Spiders trade like shares of stock. They're valued at about 1/10th of the value of the S&P 500 index (around $150 each, as of this writing).

Spiders have some advantages over their index-fund brethren. Whereas funds sometimes have minimums of several thousand dollars, you can buy and sell Spider shares as little as one at a time. And, while you have no control over when mutual funds generate taxable capital gains, with Spiders, gains or losses occur mainly when you sell your shares.

## 430 If I own shares of a mutual fund that invests in a particular company, can I attend that company's annual shareholder meeting?

Technically, you're not the shareholder — the mutual fund is. Usually, only a legal representative of the fund (such as the manager) can represent the fund as the shareholder of record. Still, it doesn't hurt to ask. Give the company a call, ask for the Investor Relations department, and inquire whether you can attend.

## 431 If I pay taxes on a mutual fund's dividends and capital gains distributions, will I be taxed again on them when I sell the shares?

To clarify, let's say you contribute to a mutual fund using money that is not in an IRA or 401(k) account. All the distributions are automatically reinvested. Each year you receive a 1099-DIV and you pay taxes on the ordinary dividends and on the capital gain distributions. You want to know whether you'll be taxed again when you cash in shares from the mutual fund, as you already paid taxes on all the distributions.

The answer is that the taxman only rings once for distributions as long as you've kept a record of your dividend and capital gains reinvestments. The cost basis for shares bought with reinvested dividends is the price at which they're purchased. You will be taxed only on the amount they have appreciated in value since the time they were added to your portfolio.

Imagine that you bought 50 shares of Carrier Pigeon Communications (ticker: SQAWK) at $100 per share. A few months later, the company paid you $150 in dividends, which was reinvested in more shares. By then, though, SQAWK was trading at $110 per share, so your $150 bought 1.36 shares.

You now have 51.36 shares. Your cost basis is $100 each for the first 50 and $110 for the 1.36 shares. Whenever you sell the shares, Uncle Sam will tax you on their appreciation beyond their cost basis. Tax rates vary by holding period, though, so make sure you keep track of exactly how long you've held each share. You may want to consult your friendly local tax professional for advice tailored to your particular situation.

---

## 432 If mutual funds pay taxes each year on capital gains of stocks they sold, why does the investor also have to pay taxes on all the capital gains when he sells the mutual fund shares? Haven't most of the capital gains taxes already been paid by the mutual fund? It seems as if Uncle Sam is double dipping here.

A mutual fund doesn't pay taxes on capital gains of stocks sold during the year. You do. Funds report distributions of income from dividends, interest, and capital gains (net of losses) to the fund's shareholders (and to the IRS) on Form 1099.

Most shareholders have those distributions reinvested in additional mutual fund shares. (Note: Even if you do this, you must still pay the taxes due on the distribution.) When you liquidate your holdings in a mutual fund, then you'll be taxed on any gain over the purchase price paid for each fund share held. This isn't double taxation. You're taxed on gains from securities the fund bought and sold — and later, when you sell your shares of a fund, you pay taxes on the difference between your purchase price and the current price of fund shares. It's smart to keep records of all purchases, including those bought with reinvested dividends and capital gains.

## 433 What does it mean to "buy the dividend" in a mutual fund?

"Buying the dividend," or "buying the distribution," happens when you invest in a mutual fund just before it declares dividends or capital gains distributions. Doing this in a taxable account will generate an unnecessary tax bill. Let's look at an example.

Imagine that on Monday, you buy 100 shares of the Ominously Overdiversified Mutual Fund (ticker: OOMFX) at $30 each, for a total of $3,000. Let's say that the fund had previously announced a $2 distribution for each share, to occur on Tuesday. This means it sends you $2 per share, or $200, and your $30 shares are now worth $28. (Note that 100 times $28 is $2,800, which when added to $200 yields your original $3,000 investment.) It's not exactly six of one, a half dozen of the other. That $200 distribution counts as *income* to you, and you'll be taxed on it.

By buying just before the distribution, you end up paying some taxes needlessly. Most stock funds declare dividends and capital gains distributions either every three or six months, or every year. It's best to find out when a fund's distribution will take place and avoid buying in right before it happens.

This isn't an issue for money market funds, bond funds, or funds in tax-deferred accounts such as IRAs or 401(k)s.

## 434 What is the difference between a mutual fund and a unit investment trust?

With a mutual fund, its manager invests in assets according to a stated set of objectives. Shares are issued and redeemed on demand at a specific net asset value that is determined at the end of each trading day (based on the total market value of the fund's holdings). There's no fixed number of shares. If many people want to buy in, the fund company will issue more shares.

Meanwhile, a unit investment trust (UIT) invests in a relatively fixed portfolio of investments. These are held until the trust is liquidated at a predetermined date in the future. Investors who want to trade shares of a UIT before it matures can often do so on the secondary market. Unlike a mutual fund, UIT share prices in the secondary market may be priced above or below the net asset value of the trust's actual holdings. When you buy shares of UITs, you typically pay a sales fee, or load, of around 4% or 5%; many mutual funds carry no sales load at all.

---

## 435 Where can I learn more about mutual funds?

Here are some websites that can help you out:
- www.ici.org
- www.sec.gov/consumer/inwsmf.htm
- www.morningstar.com
- www.indexfundsonline.com
- www.Fool.com/school/mutualfunds/mutualfunds.htm

And, here's a top-notch book by the father of the index fund:
- *Common Sense on Mutual Funds: New Imperatives for the Intelligent Investor* by John C. Bogle

# Managing Your Portfolio

*It might seem like all you need to know about investing is how to study a company's financial health and its prospects for growth. That's certainly critical, but it's also important to give a lot of thought to how you manage your portfolio. There are decisions to be made regarding how you add money to your holdings, when to sell stock, and how to evaluate your portfolio's performance, among other things. This chapter looks at these kinds of topics.*

## 436 Does the Fool offer any simple step-by-step guidance on how to plan an investing strategy?

We do, in the form of our *13 Steps to Investing Foolishly*. Here they are, paraphrased:

1. Understand Foolishness. See the myths of Wall Street debunked. Investing *isn't* too mysterious or difficult for you. You *can* take control of your financial destiny. Experts and gurus aren't likely to help you as much as you'd think. Learn what Foolish investing is all about.

2. Settle your finances. Dig your way out of any credit card debt. You're not ready to start investing until you've paid off any high interest debt.

3. Set expectations. Learn what to expect from the stock market. Evaluate how your investments have been doing compared to the market.

4.  Consider index funds. They're good places to move money that has been sitting in underperforming mutual funds and good places for you to accumulate money if you're not yet ready to select individual stocks on your own. They'll permit you to earn while you learn. Those who have no interest in learning more about investing might just stop at index funds and leave it at that. With index funds you'll be assured of performing just about as well as the overall market average.

5.  Consider investing via Drips (dividend reinvestment plans) or direct investing plans, which permit you to regularly sock away small amounts of money.

6.  Open a discount brokerage account if you haven't already done so.

7.  Plan for retirement. Assess and maximize your current retirement saving plans, and learn more about 401(k) plans and IRAs.

8.  Gather information on companies that you're thinking of investing in. This can and should come in the form of financial statements issued by the company, news releases, online discussion board posts, and more.

9.  Learn to evaluate businesses. Learn to decipher financial statements and crunch some numbers.

10. Consider Rule Maker investing, which focuses on large successful companies that are setting the rules in their industries. It's discussed a little earlier in this book, and you can learn much more about it in *The Motley Fool Rule Breakers, Rule Makers* book and at www.rulemaker.Fool.com.

11. Consider small-cap companies and the more aggressive (and risky) Rule Breaker investing strategy, which invests in companies that succeed by breaking all the rules. You can learn more about it in the book mentioned above and at www.rulebreaker.Fool.com.

12. Learn about advanced investing issues, such as options, day trading, technical analysis, margin, and shorting. You're best off steering clear of some or all of these, and using others only in moderation.

13. Get fully Foolish. Register at Fool.com if you haven't already done so, and explore whatever nooks and crannies you haven't yet discovered. Participate in our online community, sharing and gathering information.

To learn more about the *13 Steps to Investing Foolishly*, click over to www.Fool.com/school/13steps/13steps.htm.

### 437 I've heard that investors should keep a third of their investments in stocks, a third in bonds, and a third in cash. Do you recommend this?

There are many "portfolio allocation formulas" out there, and some Wall Street brokerages make headlines and incite market panic when they announce changes to their recommended mix of stocks, bonds, and cash. We chuckle when financial advisors announce they're changing the ideal portfolio mix from something like 47% stocks to 49% stocks. Such tweaking seems utterly silly, racking up commission charges when people have to buy and sell to readjust their portfolios.

*Our* basic guidelines follow investment timeframes and, of course, what you can tolerate in terms of market volatility. In general, money that you don't expect to need for five years or more (and ideally longer) can be invested 100% in stocks. Stocks can be volatile in the short term, but they generally perform well in the long term.

Any funds that you'll need to use in the near future (emergency money or money needed within five years) should be in something safe like CDs, money market funds, or perhaps bonds. Whatever's left over is likely to grow most quickly in stocks.

### 438 Are 20 stocks too many to hold in one portfolio?

When learning about investing, you'll often read about the importance of diversification. Well, true, it's important. But, it's almost as bad to be overdiversified as underdiversified.

Let's look at some examples to see how this works. Imagine that your portfolio consists of just two stocks, A and B. You have $5,000 tied up in each, for a total of $10,000. If A's stock price suddenly drops to half what you paid, your portfolio's value sinks to $7,500. It falls by 25%, just because of one stock's move. That's exposing yourself to quite a bit of risk.

At the other extreme, let's say that you hold 25 stocks, with about $2,000 in each, for a portfolio total of $50,000. Each stock represents 4% of the portfolio's value. Imagine that one of your holdings doubles! It's now worth $4,000. But, since it was such a small part of your total portfolio, its amazing 100% surge will boost your portfolio by only 4%. If you hold only 10 stocks (in equal measure) and one of them doubles in value, your portfolio will gain 10%. See the difference?

There's no absolute best number of stocks to own. Different numbers work for different people. If you have 20 stocks, and you're confident that they're all strong performers, you could do well. But, if you think that only 15 are truly outstanding companies with great growth potential, you should consider trimming your holdings to just those 15. The idea is to invest your money in your best ideas. By concentrating your portfolio this way, you set it up to grow more quickly.

A final consideration is that, to be a responsible investor, you'll need to follow your companies' progress at least once a quarter, reading news reports, financial statements, and annual reports. If you own stock in 30 companies, this can be very hard or even impossible to do. Most people find that between eight and 15 companies is a manageable number.

---

## 439 Does it make sense to buy additional shares of a stock that's falling, or is it just throwing good money after bad?

This is called "averaging down," and it often isn't a good idea. There's very likely a good reason why the stock is dropping. An exception to this rule would be if the market has significantly overreacted to some news, sending shares down to levels you don't believe are justified. This might happen when a solid company has a short-term problem, as Intel did in 1994 with its flawed Pentium chip. Before you average down on any stock, do double the homework.

---

## 440 What is a "mock portfolio"?

Mock portfolios are great tools for people new to investing and for those trying out new investing methods. You simply go through all the motions of investing, but stop short of actually plunking down your hard-earned cash. Research some companies, decide which ones you'd buy, and then set up a pretend portfolio, either on paper or online. (Many websites, including Fool.com, offer online portfolio tracking.) Keep track of details such as when you "bought" the shares and at what price. Then track your performance over time.

With a mock portfolio, you can gain confidence and comfort in your stock-picking ability. You can learn from mistakes you didn't technically make, and learn from successes, as well.

## 441 Can you explain "dollar-cost averaging"?

Dollar-cost averaging is a good way to protect yourself from a volatile market. It's the practice of accumulating shares in a stock over time by investing a certain dollar amount regularly through up and down periods.

For example, you might purchase $500 worth of a stock every three months. You'd do this regardless of the stock price, buying 10 shares when the price is $50 (10 times $50 is $500) and eight shares when it's $60 (eight times $60 is $480).

The beauty of this system is that when the stock slumps you're buying more, and when it's pricier you're buying less. It's an especially good way to accumulate shares if your budget is limited. (Buying regularly through dividend reinvestment plans, or "Drips," is a form of dollar-cost averaging.) Don't drown in commission costs, though — dollar-cost average only if you can keep commissions below 2% or if you're buying through direct-purchase plans.

## 442 A friend of mine is trying to sell me on some stock in a small company I never heard of before. Is there any way I can get more information on it?

Call the company and ask for an investor's package, which should supply a lot of information in the form of an annual report, press releases, and other reports. (You might also look up these documents online at the company's own website or at www.freeEdgar.com.) If you can't get this information, it's a bad sign. Once you get to the financial statements, scrutinize them. Check to see how much the company is generating in sales and net income (earnings). See how quickly these and other items are growing (or not growing). See how much debt the company is carrying. Find out what its prospects are. Make sure it's not a penny stock (trading for less than $5 per share) — if it is, just walk away.

You can also check on whether there have been any complaints lodged against the company (or any security) by contacting the North American Securities Administrators Association. Give them a call at 888-846-2722 or point your Web browser to www.nasaa.org.

---

### 443 How should I go about evaluating how well my investments are doing?

The math involved does scare some people, so let's run through an example. Imagine Ethel, who begins the year with a portfolio valued at $10,000. At year-end, it's worth $14,000. Let's see how it grew:

Divide $14,000 by $10,000, and you get 1.4. Subtract 1 and you have 0.4. Multiply that by 100, tack on a % sign, and *voila* — you've got a 40% increase. It's that simple, sometimes.

If Ethel added to her investment during the year, though, as many people do, things get more complicated. Let's say Ethel plunked $2,000 of her hard-earned savings into this portfolio during the year. This means her investments didn't really appreciate by 40%. The total value of her portfolio did, but partly because of the money she added. Even if the stock prices didn't budge, her contributions would have resulted in a 20% increase.

If you make intra-year contributions, it suddenly becomes difficult to calculate your actual return. Ideally, you'd need to use a computer program that can determine the "internal rate of return," or IRR. Software such as Microsoft Excel can do this, as does Fool.com's free online portfolio tracker.

Your trusty calculator can give you an approximate value. Just take the portfolio's end value and subtract half the net additions made. Divide this by the portfolio's beginning value, to which has been added half the net additions. We'd get: ($14,000 minus $1,000) divided by ($10,000 plus $1,000) equals 1.18. Subtract one, multiply by 100, tack on that % sign, and you're looking at an 18% gain.

Once you know your holdings have appreciated a certain amount, compare that to a benchmark such as the Standard & Poor's 500. If your portfolio rocketed ahead 15% in 1999, you may have rejoiced. But the market (as measured by the S&P 500) was up about 20% for the year, so you underperformed it. Aim to beat the market — or, with the help of index funds, to at least meet the market average.

---

### 444 How can I account for inflation and taxes in evaluating my returns?

Let's run through an example. If Marge buys $5,000 worth of stock in Las Vegas Light & Power (ticker: GLITZ) and sells it about a year later for $5,800, her total return is 16% ($5,800 divided by $5,000 equals 1.16, revealing a 16% gain). Many times we stop there in our number crunching, but if you want to get a more realistic number, there are a few more factors to consider.

First up, the taxman. Let's say that Marge is in the 28% tax bracket, so she forks over 28% to Uncle Sam, keeping 72%. Take her 16% return and multiply it by 0.72 and you get 11.5%. That's Marge's after-tax return. For investors in higher brackets, the effects can be even more profound. (Next time a friend who invests money short-term tells you her returns, ask her what her tax bracket is. It might look like she's earning a higher return than you are — until you figure in taxes. And commissions. One way to reduce the tax bite is to hold stocks longer than one year to qualify for long-term capital gains tax rates, which top out at 20% currently.)

Next up, Old Man Inflation. Money is worth less as time marches on and prices rise. While your investment grows and takes two or three steps forward each year, inflation makes it take one step back. Let's say inflation was 2.5% during the year of Marge's investment. Taking her 11.5% after-tax return and subtracting 2.5% yields an after-tax, inflation-adjusted return of 9%. (This effect can wipe out much of a money market fund's return.)

For returns covering multiple years, you take the annualized after-tax return and subtract the annual rate of inflation during the period. You can get more information on inflation (as measured by the Consumer Price Index) from Bureau of Labor Statistics data at your library or online at: http://stats.bls.gov/cpihome.htm.

## 445 What should I do about my investments that have gone awry — my portfolio's turkeys?

It's a very good idea to regularly reflect on your investing turkeys. Some turkeys are companies you never should have invested in. Other turkey investments can occur with solid companies, if you sell their stock for a loss. A turkey postmortem should impart some valuable lessons.

With current holdings that are in the red, you need to figure out if more patience is required or if you have a hopeless turkey on your hands. Are you holding on just hoping to decrease your loss? That reasoning, like a turkey, doesn't fly. Imagine that you bought $5,000 worth of Year-3000 Solutions Inc. (ticker: 3KFIX) and it's now worth $3,000. You realize the company has little merit and you're out $2,000. You may be hanging on, hoping for a small rise in 3KFIX to make back some of that $2,000 loss, but you're probably better off putting that remaining $3,000 to work in another stock with better prospects. You should park that $3,000 where you think it will grow the fastest. Remember: You want your money in the most promising investments you can find.

It's also very beneficial to examine your turkeys of yore. Make a list of all the stocks you've sold and the prices at which you sold them. Check and see how they're priced today. (This might be painful, so have some ice cream or cookies on hand for comfort.)

If most of the stocks have since recovered and are doing well, you probably should have hung on. Investors often jump ship prematurely, at the first inkling of possible trouble. Remember that many terrific stocks go through periodic slumps.

Take note of how many turkeys you've sold. If you've got a big flock of them, you may have jumped into too many stocks without doing sufficient research first. If most of your turkeys are actually still in your portfolio, you've probably been putting off examining your holdings. Such due diligence is time-consuming, but necessary. That's one reason why it's best to not own more than 15 or so companies — it's hard to keep up with them all.

One mark of successful investors is that they take the time to think about investing and to learn from their successes and screw-ups.

## 446 Is it really best to buy and hold stocks, or can you do well trading more frequently?

The best way to accumulate wealth appears to be to buy stock in great businesses and hold on for decades. But this is easier said than done. When the stock market is surging or plunging, or when you learn of one exciting company after another, it can be hard to refrain from actively buying and selling.

The buy-and-hold message is further challenged by the likes of day traders, who believe they can wring extra profit following the stock market by the hour. In addition, brokerage firms benefit by encouraging customers to trade frequently. (The firms take a cut of every trade. The more you trade, the more they profit. Not a great equation.)

Brad Barber and Terrance Odean, professors at the University of California at Davis business school, recently published papers demonstrating that individual investors who buy and hold generally outperform those who trade frequently.

Barber and Odean studied the trading of more than 60,000 households with accounts at a major discount brokerage from 1991 through 1996. They learned that the average household had a net annualized geometric mean return of about 15.3%, compared with a market gain of 17.1%. Bummer. Even worse, the fifth of the households that traded most often realized merely a 10% yearly gain.

The professors concluded that these folks were losing to the market because they were trading too much. The average household turned over, or "churned," 80% of its stock portfolio each year. This means that a portfolio valued at $10,000 had $8,000 worth of stocks bought and sold during the year. We're not talking small-potatoes expenses here, as things like commissions and taxes will take significant bites out of these investments.

The lesson is clear: Investors who think of themselves as committed, long-term owners of businesses are much more likely to generate enviable returns than are the active traders who try to time the market by rapidly moving in and out of stocks. In Barber and Odean's own words, "[Frequent] trading is hazardous to your wealth."

## 447 If I limit myself to just high-quality companies, would buying and selling stock frequently be so bad?

Well, first off it's not always easy to discern exactly what is or isn't a high-quality company. And, even big, established names such as Nike can experience protracted slumps. In the short term, you're never guaranteed smooth sailing.

Let's examine the disadvantages of trading frequently, though. Imagine that you bought $10,000 worth of stock in Sharma's Secret Passwords Inc. (ticker: SHHHH). It was a smart purchase — within about 10 months, it's doubled and your shares are worth $20,000. You have a choice. You can continue hanging on, or sell and buy something else.

We'll assume that you're still bullish on SHHHH, but that you also have high expectations for Terri's Tye-Dyed Togas (ticker: TOGAZ). Let's also assume that your expectations are correct —both will end up doubling within a year! Here are two possible scenarios for you:

1. You hang on to your SHHHH shares and they double, becoming worth $40,000.
2. You sell your $20,000 of SHHHH shares to buy shares of TOGAZ. Let's say that you're in the 31% tax bracket. That means $3,100 of your $10,000 gain will go to our friend Uncle Sam (unless you hold SHHHH for more than a year, in which case $2,000 of your gain would go to Uncle Sam). Out of the $20,000 of shares you sold, you now have $16,900 to reinvest in TOGAZ. You do so, and within a year, it's doubled and is worth $33,800.

This should give you an idea of what happens when you trade frequently. The more you trade, the more you surrender in the form of taxes. If you hang on to shares of a great company for decades, you *will* eventually sell and pay taxes, but the overall hit will be lower than if you'd been steadily trading all along.

Of course, if you think that SHHHH has run its course or you no longer have any faith in its future prospects, then you *should* sell your shares and move on to better prospects.

## 448 How can I keep from developing bad investing habits?

A little psychology review might help. Think back to that Psych 101 course you took freshman year in college. Dust off your memories of behavioral psychologist B. F. Skinner.

You may recall that the "Skinner box" featured a contraption that rewarded rats with food pellets when they pressed a lever. (Yes, this really relates to investing. Keep reading.) Skinner conditioned rats to expect a pellet whenever they pressed this lever. Rats also learned to expect pellets when they were dispensed according to a fixed schedule, such as for every third or ninth press of the lever.

Then he introduced variable reinforcement, so that a pellet would be dispensed at seemingly random intervals. Perhaps after five presses first, and then after 20, and then after two. The rats would never know which press would yield a reward. Amazingly, the rats kept pressing the lever, even after many presses passed without any snack. Indeed, even when pellets were no longer dispensed *at all*, the rats kept pressing the lever.

You might have guessed by now where this is heading. Think of all the bad habits that investors sometimes develop, such as buying penny stocks or studying charts of stock price movements. Chances are, there was at least one occasion that served as positive reinforcement for this behavior. Maybe you bought one penny stock and beat the odds, doubling your money with it. If so, you may be continuing to buy penny stocks over and over again, losing money each time, because you've been conditioned to expect a reward — eventually.

This effect is even more pronounced in casinos and with lottery tickets. Both offer variable positive reinforcement, enough to keep gamblers coming back for more.

Those who persist with bad habits, such as acting on hot stock tips, are likely to get burned much more often than they're rewarded. Don't let one positive reinforcement lead you to a lifetime of negative ones. Focus on fundamentals, such as a company's quality and its growth rates, and you'll take much of the guesswork out of investing.

## 449 Is it a good idea to reinvest dividends back into stock?

Reinvesting dividends is definitely a smart move. When reinvested, dividends themselves can keep growing, generating additional dividends of their own.

## 450 Why can't someone buy shares of stocks that are about to pay dividends, and then sell them the day after they pay?

That may sound good, but it won't make you rich. When a dividend is paid, a stock's price is adjusted downward to reflect the company's reduced value due to the dividend payment. With small dividends, this isn't often noticeable. But, with hefty payouts, you'll see the stock price suddenly drop, to make up for the value paid out to shareholders as a dividend.

## 451 How much difference does it make whether I buy stock in a great company at a fair price or at an overvalued price? As long as it goes up, won't I still make money in the long run?

You're right to think of the long run, but there is a difference. You may make less money if you're buying an overvalued company.

Consider the example of Holy Karaoke Inc. (ticker: HYMNS), which we'll say is trading at a fair price of $10 per share. If it's expected to grow at 12% per year for the next 10 years, we can estimate that it will be at $31 per share at that time.

If you buy it at $10 per share, your total gain over the decade will be 210%. However, if you have to cough up $15 per share, it will return only a total of 107% on its way to $31. That's about 7.5% per year. Worse still would be buying it at $20 per share. Sure, you'd make money, but your total gain would be just 55%, or roughly 4.5% annually. You can profit without considering the price you pay, but price *does* make a difference.

## 452 When should you sell a stock?

Think about selling when a company's business changes in a way that doesn't fit with your reasons for owning the stock. For example, imagine that you bought shares of Microsoft partly because of its great success running a software business with high profit margins. If it announced it was going to build and sell computer hardware, you would have to reevaluate it. Computer hardware is a lower-margin business and would likely reduce Microsoft's overall profitability. Selling might be in order.

Another reason for selling is if your stock becomes significantly overvalued relative to your assessment of its value. Don't forget to consider the tax consequences, though; you don't want to pay much of your gain to Uncle Sam. This is why Fools like to buy and hold for the long term, through periods when a stock is significantly overvalued as well as undervalued.

You could also give serious thought to selling if you find a much more compelling stock in which to invest. If your Foolish calculations suggest that a stock you own is now fairly valued and another stock appears to be undervalued by 50%, transferring your dollars might make sense. Again, though, consider tax effects.

Here are some more reasons to consider selling:
- If you think you'll need the money within three years. No one knows what the market will do in the short term.
- If the given stock is your only holding. Portfolios should be diversified. Our rule of thumb is to aim to hold eight to 15 stocks, with no more than 33% in any one stock.
- If you can't remember why you bought the shares in the first place.
- If you're only hanging on for sentimental or emotional reasons.

Successful investors learn when it's a good time to buy a stock, and when it's time to sell.

## 453 If a stock or the market is tanking, at what point should I panic and think about selling?

During stock market downswings, many investors get anxious, wondering whether they should follow the crowd and bail out on some of their investments. This is often the worst time to sell. Here are some pointers on the fine art of panicking.

People tend to panic:
- When the market tanks.
- When a stock they own tanks.
- When people around them are panicking.

None of these are particularly good reasons for panicking.

Here's when you might have cause for concern, though:
- When you don't know why you own the stocks you own. If you have no clue why you ever bought shares of Bedmobile Inc. (ticker: VROOM), you'll have a lot of trouble determining when it's the right time to sell. Did VROOM's shares just take a nosedive? It might be due to some fleeting market misunderstanding, in which case you should hang on. Or, it might be due to some serious trouble at the firm. An informed investor should have a good handle on her investments.
- When you don't understand the long-term upward trend of the market. From decade to decade, stocks in great companies and the market as a whole tend to rise in value. To keep your blood pressure down during market slumps, remind yourself of this.
- When you have a short time horizon. If your moolah is invested in stocks for just a few months, or even just a year or two, then go ahead and begin hyperventilating right now. Anything can happen in the short term. Even stocks in wonderful companies can temporarily freefall. Any money you expect to need within the next five (if not 10 or more) years should be out of stocks and perhaps in CDs or money market funds.
- When you haven't learned that it's the *percentage* of the market drop that counts, not the *points*. A 100-point drop was a big deal when

the Dow was at 1,000, because it represented a 10% drop. But when the Dow is at 10,000, 100 points is just 1%.

Well-informed Fools should rarely panic. Expect occasional market slumps and surges. Read up on investing. The more you learn, the less you'll panic.

---

## 454 There seems to be a lot of contradictory advice out there regarding investing. What's right and what's wrong?

Learning to invest successfully isn't a straightforward endeavor. You'll frequently run across seemingly contradictory advice, which will leave you scratching your head. The solution to this confusion is to understand that investing is both 1) simple and 2) complex.

At the beginning, it's simple. Your first steps should be to get out of debt, read broadly about investing, and perhaps invest your initial dollars in an index fund.

But once you begin looking into picking individual stocks on your own, you may run into some contradictions. For example:

1) Don't waste your time trying to time the market. Always remain invested in stocks.
2) Don't be afraid to stay out of the market, at least partially, for a while. Wait for the fat pitches.

Here's another pair:

1) Don't add money to a falling stock position.
2) Dollar-cost average, investing regularly in a stock no matter whether it's up or down.

There are many such dilemmas that frustrate new investors:

1) Buy and hold forever (or at least for a very long time).
2) Sell when something much better comes along.

And:

1) Let your winners run.
2) Rebalance your portfolio when one or more stocks come to dominate it in a big way.

There are some points on which most Fools will agree (penny stocks are bad, technical analysis is dubious), but there are many points on which we differ a little. Furthermore, scratch the surface of a Fool and you'll likely find that many of us are a little contradictory even within our own attitudes. That's fine. It just means we're complex, and that investing can also be complex. In some situations, buying and holding for decades might work well. In others, it might make sense to sell when something much more promising comes along.

If you're a good Foolish investor, you're always questioning, examining, thinking, and rethinking. You're continually changing your perceptions of investing, perhaps after making some regrettable moves and pondering how they came to pass. With knowledge and experience you'll develop an investing approach that you understand and are comfortable with, and that will continue to evolve over time.

Life is simple: Eat, drink, breathe, sleep.

Life is complicated: Prepare a tax return, study physics, and raise children.

Wherever you go, even in investing, there are always contradictions. But that's okay.

# How Businesses & The Economy Work

*As you learn more about investing and the stock market, it will help if you learn about the environment in which companies operate, as well. This chapter examines topics ranging from bonds, to the economy, to market crashes, to how companies "go public."*

**455** **Why does the stock market often drop when there's good economic news reported? That doesn't seem to make sense.**

It's often related to interest rates. Alan Greenspan and his buddies at the Federal Reserve set short-term interest rates, trying to keep inflation at bay and promote a healthy economic environment. When positive economic news is released, such as lower unemployment figures, rising wages, or growing national productivity, the specter of possible inflation is raised. Economies growing too quickly can spur inflation, with too much currency in the marketplace leading to the weakening of the dollar and rising prices.

To stem inflation, the Fed sometimes notches up interest rates to decrease the amount of borrowing and slow down the economy. Rising interest rates render bonds more attractive, as they offer fixed incomes. Investors pull money back from stocks, which are hit doubly with the threat of shrinking corporate earnings and the attractiveness of growing bond yields.

## 456 Why do bonds fall in value when interest rates rise?

To be precise, the prices of *existing* bonds will fall when interest rates rise. The prices of newly issued bonds are fixed. But let's back up a bit.

Higher interest rates mean that companies are likely to borrow less, produce less, and thus earn less. (This is because higher interest rates make it more expensive to borrow.) Since stock prices are tied to how much a company can earn, higher interest rates theoretically cause stock prices to fall. This, coupled with rising bond interest rates, makes bonds more attractive to investors.

Imagine 5% bonds with 10 years left until maturity that originally sold for $1,000 each. If you buy these bonds now, you'll be getting $50 per year from each of them and then $1,000 at maturity. But, if interest rates have risen since those bonds were issued, and you can buy new 10-year bonds that pay you 10%, that amounts to $100 per year per $1,000 invested. You would obviously be willing to pay more for the 10% bonds than the 5% ones. So, the price of 5% bonds will fall. It will fall to the point where $1,000 invested in the 5% bond will bring you same total yield-to-maturity as $1,000 invested in the new 10% bond.

## 457 What causes recessions?

By one common definition, you have a recession when the nation's economic output (Gross Domestic Product) declines for at least two consecutive quarters. Recessions are often accompanied by rising unemployment and decreasing consumer spending. To answer the question of what causes them, I thought I'd see what an online search engine would offer me when I typed in "cause recession." Here are just some of the many articles and Web pages it returned:

- Y2K may cause global recession...
- Fed mistake could cause recession...
- Increase in oil prices can cause recession...
- Stock market fall unlikely to cause recession...
- Analysts say stock sell-off may cool the economy and cause recession...
- Households saving more will cause recession...
- Overspending and high taxes could cause recession...

- Asian contagion could cause U.S. recession...
- Hard brushing can cause gum recession...

Hmm... well, that last item appears to be dental and not economic in nature... but, otherwise, the tidbits above should demonstrate that a wide variety of things are often linked to recessions. Causes might be internal (e.g., interest rate changes) or external (e.g., wars, financial crises elsewhere in the world, etc.). Economists vary on their views of what causes recessions. At any given time, you'll likely find some people who think we're heading toward a recession and some people who think we're moving away from one.

## 458 Is a strong dollar good or bad for stocks?

You'd think that a strong dollar would be good for American companies — but that's not always the case. A strong dollar can cause trouble for companies with extensive international operations, such as Procter & Gamble or McDonald's. These firms receive a big chunk of their revenues in the form of rubles, pesos, and francs. If the dollar is strong, when the time comes to exchange those currencies for U.S. dollars, they'll get fewer dollars for the foreign currencies — and fewer dollars means lower earnings.

Major international enterprises typically take steps to protect themselves to some degree from currency exchange risks.

## 459 I keep hearing about teenagers in Silicon Valley becoming millionaires thanks to venture capitalists. Who are these venture capitalists?

Venture capital ("V.C.") firms generally invest money in young start-up companies that need cash to grow. The venture capitalists pool large sums of money, review many businesses each year, and select the most promising ones for their investments. In exchange for the funds they provide, venture capitalists receive a percentage of the company, and often become involved in its management. They hope for the company to go public or be acquired in a few years so that they can cash out at a premium.

Silicon Valley, in the San Francisco Bay area, is home to many very large venture capital firms that grew large by funding tiny high-tech start-ups that became the giants we all know today (e.g., Apple Computer, Intel, Sun Microsystems, 3Com, Adobe, Cisco Systems, etc.) Many high-tech company founders once helped by venture capitalists have gone on to do the same thing on a smaller scale to help today's start-up companies. They are referred to as "angels."

## 460 Can you explain how companies go public?

Companies "go public" via initial public offerings (IPOs) — issuing shares of stock to be traded in public stock markets like the New York Stock Exchange or the Nasdaq.

Consider PieMart Inc. (ticker: GOBBL). Stores can't keep these pies in stock. To meet demand, it needs to make a heck of a lot more pies. It should hire more workers and build more factories, but poor PieMart doesn't have much cash.

The company isn't doomed, though. It can borrow from a bank. It can issue bonds (borrowing money from individuals or institutions and promising to pay the lenders back with interest). It can find some wealthy person or company interested in investing in PieMart. Or, it can go public, issuing shares of stock. Companies often use many or all of these options. They frequently secure venture capital funding, for example, a few years before going public. And until they attract venture capital dollars, they may rely on bank loans.

To go public, PieMart will need to hire an investment banking firm, which underwrites stock and bond offerings. (Examples include Goldman Sachs and Morgan Stanley Dean Witter.) The bankers will study PieMart's business and, if they think the company is worth around $150 million, they might recommend that PieMart sell 10% of its business as stock, issuing 1 million shares priced at $15 per share. Once it is announced that PieMart is going public, if it seems that people will be scrambling to buy shares, the bank might raise the opening price. A lack of interest might cause the price to be lowered, or PieMart might even decide to postpone the offering.

If all goes as planned, $15 million will be generated. The investment bank will keep roughly 7% for its services and PieMart will get the rest. From now on, people will buy and sell PieMart shares from each other on the open market, and PieMart will not receive any more proceeds from these shares. The company got its money when it issued them.

If PieMart later decides to raise more money by offering additional shares of stock to the public, that will be a "secondary offering."

Public companies such as PieMart have obligations to shareholders and the Securities and Exchange Commission (SEC). For example, they have to announce earnings four times a year. Remember that they're partially owned by the public, by shareholders like you. When they spend their new money to grow the business, they're spending your money. That's why you have a right to know what they've been up to.

---

**461 Is it true that when a company goes public, its insiders can't sell their shares for a certain period of time? Why is this?**

This is called the lock-up period. It typically runs for 90 days to a year and offers outside investors some measure of protection. If the newly public firm has some skeletons in the closet, insiders who know about them can't act on their "inside" knowledge and quickly sell shares before the public learns the bad news. Some companies set extra-long lock-up periods, to show their faith in the company and to inspire confidence in public shareholders.

---

**462 When I tried to purchase shares of a company at its IPO price, my broker told me this was impossible because his firm would not be issued any shares. How are IPO shares allocated?**

When going public via an IPO, a company typically selects one or more lead investment banks to complete the offering, or "underwriting," process. The lead underwriters typically select a "syndicate" — a group of other investment banks and brokerages (perhaps 10 or so) to help sell and distribute the shares. Each syndicate bank usually receives a small portion of the shares being offered to the public.

If a million shares of Pearls for Swine Barnyard Jewelry (ticker: OINK) are being offered, the lead underwriters may keep 800,000 shares to sell and allocate the remaining 200,000 to the syndicate banks. Syndicate banks may be selected because they have a desired customer base (individuals/retail, institutional, or regional, for example), or perhaps because of inter-firm relationships.

When you look at an IPO announcement in a newspaper (the notice is called a "tombstone"), the lead underwriters are the ones listed on top in the biggest print. The syndicate banks are listed below.

Your brokerage was probably not in the syndicate for the IPO you were interested in. Note that, even if it were, you might not have been deemed worthy of some shares. Since each syndicate member only gets a relatively small number of shares, they may just go to major customers (usually institutional investors). The rest of the customers who desperately want shares will have to buy them on the open market from investors who got some initial shares and want to sell them immediately.

Most IPOs don't do well at first. Some spike up quickly, and then slump for a year or two, while others never really spike much at all. We avoid investing in IPOs, preferring to observe how the business does in its first public year. With thousands of public companies out there, why pin your hopes on a firm that usually doesn't have much of a track record?

## 463 It seems like you can make a lot of money investing in IPOs. Is that right?

Few things can work investors into a frenzy like the prospect of a company's first foray into the stock market. Feeding the excitement are spectacular debuts like that of Internet software company Netscape in 1995. Shares were priced at $28 each, but due to high demand they began trading at an incredible $71 per share before settling down to $58 per share at the end of the day.

There are many reasons why Fools should avoid IPOs:
- They're considerably more volatile than other stocks.
- Many are young companies with unproven operating histories. Better to let a firm get a few quarters under its belt before investing.

- IPOs tend to underperform. Finance professors Tim Loughran and Jay R. Ritter examined the performance of 4,753 IPOs between 1970 and 1990. In their second six months on the market, the new issues lost 1.1% vs. a 3.4% gain for other firms of the same size. In the five years following the offering, the average annual return for IPOs was 5.1% vs. 11.8% for their counterparts.

There's no need to scramble for IPOs. Although many do skyrocket in value in their first days, others don't. And even the much-hyped high-flyers often come back down to earth, permitting Fools to buy when the shares are priced closer to their fair value. While shares of Netscape approached $90 each in its first few months, they traded around $20 a few years later. When America Online announced in 1998 that it was planning to buy Netscape, Netscape shares traded around $40.

Plus, remember that individual investors seldom are able to buy IPOs at their offering price. The IPO shares of decent companies largely go to institutional investors and mutual funds. This means you'll be buying the shares on the open market and not at the offering price. In cases where a popular IPO's price skyrockets, you'd likely be buying near the high, not the low.

There are many great companies that have been trading for a year or longer; we prefer to dig for our truffles in that field instead of chasing after IPOs.

---

## 464 Isn't it unfair to shareholders for corporate executives to be given stock options? They already receive high salaries. How is this justified?

It's true that executive salaries can seem astronomical, and stock options are often considered in the numbers you see reported. (Indeed, many small start-up firms compensate executives *primarily* through stock options, as it conserves cash and can be tax-advantageous to the executives, too.)

America Online CEO Steve Case, for example, received $575,000 in salary, $1 million as a bonus, and $11 million in stock options in 1999. Case's stock options are meant to motivate him to make the company succeed and to build wealth for shareholders. If the options do motivate management and help in retaining top talent, then they can help create value for the company that is then passed on to all shareholders.

Some, like Warren Buffett, don't buy this reasoning, though. They argue that option-holders are not exposed to the downside risk of owning a piece of the company, like shareholders are. They explain that management might add little value, but still see earnings (and most likely the stock price) increase. These folks would rather see executives paid based on how well they maximize a company's growth and profitability.

## 465 Companies often offer stock options to employees. Where does the stock for these options come from?

Companies generally create more stock by asking shareholders to authorize an increase in the number of shares outstanding. Frequently the company will specify that a certain number of new shares will be held for employee stock option grants. Once they get the okay, new options will be minted as needed. Sometimes the company repurchasing some of its own publicly traded shares offsets any dilution caused by this increase in the number of shares outstanding.

## 466 Can you tell me what a CFO does? I find many of these top executive positions mysterious.

The chief financial officer (CFO) is responsible for all things financial at the firm. This includes determining what the company's financial needs are and will be, how best to finance those needs, and informing all stakeholders (investors, creditors, analysts, employees, management) of the firm's financial condition.

She is also focused on creating and maintaining the best mix of internal cash, debt financing, and equity financing for the company (this is the company's "capital structure"). As part of those responsibilities, she plans and oversees the forecasting and budgeting process, maintains relationships with funding sources such as commercial and investment banks, and oversees the process of developing and communicating the quarterly and annual financial statements.

### 467 What is a "hostile takeover"?

Well, a friendly takeover involves one company agreeing to be bought by another, and is often referred to as a "merger" rather than a "takeover." Managers from each firm will typically meet and freely share information about the companies. As you might imagine, in a hostile takeover, the acquisition target is not too thrilled or cooperative.

In a hostile takeover, a would-be acquirer typically sees some strategic value in another company. It may make friendly overtures about a possible merger and be rebuffed. If so, it may then move on to dealing directly with the target company's shareholders by offering to buy their shares for a certain amount in cash or an exchange of stock, or both. If enough shareholders respond, the acquirer can gain control. To entice shareholders, the offer will certainly be for a price significantly higher than the target's current stock price. Companies whose share prices have slumped are extra-vulnerable to takeovers.

Some high-profile hostile takeover bids have included IBM for Lotus, Johnson & Johnson for Cordis, and Hilton for ITT.

### 468 What happens when a company in which I own shares files for Chapter 11 bankruptcy protection? How do I determine whether I have a total loss for tax purposes?

When companies spot the grim reaper in their rearview mirror, they can file for Chapter 11 bankruptcy protection. This allows them to continue operating while a trustee is appointed to develop a plan to turn the company around. If you think the company will get its act together, you might want to hang on to those shares. If you're skeptical or have a better place to invest the money, you should consider selling. Roughly half of the companies that enter Chapter 11 protection ultimately recover; however, stockowners are often diluted by the bankruptcy actions.

With any stock holding, you never have a tax loss until you actually sell the shares. Up to that point, the loss hasn't technically happened yet and is called a "paper loss" (though the sleepless nights it may cause are very real).

# Un-Foolish Investing

*At The Motley Fool, we embrace a range of investing styles and principles. Online, we maintain several real-money portfolios that employ different strategies. Our Rule Maker strategy seeks out growing giants that manage their cash well. Our Rule Breaker strategy is more aggressive, seeking out upstart companies that promise to change their industries — or the world. We also support investors seeking out companies trading at attractive valuations, and we believe that investing via dividend reinvestment plans (or "Drips") can be effective. Is there anything we* don't *believe in? You bet. This chapter covers some of the many approaches to investing that we avoid.*

**469** **It seems that a lot of people are day trading these days. Is it worth learning more about?**

Day trading may look like investing, but it's far from it.

Investors (at least good Foolish ones) study businesses, carefully buy stock, and hold on for the long term — usually years or decades. They consider themselves part owners of real businesses. Day traders, meanwhile, spend most hours that the market is open glued to monitors — tracking stocks and placing orders. They typically place scores of orders each day and hold each stock for no more than a few hours. Many ignore company fundamentals, focusing only on what might make the stock price move in the very short term.

So, how well do day traders perform? A recent study by the North American Securities Administrators Association suggests that only about 11.5% might trade profitably. (Of course, trading "profitably" does not even mean that they will beat the S&P 500, a performance available via the purchase of an index fund at very low cost.)

According to managers of day trading firms cited in a recent *Washington Post Magazine* article, about 90% of day traders "are washed up within three months." David Shellenberger of the Massachusetts Securities Division has noted that, "Most traders will lose all of their money." A principal of a day trading firm even admitted, "95% will fail in the first two years." Former Securities and Exchange Commission Chairman Arthur Levitt recommends that people only day trade with "money they can afford to lose."

The people who appear to be making the biggest killing in day trading are those running day trading firms. These outfits provide day traders with trading equipment and charge them commissions for each trade. With each customer trading all day long, the coffers fill quickly. Regulators are investigating this industry.

Understand that people who trade stocks online are by no means necessarily day traders. Accessing brokerages online makes sense for most people, especially when commissions for online trades are so low.

Resist articles you may see here or there profiling a successful day trader. Know that for every success there are countless failures. Don't let yourself or those you care about get sucked into day trading.

## 470 If most people who day trade lose most or all of their money, why would anyone in their right mind ever do it?

You can blame the usual suspects — greed and ignorance. You can also throw in overconfidence. The research of finance professors Terrance Odean, Brad Barber, and Simon Gervais has linked overconfidence to frequent trading, and frequent trading to diminished investment returns. They suggest that traders tend to give themselves more credit for successful trades than unsuccessful ones, thereby becoming overconfident.

Desperation might also be at work. Once you've lost most of your money, you might frantically trade with what's left, trying to recover your losses. A grisly scenario, no? This Fool prefers decade trading to day trading.

---

## 471 Why shouldn't I listen to investing experts on TV when they recommend getting in or out of the market? Why isn't it good to time the market?

Many financial prognosticators like to predict when the market will surge and when it will crash. Unfortunately, they're often wrong. No one can consistently and accurately know what the market will do in the short term. That's why you're not likely to ever see Fools making such pronouncements. In the long term, though, the trend is clear: The market rises.

Shedding some very useful light on the question is a study conducted by University of Michigan finance professor H. Nejat Seyhun for Towneley Capital Management. Here are some of his findings:

If you invested in the stock market from 1963 through 1993, it would have yielded an average annual return of 11.83%. That should seem pretty good.

But here's the amazing part. The period of 1963 through 1993 includes 7,802 days. If you were out of the market (not invested in it) for the 10 days when the market rose the most, your average annual return would only be 10.17%. If you sat out the 30 best days, your return would plunge to 8%. Up that to the 90 best days, and you're down to a mere 3.28%.

Most of the market's gains seem to occur on just a few days. This means anyone who tries to time the market is at risk of missing out on substantial gains. While some will suggest that there are dangerous times to be in the market, it's probably more dangerous to be out of it.

In 1995, the market (as measured by the S&P 500) advanced a whopping 37.5%. Some prognosticators suggested that 1996 would give back some of that gain. Had you sat out 1996, you'd have missed out on a rise of just under 23%. In 1997, the S&P advanced 33%. Considering that the market's historical annual average return is 11%, those were heady years. Many predicted that we were surely due for a crash. Yet 1998 offered a jump of 28.6%. You just never know.

The lesson is clear: If you hang on for the long term, you'll be in the market on days when it counts — and able to ride out the occasional downturns.

## 472 I've heard a lot about penny stocks, but I am not sure what they are. Do they really cost a penny? Are they a good idea for someone who doesn't have a lot of money to invest?

In the days of yore, these stocks often did cost only a penny per share. Today, any stock selling for under $5 per share might be considered a penny stock. They often represent companies with less-than-stellar track records promising great success around the corner. (Revolutionary gold deposit detectors! A cure for the common cold!)

Penny stocks are dangerous because people think low prices mean bargains and that they'd be better off spending their $250 on 100 shares of a penny stock than on seven shares of, say, McDonald's.

It can be hard to believe, but a stock might be grossly overvalued at $1.50 per share but significantly undervalued at $150 per share. Many people don't understand this, and they often gravitate toward the $1.50 stock, thinking it'll more quickly double in value. That's a risky assumption, though. Your performance holding a stock really depends on the stock's intrinsic value, not its trading price, and the amount of money you invest, not the number of shares you own.

Imagine that you buy 100 shares of a $0.60 stock and one share of a $60 stock. If each of them double in value, you'll have 100 shares of a $1.20 stock, worth $120, and one share of a $120 stock, worth $120. You would have gained no advantage by buying the lower-priced stock. A $60 or $25 or $100 stock is more likely to double in value and hold its value for the long term than a typical penny stock.

Most penny stocks are selling for a low price for a reason. Because of their low price, they are often used in various stock scams. They occasionally get hyped and soar briefly, before plummeting back to earth. Steer clear of the pennies.

---

## 473 What is the Foolish take on technical analysis? What is it, and is it worth learning?

"Beware of technical analysis, my son! The jaws that bite, the claws that catch!" Had Lewis Carroll been an investing aficionado, he might have cautioned investors about technical analysis, instead of the Jabberwock and Jubjub bird. He didn't, though, so permit me.

Technical analysis is often contrasted with fundamental analysis. Technical analysis dwells on charts of stock price movements and trading volume. Fundamental analysis, on the other hand, focuses on the value of companies, studying such things as a firm's business, earnings, and competition. While investors from the fundamental school want to understand a business from the inside out, technicians mostly remain on the outside, observing how the stock behaves in the market.

Technicians have defined many patterns in the charts they study, imbuing them with much significance. There's a head-and-shoulders pattern and a cup-and-handle pattern. Perhaps next we'll see an ostrich-and-eggbeater pattern. These patterns do exist, but they don't necessarily mean anything. Imagine someone discovering that on presidential election days, whenever the skies above Fresno were cloudy, Republican candidates won. Like many patterns, this would be a randomly occurring one, a coincidence. For you to bet any of your hard-earned savings on this would be nothing more than gambling.

Investors who use technical analysis are really betting on the psychology of the market, as they scrutinize investor behavior. They try to determine where the big, institutional money is going so they can put their cash in the same places. Imagine Warren Buffett trying to follow this short-attention-span crowd instead of seeking, buying, and holding great companies for the long-term. Imagine the taxes and commissions.

It's amazing to think that technicians might study a stock chart, see a particular pattern, determine that the stock is "breaking resistance," and then buy shares. All this would very possibly be done without understanding what the company does or what its prospects and circumstances are.

While we're not fond of technical analysis, many investors do claim it helps them find appropriate places to buy and sell stocks, and some investors use technical analysis in combination with other investing approaches.

We recommend that you focus on the fundamentals. If you find a company quietly selling more and more prefab igloos, increasing its profit margins and earnings, and going unnoticed by Wall Street, consider snapping up shares. Don't worry about what others are doing. The true value of great companies is eventually recognized.

---

### 474 I've seen come-ons from various gurus who claim that they can teach me ways to get rich quick. Are they worth investigating?

If someone offers to show you, for a fee, how to get rich in a few weeks or months, we hope that you'll turn and run away. Unfortunately, some Americans are doing the opposite. They're buying how to make-millions books, attending expensive seminars, calling 900-numbers for financial guidance, and subscribing to costly newsletters.

A man named Wade Cook, for example, has spoken of earning 20% to 40% returns — monthly. Let's do a little math and see how realistic this is. If you take a single dollar and compound it at 20% monthly for 15 years, you'll have $179 *trillion*. Last time we checked, that was more than seven times the Gross Domestic Product of the entire world, more than the total market value of all goods produced and services rendered globally in an entire year. This kind of result from investing a single dollar should seem a little unrealistic.

If any of these financial gurus were using their own systems to invest their own money for any significant period of time, they would long ago have appeared on lists of the richest Americans. Indeed, they'd have purchased most of our solar system. Instead, they appear to be making most of their money from selling their products, not from their stock purchases.

Since Cook appears to know how to make billions, we find it surprising that he spends any time offering investing seminars that cost several thousand dollars. Last time we checked, his "Wall Street Workshop" cost a whopping $5,695 and his "Zero to Zillions" audiocassette tape set was $1,295. At the same time, Cook's company was (and likely still is) a penny stock, with a measly total market value of roughly $15 million.

While the Fool recommends investing in stocks and holding for decades, these investing gurus often urge you to use money you've borrowed for high-risk options trading. We avoid options, as they can (and often do) end up worthless. And, we realize that investing with borrowed cash means that any mistakes translate into magnified losses. Gurus tend to rely heavily on predictions of short-term movements of stocks. We know that no one can consistently and successfully make such predictions — even Dionne Warwick (as far as we know).

For the best way to accumulate wealth, look at two of America's greatest financial successes. Bill Gates snagged the top spot by hanging on to shares of his ever-growing Microsoft stock. Warren Buffett bought into great businesses and held on. Both have publicly stated that among the qualities that have driven them to success, two stand out: patience and perseverance. How reassuringly Foolish.

---

## 475 Can you explain options to me? I don't mean employee stock options, but the other kind.

Imagine you want to invest in Legal Beagles (ticker: WOOFF), a new company providing legal advice for house pets. You can buy shares the usual way — or you can buy options.

There are two main types of options: calls and puts. A call gives you the right to buy a set number of shares, at a set price, within a certain period of time (often just a few months). For this right, you pay a price premium. Puts are similar, but give you the right to sell shares.

If WOOFF is selling for $50 per share and you expect it to rise, you could buy "October $55" call options for it. Let's say you snap up call options and pay $6 each ($600 total) for options to buy 100 shares of WOOFF at $55 apiece. If, just before your options expire, WOOFF is selling for $65 per share, you can exercise your options and buy 100 shares for $5,500. Then you can keep them or sell them for $6,500.

If you sell, you make a $1,000 profit, right? Nope. You paid $600 for the options alone, remember? So, your profit is down to $400 — less, when you account for trading commissions.

Options can be risky. If WOOFF stays at $55 or falls, your $600 would be entirely lost. It has to top $61 per share — $55 plus $6 — by October for you to profit.

Some folks like options because of the leverage they offer. They point out that, if you only have $1,000, you can only buy 20 shares of a $50 stock. Alternatively, that $1,000 could buy many more options tied to hundreds of shares of stock. True enough. With options, though, timing is critical. If things don't go your way in a short time frame, your option will expire worthless.

*Most* options expire unexercised and worthless, in fact. (Those most likely to profit from options are the ones who "write" or sell the options.) That's because options are really about buying time, not stocks. If you're sure that WOOFF's stock will rise, you're probably best off buying its stock. Then, if it doesn't behave as you expected it to, you can either sell the shares or hang on patiently.

Options are not for beginning investors, and only those who understand the ins and outs of options should even consider them.

## 476 What about covered call options? Aren't those safe?

We're getting into advanced investing stuff here. Selling covered calls is indeed not as risky as buying call options. For example, imagine that you own 100 shares of Amalgamated Thought Co. (ticker: HMMMM), and you "write" a covered call option for those 100 shares. This means you sell the call to someone (let's say for $5 per share, or $500) giving them the right to buy your shares within a certain time frame for a certain price (let's say $80 per share).

You're betting that the shares won't trade above $80 within the life of the option. If Amalgamated Thought only rises to, say, $70, in the time period, the call buyer won't exercise the option and you'll get to keep that $500. The buyer, meanwhile, is betting the stock will surge soon. If it does, perhaps passing $90, she'll exercise the option, paying you $80 per share. Your upside on the option is a $500 profit regardless of how the stock performs. But, if the option is exercised, you lose those shares. Worse, you have to sell them at a below-market rate and must pay any capital gains taxes that apply, too. Rats.

## 477 Can you explain what futures are and why they're important?

Futures are typically for commodities such as lumber, soybeans, and orange juice. They represent contracts between two parties to buy or sell a certain amount for a specified price at a set future date. (Buy some and fail to pay attention, and you risk having to take delivery of truckloads of pork bellies!)

There are also S&P 500 futures, based on the S&P 500. Each day the party who bet wrong is obligated to pony up cash based on the price of the S&P 500. Futures are bought by some investors to protect themselves against unfavorable price swings or by speculators betting on where the market is going. They can be very risky.

Some short-term investors pay a lot of attention to S&P futures, as they can indicate the market's likely moves before trading begins for the day.

## 478 What is the Fool's take on lotteries?

One lottery ticket here and there won't hurt anyone, but too many people are buying too many tickets. It's a massive and destructive industry.

When lottery jackpots get gargantuan, lottery organizers get excited. Convenience store owners get excited. And people across the nation get excited, too, dreaming of early retirement. There's a much more reliable way to retire early, though.

Consider Abner, who spends $50 per month on the lottery. That's $600 per year. If that money were invested and grew at the stock market's 11% average annual growth rate, it would become more than $100,000 after 30 years (and some $350,000 after 40 years!). That's just the average return of the stock market. Fools who carefully select individual companies to invest in should be able to beat that.

But Abner is buying lottery tickets. Lotteries typically pay back 50 cents for every dollar bet. On average, if Abner plays $50 every month, he'll lose half of his investment the first month, leaving him with $25. The following month he'll try again, and again lose half. After 40 years, having poured $24,000 into the lottery, the typical player, on average, will have just $12,000 left.

Lottery gamblers are ignoring mathematical realities. They're tens of times more likely to die from flesh-eating bacteria than to win a Powerball jackpot. And the vast majority of players will lose most of what they wager over the years. They keep playing because the "who knows — you could be next" message is heavily promoted by our states.

State governments have a higher calling. They'd serve the public better by scaling back or eliminating their lottery advertising. Oddly enough, casinos, which typically take 10 times less from a bet than lotteries do, live with tight advertising regulations.

Foolish investors shouldn't buy lottery tickets, except as infrequent amusements. Playing Powerball regularly means hurting your chances of methodically becoming wealthy. Long-term investors, not short-term speculators, will retire early.

# CHAPTER TWENTY-THREE

# Potpourri

*You can't categorize everything in life. A stroll through your local video store, for example, may have you scratching your head, wondering to yourself, "Why is* Tootsie *a drama? Shouldn't it be filed as a comedy?" In this chapter you'll find answers to questions that don't fit easily in any other chapter. They're not less important, just less classifiable, involving topics such as tulips, REITs, and foreign stocks.*

## 479 What kinds of financial records should I keep?

Take a deep breath. There are a lot of things you should keep track of. Ideally, you might get a fireproof box to store them in, or perhaps a safe deposit box at your bank for some of them. You might also consider making a set of copies of them and storing them at a family member or friend's home. That way, if something happens to your home, you'll have these important papers. Here are the kinds of things you'll want to keep:

- Real estate paperwork. This includes mortgage papers, the deed/title to your home, and records of any major capital improvements or repairs to your home.
- An inventory of your valuable possessions. Go through your home and make a list of all your furniture, jewelry, electronics, and more. Jot down what you paid for them and keep any receipts for them that you may have. Better still, consider taking photos or a videotape of these items, too. These will all prove invaluable should you have to fill out insurance papers after a fire or burglary.
- Tax papers. Keep copies of your tax returns for the past several years

— ideally you might keep copies for every year that you file. They may prove useful or at least interesting one day. Hang on to supporting documentation for three to seven years, as well.
- Insurance policies that are still active. (You needn't keep records of expired policies.)
- Investment records — keep statements from your broker, and trade confirmations, too.

Remember that some of your financial records might reside on your computer, such as in Quicken files or spreadsheets. If this is the case, you should back up that data regularly, and perhaps keep a copy of the data on a disk in another location.

---

### 480 How can I research whether a company I'd like to invest in is involved in an objectionable activity? I don't want to invest in companies that test products on animals.

This is sometimes called "socially responsible investing" (SRI). The more socially responsible you try to be, the more difficult it can become to find acceptable companies, as there are many different ways that a business can be perceived to hurt man or nature. A company may not pollute, but it might have a record of discriminating against female employees. Another firm may not make cigarettes, but it might sell junk food that could clog arteries and cause disease. It's hard to find objection-free organizations.

That said, there are lots of resources online where you can learn more about SRI. Click over to these sites, for example:
- www.socialinvest.org, www.socialfunds.com
- www.betterworld.com/BWZ/9604/product.htm

Some other useful sites are:
- www.greenmoney.com
- www.goodmoney.com
- www.srinvest.net.

There are many mutual funds catering to this niche, too. (As with most funds, not all have stellar records.)

If you're not online, check out these books:
* *Investing With Your Values: Making Money and Making a Difference* by Hal Brill, Jack A. Brill, and Cliff Feigenbaum
* *The Mindful Money Guide* by Marshall Glickman

---

## 481 I have some employee stock options from my employer. Can you explain the term "strike price" for me?

Let's say that you work for Rubber Chicken Catering Inc. (ticker: CHEWY). You're issued 1,000 employee stock options with a strike (or "exercise") price of $10 each. A few years later, the shares are trading at $35. At this point, you decide to "exercise" your options.

Since your options carry a strike price of $10, you're entitled to buy up to 1,000 shares at $10 each — not the $35 that they're currently going for on the open market. If you exercise all of them, you'll fork over to your company $10,000 for 1,000 shares and they'll immediately be worth $35,000. You can hang on to them as long as you like, or quickly cash out for a $25,000 profit.

As you might suspect, it's not exactly quite this simple. There are many tax issues to consider, and your option plan might have some special features. Read the plan carefully. You might also read Kaye Thomas's book, *Consider Your Options*, or drop by his website at www.fairmark.com.

---

## 482 What does it mean when a Nasdaq company's ticker symbol ends in "F"?

Nasdaq stocks have four-letter ticker symbols. If there's a fifth letter, it's there to signify something. Here are the letters you're most likely to see:
* A and B refer to class A or B of the company's stock.
* E is for companies delinquent in filing reports with the Securities and Exchange Commission.
* F designates a foreign company.
* Q indicates that the firm is in bankruptcy proceedings.
* Y is for foreign stocks trading as American Depositary Receipts (ADRs).

## 483 What is "beta"?

Beta is a measure of a stock's volatility. A beta of 1.0 indicates a stock that rises and falls in sync with the overall market. A beta greater than 1.0 suggests wider swings, while beta less than 1.0 indicates a sleepier stock.

Let's say the stock of Wart-B-Gone (ticker: XWART) has a beta of 1.2. If the market as a whole advances 10% in a given period, we can expect Wart-B-Gone to advance 12%. If the market falls 20%, Wart-B-Gone can be expected to fall 24%.

Conversely, if United Velcronics (ticker: UVELC) has a beta of 0.50, it is roughly half as volatile as the market. A market drop of 8% can be expected to depress UVELC about 4%. A market surge of 10% should move the company about 5%.

That seems relevant enough and sounds professional enough that The Motley Fool ought to support an intense focus on beta, right? Nope. We're contrary here, as well. Since we prefer to hold stocks for the long term, short-term volatility doesn't faze us. Wart-B-Gone could have a beta of 2.5, even, and we might still happily buy it — if we planned to hang on for years and years and had high expectations. Many stocks that have proven to be wonderful long-term investments have been very volatile in the short run.

## 484 What are REITs?

REITs are Real Estate Investment Trusts, organizations that combine the capital of many investors to acquire or finance all kinds of real estate, such as offices, hotels, or apartments. A REIT is a little like a mutual fund. Its portfolio is professionally managed and diversified, holding many properties. REITs typically trade like stocks on major stock exchanges.

REITs are unique in many ways. For starters, corporations or trusts that qualify as REITs generally don't pay corporate income tax and are often exempt from state income tax, as well. They're required to invest at least 75% of their assets in real estate and pay out 90% of their distributable net income as dividends. In some years, REIT dividends can run quite high, topping 10%.

The popularity of REITs has increased in recent years, as people have discovered this way to invest in real estate without actually buying any.

You can learn more about REITs at these sites:
- www.nareit.org
- www.reitanalyst.com
- www.reitnet.com

And in this book:
- *Investing in REITs: Real Estate Investment Trusts* by Ralph L. Block

---

## 485 I'm interested in REITs, but I don't understand what "FFO" refers to. Can you explain?

With most companies, net income is a useful number to evaluate, reflecting the profits left over from sales after all expenses have been subtracted. With REITs, though, net income isn't as meaningful.

According to accounting rules, the value of REIT properties is decreased over time, with depreciation charged against net income, reducing it. In reality, however, these properties are probably not falling in value, and may even be appreciating, so a REIT's net income tends to understate its health. This is why, with REITs, you should look at the "funds from operation," or FFO, instead. The FFO ignores the effect of depreciation and other non-cash charges to help you see a REIT's true performance.

---

## 486 Why do some REITs have terrific dividend yields while others don't? Is there any reason not to invest in high-yield REITs?

If a yield looks too good to be true, it probably is. Remember that the market sets the price of the stock, and as a stock's price drops, its yield rises.

For perspective, consider that a 30-year U.S. Treasury bond is priced to yield around 6% because investors are pretty sure the dividend will be paid. However, Russian government bond yields have hovered around 30% or more. Since investors are not so sure they'll end up being paid, they'll demand a higher yield before taking the chance.

The same goes with REITs. As an example, consider Kranzco Realty Trust. Before merging with CV REIT and becoming Kramont Realty Trust, it was the highest-yielding shopping center REIT, with a yield of around 15%. Because of weak earnings, it had been forced to cut its dividend. This development caused many investors to sell, sending the stock price south and the yield up. Management's dividend cut may have been enough to reposition the firm on steady ground, but investors were understandably nervous about what the future held.

If you invest in a REIT yielding 10%, things may well turn out hunky-dory (or not). But, if you go for one kicking out 18% to 30%, you're buying into income streams that other folks find rather doubtful. You'll want to do enough research to be pretty sure you're right.

## 487 Is it a good idea to invest a portion of your money in foreign stocks?

Conventional wisdom holds that you'd do well to invest a portion of your nest egg in foreign stocks. International holdings might be alluring, too. Imagine exotic annual reports issued by Yurt Retirement Villages of Mongolia (ticker: YURTS) or the Uzbekistan Cotton Barn (ticker: PICKN). Global investing might even seem prudent, given that the American stock market has risen so much in recent years.

But, think again. There are compelling reasons to be wary of foreign stocks. For starters, the United States is one of the most demanding countries when it comes to the information that publicly traded companies are required to disclose. However, most other countries don't have as demanding a regulatory environment as we have in the U.S. for financial disclosure. In addition, different countries have different accounting practices, which can make assessing their financial performance very difficult.

Also, most countries aren't as economically or politically stable as the United States. It would be a shame to invest in a promising Freedonian company, only to see Freedonia erupt in a nasty and lengthy civil war. Currency risk is another issue. To profit with foreign stocks, you not only need appreciating securities, but also favorable currency exchange rates. Your Freedonian stock might have gone up 10%, but if the Freedonian flurgle has dropped 20% against the American dollar, you lose. Remember also that if the American economy tanks, the rest of the world's markets will likely be hit, too. So "diversifying" by purchasing stock in overseas companies doesn't necessarily offer that much protection.

There's good news, though. You can invest internationally without leaving home. Many American companies generate a large chunk of their sales overseas. By buying shares of these firms, you can benefit from the growth in emerging economies and also diversify your portfolio. Many American companies generate more than half their revenues internationally. In 1999, for example, 71% of ExxonMobil's sales came from abroad. For Dole Food and IBM, it was 58%; for Gillette, 60%; Motorola, 57%; Eastman Kodak, 52%; and for Coca-Cola, more than 62%. Tupperware generated fully 85% of its sales abroad. Investments in these kinds of companies do expose you to some currency risk, but most global companies take steps to minimize it.

Investing directly in emerging markets does offer rewards, but at considerable risk in many cases, given the lower regulatory standards and the challenge of digging up information. When you have a yen for foreign companies, consider large American companies with substantial foreign operations. Investing directly in international stocks is less problematic if you happen to be extremely familiar with a particular foreign company and the country it operates in.

## 488 What is the FOOL 50 index?

It's an index that came to life in January of 2000. We created it so that we could group and track the performance of the 50 companies we think will most likely define commerce in the decades ahead.

In the words of my fellow Fool Bill Mann, "The companies that make up the FOOL 50 are in the vanguard of the trends that will define commerce in the next decades. They possess a gold-plated brand name, a tradition of innovation, a superior use of technology, and a culture of accountability to their shareholders. They also, as a group, represent the globalization of the American economy. The FOOL 50 contains eight companies that are domiciled outside of the United States, and an additional 19 that are American companies that derive more than 50% of their income from international operations. As the economies of the world continue to meld into one, we expect that, more and more, this index will reflect the composite nature of the global marketplace."

Some of the FOOL 50 component companies include: American International Group, Amgen, Berkshire Hathaway, Citigroup, Costco, eBay, EMC, Enron, HSBC Holdings, Medtronic, News Corp., Nokia, Oracle, PepsiCo, Schwab, Sony, United Parcel Service, Wal-Mart, and Yahoo!

You can learn more about the FOOL 50, by popping over to www.Fool.com/now50/now50.htm.

## 489 Do variable annuities make sense for some people?

Insurance salesmen often push these mutual fund-like instruments (which generate hefty commissions), but they usually aren't the wonder investments they're cracked up to be. Here are some reasons why:

- Variable annuity fees are steep. They typically scarf up more than 2% of your holdings *each year*, according to Morningstar. That's negative growth. On a $50,000 account, you'd be forking over some $1,000 annually. (These fees seem to be dropping in recent years, though.)
- Earnings grow tax-deferred in a variable annuity, but when the tax is ultimately paid, it's at your normal rate, which can reach 39.6%. Compare that with the long-term capital gains rate of just 20%. Even if your tax bracket isn't very high, if you choose to withdraw most of your funds at one time, that will likely kick you into a higher bracket.
- It usually takes at least 15 years before the performance of your variable annuity will match the after-tax returns of investments in a taxable account. You'll be tying up your money for a long time.
- The "death benefit" that will pay your beneficiaries at least as much as you put into the annuity is often a selling point, but it usually costs more than it's worth. Long-term investments in good stocks are likely to increase, not just maintain, their value.
- If you don't draw out the money before you die, your beneficiaries will be taxed on it. Mutual funds and individual stocks will cost your

heirs a lot less.

- As with instruments such as IRAs, if you withdraw funds before age 59½, you'll be charged a 10% penalty. Better be sure you won't need that money soon.
- Variable annuities offer the option of annual payments. But you could achieve annual income effectively in other ways, such as by selling off small portions of stock holdings each year.

Plans such as 401(k)s and IRAs are generally more effective for socking away money for retirement. Consider maxing those out before looking at variable annuities. Take the time to learn more about annuities before putting any money into one.

## **490 Do you recommend any investment newsletters?**

Newsletters in general don't have a spectacular track record, and we pay attention to few, if any, of them. They typically make for dry reading and generally do not compare their returns to the market averages. They're often bent on getting you to subscribe for their "Hot List" of picks — encouraging you to invest on a daily or weekly basis.

This is exactly the way *not* to invest. Even if you make some money at it, brokerage commissions and taxes will kill you. Investors are better served finding their own stock ideas within industries they understand well than in gathering ideas from the typical newsletter.

There's also very little teaching going on in the newsletter industry. Most would prefer that you never quite learn enough, so you'll have to keep subscribing. The Motley Fool aims to do all the things investment newsletters don't do: stressing the importance of learning, intellectual flexibility, and long-term investing, and deriving some wholesome amusement from one's reading.

One newsletter we do like is *Outstanding Investor Digest*. It frequently runs interviews with investing greats like Warren Buffett and Charlie Munger. Unfortunately, it's rather pricey. Read more about it at www.oid.com or call (212) 925-3885 for more information.

## 491 What is the "random walk theory"?

It says that a stock's next move is not predictable and not based on past moves. Burton Malkiel discusses it in detail in *A Random Walk Down Wall Street*. He concludes that people (or animals, presumably) choosing stocks randomly could do as well as the pros — and advocates investing in index funds.

## 492 What is the "efficient market theory"?

It's a theory suggesting that all available information about a stock is known and factored into its price. Thus, an investor shouldn't be able to find undervalued or overvalued stocks. There are strong and weak forms of the theory, and it's not embraced by all. Many Fools tend to think that the market is generally efficient, but there are still occasional pockets of inefficiency that an alert investor can take advantage of.

## 493 Why do I sometimes hear people chuckling knowingly about tulips when they're discussing investing?

While the pilgrims were settling in Massachusetts, people in Holland were bidding higher and higher prices for tulip bulbs. This great "tulip-mania" episode of the mid-1600s is one of the first documented cases of speculative investing frenzy. Incredibly, people were taking out loans on their homes to buy bulbs they didn't even intend to plant, but to re-sell. Prices soared to the modern-day equivalent of tens of thousands of dollars per bulb. Eventually, the proverbial bubble burst, wiping out many investors.

Today, whenever the stock market is deemed to be getting way ahead of itself, it's often referred to as a "bubble" (about to burst). Likewise, when some people see a certain group of stocks surging higher and higher in value, they may murmur something about how it's just like what happened with tulips.

## 494 Why do you often recommend that kids get into investing? I would think that they could just wait until they've been out of college a few years and then begin buying stocks. No?

Well, if you want to make sure you end up in a first-class nursing home with round-the-clock care, you should think about getting your kids involved in investing — now. Kids have a colossal edge over the rest of us when it comes to investing: They have time.

Consider that if you're 35 years old, you might stay invested in stocks for only 30 to 40 years. But, if you're 15, you've got 50 to 60 years.

Here's an example: Let's say that Tiffany saves part of her allowance and flips burgers or baby sits to earn even more. She manages to save about $10 per week and invests $500 each year for 11 years, from age 14 to 24. She socks it away in the stock market and forgets about it until age 65. (We'll assume that the investments in this example grow at the historical market average of 11% per year.)

Now, her friend Trevor, who's the same age, puts off investing until much later. Beginning at age 40, he invests $5,000 each year for 25 years. Believe it or not, Trevor won't be able to catch up with Tiffany. It's mathematically true. In her 11 years, she saved and invested a total of $5,500, and poor Trevor saved and invested a whopping $125,000. By the time they turn 65, Tiffany's money will have grown to $705,688, beating Trevor's $634,994.

How can she possibly have come out ahead? It's because of time. Tiffany's money grew for 50 years, roughly twice as long as Trevor's did. And she was ahead of him every single year.

Mathematically speaking, when you leave money to compound year after year, the really big changes happen in the later years. A nest egg may grow by just hundreds of dollars per year in the earlier years, but in later years, it may grow by hundreds of thousands of dollars per year.

This eye-popping example demonstrates that it's never too early to start investing. How much money you start with isn't as important as how many years you have to invest that money — each year can make a big difference at the back end.

## 495 If I want to get my kids interested in investing, what are some things I should do?

It might be too late to get your kids into that prestigious kindergarten, but you can still give them a great edge in life by introducing them to investing when they're young. With time on their side, they're positioned to reap the greatest benefit from the magic of compounded growth.

Before plunking actual money into stocks, though, play and experiment together. Here are some suggested activities:

1. Build a mock portfolio. Have your kids make a list of companies that interest them. At home, in their classrooms, at the mall, and on TV, they'll find ideas such as America Online, Nike, Gap, Disney, Ford, Coca-Cola, Mattel, Hasbro, McDonald's, Wal-Mart, ExxonMobil, General Electric, Black & Decker, Nordstrom, and more. Have them list 10 to 20 companies on a sheet of paper, with ticker symbols, current stock prices, and today's date. Every week or so, have them record the latest prices. Calculate the gains or losses regularly. Such short-term stock price movements aren't terribly meaningful, but they can help a child understand how the market works.

2. Follow the companies together. Scan newspapers and magazines for stories about the businesses. If McDonald's is promoting 55-cent burgers, watch to see if this will be a good move that brings in more sales, or a bad one that decreases total profits. Note how news affects stock prices.

3. Eventually, help your child actually invest money. You can open a joint brokerage account, with you acting as custodian. Or informally "sell" some of your own shares to your child. If you own some shares of PepsiCo, for example, you can "sell" two shares to your child at its current price. If you're about to buy 100 shares of ExxonMobil and your child wants to buy a share or two herself, you can buy 101 or 102 shares. (Yes, really. You don't have to buy in "round lots" of 100.) Once your child turns 18, she can open her own brokerage account and you can transfer her shares into it.

Get your kids started learning about investing today, and they might end up helping pay for their own college tuition. Appreciating its dollar value might inspire them to read a few more books and attend a few less all-night parties in their freshman year, too!

## 496 Can kids have brokerage accounts?

Kids can't have brokerage accounts of their own. You can still get them started early, though. Here's how:

You can set up a trust fund. You'll have to manage it yourself or pay someone to do so. It eventually becomes the property of your child, but he or she can't take control of it until reaching an age you specify (even something like 43).

Stocks bought for youngsters are frequently set up in UGMA (Uniform Gift to Minors Act) accounts. The investments belong to them, but they can't take control of them until age 21. Until then, the custodian (probably you) calls the shots. Custodians can withdraw money from the account for the benefit of the youngster. (Learn more about investing for your kids at www.Fool.com/money/investingforkids/investingforkids.htm.) You could also set up a joint account, with you controlling the account until the child reaches age 18.

A great way to get kids started is through dividend reinvestment plans (Drips) and direct stock purchase plans (DPSs). They allow you to buy small amounts of stock directly from the company, bypassing brokers, and often operate like an UGMA or joint account. Just ask a company you're interested in if it offers such plans. Before opening an account, learn more about these plans at (take a deep breath) www.Fool.com/DRIPPort/WhatAreDRIPs.htm.

## 497 Where can teens learn about stocks, mutual funds, and investing?

It's hard to go wrong with Peter Lynch's books. For many years Lynch managed Fidelity Investments' mammoth mutual fund, Magellan, with stellar results. All his books are very readable, but his *Learn to Earn* is the one geared to young people.

Have your youngsters click over to our online area for young investors, too — it's at www.Fool.com/teens.

## 498 What are you referring to when you criticize companies for "selective disclosure"? What are they disclosing, and to whom?

A lot has changed recently regarding selective disclosure. Widely practiced in the past, it involves companies telling a few favored people some critical information. You read that right — unbeknownst to many investors, stock prices have often moved based on information given to *some* people but not to all. Here's how it's worked:

Several times a year, major conferences are held, often sponsored by brokerages. At these pow-wows, invited company executives discuss their businesses with big-money investors and analysts. This might sound innocent enough, but if very bullish comments are made or caution is advised, shares on the market would soon be spiking sharply up or down, with individual investors left in the dark as to why.

A similar scenario has often played out with analyst conference calls. Each quarter, publicly traded companies report earnings, issuing press releases. Within a few hours (and sometimes even before the release), executives of these companies would be on the horn with Wall Street analysts, answering questions and offering additional information in private conference calls.

The good news for individual investors is that the times have been changing. It's now common to see a company publish a phone number that anyone can use to hear a replay of the conference call. Some companies offer transcripts or recordings of calls on their websites.

Better still, the Securities and Exchange Commission (SEC) has also been on board with the Foolish mission of leveling the playing field for the individual investor. The SEC recently approved a new "Fair Disclosure" rule that bans public companies from alerting analysts and major investors to important changes before disclosing that information to the general public. The proposal to ban selective disclosure received more than 6,000 comments, most of them from individual investors in favor of the ban. Perhaps not too surprisingly, many (possibly most) of these comments came from Fools like you.

It's still a little unclear exactly how companies will respond to the new ruling. Some may decide to share less information with anyone. We hope that most companies will simply begin disclosing information more fairly, to all.

## 499 Who was Benjamin Graham? I hear his name now and then, but am not familiar with him.

Many investors hold Warren Buffett, arguably America's greatest investor, in the highest esteem. But whom might you find on Warren's own pedestal? Probably a guy named Benjamin Graham, under whose tutelage Warren worked many moons ago. Although Graham's record doesn't beat Buffett's, he was no slouch. Between 1929 and 1956, a period spanning the Great Depression and several major wars, Graham's investments grew an average of about 17% per year.

Ben Graham is known as the father of value investing. Value, or "defensive," investors quietly seek out bargains among underpriced companies, buy into them, and then patiently wait for their fair value to be realized. Growth investors are more aggressive. They aim to buy businesses that are booming, often due to high demand for their products. While growth investors will buy a dollar hoping for it to become two dollars, value investors will try to buy a dollar for fifty cents.

Graham was a pioneer in driving home to investors the importance of crunching numbers. After experiencing the devastation of the 1929 crash, he sought to develop resilient techniques that could be used by any investor. He popularized examining price-to-earnings (P/E) ratios, debt-to-equity ratios, dividend records, net current assets, book values, and earnings growth. Graham knew what he was looking for and demanded high quality on every count.

Graham's focus was on objective numbers rather than more subjective things such as management, trends, brand names, and new products.

The data he tapped was publicly available via corporate financial statements and the *Standard & Poor's Stock Guide* (available for free from many brokerages).

In 1934, Graham co-authored with David Dodd a hefty textbook called *Security Analysis*. Nearly seven decades later, it's still widely used in business schools. As it's not the easiest read, we recommend his more concise work, *The Intelligent Investor*. Warren Buffett himself has referred to *The Intelligent Investor* as "by far the best book about investing ever written." Pick up a copy at your local library and check it out, Fool.

---

## 500 Are there really 500 questions and answers in this book?

There are now. Thanks for reading this far! I hope you enjoyed the book and found it useful.

**PART THREE**

# Appendices

## APPENDIX A

# Resources for More Information

*I hope that you've enjoyed this book and that it has helped you become savvier in managing your money. Here are some more resources that might be useful:*

**Motley Fool Books** (available at www.FoolMart.com):

*The Motley Fool You Have More Than You Think* by David and Tom Gardner
This is a great introductory book, focusing primarily on personal finance topics such as getting out of debt, saving money, spending prudently, and beginning investing. It's perfect for anyone who's not sure they have what it takes to take control of their financial future. It makes a strong case for *why* you should plan and invest.

*The Motley Fool Investment Guide* by David and Tom Gardner
This book introduces Foolish investing in some detail. It covers topics such as why you might avoid most mutual funds, why you should consider index funds, how to go about finding companies to invest in, how to read financial statements, how to evaluate companies, and how to manage a portfolio. It also introduces Rule Breaker and Rule Maker investing.

*The Motley Fool Rule Breakers, Rule Makers* by David and Tom Gardner
This book offers a detailed explanation of how brothers David and Tom Gardner go about choosing companies in which to invest. One looks for companies that break rules and the other for firms that make rules. This book will teach you a lot about how to evaluate businesses by looking at the big picture and by drilling down into some numbers.

*The Motley Fool Investment Workbook* by David and Tom Gardner
Grab a pencil before reading this book. It covers topics ranging from personal finance and budgeting, all the way to how to read an annual report. In it you're expected to do some exercises and crunch some numbers — it's full of worksheets.

*The Motley Fool's Investing Without a Silver Spoon* by Jeff Fischer
In these pages is just about everything you need to know about dividend reinvestment plans (Drips) and direct stock purchase plans (DSPs). Included is a comprehensive directory of companies that offer these plans, along with details on the plans (such as phone numbers, fees, minimum investment amounts, etc.).

*The Motley Fool's Investment Tax Guide* by Roy Lewis and Selena Maranjian
To minimize the amount you fork over to Uncle Sam each April, you should really be attending to various tax matters *throughout* the year. This book is a fairly comprehensive introduction to tax issues relevant to most Fools: investing, children, education, homes, retirement, home offices, and more. It's written in an amusing manner and explains many tax issues in an easy-to-understand way, employing many examples.

*Investment Clubs: How to Start and Run One the Motley Fool Way* by Selena Maranjian
If you're thinking of starting an investment club, this short book will prove very helpful. It offers a long list of issues for you to consider and topics to discuss with your friends both before and after you form your club. It also includes a sample partnership agreement, bylaws, agenda, and tax forms.

## Other Useful Books

### Personal Finance:

Note that you'll find many more book (and website) recommendations in the Personal Finance section of this book. The books on this list offer more general, less targeted information.

- *The Wealthy Barber* by David Chilton
- *The Millionaire Next Door* by Thomas J. Stanley and William D. Danko
- *Making the Most of Your Money* by Jane Bryant Quinn
- *Consider Your Options: Get the Most from Your Equity Compensation* by Kaye A. Thomas
- *Ask the Headhunter* by Nick A. Corcodilos
- *The Cathedral Within: Transforming Your Life by Giving Something Back* by Bill Shore and William H. Shore

### For Beginning Investors:

- *One Up on Wall Street* by Peter Lynch with John Rothchild
- *Learn to Earn* by Peter Lynch and John Rothchild
- *The Richest Man in Babylon* by George S. Clason
- *Wall Street Words: An Essential A to Z Guide for Today's Investor* by David Logan Scott
- *Common Sense on Mutual Funds: New Imperatives for the Intelligent Investor* by John C. Bogle
- *How to Make Money in Stocks* by William J. O'Neil
- *Where Are the Customers' Yachts?* by Fred Schwed, Jr.

### For Intermediate Investors:

- *Common Stocks and Uncommon Profits* by Philip A. Fisher
- *The Intelligent Investor* by Benjamin Graham
- *Tricks of the Trade: An Insider's Guide to Using a Stockbroker* by Mark Dempsey
- *A Random Walk Down Wall Street* by Burton G. Malkiel
- *How to Read a Financial Report* by John A. Tracy
- *Super Stocks* by Kenneth L. Fisher
- *The Gorilla Game: The Investor's Guide to Picking Winners in High Technology* by Geoffrey A. Moore, Paul Johnson, and Tom Kippola
- *The Money Masters* by John Train
- *The New Money Masters* by John Train
- *What Works on Wall Street* by James P. O'Shaughnessy
- *Stocks for the Long Run* by Jeremy J. Siegel
- *Stock Picking* by Richard J. Maturi
- *How the Stock Market Works* by John M. Dalton, Esq.

- *Confessions of a Stockbroker: You, Too, Can Find Tomorrow's Blue Chips Before Wall Street Finds Them* by Andrew A. Lanyi
- *Liar's Poker: Rising Through the Wreckage on Wall Street* by Michael Lewis

**For Seasoned Investors:**

- *Security Analysis* by Benjamin Graham & David Dodd
- *The Quest for Value: The EVA™ Management Guide* by G. Bennett Stewart, III
- *The Real Key to Creating Wealth* by Al Ehrbar
- *Analysis of Financial Statements* by Leopold A. Bernstein
- *Valuation: Measuring and Managing the Value of Companies* by Tom Copeland et al.

**Books on Business, for Anyone:**

- *Buffett: The Making of an American Capitalist* by Roger Lowenstein
- *Built to Last: Successful Habits of Visionary Companies* by James C. Collins and Jerry I. Porras
- *Capital Ideas: The Improbable Origins of Modern Wall Street* by Peter L. Bernstein
- *Morgan: American Financier* by Jean Strouse
- *The Lexus and the Olive Tree* by Thomas L. Friedman
- *Selling the Invisible: A Field Guide to Modern Marketing* by Harry Beckwith
- *Maverick: The Success Story Behind the World's Most Unusual Workplace* by Ricardo Semler
- *How to Drive Your Competition Crazy* by Guy Kawasaki
- *Rules for Revolutionaries* by Guy Kawasaki
- *Against the Gods: The Remarkable Story of Risk* by Peter L. Bernstein
- *The Roaring 2000s* by Harry S. Dent
- *The Experience Economy* by B. Joseph Pine II and James H. Gilmore
- *Made in America: My Story* by Sam Walton and John Huey
- *Pour Your Heart Into It: How Starbucks Built a Company One Cup at a Time* by Howard Schultz, Chairman and CEO of Starbucks, with Dori Jones Yang
- *The Entertainment Economy: How Mega-Media Forces Are Transforming Our Lives* by Michael J. Wolf
- *Built from Scratch: How a Couple of Regular Guys Grew the Home Depot from Nothing to $30 Billion* by Bernie Marcus and Bob Andelman
- *Living on the Fault Line* by Geoffrey Moore
- *The 12 Simple Secrets of Microsoft Management: How to Think and Act Like a Microsoft Manager and Take Your Company to the Top* by David Thielen
- *Intellectual Capital: The New Wealth of Organizations* by Thomas A. Stewart
- *Enterprise One to One: Tools for Competing in the Interactive Age* by Don Peppers and Martha Rogers
- *The Price of a Dream: The Story of the Grameen Bank* by David Bornstein

**Online Motley Fool Resources:**

- The 13 Steps to Investing Foolishly: www.Fool.com/school/13steps/13steps.htm
- Register with the Fool — it's free: www.Fool.com/community/register/register.asp
- Online tour of Fooldom: www.Fool.com/about/site/tour.htm
- The Fool Advisor, which will help you find useful areas on Fool.com: www.Fool.com/help/advisor/advisor.htm
- Stock quotes and data/research center: http://quote.Fool.com
- Fool discussion boards: http://boards.Fool.com
- Set up a portfolio and track your stocks: http://quote.Fool.com/portfolios
- Investing basics area: www.Fool.com/school/basics/investingbasics.htm
- Investing strategies — meet our portfolios: www.Fool.com/strategies.htm

- Mutual fund info: www.Fool.com/school/mutualfunds/mutualfunds.htm
- Planning for and living in retirement (annuities, IRAs, 401(k)s, etc.): www.Fool.com/retirement.htm
- Market news and commentary on companies: www.Fool.com/news.htm
- Personal finance topics (buying a car, buying a house, investing for kids, brokerage info, paying for college, banking, careers, insurance, and more): www.Fool.com/pf.htm
- Dealing with debt: www.Fool.com/credit/credit.htm
- The Fool Mortgage Center: www.Fool.com/house/mortgage/index.htm
- The Fool Discount Broker Center: www.brokerage.Fool.com
- How to value stocks: www.Fool.com/school.htm
- Forming and running investment clubs: www.Fool.com/InvestmentClub/InvestmentClub.htm
- Motley Fool Stock Research: www.Fool.com/research/research.htm
- Tax strategies: www.Fool.com/taxes/taxes.htm
- Web resource list featuring links to countless helpful research sites: www.Fool.com/community/resource

### Other Useful Online Resources:

- www.investorwords.com — An extensive online glossary of investing terms.
- www.freeEdgar.com — Find the financial reports that companies file with the SEC.
- www.multex.com — Access research reports prepared by Wall Street analysts (and some Fools, too). Most of these will cost you a few dollars, though.
- www.company.sleuth.com — Check out SEC filings and also domain name and trademark registration.
- www.companiesonline.com — A good resource for looking up companies in various industries, as well as for quickly finding company phone numbers.
- www.berkshirehathaway.com — Where you'll find Warren Buffett's annual letters to shareholders, which impart many valuable lessons. Good for investors of all levels.
- www.google.com — This is one of the best search engines on the Web and can help you find information on just about anything.
- www.wsrn.com — A useful assortment of company research tools.
- http://web.utk.edu/~jwachowi/wacho_world.html — A finance professor's incredibly comprehensive directory of financial, business, and investing websites.
- www.hoovers.com — A handy site for quickly looking up information on a company. Pay a little extra and you'll be able to access even more information.
- www.better-investing.org — A great site, replete with info on and for investment clubs.
- www.bivio.com — Another useful investment club website.
- www.capatcolumbia.com — For those serious about delving deeply into evaluating companies, this is material from the Securities Analysis and Investment courses at the Graduate School of Business, Columbia University. Some of it may go over your head, but some of it might sink in.
- www.newspaperlinks.com — Don't forget local newspapers. They can be a great source of information on companies in which you may be interested. This site is a directory of newspaper websites.
- www.newsdirectory.com — This site will help you locate many magazine websites, among other things.
- www.refdesk.com — A great all-purpose online reference desk.

## APPENDIX B

# A Glossary
# for Investors

**10-Q** — A financial report companies submit on a quarterly basis to the SEC. It's unaudited.

**10-K** — An audited report that public corporations file annually with the SEC. It contains detailed year-end financial results and discussions of the company's operations.

**12b-1 Fee** — A mutual fund fee that covers promotional expenses such as advertising.

**401(k)** — A retirement savings vehicle offered by many employers. Given their tax advantages and the possibility of corporate matching (read: FREE MONEY), 401(k) plans are well worth considering. Nonprofits have almost identical 403(b) plans, and local and state governments offer 457 plans.

**Accounts Payable** — Money owed by a company to suppliers, creditors, and others. This appears as a liability on the balance sheet.

**Accounts Receivable** — Money owed to a company by customers that have purchased goods and/or services on credit. Accounts receivable is listed as an asset on the balance sheet, as it is a number that will (presumably) be turned into cash by the company as the receivables are paid off.

**American Depositary Receipt (ADR)** — A negotiable certificate representing shares of a foreign stock. It's typically held by a U.S. bank and traded on a U.S. stock exchange.

**American Stock Exchange (AMEX)** — The AMEX is the United States' second-largest floor-based stock exchange. In 1998, the AMEX merged with the Nasdaq, to form the Nasdaq-Amex Market Group.

**Amortization** — The systematic repayment (e.g., monthly, quarterly, or yearly) of a debt or loan, such as a bond or mortgage, over a specific time period. Amortization also refers to the gradual reduction in book value of an intangible asset, to reflect its resale or redemption value.

**Annual Report** — Report issued each year by public companies that includes information about the company's business and its financial performance.

**Asset** — Anything that has monetary value and could be sold or converted into money. Typical personal assets include stocks, real estate, jewelry, art, cars, and bank accounts.

**Asset Allocation** — Dividing investment dollars among various asset classes — typically among cash investments, bonds, and stocks — to best match your goals, time horizon, and temperament.

**Back-End Load** — A back-end load is a sales fee charged by some mutual funds when an investor sells fund shares.

**Basis (or Cost Basis)** — The total amount paid by an investor for a security. It's used, together with the proceeds from the sale of the security, to calculate capital gains for tax purposes.

**Basis Point** — Most often used when discussing changes in interest rates. One basis point is 1/100th of a percentage point. Twenty-five basis points is 0.25%, or a quarter of a percentage point.

**Bear** — A person with a generally pessimistic outlook on the market, a market sector, or a specific stock.

**Bear Market** — When the overall market loses value over a period of time. There is no "official" definition of what makes a bear market, though many feel a drop of at least 10% is needed. A drop of something less than 10% is often called a "correction" (even though the term "correction" is never used when the market moves up 10%).

**Beta** — A measure of the relative volatility of a stock or other security as compared to the volatility of the entire market. A beta above 1.0 shows greater volatility than the overall market, and a beta below 1.0 reflects less volatility.

**Bid-Ask Spread** — The difference between what a buyer is willing to pay (bid) for a security and the seller's asking price (ask).

**Blue-Chip Stocks** — Stocks of established companies with strong records of rewarding shareholders. Examples include General Electric, Coca-Cola, Ford Motor Company, and Johnson & Johnson.

**Board of Directors** — A group of people elected by a corporation's shareholders to oversee the management of the company. The board members meet several times each year, are paid in cash and/or stock, and take on legal responsibility for corporate activities.

**Bond** — An interest-bearing or discounted debt security issued by corporations, governments, or others (such as David Bowie — really). A bond is essentially a loan made by an investor to an issuer.

**Book Value** — A company's assets, minus any liabilities and intangible assets, divided by the number of shares outstanding. It's an accounting concept, not a measure of the company's true value.

**Broker** — One who sells financial products. (Whether in insurance, real estate, or stocks, most brokers work under compensation structures that often are at direct odds with the best interests of their clients. When using a broker, you should always find out how he or she is compensated.)

**Bull** — A person with a positive or optimistic outlook toward the general market, a market segment, or a particular stock.

**Bull Market** — A market that has been gaining value.

**Buy-and-Hold** — A strategy that involves buying shares of companies with the intention of keeping those holdings for a long time, preferably decades, and participating in the long-term success of being a partial owner of the business underlying the stock.

**Capital** — A business' cash or property, or an investor's pile of cash.

**Capital Appreciation** — One of the two components of total return, capital appreciation is how much the underlying value of a security has increased. If you bought a stock at $10 per share and it has risen to $13, you have enjoyed a 30% return or appreciation on the original capital you invested. Dividend yield is the other component of total return.

**Capital Expenditures** — The cost of purchasing long-term assets, such as property, plants, and equipment, during a particular period.

**Capital Gain/Loss** — The difference between the proceeds from the sale of an asset and its original purchase cost (or "basis").

**Capital Gains Distributions** — Payments made to mutual fund shareholders for gains realized through purchases and sales by the mutual fund. (Because these capital gains distributions are sometimes substantial, check with the mutual fund you are considering investing in and avoid buying shares of a mutual fund just prior to its capital gains distribution.)

**Capitalization** — See Market Capitalization.

**Cash Account** — A brokerage account that settles transactions on a cash basis with no opportunity for the account holder to use credit (margin).

**Cash and Cash Equivalents** — This is usually the first item on a balance sheet. It refers to the amount of money that a company has sitting in the bank. It may also include marketable securities, such as government bonds and banker's acceptances — things that can be quickly converted into cash.

**Cash Flow** — Cash flow is the cash that flows through (i.e., is generated or used by) a company during a specified period.

**Cash Flow Statement** — A financial statement reflecting the cash inflows and outflows in a company's operations, investments, and financing activities. Also called the "statement of cash flows."

**Certificate of Deposit (CD)** — An insured, interest-bearing deposit at a bank, requiring the depositor to keep the money invested for a specific length of time.

**Churn** — Churning is overtrading by a broker in a customer's account. This generates lots of trading commissions and often leads to deteriorating returns.

**Closed-End Fund** — A mutual fund that has a fixed number of shares and is typically listed on a major stock exchange. Since the number of shares is limited, the fund company can't just create new shares for you when you want to buy in. So, you have to buy shares on the open market. See also: Open-End Fund.

**Closing Price** — The last trading price of a stock when the market closes for the day.

**Commercial Paper** — A promissory note issued by a large company to secure short-term financing.

**Commission** — A fee charged by a broker for executing a transaction.

**Commodities** — Goods such as grains, precious metals, and minerals traded in large amounts on a commodities exchange.

**Common Stock** — A security representing partial ownership in a corporation.

**Compounding** — When an investment generates earnings on reinvested earnings.

**Convertible Security** — A preferred stock or corporate bond that can be exchanged for shares of the company's common stock at a specified price or rate.

**Correction** — A modest drop in a stock or the stock market. The term is based on the notion that, when this happens, an overpriced individual stock or stocks in general return back to their "correct" values. The term, for reasons that elude us, is never used for a return to a higher level from a lower level. See also: Crash.

**Cost Basis** — The original price paid for an investment (including commissions).

**Coupon/Coupon Rate** — The interest rate that a bond issuer is obligated to pay the bond holder until the bond matures.

**Crash** — A market crash is a big drop in market value. It's what many shorter-term-focused investors always worry about. The stock market never goes up in a straight line, so there will always be crashes. It can take a few days, months, or even years for a market to recover after a crash.

**Current Assets** — Listed on the balance sheet, these are assets easily convertible to cash. Cash, short-term investments, and accounts receivable are asset categories that should result in cash within the next year.

**Current Liabilities** — Also listed on the balance sheet, these are debts or other obligations payable within a year.

**Day Trader** — Day traders are in and out of the market many times during the course of one trading session and often do not hold a position in any stocks overnight.

**Depreciation** — This is an accounting action requiring no cash. It involves gradually decreasing the recorded value of an asset over its useful life by charging amounts against earnings.

**Discount Broker** — A brokerage that executes orders to buy and sell securities at lower commission rates than a full-service brokerage. See www.brokerage.Fool.com for more info.

**Diversification** — The strategy of buying a range

of different assets in an attempt to lower overall investment risk. (Diversification can occur across asset classes — such as stocks and bonds — and also within the stock universe, across different industries.)

**Dividend** — A distribution from a company to its shareholders from its earnings. Typically, dividends are paid on a quarterly basis.

**Dividend Reinvestment Plan (Drip)** — A plan permitting investors to invest small amounts of money in a company's stock, with the option of having dividends automatically reinvested in additional stock.

**Dividend Yield** — Calculated by dividing a stock's annual dividend by its current share price. This measure reflects the return you'd earn (from dividends alone) in a year if you bought a given stock at its current price.

**Dollar-Cost Averaging** — Regularly plunking equal amounts of money into an investment. The money deducted from your paycheck if you participate in your company's 401(k) program is an example of dollar-cost averaging. The idea is that regular periodic investments allow you to buy more shares when a stock price is low and fewer shares when a stock price is high.

**Dow Jones Industrial Average (Dow or DJIA)** — The oldest and most widely known index of the stock market. The "Dow" represents the average of 30 actively traded major American companies.

**Earnings (or Losses)** — Earnings, also known as net income or net profit, are what's left over from revenues after a company covers all its costs and pays all its bills. (In the case of some companies, this will result in losses.)

**Earnings Per Share (EPS)** — To allow for apples-to-apples comparisons, those who look at earnings use EPS. You calculate the earnings per share by dividing a company's net income by the number of shares it currently has outstanding — but you shouldn't even have to bother, as most companies report their EPS.

**Emerging Markets Fund** — A mutual fund that invests in countries with developing economies such as those in Latin America and Asia (excluding Japan).

**Endless Loop** — *See* Loop, Endless.

**Equities (Stock)** — A name that comes from "equitable claims." Equities are just shares of stock. Because they represent a proportional share in a business, they are equitable claims on the business itself.

**Ex-Dividend Date** — The date during the quarter before which you must buy a stock to get its quarterly dividend payout. This is because a company needs some time to get its records straight; it cannot pay a dividend to someone who buys the stock the morning the checks go out.

**Expense Ratio** — The percentage of a mutual fund taken out of the pockets of shareholders to pay expenses — much of which goes to the salesmen and managers of the fund. If you're investing in mutual funds, look for those with an expense ratio of less than 1%.

**Fair Value** — This is the theoretical price at which a company is valued "correctly." Analysts often disagree about what this number is for any given company. A company's stock may be trading above or below its perceived fair value.

**Federal Reserve** — The central bank of the United States. The Federal Reserve (or "Fed") oversees money supply, interest rates, and credit. The Federal Open Market Committee (FOMC) is the 12-member policy-making arm of the Fed that sets monetary policy, chiefly by setting interest rates. It also buys and sells government securities, which increase or decrease the nation's money supply.

**Fiscal Year** — A 12-month accounting period that may or may not correspond to the calendar year. Many companies begin and end their "fiscal" years on dates other than January 1st and December 31st. Often this is done to facilitate financial reporting or perhaps to better represent cyclical or seasonal characteristics of the company's revenues. Sometimes it is just management preference not to have the fiscal year-end accounting chores (which are more substantial than for quarterly reports) falling in the traditional winter holiday season.

**Fixed-Income Fund** — A mutual fund that invests in bonds.

**Front-End Load** — A sales commission charged by a mutual fund — typically around 3% to 5%. You can avoid this fee with no-load funds.

**Full-Service Broker**— Full-service brokers earn their name because they offer their customers not only executions of trades, but also investment guidance, research, and other services. For this, they've traditionally charged hefty commissions.

**Fundamental Analysis** — The method of studying a company through its income statements, balance sheets, and other financial statements to determine whether it is a suitable investment. It also takes into account factors such as competitive position and growth prospects. Fundamental analysis stands in stark contrast to technical analysis.

**Futures/Futures Contract** — A contract to buy or sell a specific amount of a commodity or security for a specific price at a specific point in the future.

**Gross Margin** — This is a preliminary profit measure, reflecting how much of every dollar of sales a company keeps after the cost of sales is subtracted. Calculate it by taking gross profits (revenues minus cost of goods sold) for a period, and dividing by the revenues for the same period.

**Growth and Income Fund** — A mutual fund that pursues long-term growth of capital, as well as current dividend income from stocks. This describes most stock mutual funds at some level, but the term is used to distinguish these funds from ones that are more exclusively aimed at investing in growth stocks ("aggressive" or "growth" funds) or more stable funds, designated as income funds.

**Growth Stock Fund** — A mutual fund that emphasizes acquiring companies believed to be rapidly growing earnings and sales. Growth stocks usually have little or no dividend, as they are still at a stage in their businesses where they are reinvesting most or all of their earnings into the further development of the business.

**High-Yield Bonds** — See junk bonds.

**Income Fund** — A mutual fund that invests in bonds and companies paying significant dividends.

**Index** — A selection of securities whose collective performance is used as a standard to measure the stock market. Some indexes reflect a specific sector, industry, or region. Examples include the Dow Jones Industrial Average, the Standard & Poor's 500, the Wilshire 5000, and the FOOL 50.

**Index Fund** — A passively managed mutual fund that seeks to essentially duplicate the performance of a particular market index. They typically charge very low fees, compared to actively managed mutual funds.

**Individual Retirement Account (IRA)** — A tax-deferred retirement account set up with a financial institution such as a bank or brokerage, in which contributions may be invested in many types of securities.

**Initial Public Offering (IPO)** — A company's first offering of common stock to the public.

**Institutions** — Institutional investors include pension funds, insurance funds, mutual funds, and hedge funds. These are the big players in the stock market.

**Inventory** — Inventory represents raw materials, near-finished products, and finished goods that a company has not yet sold. You'll find it listed as an asset on a company's balance sheet.

**Junk Bond (High-Yield Bond)** — A bond issued by a company with relatively high chances of defaulting. To compensate for the extra risk, the interest rate is set relatively high.

**Liabilities** — Outstanding debts.

**Limit Order** — An order to buy or to sell a security at a specific price or better. Example: "Buy 200 shares of Microsoft at $65." This would be placed when Microsoft is trading above $65 a share, and the purchaser is interested in waiting for a better price, and accepting the possibility that his preferred price will not ever be available, in which case the order will not be filled. See Market Order.

**Load** — A sales fee or commission charged when you buy or sell mutual fund shares. When a fund's (front-end) load is 5%, for every $100 you invest, you're only getting $95 invested into the market, as $5 goes to the salesperson and/or mutual fund company. You can avoid loads by choosing no-load funds.

**Loop, Endless** — *See* Endless Loop.

**Margin Account** — A brokerage account that allows you to buy securities by borrowing from your broker. Margin accounts should not be used by inexperienced investors, or those who are putting money at risk that they can't afford to lose.

**Market Capitalization (or "Market Cap")** — A company's total stock market value, calculated by multiplying the current price of a single share of stock by the total number of shares outstanding. This can be viewed as sort of a price tag for the company.

**Market Order** — An order to buy or sell immediately at the best price available at that moment.

**Market Timing** — An investment strategy based on predicting market trends — something that any intelligent, experienced investor should tell you cannot be consistently done. The goal is to outguess the other participants in the market, jumping out before downturns and back in before upturns.

**Money Market Fund** — A mutual fund that invests in very-short-term, high-liquidity investments. Essentially akin to a savings account, though usually offering better interest rates than a passbook savings account.

**Mutual Fund** — An investment company that takes the cash of many shareholders and invests it in a particular way, as defined by the fund's prospectus.

**National Association of Securities Dealers (NASD)** — The largest securities industry self-regulatory organization in the United States. Through its subsidiaries, NASD Regulation, Inc., and the Nasdaq Stock Market, Inc., the NASD develops rules and regulations and conducts regulatory reviews of members' business activities, to protect investors.

**Nasdaq Stock Market** — The Nasdaq began as the world's first electronic stock market, and today is where investors trade stock in more than 5,000 companies. It's often seen on television as a large wall of video screens showing individual stock price movements.

**Net Asset Value (NAV)** — The market value of a mutual fund's total assets, minus liabilities and fees, divided by the number of shares outstanding. The NAV is the amount of money that an investor would receive for each share if the mutual fund sold all of its assets, paid off all of its outstanding debts, and distributed the proceeds to shareholders.

**Net Income** — Start with a company's revenues, subtract all expenses, and you'll end up with net income, a.k.a. earnings. Net income is listed on a company's income statement.

**Net Margin** — Net income divided by revenues. This measure of profitability indicates how much of the company's sales make it to the bottom line as profits. Expressed as a percentage, it tells you how many cents on each dollar of sales is pure profit.

**New York Stock Exchange (NYSE)** — The oldest stock exchange in the United States, this Wall Street haunt is the one frequently featured on television, with hundreds of traders on the floor staring up at screens and answering phones, ready to trade stocks on command from their firms.

**No-Load Fund** — A mutual fund that charges no sales commission or load.

**Odd Lot** — A number of shares that's fewer than 100. Trading in odd lots used to incur higher transaction fees. Today, with online computerized discount trading, buying and selling stock in odd lots no longer involve higher transaction costs.

**Open-End Fund** — A mutual fund that has an unlimited number of shares available for purchase. Most mutual funds are open-ended. *See* Closed-End Fund.

**Operating Income** — A company's net sales minus its cost of goods sold (COGS), depreciation, and selling and administrative (SG&A) costs. This reflects how much of the company's profits are generated by its principal business. Look for this number on the income statement.

**Option** — A "call" option is a contract in which a seller gives a buyer the right, but not the obligation, to buy the optioned shares of a company at a set price (the "strike price"), for a certain period of time. If the stock fails to meet the strike price before the expiration date, the option expires worthless. A "put" option is a contract that gives the buyer the right, but not the obligation, to sell the stock underlying the contract at a predetermined price (the strike price). The seller (or writer) of the put option is obligated to buy the stock at the strike price.

**Over-the-Counter (OTC)** — A geographically decentralized market in which stock and other securities transactions are not conducted in person — as on the much-televised floor of the New York Stock Exchange — but through a telephone and computer network. The over-the-counter market is regulated by the National Association of Securities Dealers (NASD).

**Penny Stock** — This term is generally applied to stocks trading for less than $5 per share. Penny stocks are notorious for their volatility and riskiness. Fools should steer clear of them.

**Portfolio** — All the securities holdings of an individual, an institution, or a mutual fund.

**Preferred Stock** — A class of stock that is given preference over common stock in regard to the payment of dividends or — heaven forbid — any liquidation of the company. Preferred stock is paid dividends at a specified rate, but will generally not carry the voting rights that common stock does.

**Price-to-Earnings (P/E) Ratio** — The share price of a stock divided by its earnings per share (EPS) over the past year.

**Prime Rate** — The interest rate that lenders charge their very best, most-reliable customers.

**Principal** — The original cash placed into an investment.

**Prospectus** — A legal document usually written in extraordinarily tedious language that provides information about a potential investment, such as discussions of its investment objectives and policies, past performance, risks, and costs.

**Real Estate Investment Trust (REIT)** — REITs are a specialized form of equity that allows investors to own a portion of a group of real estate properties.

**Real Return** — The inflation-adjusted returns of

an investment. For example, the returns for stocks during the 20th century were approximately 11% annually; however, that does not factor in the roughly 3% annual inflation rate over the same time period. Therefore, the real return of stocks was approximately 8% annually.

**Relative Strength (RS)** — Relative strength rates the performance of every stock listed on the major U.S. exchanges, giving a numerical grade (from 1 to 99) to the performance of a stock over the past 12 months. Thus, it's a momentum indicator. A relative strength of 95, for example, indicates that a stock has outperformed 95% of all other stocks over the past year. A high RS rating does not necessarily promise future appreciation, but many investment strategies include the use of relative strength as a factor in evaluating stocks.

**Retained Earnings** — Income a company has earned since it began, less the dividends it has paid. Retained earnings appear as an item on the balance sheet, in the shareholder equity section.

**Return on Equity (ROE)** — Return on equity is a measure of how much in earnings a company generates in four quarters compared to its shareholder's equity. It is measured as a percentage and serves as one measure of profitability.

**Revenues (Sales)** — Revenues are monies that a company collects from customers in exchange for products or services.

**Roth IRA** — Roth IRAs are retirement accounts in which contributions to the account are not tax-deductible, but withdrawals are tax-free as long as certain conditions are met.

**Round Lot (Even Lot)** — A group of shares of stock traded in a multiple of 100, or $1,000 or $5,000 worth of bonds.

**S&P 500 Index (Standard & Poor's 500 Index)** — An index of 500 of the biggest publicly traded companies in the United States. The S&P 500 is generally thought of as the best measurement of the overall U.S. stock market, though the Wilshire 5000 is a more complete index.

**SEC** — *See* Securities and Exchange Commission.

**Secondary Offering** — When a company offers a

large block of stock for sale anytime after its initial public offering, it's called a secondary offering.

**Secondary Market** — This is what we most often refer to when we use the words "the market." This is the market in which stocks and other securities are traded after they are initially offered. The New York Stock Exchange, the Nasdaq stock market, the bond markets, and so on are all secondary markets. On these markets, you're buying from other investors, not from the companies or entities that issued the securities. Also known as the aftermarket.

**Sector** — A group of companies with shared characteristics — usually operating in a common industry.

**Sector Fund** — A mutual fund that invests in a relatively narrow market sector (e.g., technology, energy, the Internet, or banking).

**Securities** — A fancy name for shares of stock or bonds, "securities" is just a blanket way to refer to any kind of financial asset that can be traded.

**Securities and Exchange Commission (SEC)** — The federal agency charged with ensuring that the U.S. stock market is a free and open market. All companies with stock registered in the United States must comply with SEC rules and regulations, which include filing quarterly reports on how the company is doing. The SEC, headed by five appointed members, was created under the Securities Exchange Act of 1934.

**Settlement Date** — The date by which a broker must receive payment for a sale or receive an asset that has been sold. The settlement date for stocks is generally three business days from the execution of the trade.

**Shorting** — To aim to profit from a stock's fall in value. To short, you borrow shares via a broker and sell them. If all goes well, you profit by buying them back on the open market later, at a lower price, to replace the shares you borrowed.

**Spiders** — S&P 500 Depositary Receipts, trading under the ticker symbol SPY, are colloquially known as "Spiders." They're stock-like securities made up of the components of the S&P 500 index, trading at one-tenth of its value. You can buy and sell shares of Spiders just as you would stocks.

**Spread** — *See* Bid-Ask Spread.

**Stock** — An ownership share in a corporation. Each share of stock is a proportional stake in the corporation's assets and profits. If you buy stock in a company, you own a share of the successes and failures of that business.

**Stock Certificate** — A document designating and verifying shareholder ownership in a corporation.

**Stock Split (or Split)** — A company-initiated increase in the number of shares of the company's stock. A stock split simply involves a company altering the number of its shares outstanding and proportionally adjusting the share price to compensate. This in *no way* affects the intrinsic value or past performance of your investment, if you happen to own shares that are splitting. In a typical example, a company will announce a 2-for-1 split and a few months later, if you owned 100 shares at roughly $60 each, you'd suddenly have 200 shares, trading around $30 each. Before and after the split, the value of your holdings was $6,000.

**Street Name** — Registration of securities in the name of the owner's broker to facilitate share transfers at the time of sale.

**Technical Analysis** — Technical analysis involves investors dwelling on charts of stock price movements and trading volume. Investors who use technical analysis focus on the psychology of the market, guessing whether various stocks will rise or fall in the short term. Fools aren't big believers in technical analysis — we prefer fundamental analysis.

**Ticker Symbol** — An abbreviation for a company's name that is used as shorthand by stock-quote reporting services and brokerages. For example, Kellogg's ticker is K, Coca-Cola's is KO, and the Dynamic Materials ticker is BOOM.

**Trade** — The purchase or sale of a stock, bond, or other security.

**Treasury Bill (T-bill)** — A short-term discounted security issued by the U.S. government, maturing in 13, 26, or 52 weeks.

**Treasury Bond (T-bond)** — A long-term security issued by the U.S. government, with a maturity of 10 to 30 years. The 30-year Treasury bond is also referred to as the "long bond."

**Treasury Note (T-note)** — An intermediate-term security issued by the U.S. government, having a maturity of 1 to 10 years.

**Turnover Ratio** — A measurement of a mutual fund manager's trading activity during the past year. A fund with $10 billion in assets and a turnover ratio of 100% bought and sold $10 billion worth of securities during the year. (Mutual funds with lower turnover rates generally leave their shareholders with lower tax bills and higher returns at the end of the year.)

**Underwriter** — An investment bank or brokerage that helps a company execute an initial public offering or secondary offering of its stock.

**Uniform Gifts to Minors Act (UGMA)** — A law that provides a method for giving irrevocable gifts to children while maintaining custodial control over the account. UGMA accounts are managed by you or some other custodian who acts on behalf of a minor. Eventually (at age 18 to 25, depending on the state) the assets have to be turned over to the child.

**Uniform Transfers to Minors Act (UTMA)** — Similar to the UGMA, this law permits the transfer of gifts other than money (such as real estate or art) to children, while maintaining custodial control over the account.

**Valuation** — The determination of a fair value for a security.

**Volatility** — The degree of movement in the price of a stock or other security.

**Volume** — The amount (expressed in shares or dollars) of a stock that is traded during a specified period.

**Wall Street** — The main drag in New York City's financial district and the street on which the New York Stock Exchange is located, although the term is used mostly to refer to the professional investing establishment.

**Working Capital** — The lifeblood of a company, this is the money it has sloshing around, ready to reinvest in the business. Take the total current assets and subtract the total current liabilities. This measure compares money the company has at its disposal to money it needs to pay out in the near future.

**APPENDIX C**

# Index

Bear, defined, 394
Bear market, defined, 195, 394
Ben & Jerry's, Inc., 258
Berkshire Hathaway Corp., 198, 239, 272, 378
Bernstein, Leopold A., 298
Beta, defined, 374, 394
Bid-ask spread, defined, 394
Bid price, defined, 248
Block trades, defined, 228
Board of directors, defined, 394
Bonds
  calls, 179–180
  corporate, 179
  defined, 179–180, 394
  junk, 179, 397
  long, 181
  municipal, 179
  performance (vs. stocks), 180, 194–195
  price of, and interest rates, 352
  Treasuries, 179
  Treasury bills, 181, 400
  Treasury bonds, 181, 400–401
  Treasury notes, 181, 401
  U.S. Savings Bonds, 180–181
  yield calculations, 180
  zero-coupon, 180–181
Book value
  as company evaluation tool, 283–284
  defined, 394
Brand names
  importance of, 252, 257
  market value of, 252–253
Braze, Dave, 33, 35, 140–141
Broker. See Stockbrokers
Brokerage(s). See also Commissions; Stockbrokers
  banking services, 103–104
  and company ratings, 220, 235
  conflicts of interest, 210, 221, 231
  coverage of stocks, defined, 220
  discount, 205
    advantages of, 336
    evaluation of, 313
    services and commissions, 309–310
  full service
    defined, 397
    services and commissions, 309–310
  information sources on, 392
  online
    deposits to, 312
    reviews of, 313
    and trading price, 313
  orders, types and functions, 313–315
Brokerage accounts

for children, 383
  idle funds in, 211
  insurance on, 312
Budgets, personal. See also Money-saving ideas
  calculation of percentages, 8
  importance of, 3–4
  information sources on, 11, 390
  living within, 10–11
  psychology of, 4
  savings, locating, 5
  setting up, 4–5
  software for, 7
  teaching children about, 10
  typical, 7–8
  worksheet for, 5–7, 6f
Buffett, Warren, 182–183, 198, 229, 237, 238, 239, 358, 365, 367, 385–386
Bull, defined, 394
Bull market, defined, 195, 394
Burger King, Inc., 258
Burial. See Funeral and burial
Burn rate, defined, 307
Business model, defined, 253
Buy-side analysts, defined, 219–220

## C

Calculations
  asset turnover, 306
  avoiding errors in, 255
  bond yield, 180
  credit card interest, 18
  days sales outstanding (DSO), 286
  earnings yield, 300–301
  enterprise value (EV), 301–302
  estimated taxes, 128
  flow ratio, 292–293
  growth rates, 274–275
  income taxes, 121–123
  inventory turnover, 285
  net asset value (NAV), 323
  percentages, 8
  profitability, 270
  profit margins, 270
  return on assets (ROA), 305–306
  return on equity (ROE), 288–289
  return on portfolio, 340–341
  working capital, 306–307
Campbell Soup Co., 295
Capital appreciation, defined, 394
Capital, defined, 394
Capital expenditures, defined, 394
Capital structure
  as company evaluation tool, 291–292
  defined, 291

credit repair services, 14
getting copies of, 13–14
and home purchase, 64–65
negative information in, 14
Credit unions. *See under* Banks and banking
CUSIP number, defined, 315
CV REIT, 376

**D**

Day orders, defined, 314
Days sales outstanding (DSO), calculation of, 286
Day trading, 343–344, 361–363
Death. *See* Estate planning
Debt
  professional help with, 17
  reduction of, 15, 16–17, 22
  types of, 14–15
Defensive investing, 385
Dell Computer, 258, 282, 295
Depreciation, defined, 395
Diageo Corp., 258
Direct stock purchase plans (DSPs), 191–192, 193–194
  for children, 383
  information sources on, 383
Disability insurance. *See under* Insurance
Disclosure, changing rules on, 384–385
Disney Co., 252, 267
Dividend(s). *See under* Mutual funds; Stock(s)
Dividend reinvestment plans (Drips), 191–192, 193–194, 336
  advantages of, 336
  for children, 383
  information sources on, 383
Dodd, David, 386
Dole Food, Inc., 377
Dollar cost averaging, 192, 339, 396
Dollar, strong, effect on stocks, 353
Dow, Charles, 214
Dow Jones Industrial Average (DJIA)
  calculation of, 215–216
  companies in, 214, 215
  defined, 214, 396
  and market circuit breakers, 229–230
  volatility in, 185–186
Dreyfus S&P 500 Index fund, fund information, 329
Drips. *See* Dividend reinvestment plans
DSPs. *See* Direct stock purchase plans
Dunnan, Nancy, 166

**E**

Earnings per share (EPS)

defined, 396
diluted *vs.* basic, 244–245
in evaluation of stock, 280–282
Earnings reports
  10-K and 10-Q reports, 262, 263, 297, 393
  annual reports (10-Ks), defined, 393
  components of, 264
  Internet access to, 297
  interpretation of, 254
    balance sheet, 264–269, 284–285, 295
    cash flow statement, 271–272, 295, 395
    income statement, 269–271
  locating, 262, 263
  release schedule, 262, 263
  risk analysis in, 263–264
  and stock price, 235
  terminology, 272–274, 273t
Earnings, retained, 399
Earnings yield, calculation of, 300–301
Eastman Kodak Corp., 250, 377
eBay, Inc., 258, 378
Economy. *See also* Interest rates
  exchange rates, effect of, 353
  recession
    causes of, 352–353
    defined, 352
EDGAR database, 263
Education. *See* College
Efficient market theory, 380
EMC, Inc., 378
Emergency funds
  and 401(k)s, 147–148
  need for, 9
  sources of, 9–10
  storage of, 9
Emerging market funds, 396
Enron, Inc., 378
Enterprise value (EV), calculation of, 301–302
Enterprise value-to-sales ratio (EVSR), defined, 305
Equities, defined, 396
Equity fund, defined, 322
Estate planning. *See also* Funeral and burial arrangements
  financial records and, 167–168
  401(k)s in, 163
  heirs, selection of, 164
  importance of, 161–162
  information resources on, 165
  intestate death, 164
  IRAs, 163
  life estate trusts, 163
  living trusts, 163
  payable on death accounts, 163

shorting of, 317
splits information, 241
stock analyst's reports, 220
valuation of, 392
taxes, 125, 137–138
Tax Identification Numbers (TINs), 200
terminology, 392
tracking stocks, 260
Intrinsic value, defined, 302–303
Intuit, Inc.
money management software, 7
tax preparation software, 127, 128
Inventory
as company evaluation tool, 284–286
defined, 397
turnover, defined, 285
Investment(s). *See also* Bonds; 401(k) plans;
    IRAs; Portfolio; Stock(s)
advice, evaluation of, 349–350
asset allocation, 141–142
bad habits in, avoiding, 345–346
bear market, defined, 195, 394
beginning, 177–178
bull market, defined, 195, 394
buy and hold strategy, 343–345, 394
and charitable donations, 155–156
by children, 381–382, 383
commodities, 182
diversification, 207, 337–338, 395–396
dollar cost averaging, 192, 339, 396
education resources, 298
in emerging markets, 377
errors, common, 207
frequent trading, 222, 343–344, 344–345
futures, 182, 369, 397
for home purchase, 82
information sources on, 178, 183, 389–392
institutional investor, defined, 224
knowledge, importance of, 182–183
long-term, wisdom of, 182, 190, 205
online chat/discussion boards, 206, 391
online investing services, 194, 312–313
overseas, 376–377, 378
and ADRs, 219
and currency risk, 377
via U.S. companies, 377, 378
records, retention of, 126, 371–372
for retirement
asset allocation, 141–142
income *vs.* safety, 140–141
and inflation, 140–141
and stocks, 182
risk
currency risk, 377

nature of, 181–182
reduction of, 182–183
researching, 263–264
stocks *vs.* bonds, 195
rules, general, 207–208
savings accounts, 100–101
small investors, 191–192, 202
stocks *vs.* bonds, 194–195
strategy for, 335–336
time value of money, 381–382
value investing, 385
for women, 198–199
Investment banking firms, role of, 354–355
Investment clubs
focus of, 201
forming of, 200–201
information sources on, 201–202, 390, 392
for teenagers, 201
value of, 199
Investment gurus, 366–367
Investor's newsletters, recommended, 379–380
IPOs. *See* Initial public offerings
IRAs (Individual Retirement Accounts)
allowable investment types, 145
changing investments in, 146
defined, 144, 397
in estate planning, 163
Roth IRAs, 144–145
defined, 399
stock trading in, 145
stock trading in, 145
ITT Corp., 359
Iverson, Ken, 256
iVillage, Inc., 307

**J**
Johnson & Johnson Corp., 359
Junk mail, stopping, 20–21

**K**
Kmart Corp., 283, 302
Koch, Steve, 21
Kramont Realty Trust, 376
Kranzco Reaity Trust, 376

**L**
Layoffs, and stock price, 249–250
*Learn to Earn* (Lynch), 384
Levitt, Arthur, 362
Liabilities, defined, 397
Liability insurance. *See under* Insurance
Liberty Media Cable, 260
Life insurance. *See under* Insurance
Limit orders

calculation of, 277
defined, 399
industry variations in, 278
interpretation of, 278–280
Personal property insurance, 38–41
Pfizer, Inc., 293
Philanthropic Advisory Service of the Council of Better Business Bureaus, website, 154
Porter, Michael, 299
Portfolio. *See also* Investment(s)
  asset allocation in, 337
  defined, 399
  establishing, information on, 391
  losing stocks, analysis of, 342–343
  mock portfolios, 338–339
  performance evaluation, 340–341
    and commissions, 341
    and inflation, 341–342
    and taxes, 341–342
  return on, calculation of, 340–341
  sample, 256, 391
  size of, recommended, 337–338
  tracking, online, 339
Price-to-earnings ratio. *See* P/E (price-to-earnings) ratio
Price-to-sales ratio (PSR)
  defined, 303–304
  limitations of, 305
Prime rate, defined, 399
Principal, defined, 399
Procter & Gamble Corp., 257, 295, 353
Profitability, calculation of, 270
Profit margins, calculation of, 270
Pro forma, defined, 272
Prospectus, defined, 323, 399
PSR. *See* Price-to-sales ratio
"Pump and dump," 222
Pure-play companies, defined, 258

**Q**
Quantum Fund, 223
*Quicken* (Intuit), and budgeting, 7
Quick ratio, defined, 283

**R**
*A Random Walk Down Wall Street* (Malkiel), 380
Random walk theory, 380
Real return, defined, 399
Realtors
  commission structure, 72, 74
  information sources on, 82
  multiple agents, 76
  *vs.* real estate brokers, 73–74

selection of, 75–76
  working with, 76
Recession
  causes of, 352–353
  defined, 352
Records
  financial
    estate planning, 167–168
    home improvement, 126
    house purchase, 126–127, 371
    income taxes, 124–125, 126–127, 372
    insurance, 371–372
    investments, 126, 371–372
    storage of, 371
    types, 371–372
  of property owned, for insurance purposes, 39–40, 371–372
Redemption fees, in mutual funds, 326
REITs (Real Estate Investment Trusts)
  defined, 374–375, 399
  dividends, 375, 376
  evaluation of, 375
  information sources on, 375
Relative strength, defined, 399
Retirement. *See also* 401(k) plans; Investment(s), for retirement; IRAs
  assets
    adequate, 139–140
    drawdown rates, safe, 142–143
    information sources on, 149, 392
    learning about, 336
    saving for, 370
    Social Security income, estimating, 148–149
Return on assets (ROA)
  calculation of, 305–306
  as company evaluation tool, 296
  significance of, 305–306
Return on equity (ROE), 296
  calculation of, 288–289
  as company evaluation tool, 288, 296
  defined, 399
Revenues, defined, 399
Ritter, Jay R., 357
ROA. *See* Return on assets
ROE. *See* Return on equity
Roll-ups, defined, 258–259
Roth IRAs. *See under* IRAs
Round lot, defined, 399
Rule Breaker companies
  advantages of, 336
  identification of, 255–256
Rule Maker companies, 257–258, 336
Rumors, buying on, 236–237
Run rate, defined, 274

**Y**
Yahoo!, Inc., 263, 293, 378

**Z**
ZDNet, Inc., 260